WINDOWS 2000

Active Directory

WINDOWS 2000

Active Directory

Joe Casad, MCSE

Osborne/**McGraw-Hill**

Berkeley   New York   St. Louis   San Francisco
Auckland   Bogotá   Hamburg   London   Madrid
Mexico City   Milan   Montreal   New Delhi   Panama City
Paris   São Paulo   Singapore   Sydney
Tokyo   Toronto

Osborne/**McGraw-Hill**
2600 Tenth Street
Berkeley, California 94710
U.S.A.

For information on translations or book distributors outside the U.S.A., or to arrange bulk purchase discounts for sales promotions, premiums, or fund-raisers, please contact Osborne/**McGraw-Hill** at the above address.

Windows 2000 Active Directory

1234567890 DOC DOC 019876543210

ISBN 0-07-212323-0

Publisher
Brandon A. Nordin
Associate Publisher and Editor-in-Chief
Scott Rogers
Acquisitions Editor
Jane K. Brownlow
Project Editor
Lisa Theobald
Acquisitions Coordinator
Tara Davis
Technical Editor
Ron Ellenbecker
Copy Editor
Dennis Weaver
Indexer
Karin Arrigoni

Proofreaders
Jenn Tust
Tandra McLaughlin
Linda Medoff
Doug Robert
Computer Designers
Jani Beckwith
Michelle Galicia
Elizabeth Jang
Illustrators
Michael Mueller
Beth Young
Cover Design
Matthew Willis
Series Design
Peter F. Hancik

This book was composed with Corel VENTURA™ Publisher.

About the Author

Joe Casad is an MCSE, engineer, and consultant who has written extensively on computer networking and systems administration. Formerly managing editor of *Network Administrator* magazine, he is currently the technical editor of *SysAdmin* magazine and UnixReview.com.

About the Technical Editor

Ron Ellenbecker has worked with personal computers for more than 20 years. He earned his MCSE in 1996 and has kept up to date, passing all the Windows 3.11 and 9.x tests along with the NT 3.51 and NT 4.0 tests. Ron is currently a senior systems engineer with Tushaus Computer Services and assists with designing and implementing networks of all sizes. He also assists with the maintenance and upgrading of Tushaus's internal network, consisting of more than 15 servers and numerous workstations in various locations.

AT A GLANCE

Part I	Introducing Active Directory	
▼ 1	The Active Directory Environment	3
▼ 2	Active Directory Concepts	17

Part II	Setting Up Your Network	
▼ 3	Active Directory with TCP/IP and DNS	39
▼ 4	Understanding Replication	81
▼ 5	Users and Groups	133
▼ 6	Group Policy	173
▼ 7	Setting Up Active Directory	205
▼ 8	Managing Active Directory	257
▼ 9	Active Directory Clients	305

Part III	Mastering Active Directory	

▼ 10   Active Directory Schema 337
▼ 11   Active Directory Security 377
▼ 12   Scripting Active Directory 433
▼ 13   Interoperating Windows 2000 459
▼   Index 537

CONTENTS

Acknowledgments xxi

Intoduction xxiii

Part I
Introducing Active Directory

▼ 1 The Active Directory Environment 3

What is Active Directory? 4

    Flexible Security 6

    DNS Integration 8

    Fault Tolerance and Bandwidth Management 10

    The Data Storehouse 12

    Uniform Interface 15

Summary 16

▼ 2 Active Directory Concepts 17

Mixed Mode and Native Mode 19

A Closer Look at the Active Directory Network 21

    Operations Masters 23

    Multiple Domains 27

Naming Objects in Active Directory   31
Summary   36

Part II

Setting Up Your Network

▼ **3** Active Directory with TCP/IP and DNS   39
Active Directory and DNS   40
    How DNS Works   40
    The DNS Namespace   45
    Understanding Zones   46
    Active Directory—Integrated Zones   48
    Dynamic Updates   48
    How Active Directory Uses DNS   50
    Installing DNS Server   52
    Configuring DNS   53
    Migrating DNS Data to Windows 2000 DNS Server   67
    Interoperating with Other DNS Servers   68
Sites and Subnets in Active Directory   69
    Subnets and Sites   70
    Configuring Active Directory Sites   71
    Defining Active Directory Subnets   74
    Placing Servers in Sites   76
Summary   79

▼ **4** Understanding Replication   81
Replication and Active Directory   82
    Replication Topology   91
    Replication and the KCC   92
    Connection Objects   93
Managing Intrasite Replication   94
    Viewing Connection Objects and Properties   96
    Creating a New Connection Object   98
    Checking the Replication Topology   100
    Forcing Replication Manually   101
Intersite Replication   102
Configuring Site Links   104
    Configuring Site Link Bridges   109
    Configuring a Preferred Bridgehead Server   113
Managing and Monitoring Replication   115
    Repadmin   115

Replication Monitor   117
Performance Monitor   129
Network Monitor   131
Summary   132

▼ 5 Users and Groups   133
A Quick Look at Windows NT and Windows 2000 Security   134
Understanding Groups   135
Distribution Groups   136
Security Groups   136
Predefined and Built-In Groups   140
Managing Users and Groups   142
Creating New Users   143
Adding or Removing Users from Groups   146
Viewing and Modifying User Properties   149
Moving Users   154
Deleting, Disabling, and Renaming User Accounts   156
Creating or Deleting a User Principal Name (UPN) Suffix .   157
Creating Groups   159
Adding or Removing Groups from Other Groups   161
Viewing and Modifying Group Properties   162
Moving Groups   163
Deleting Groups   163
Assigning Permissions   164
Ownership   167
Setting Inheritance   168
Delegation of Control   170
Summary   172

▼ 6 Group Policy   173
What Is Group Policy?   174
A Look at Policy in Active Directory   176
Local Policy   176
Default Policy   178
Group Policy Objects   179
System Policy   179
Setting Up Group Policy   180
How Group Policies Are Processed   184
Where Group Policies Are Stored   186
How Group Policies Interact   187
Creating a Group Policy Snap-In   188
Understanding Group Policy Options   191
Templates   192

Links 194
Filtering Group Policy 195
Setting Group Policies that Control Group Policy 197
Specifying a Domain Controller 197
Group Policy Strategies 201
Summary 203

▼ 7 Setting Up Active Directory 205
The Deployment Process 206
Do You Really Need Active Directory? 207
Planning and Implementing a Test Site 209
Planning and Implementing a Pilot Site 211
Planning Your Active Directory Network 212
Axioms, Tips, and Best Practices 215
Planning Your Active Directory Rollout 222
Executing Your Active Directory Rollout 230
Active Directory System Requirements 231
Installing Windows 2000 232
Important Setup Procedures 250
Installing the Windows 2000 Support Tools 250
Switching to Native Mode 251
Configuring Global Catalog Servers 252
Creating an OU 252
Delegating Control of an OU 253
Moving Objects 254
Demoting a Domain Controller 254
Summary 255

▼ 8 Managing Active Directory 257
Backing Up and Restoring the Active Directory 258
Backing Up System State Data 260
Replication Restore 261
Nonauthoritative Restore 262
Authoritative Restore 264
Modifying the Directory 265
Managing Files and Folders in Active Directory 280
Publishing Folders 280
Managing Files and Folders through Group Policy 283
Managing Printers in Active Directory 286
Managing Software in Active Directory 289
Assigning Software 291
Publishing Software 293
Creating a .zap File 294

Configuring Software Installation Policy Properties 295
Managing the User Desktop Through Group Policy 297
Folder Redirection 298
Managing Operations Masters 300
Reassigning the Schema Master 300
Reassigning the Domain Naming Master 301
Reassigning the RID Master, PDC Emulator, or
Infrastructure Master 302
Summary 303

▼ 9 Active Directory Clients 305
Understanding Client Options 306
Windows 2000 Professional Hardware Requirements 308
Windows 2000 Clients 311
Windows NT Clients 312
Windows 95/98 Clients 312
Clients from Other Networking Systems 314
Address Book 315
Managing Clients 316
Computer Management Tool 317
AD Users and Computers 318
Managing the Network from Clients 331
Summary 333

Part III

Mastering Active Directory

▼ 10 Active Directory Schema 337
What Is the Schema? 338
Attributes, Syntaxes, and Schema Classes 341
The Schema Cache 346
Modifying the Schema 349
Schema Changes and the Schema Master 351
Generating an X.500 Object ID 354
Working with Active Directory Schema 356
Working with ADSI Editor 372
Summary 376

▼ 11 Active Directory Security 377
Kerberos 378
What Is Kerberos? 379
How Does Kerberos Work in Windows 2000? 384

Configuring Kerberos 387
Interoperating Windows 2000 Kerberos 394
What Kerberos Doesn't Prevent 397
Understanding Security Policy 398
Account Policies 400
Local Policies 402
Event Log 405
Restricted Groups 405
System Services 407
Registry 408
File System 410
Public Key Policies 411
IP Security Policies 411
Summary 432

▼ 12 Scripting Active Directory 433
Scripting in the Active Directory Environment 434
Interfaces 435
What Is Windows Scripting Host? 438
Configuring Script Files 439
cscript.exe 442
wscript.exe 443
Setting the Default Scripting Host 444
Debugging Scripts 444
Logon Scripts 446
User Logon Scripts 447
Policy Scripts 448
Built-in Scripts 451
Executing Scripts Automatically 452
Running UNIX Scripts in Windows 2000 457
Summary 458

▼ 13 Interoperating Windows 2000 459
Windows 2000 and NetWare 460
Configuring Windows 2000 for NetWare 460
Services for NetWare 473
Windows 2000 and UNIX-Based Systems 474
Connectivity Utilities 476
Interoperating Printers with UNIX 488
Telnet Server 490
Simple TCP/IP Services 496
Services for UNIX 497

Windows 2000 and Macintosh 498
    File Services for Macintosh 500
    Print Services for Macintosh 510
    Supporting AppleTalk 515
Active Directory in the Microsoft Exchange Environment 519
    Organizing and Optimizing Connection Agreements 524
    Implementing an Exchange Server Connection 525
    Managing the Active Directory Connector 532
Summary 535

▼   Index 537

ACKNOWLEDGMENTS

Thanks to all who helped with this book. My thanks must begin with my wife, Barb Dinneen, and my kids, Xander, Mattie, and Bridget, for their support and patience throughout the project. I would also like to thank the professionals at Osborne/McGraw Hill for lending their expertise. Thanks to Ron Ellenbecker for keeping me on task, to Dennis Weaver for keeping things proper, and to Lisa Theobald for her good judgement and uncanny ability to adapt to an author's eccentricities. Thanks to Jane Brownlow and Tara Davis for their patience in difficult times.

INTRODUCTION

I n the computer industry, where 18 months is a generation and 8 years is an era, software vendors must anticipate the future as they build their systems. Microsoft looked into the future and saw Windows 2000—a hugely complex and versatile operating system that has been billed as the most expansive piece of software ever written. And at the center of this towering edifice is a mysterious, self-replicating, multi-master database known as Active Directory. Active Directory is the most significant innovation of Windows 2000, and it totally rewrites the rules for deploying and administering Microsoft networks. But what is it? The short answer is that Active Directory is Microsoft's attempt to simultaneously integrate the emerging X.500 and Lightweight Directory Access Protocol (LDAP) Internet technologies with DNS and the Windows network security model. The long answer to the question "What is Active Directory?" is this book. This book is your guide to the Active Directory environment.

Who Should Read This Book

This book is designed for the technical user who is now or will soon be exploring the world of Active Directory networks. If you're a Windows NT administrator and you want to quickly become an expert on managing and deploying Active Directory, this book is for you. If you're a developer or a power user who wants a deeper knowledge of what Active Directory is doing than you're getting from off-the-shelf Windows 2000 books, you'll find answers to many of your questions in these pages. If you're new to Windows networks—either because you've spent more time with other systems or because you're starting out in the administrator profession—this book will help bring you in line with the latest Microsoft networking technology with minimal diversions and historical asides. Lastly, if you are a manager who has a role in purchasing and deploying information technology within your organization, this book will give you the background you need to determine whether Active Directory is the best solution for your network.

What This Book Covers

Chapter 1, "The Active Directory Environment," introduces the Active Directory environment by discussing some of the problems with Windows NT and describing the solutions that Microsoft envisioned for those problems. Along the way, you'll learn about some important Active Directory concepts, like trees, forests, sites, and organizational units (OUs).

Chapter 2, "Active Directory Concepts," discusses some important concepts you'll need to understand to get around in the Active Directory environment. You'll learn about mixed mode and native mode. This chapter also describes the structure of the Active Directory network and discusses the roles of Active Directory operations masters—single-master roles for special domain controllers in the multi-master world of Active Directory. You'll also learn about Active Directory naming conventions.

Chapter 3, "Active Directory with TCP/IP and DNS," examines some important networking issues. Specifically, the chapter takes a close look at how Active Directory works with DNS to resolve names and find resources in the Active Directory environment. You'll learn about Active Directory–integrated zones and dynamic integration with DHCP. This chapter also shows you how to set up Active Directory sites and how to associate sites with TCP/IP subnets to optimize directory replication.

Chapter 4, "Understanding Replication," takes on the important subject of Active Directory replication. Active Directory domain controllers use the replication process to communicate directory changes to one another, thus allowing the flexible and versatile multi-master architecture that is one of the central features of the Active Directory environment. You'll learn about the Knowledge Consistency Checker (KCC) and about the concept of replication topology. You'll also read about intersite versus intrasite replication, and you'll learn how to configure site links, site link bridges, and bridgehead servers. This chapter also shows you the tools you'll need to manage, configure, and monitor directory replication.

Chapter 5, "Users and Groups," describes Active Directory user and group objects. You'll learn the different types of Active Directory groups. You'll learn how to create and configure user and group accounts and how to manage user and group accounts through the Active Directory interface. You'll also learn to configure permissions, ownership, inheritance, and delegation of authority.

Chapter 6, "Group Policy," discusses Active Directory's powerful group policy feature, which lets you apply layers of configuration settings to computers, sites, domains, and organizational units. You can use group policy to standardize administration, improve security, and reduce the total cost of ownership.

Chapter 7, "Setting Up Active Directory," describes Microsoft's recommended process for deploying Active Directory. You'll learn about how to install Active Directory, how to upgrade an existing Windows NT network, and how to build a new Active Directory network from scratch. This chapter discusses some important deployment tools and options and provides a summary of recommended practices for locating domain controllers, DNS servers, and other network services. The chapter also discusses Active Directory trusts and shows how to create explicit trusts for Active Directory networks.

Chapter 8, "Managing Active Directory," describes some important directory-related management issues. You'll learn how to back up and restore the Active Directory. You'll also learn how to search and edit the directory using directory editing tools such as ADSI Editor and LDP. This chapter also shows how to manage resources such as files, printers, and software through Active Directory policies and how to seize operations master roles.

Chapter 9, "Active Directory Clients," discusses issues related to managing clients on Active Directory networks. You'll learn what directory services you can and can't use with Windows 2000, Windows NT, and Windows 95/98 clients. You'll learn how to install Active Directory Client for Windows 95/98.

You'll learn how to check client compatibility, how to search the directory from a client computer, and how to join a Windows NT or Windows 2000 client to an Active Directory domain. You'll also learn some important client management tools and how to install Active Directory management tools onto a client computer.

Chapter 10, "Active Directory Schema," describes the schema—the object-oriented structure of classes and attributes at the heart of the Active Directory. You'll learn about the different types of classes and attributes. You'll learn how to add and modify classes and attributes. And you'll learn how to manage the schema using the built-in Active Directory Schema utility and the ADSI Editor. You'll also learn about the schema cache and the X.500 Object ID Generator.

Chapter 11, "Active Directory Security," discusses some important security features of the Active Directory environment. You'll learn how Kerberos authentication works and how Active Directory domain controllers act as Key Distribution Centers (KDCs) to provide authentication for network services. This chapter also provides a detailed description of some Active Directory security-related policies, including the important new IP Security (IPSec) feature.

Chapter 12, "Scripting Active Directory," describes Windows scripting host and shows how you can use the scripting host to execute custom scripts in the Active Directory environment. You'll also learn how to deploy layered logon scripts through Active Directory group policy, and you'll learn about some of the important management scripts included with Windows 2000.

Chapter 13, "Interoperating Windows 2000," shows how to interoperate Active Directory networks with NetWare, Macintosh, and UNIX systems. You'll also learn about the Active Directory Connector service, which provides integration of Active Directory with the Microsoft Exchange directory service.

How to Read This Book

Unlike many computer books, this book is designed to be read cover to cover. Just pick it up and read it. When you're finished, you'll know quite a lot about how Active Directory works and how to work *with it*. This book is also designed to serve as a special desktop reference for users who are serious about deploying Active Directory and can't get the necessary answers from the cursory coverage in other texts. Keep this book close to your desk when you're planning, installing, and administering your Active Directory network. You'll find detailed procedures describing everyday tasks and detailed explanations of fundamental Active Directory components. Read it early to gain the background you'll need to set up and manage Active Directory, and then refer back to it when want to try something you haven't done before, such as changing the replication topology or adding a new attribute to the schema.

PART I

Introducing Active Directory

CHAPTER 1

The Active Directory
Environment

Active Directory is a vast and intricate architecture designed to simplify the life of the network administrator. Microsoft insists that Active Directory makes a Windows 2000 network easier to understand and manage. But *what is it*? According to Microsoft, Active Directory is a *directory service,* and a directory service is "an information source and the services required for making that information source available to users." But this is only part of what Microsoft means by Active Directory. The real Active Directory is a structure—a paradigm for the network and a way of doing business.

WHAT IS ACTIVE DIRECTORY?

Simply put, Active Directory is three things:

▼   A database

■   A collection of services that access that database

▲   A network environment that exploits the possibilities of that database to provide better, more manageable, and more logical Microsoft networks

The rest is details, and those details are the subject of this book. Active Directory is so big, so all encompassing, and so different from anything that preceded it, that it is difficult to know where to begin to describe it. Most descriptions begin with a long list of terms and concepts related to the Active Directory infrastructure. Those terms and concepts are certainly important, and you'll be learning more about them in later chapters. But concepts are of little use without a context, and the best context to begin this study of Active Directory is the context from which it arose: the Windows NT domain.

Active Directory grew out of Windows NT's domain architecture, and many elements of the NT domain are present in its framework. But Active Directory is something more than NT domain architecture. It isn't just an update—it's a whole new approach to networking.

Windows NT went far for an operating system developed wholly from scratch only a few years ago. Windows NT Server 4 was a huge seller that captured a large percent of the corporate networking market. And yet, Microsoft was well aware that NT had certain limitations, like these:

▼ **Inflexible security system**   The permission system offered only limited granularity. It was difficult to organize the domain into smaller units. NT did allow *resource* domains, in which an administrator could control the resources in a local area, but the domain trust system was confusing and anything but seamless, and all the little clouds with one-way arrows in NT Enterprise classes ultimately did not clear up the confusion.

■ **Outdated naming system**   The NetBIOS naming system built into Microsoft networks was out of step with the world. Microsoft supporters and detractors often share the presumption that Microsoft's conventions will someday become the world's conventions, but when it comes to naming resources, the world and the Internet were too big even for Microsoft. The growth of the Web-based technologies has made it increasingly difficult for Microsoft to justify basing its networks around NetBIOS rather than universally accepted and Internet-ready Domain Name System (DNS).

■ **Insufficient fault tolerance and bandwidth management** The special status of the primary domain controller (PDC) caused special problems when the PDC went offline. A backup domain controller (BDC) could be promoted, but promoting the BDC required human intervention. The PDC/BDC system also posed additional limitations for domains with multiple sites connected through slow wide area network (WAN) links.

■ **No informational context**   The NT domain, with its focus on network security, did only part of what a modern directory service is capable of doing and suffered from the missed opportunity to use its elaborate structure and services to support other types of functions.

▲ **Inelegant interface**   Objects, and the tools that managed objects, were confusing and conceptually inconsistent.

A look at how Active Directory addresses these limitations is the best way to begin this study of the Active Directory environment.

Flexible Security

As Figure 1-1 shows, Active Directory supports a new feature that was entirely missing from Windows NT: the *organizational unit* or OU. An OU is a container that you can create at any time just because you need a container. This container concept is reminiscent of Novell NetWare. You can place many different types of objects inside an OU container: printers, computers, domain controllers, and even users.

OUs create opportunities for subgrouping within a domain that were missing from Windows NT. You can place all users and computers of a single office into a separate OU and delegate authority for those objects to an OU administrator. The OU administrator can then manage users and resources even though he or she may not have access to similar resources in other parts of the domain. Alternatively, you can create position-based OUs, in which users and resources are organized by department rather than by geography. You can even place OUs inside other OUs. Through the Windows 2000 group policy

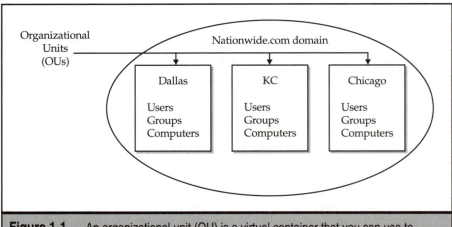

Figure 1-1. An organizational unit (OU) is a virtual container that you can use to subdivide the domain

feature, you can assign inheritable properties to users in the OU, including OU-based logon scripts.

Like Windows NT, Active Directory supports trust relationships for multidomain networks. But Microsoft has gone to considerable effort to organize and systematize the multidomain environment. Active Directory provides the one-way, nontransitive trust relationships used with Windows NT 4, but by default, Active Directory trusts are transitive and two-way (see Figure 1-2).

Windows 2000 domains can actually be structured in a hierarchy of domains. This hierarchy, which, as you'll see later, parallels the structure of domains and subdomains within the DNS namespace, is called a *domain tree*. A single Active Directory can even support multiple domain trees in what Microsoft refers to as a *forest*.

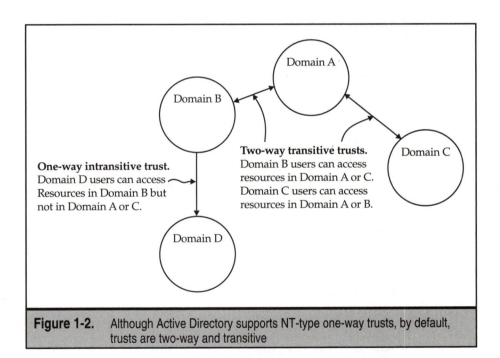

Figure 1-2.   Although Active Directory supports NT-type one-way trusts, by default, trusts are two-way and transitive

Windows 2000 native-mode Active Directory supports three kinds of groups:

▼ **Domain local groups**   Can contain user accounts, global groups, and universal groups from any domain. Can assign permissions only to objects in the domain in which the group exists.

■ **Global groups**   Can contain global groups and user accounts from the domain in which the group resides. Can assign permissions for all domains.

▲ **Universal groups**   Can contain accounts, global groups, and universal groups from all domains. Can assign permissions to all domains.

The group policy feature in Windows 2000 has an entirely new role and is better integrated with other security components than in previous Windows versions. This increased integration contributes to the increased granularity of the Active Directory permission system. You also have the option of disabling the security features of groups completely so that you can use the group as something more like e-mail distribution lists.

NOTE: The concept of a *nonsecurity group* is a good example of Microsoft's effort to position the Active Directory broadly as an *information database* rather than specifically as a *security information database*.

You'll learn more about trees, trusts, OUs, groups, and delegation of authority in later chapters.

DNS Integration

On Windows NT networks, it was easy enough to reference a computer using the Internet-based DNS name. Certain network resources, however, cannot be referenced by DNS, but instead must be referenced through a NetBIOS computer name using Microsoft's Universal Naming Convention (UNC). Indeed, a Windows NT or

Windows 9X computer must have a NetBIOS computer name to function on the network, and the NetBIOS naming system (with its WINS servers, b-node broadcasts, and LMHOSTS files) operates as a wholly separate and parallel system that must be maintained instead of (or in addition to) DNS.

Windows NT 4 introduced what Microsoft called DNS/WINS (Windows Internet Naming Service) integration, and this integration bridged the gap somewhat between the DNS and NetBIOS namespaces. But the need for this integration was an artifact of history, and eventually the task of maintaining the NetBIOS system began to look pointless even for Microsoft. Active Directory fully supports WINS name resolution, but according to Microsoft, on a fully compliant, native-mode Windows 2000 network, WINS is unnecessary.

Active Directory is built around DNS. If you don't have a DNS server, you can't even install Active Directory and, as mentioned, the Active Directory domain structure parallels the DNS domain structure.

Active Directory is a database of objects, and each object is classified and located through Microsoft's extensions of the DNS namespace. Though Active Directory is fully integrated with the DNS namespace, DNS handles only part of the task of locating Active Directory objects. The details of locating objects are left to domain controllers running the Lightweight Directory Access Protocol (LDAP) service. DNS servers identify LDAP servers operating on the network. An LDAP server is then used to locate the Active Directory object. This process is shown in Figure 1-3.

The Active Directory system is designed to exploit the advantages of dynamic DNS. (A dynamic DNS server does not require static mappings of IP address to host name but instead lets clients register host names and IP addresses automatically.) Active Directory does not specifically require the DNS implementation included with Windows 2000. Although Microsoft would love to see you use the Windows 2000 DNS (which was specifically designed to operate with Active Directory), the official Microsoft word on choosing a DNS server is that the DNS implementation *must* support SRV records, and it is highly recommended that the DNS server support dynamic updates and incremental zone transfer.

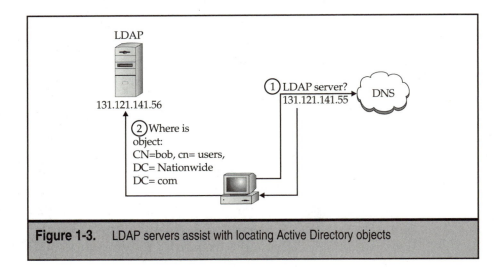

Figure 1-3. LDAP servers assist with locating Active Directory objects

NOTE: If your DNS server lives in the UNIX world, BIND 8.1.1 is Microsoft's recommendation for a DNS server that supports dynamic updates and SRV records.

Fault Tolerance and Bandwidth Management

On an Active Directory–based Windows 2000 network, all domain controllers have a writable copy of the directory. This equality of domain controllers increases fault tolerance and, in the case of networks divided with WAN links, improves performance by reducing the number of operations, which in NT 4 would have required access to the primary domain controller.

NOTE: Active Directory networks still have domain controllers with special roles. In Chapter 2, "Active Directory Concepts," you'll learn about Windows 2000's operations masters: the schema master, the domain naming master, the RID master, the infrastructure master, and the PDC emulator.

With all domain controllers writing to the directory, the task of managing and replicating directory changes becomes vastly more complicated. Replication traffic can command a major share of bandwidth in some situations. Add to this the much grander scale of the Active Directory database. For reasons of efficiency, Microsoft has had to become more sophisticated about managing directory replication traffic.

Active Directory includes the concept of a *site*, which, according to Microsoft, is "one or more well-connected IP subnets." In essence, a site consists of a group of computers connected through relatively fast LAN-type network connections. Sites are connected to other sites through relatively slow WAN connections. Through this feature, the Active Directory knows where each domain controller is in relation to the network and can time the replication traffic to maximize efficiency and minimize bandwidth. Domain controllers use one schedule for updating and synchronizing the directory within the local site and a different schedule for updating and synchronizing the directory with other sites across the WAN link.

A *bridgehead server* is a domain controller that is specifically assigned the role of passing replication traffic to other sites. Only the bridgehead server participates in replications across WAN links; other domain controllers do not (see Figure 1-4). Because the bridgehead server stays in equilibrium with other domain controllers within its own site, changes made on any domain controllers will eventually propagate to all parts of the network.

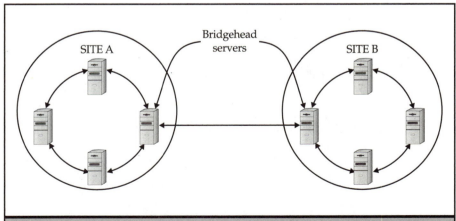

Figure 1-4. Active Directory can assign the role of replicating across WAN links to a bridgehead server

The Data Storehouse

Perhaps most the important thing to remember about Active Directory is that at the bottom of it all is a big directory—an information database. Active Directory is a storehouse of network information and a systematic means for retrieving that network information. If there is a new paradigm with Windows 2000, it is that the business of the network operating system is not security but *information*. Windows 2000 uses the Active Directory database to maintain security and manage resources. Active Directory–enabled domain controllers use the tools of Active Directory to maintain the logical structure of the network itself. Applications invisibly access Active Directory to adapt to the current environment. Administrators and users interactively search the directory for objects and attributes associated with those objects.

Active Directory plays a role in so many different types of activities that it is tempting to guess that Active Directory *is* Windows 2000. But this is something of an oversimplification. You can install Windows 2000 with or without Active Directory; without it, you still get some of the new tools and features discussed in this book, but you won't get the information-rich Active Directory environment. And you won't get the layered and logical network structure Active Directory provides.

Each object in the Active Directory database belongs to a class. A *class* is a definition for the object, a description of the types of data with which the object will be associated. Each class comes with a collection of attributes. An *attribute* is a single parameter associated with the class. For example, let's say that a user object called bob is a member of the built-in Active Directory class called *user*. An attribute associated with the class *user* is *TelephoneNumber*. The value of the attribute *TelephoneNumber* for the user object bob is 123-321-1230 (see Figure 1-5). The class user also has other attributes, each representing a parameter associated with a network user (*userPassword*, *employeeID*, *name*). This object-oriented approach to organizing data is not new to programmers, but previous versions of Windows did not expose the object model to users as openly as Microsoft has done with Active Directory. Essentially, two objects that may seem very different on the surface (say, a printer and a user) are considered logically similar within the Active Directory database. The only distinction is that each belongs to a different class with different attributes.

The collective definition of all classes and attributes for the directory is called the *schema*. The schema is a blueprint for the directory database, and Microsoft is careful to ensure that the schema remains safe and consistent. It is interesting to note that, even though an Active Directory network can have more than one domain tree, it can have only one schema. One of the domain controllers on the network serves as the schema master, which maintains a master copy of the schema for all domain controllers (see Figure 1-6).

It is possible for users and applications (with sufficient privilege) to modify the schema. This ability to customize the schema is a powerful feature that lets you harness the tools of Active Directory to organize almost any kind of information you want. In this book you'll learn how to modify the schema and you'll learn how and when you may wish to adapt the schema for your own administrative needs.

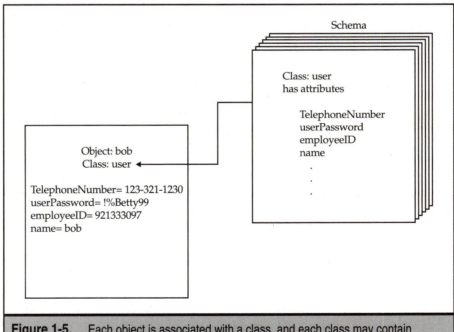

Figure 1-5. Each object is associated with a class, and each class may contain several attributes

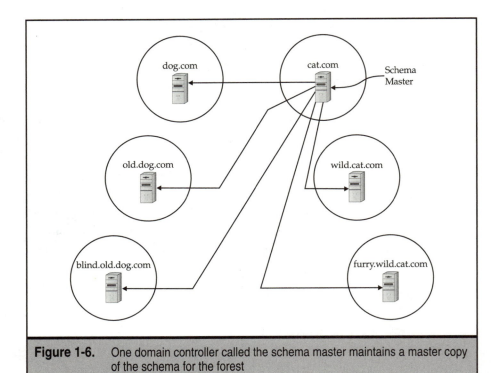

Figure 1-6. One domain controller called the schema master maintains a master copy of the schema for the forest

Some class and attribute values are stored in what is called the *global catalog*. The global catalog, according to Microsoft, is "a subset of the attributes for all objects in the Active Directory." Because the global catalog contains only some of the attributes associated with each object, it is smaller and queries run more efficiently than queries to the full directory. The global catalog contains enough information about an object to locate the object in the directory, and it is designed to provide a fast response for common queries. The first Active Directory domain controller is automatically a global catalog server. You can add additional global catalog servers later to help with resolving queries.

Some of the queries the global catalog resolves are invisible to the user. The global catalog maintains information on universal groups, for instance. (Universal groups, as described earlier in this chapter, are groups that provide access to resources in all network domains.) Active Directory services use the global catalog for fast location of resources. And users can query the global catalog directly to locate printers, users, computers, and other network objects. Through Active

Directory's schema customization features, you can add additional attributes to the list of attributes available for global-catalog queries.

Uniform Interface

The logic and uniformity of Windows 2000's object-oriented design is reflected in its more uniform and intuitive management tools. As you begin to explore your Active Directory–enabled Windows 2000 Server system, your first thought may be "What happened to User Manager?" Windows 2000 still has a big collection of management tools, but on Active Directory systems, many of the task-oriented utilities of NT have been integrated into more object-oriented, hierarchical utilities that reinforce the underlying philosophy that all objects are conceptually similar. These tools, designed to serve as snap-ins for the Microsoft Management Console (MMC) meta-tool, offer a treelike view of domains, OUs, computers, users, and devices.

NOTE: Microsoft Management Console, which made its debut sometime in the NT era, is a tool that acts as an interface to other tools.

When you first install Active Directory on a Windows 2000 system, you'll find some new tools in the Administrative Tools group. The three most central to daily operations are

▼ Active Directory Users and Computers

■ Active Directory Domains and Trusts

▲ Active Directory Sites and Services

These tools offer a view of the network, and an interface for managing the network, that have no equivalent in Windows NT. You can browse through all levels of the network structure and initiate a variety of management activities.

Active Directory Users and Computers, for instance, displays a hierarchical view of domains and lets you manage users, groups, domain controllers, organizational units, and computers within each of the domains (if you have the permissions to do so). By selecting a domain and choosing New from the right-click context menu, you can choose to add a new computer, contact, group, OU, printer, user, or shared folder to the domain (see Figure 1-7).

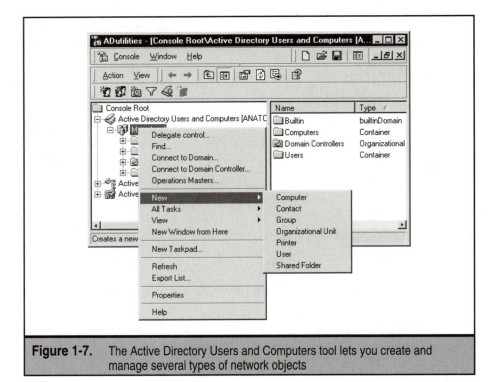

Figure 1-7. The Active Directory Users and Computers tool lets you create and manage several types of network objects

Other Active Directory management tools organize objects and tasks in a similar Explorer-like structure.

SUMMARY

This chapter introduced Active Directory and described how many important Active Directory features arose from limitations of Windows NT. But now that you've taken these first steps into the Active Directory environment, the best thing you can do is forget about NT. Active Directory is something bigger. It is a superstructure that fits around domain architecture and includes domains, users, groups, policies, and logons—but also many other things.

And now for the real story…

CHAPTER 2

Active Directory Concepts

The installation section fills the second chapter of most computer books. However, Active Directory is as wide and as deep as the whole network, and if you glean one gem of wisdom from this book, it should be that you will surely limit your possibilities if you rush to install Active Directory without a thorough understanding of how it functions. *Installing* Active Directory is easy. *Planning* for Active Directory is the hard part, and you must certainly plan before you install if you want to maximize the effectiveness of Active Directory.

The next few chapters cover some important topics you'll need to know about before you set up your own Active Directory network, including replication, users and groups, and Active Directory's relationship with Transmission Control Protocol/Internet Protocol (TCP/IP). This chapter addresses some fundamental concepts that form a foundation for understanding the Active Directory environment, including

▼ Mixed mode and native mode

■ The structure of the Active Directory network, including the roles of operations masters and the reasons for configuring multiple domains

▲ Active Directory naming conventions

An understanding of these concepts will help you prepare for the daunting task of setting up Active Directory and tailoring it for your own environment.

NOTE: If you're in a hurry, you'll find a discussion of planning and installing the Active Directory network in Chapter 7, "Setting Up Active Directory."

MIXED MODE AND NATIVE MODE

An Active Directory domain can operate in either of two modes:

▼ **Mixed mode** An operating mode that allows Windows NT 4 and Windows 2000 domain controllers to coexist on the network.

▲ **Native mode** An operating mode designed to provide a full complement of Windows 2000 features on networks where all domain controllers are running Windows 2000 and Active Directory.

Mixed mode is Active Directory's default operating mode. When you first install Active Directory on a domain, the domain will be a mixed-mode domain. It will remain a mixed-mode domain until all domain controllers are upgraded to Windows 2000 domain controllers and the operating mode is deliberately changed to native mode by a network administrator (as described later in this section).

As you might guess, mixed mode is primarily designed to facilitate the transition from an existing Windows NT 4 domain to a Windows 2000 domain. You'll learn more about the network upgrade process in Chapter 7. For now, a brief look at that process will help explain the distinction between mixed mode and native mode. Schematically, the upgrade process is as follows:

1. The domain is officially considered a Windows NT 4 domain until the Primary Domain Controller (PDC) is upgraded. As described in Chapter 7, the upgrade to a Windows 2000 domain should begin with the NT 4 PDC.

2. Once the PDC is upgraded and Active Directory is installed, the domain becomes a mixed-mode domain. In mixed mode, Windows NT 4 Backup Domain Controllers (BDCs) continue to function as before.

3. While the domain operates in mixed mode, you can gradually upgrade the BDCs to Windows 2000.

4. Once all domain controllers have been upgraded to Windows 2000 Active Directory domain controllers, you can switch the operating mode to native mode using the Active Directory Users and Computers utility (as described later in this chapter).

CAUTION: The transition from mixed mode to native mode is one-way. You cannot change a native-mode domain back to a mixed-mode domain.

The details of a particular network upgrade plan will define whether an organization should be in a hurry to transition to native mode. Microsoft has said that you can leave a domain in mixed mode "indefinitely." The Windows 2000 domain management tools and a wide range of other Windows 2000 features are available through mixed mode. Still, a few of the more innovative Active Directory features are incomprehensible to Windows NT domain controllers and thus are not available on mixed-mode domains. If you are planning a complex network and you wish to exploit the full range of Active Directory features, your upgrade plan should provide for an eventual transition to native mode.

A few important points to keep in mind about mixed mode:

▼ *Mixed mode does not support universal groups.* (A universal group can include members from any domain in the forest and provide access to resources on any domain in the forest.) See Chapter 5, "Users and Groups."

■ *Mixed mode does not support nested groups.* See Chapter 5.

■ *Mixed mode does not provide the full range of management options for Windows NT 4 domain controllers through the Windows 2000 management tools.*

■ *Mixed mode does not permit you to control remote access through Windows 2000's access-by-policy administrative model.*

▲ *Mixed mode does not automatically provide password filtering on all domain controllers—you have to configure password filtering separately.*

Administrators of very large networks should also be aware that mixed-mode domains have size constraints similar to those of Windows NT 4 domains. Specifically, the total number of computers, groups, and users for a mixed-mode domain should not exceed 40,000.

It is worth noting that this need to upgrade to Windows 2000 before switching to native mode applies specifically to domain controllers. A Windows NT Server 4 member server and pre–Windows 2000 client can continue to operate in a native-mode domain.

A CLOSER LOOK AT THE ACTIVE DIRECTORY NETWORK

A Windows 2000 domain is shown in Figure 2-1. Chapter 1 introduced many of the elements you see in this figure.

The *domain* is the fundamental security structure of a Windows 2000 network. The boundaries among domains are better integrated and less restrictive in Windows 2000 than they were in Windows NT, but users, groups, and computers still maintain a domain affiliation.

The domain controllers on a Windows 2000 domain act as equals, authenticating users and husbanding the Active Directory database. Domain controllers synchronize the Active Directory database through a complex replication process. You'll learn more about directory replication in Chapter 4, "Understanding Replication." Every domain controller does not replicate to every other domain controller. Instead, the Active Directory infrastructure for the domain maintains a *replication topology* for the domain—a network of pathways among the domain controllers describing how the directory will be replicated. Changes to the Active Directory are passed along the replication pathways, and eventually a change made through one domain controller passes to all domain controllers.

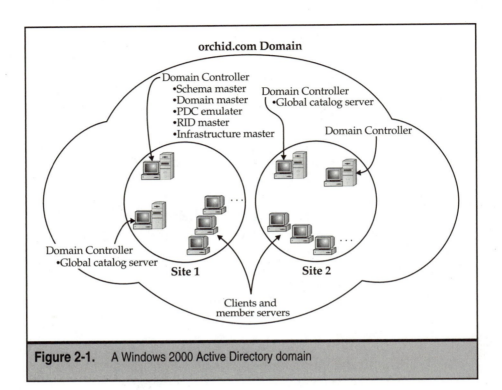

orchid.com Domain

Domain Controller
•Schema master
•Domain master
•PDC emulater
•RID master
•Infrastructure master

Domain Controller
•Global catalog server

Domain Controller

Domain Controller
•Global catalog server

Site 1

Site 2

Clients and
member servers

Figure 2-1. A Windows 2000 Active Directory domain

Figure 2-1 shows the domain divided into two *sites*. A site is
a logical division of the domain that coincides with the physical
division imposed by a slow WAN link. As Chapter 4 describes in
detail, you can define a different replication interval for replications
that must pass between the sites. A bridgehead server is a domain
controller that replicates across the WAN link on behalf of a given site.

It is important to note that the site topology, as shown in Figure
2-1, has nothing to do with the domain as a security and information
structure. In the figure, Site 1 and Site 2 are in the *same* domain, and,
when all changes are replicated, the Active Directory database for
domain controllers in Site 1 will be identical to the Active Directory
database for domain controllers in Site 2. When a change is made to
the directory, however, it may take longer for that change to be
replicated to domain controllers on other sites.

Microsoft divides the data in the Active Directory into what it calls *partitions.* The Active Directory partitions are as follows:

▼ **Domain partition**   Information about objects in the domain, including organizational units, computers, users, groups, and printers.

■ **Configuration partition**   Information about the network, including domains, sites, available network services, and the locations of domain controllers on all domains of the network.

▲ **Schema partition**   Information on the structure of the Active Directory itself. The schema partition contains object class and attribute data, as described in Chapter 1, "The Active Directory Environment."

NOTE: In this case, the term "partition" refers to a data structure within the directory. This should not be confused with the term "partition" that commonly refers to a logical division of a hard disk.

The schema and configuration partitions are replicated through all domains in the network. The domain partition is replicated only within the domain. (See Figure 2-2.) A scaled-down version of the domain partition is replicated to global catalog servers. As Chapter 1 describes, a global catalog server holds a limited collection of object attributes for all domains on the network and is designed to provide efficient responses to queries. A global catalog server keeps a copy of the partial domain directory partition for all domains in the forest. (See Figure 2-3.) Because a global catalog server is itself a domain controller, it keeps the full domain partition for its own domain. A network can have multiple global catalog servers. Each global catalog server has the full domain partition for its own domain and a partial domain partition for all other domains.

Operations Masters

The multimaster strategy for maintaining the Active Directory (in which multiple domain controllers each hold a writable master copy of the database) works well for most varieties of directory information,

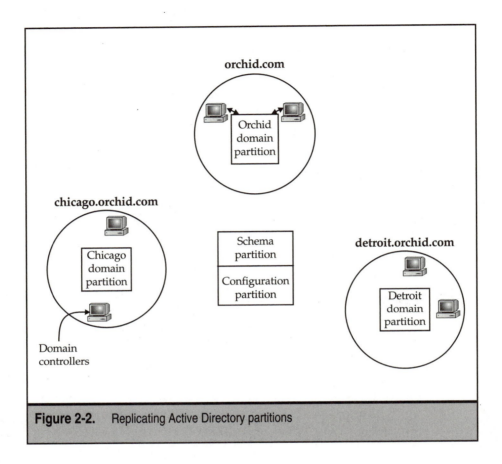

Figure 2-2. Replicating Active Directory partitions

but some types of data require tighter control. For that reason, some directory functions are overseen in single-master format, in which a single domain controller called an *operations master* assumes sole responsibility for that function.

Each Active Directory domain has an operations master serving in all of the following roles:

▼ **PDC emulator** In mixed mode, the PDC emulator accepts password changes and replicates the security database to Windows NT BDCs. (As its name describes, the PDC emulator acts as a PDC for pre–Windows 2000 computers that require a PDC to function.) In native mode, the PDC emulator still performs a role in processing password changes. When a

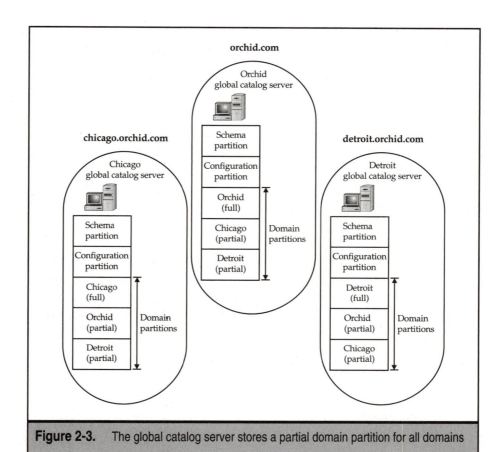

Figure 2-3.   The global catalog server stores a partial domain partition for all domains

change is made to a password, the change is forwarded to the PDC emulator through what Microsoft calls *preferential replication*. The PDC emulator thus learns of the change in advance of the replication cycle, which can sometimes take several hours. Before denying a logon request because of an incorrect password, domain controllers will forward the request to the PDC emulator to ensure that the password hasn't changed since the last replication.

■ **Relative identifier (RID) master**   As you'll learn later in this chapter, when a new object is created, it receives a unique ID. Part of that ID consists of the security identifier for the domain, and part of it consists of a *relative ID* that distinguishes the object within the domain. The RID master allocates relative IDs to each domain controller that will be issuing globally unique identifiers (GUIDs) to objects. The RID master is also used when an object is moved from one domain to another domain.

▲ **Infrastructure master**   The infrastructure master updates group membership lists to reflect to reflect name changes. If a username changes, the Infrastructure master will ensure that the groups to which the user belongs will be updated to reflect the change.

Certain operations are so critical and sensitive that only one domain controller in the entire forest can perform them. (As you learned in Chapter 1, a *forest* is a collection of all domains in a multidomain Active Directory network.) Each Active Directory forest has one and only one domain controller performing all of the following roles:

▼ **Schema master**   Maintains the master copy of the schema.

▲ **Domain master**   Oversees the creation and deletion of domains in the forest.

You do not need five domain controllers on your network to support these five special server roles. A single domain controller can (and typically does) serve multiple operations master roles.

The first Active Directory domain controller in a new forest assumes *all* operations master roles (PDC emulator, RID master, Infrastructure master, schema master, domain master). If additional domains are added to the forest, the first domain controller in the new domain assumes the domain-level operations master roles for the new domain (PDC emulator, RID master, infrastructure master).

Windows 2000 lets the administrator reassign operations master roles. For small networks, it is rarely necessary to change the default operations master assignments. On large and busy networks, though, or on networks where an operations master has gone offline, it is often necessary to change an operations master assignment. For purposes of planning your network and understanding the interaction of its various components, it is worth noting the following Microsoft recommendations for operations master assignments:

1. In most domains, it is better to let the same domain controller serve as both RID master and PDC emulator. On very large domains, especially in a mixed environment, you may wish to separate these roles to reduce demand on the PDC emulator.

2. Give the role of infrastructure master to a domain controller that is not a global catalog server but is located on the same site as a global catalog server.

3. The same domain controller should serve as both the schema master and the domain naming master. Demand for these forestwide masters is small. The dissemination of changes will be most efficient if the domain controller that performs these functions is on the same site with the users or groups that are most likely to create a domain or alter the schema.

NOTE: You can view and change domain-level operations master assignments using the Active Directory Users and Computers utility. Right-click on the domain and choose Operations Masters. The Operations Master dialog box appears, with tabs for managing the RID, PDC, and Infrastructure masters. (See Figure 2-4.)

Multiple Domains

New Active Directory features such as sites and organizational units are designed to reduce the need for multidomain networks, but, at the same time, Microsoft has designed Active Directory to support and even encourage multiple-domain configurations. Microsoft's goal was not to create confusion through this apparent paradox, but rather to make Windows 2000 flexible and adaptable to a diverse range of network designs.

You'll learn more about planning an Active Directory network in Chapter 7, but in the meantime it is important to be aware that before you even begin migrating your network to Windows 2000 and Active Directory, you should decide whether you want to employ Windows

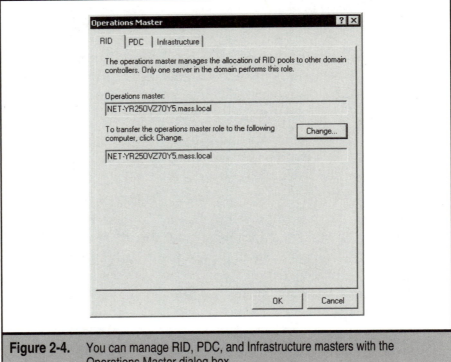

Figure 2-4. You can manage RID, PDC, and Infrastructure masters with the Operations Master dialog box.

2000 in a multidomain configuration and, if so, how you would like these domains to be organized. Of course, a healthy design is always approached from all sides at once. Your choice of a domain configuration may depend on other factors explored in upcoming chapters, such as the physical network, the TCP/IP and DNS configuration, and your system for managing users and groups.

But you may be wondering why anyone would even *want* to create multiple domains, since domains are not necessary to define an internal LAN or delegate authority for resources.

Most situations that would have required a resource (trusting) domain in Windows NT 4 can be addressed using an *organizational unit* (OU) in Windows 2000. There are, however, still reasons for implementing a multiple-domain network. Microsoft suggests the following reasons for creating multiple domains:

▼ **Separable security**   It is possible to delegate authority for an OU to an OU-level administrator, but an OU still falls within the security structure of its parent domain. If two entities with entirely separate security policies and structures are located on the same network, you may wish to place them in separate domains.

■ **Namespace**   As Chapter 1 described, Active Directory is designed to operate within DNS naming conventions, and Active Directory domain names follow the format of DNS names. You may wish to implement a multidomain network to reflect an existing DNS zone structure.

■ **Replication**   Active Directory's site feature (described earlier) makes replication more efficient, but, on a multisite domain, the full directory database must still be replicated across a slow WAN link. Replicating the full directory across the WAN link absorbs considerable bandwidth. Also, the longer interval used for intersite directory replication means that it takes longer for a change to be reflected throughout the domain. If two geographically separate sites are configured as separate domains, the full domain partition is not replicated across the WAN link—only a partial domain partition is replicated to global directory servers. (In either a multiple- or a single-domain configuration, the schema and configuration partitions are replicated.)

▲ **Migration**   A Windows 2000 multidomain environment is sometimes the result of an upgrade from a Windows NT 4 multidomain environment. It is possible to consolidate a multidomain Windows NT 4 environment into a single Windows 2000 domain, but, in some cases, it is logistically more appropriate to maintain the existing structure.

Microsoft recommends that domains *not* be used to define an organizational structure within the network if the preceding considerations do not apply. For instance, a separate domain *should not* be used to subdivide the marketing department within a corporate organization unless there is some overriding security interest requiring the marketing department to have a wholly separate system.

Another reason for implementing (or not implementing) a multidomain environment is that a separate domain lets you apply separate domain-level group policies. Active Directory's group policy feature (which you'll learn about in Chapter 6, "Group Policy") lets you apply a set of policy settings to a site, domain, or OU. Some of the group policy settings are reminiscent of system policy settings in the Windows NT 4 environment. Other aspects of Active Directory group policies are new with Windows 2000: startup and logon scripts, folder redirection, and preconfigured software installations. (See Figure 2-5.)

In a multidomain environment, you can use the group policy feature to apply separate domain-based policies to each domain. (See Figure 2-6.) You can, of course, alternatively apply nested OU policies to achieve a similar result, but since the domain is the fundamental security structure on a Microsoft network, applying

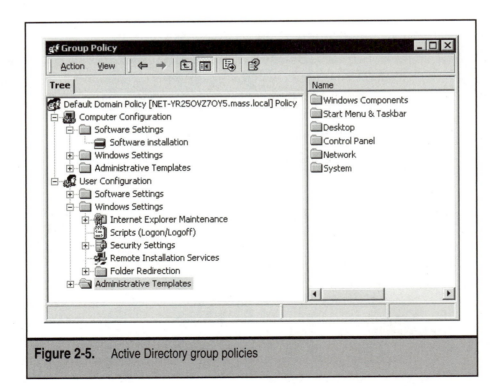

Figure 2-5.   Active Directory group policies

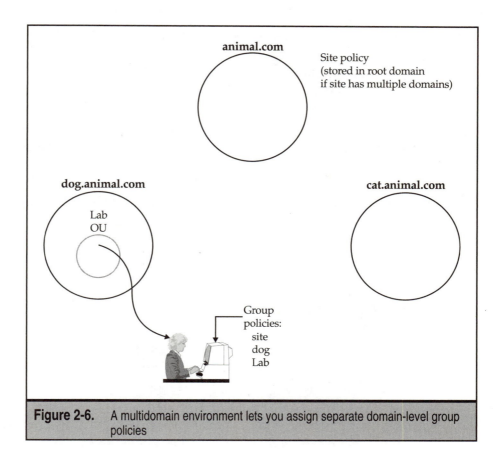

animal.com

Site policy
(stored in root domain
if site has multiple domains)

dog.animal.com

cat.animal.com

Lab
OU

Group
policies:
site
dog
Lab

Figure 2-6.   A multidomain environment lets you assign separate domain-level group
policies

distinctive security policies at the domain level is the best approach
in some situations.

Whatever the design of your network, the interaction of site, domain,
and OU group policy is a tricky subject that you must study carefully.
See Chapter 6 for more on group policy.

NAMING OBJECTS IN ACTIVE DIRECTORY

Chapter 1 revealed that Active Directory makes extensive use of DNS
for naming objects on the network. DNS, however, is not designed
for the exotic detail of a full-featured directory service like Active
Directory. DNS was originally intended only for locating computers
and other network devices. Extensions to DNS have made it possible

to locate printers, files, directories, and other shared objects, but DNS has no facility for locating a directory attribute such as, say, a user's telephone number.

The hierarchy of the DNS namespace solves only part of the problem of naming and locating objects on a directory-based network. The Internet community has for some time been aware of the need for a more general directory-based naming system that would include DNS within its functionality but would also support names for a wider range of objects and provide interoperability among the various proprietary directory systems. OSI developed a standard called X.500 for naming and referencing network objects. The Internet community applied the X.500 standard to the TCP/IP environment through protocols such as the Lightweight Directory Access Protocol (LDAP). Active Directory uses X.500 naming conventions to specify and locate network objects.

The LDAP/X.500 format may seem foreign to those who have worked in NT and other Microsoft systems, but those who have worked with NetWare 4.X and other directory-based naming systems will find the style of LDAP/X.500 names a bit more recognizable.

The LDAP naming system uniquely identifies every object on the network through a comma-separated list of name values. The values represent positions within the namespace hierarchy, with the root component on the right. The full name (called the *distinguished name*) for the user object shown in Figure 2-7 is

```
cn=Bill,ou=martians,ou=aliens,dc=sci_fi,dc=heros,dc=com
```

Note that each part of the name is associated with an object class attribute. The naming class attribute values available through Active Directory are shown in Table 2-1. Active Directory inherited this vigorous naming scheme from LDAP. This format seems incredibly confusing at a glance and, even at a long look it is never what one would call intuitive. However, the task of assigning a class attribute to each name value can be reduced to a few simple rules:

1. Anything that is part of a DNS domain name gets the *dc* attribute.

2. Organizational units get the *ou* attribute.

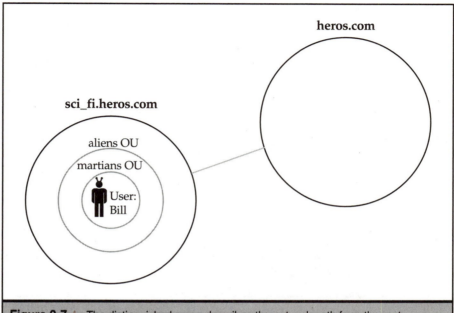

Figure 2-7.   The distinguished name describes the network path from the root
container to the object you're naming

3.   All other values get the *cn* attribute.

The distinguished name must uniquely identify the object in the
Active Directory.

NOTE: RFC 2253 specifies additional naming class attribute values
that aren't used in Active Directory.

Recall from Chapter 1 that the Active Directory is composed of
objects and attributes. Each value in the distinguished name is a
name attribute associated with an object. The path shown in Figure
2-7, for instance, includes an organizational unit object with the name
Martians and a user object with the name Bill. The distinguished
name is essentially a path through the container objects to a leaf
object you wish to locate or specify.

Microsoft uses the term *relative distinguished name* (RDN) to refer
to the portion of the name that is a name attribute of the object being

Naming Class Attribute Value	Full Name	Description
dc	Domain component	Designates a value within the distinguished name path that is a component of the DNS domain name
ou	Organizational unit	Designates the name of an organizational unit
cn	Common name	Designates other Active Directory object names

Table 2-1. Naming Class Attribute Values for Distinguished Names

named (as opposed to the path of the container in which the object resides). In Figure 2-7, for instance, the relative distinguished name of the object *cn=Bill, ou=martians, ou=aliens, dc=sci_fi, dc=heros, dc=com* is *Bill*. The maximum length for an RDN is 255 characters. However, the directory schema may impose shorter name limits for some objects.

NOTE: For a complete discussion of LDAP/X.500 naming conventions, see RFC 1779, RFC 2247, RFC 2251, or RFC 2253. The Internet RFCs are posted at numerous locations on the World Wide Web. To find an RFC, just enter its name (e.g., RFC 2251) into one of the Internet search engines, such as Lycos or Yahoo.

The common name attribute used for an object in the distinguished name or RDN is mostly for the benefit of humans. Internally, Windows refers to an object by a unique 128-bit *globally unique identifier* (GUID). The GUID is sometimes referred to as the object's *identity*. The GUID value is assigned to an object attribute called *objectGUID*. Every object in the directory has an objectGUID attribute that is unique in the directory. The distinguished name of an object changes if the object is moved to a different container. The RDN changes if an object is renamed, but the GUID is constant throughout the life of the object.

Active Directory does not require that you use the ungainly distinguished name to reference resources. In fact, a different format, called the *Active Directory canonical name format,* is the default format for displaying object names in the Windows 2000 user interface. An Active Directory canonical name starts with the dotted DNS name and then traces through the container hierarchy to the object name with the forward slash (/) as a separator, like so:

```
sci_fi.heros.com/aliens/martians/Bill
```

The Active Directory canonical name is reminiscent of the integrated DNS/WINS name path used in Windows NT 4.

You can also refer to an Active Directory object through a URL. The URL-based name format is useful in scripts and Web-based tools that may require access to the Active Directory. The URL format tacks the complete distinguished name on the end of the dotted DNS name, like so:

```
LDAP:// sci_fi.heros.com/cn=Bill,ou=martians,ou=aliens,dc=sci_fi,dc=heros,dc=com
```

Note the *LDAP* before the colon, which signifies that access will be through the LDAP protocol.

In some circumstances, Windows 2000 is capable of working with less than the full hierarchical path of the object name. The *user principal name,* for instance, is a shortened version of the full user object name that can be used as a logon name. By default, the user principal name consists of the username and the domain on which the user account resides (separated with an @ sign): Attila@pillage.com.

The user principal name may look like a condensed version of the distinguished name, but it is actually the value for a separate attribute called *userPrincipalName* that is associated with the user object. The portion of the user principal name after the @ sign is called the *user principal name suffix.* By default, the user principal name suffix matches the DNS name of the domain on which the user account resides. As you'll learn in Chapter 5, you can preconfigure other optional user principal name suffixes for the domain and select an alternative logon name and user principal name suffix for a user account. (This feature is useful when the actual domain name may be long and difficult to remember.) Because the user principal name is independent of the distinguished name, it is not affected if the user object is moved to a different container.

NOTE: It is worth noting that you can perform a great many administrative functions through Active Directory's graphics-based utilities (such as Active Directory Users and Computers and Active Directory Domains and Trusts) without ever running across a distinguished name or a canonical name. A foundation in the naming formats is nevertheless essential for understanding Active Directory and its object-oriented architecture.

SUMMARY

This chapter examined a few important concepts you'll need to study and understand to get the full picture of Active Directory, such as mixed mode and native mode, operations masters, multidomain environments, and Active Directory naming formats. These concepts appear frequently in later parts of the book as the story of Active Directory unfolds.

PART II

Setting Up Your Network

CHAPTER 3

Active Directory with TCP/IP and DNS

ACTIVE DIRECTORY AND DNS

The Domain Name System (DNS) is an integral part of the Active Directory environment. In fact, you can't even install Active Directory unless a suitable DNS server is present on your network—and not just any DNS server. Active Directory clients use DNS servers to locate Active Directory domain controllers, and the DNS server must support the SRV record in order to list domain controllers. Microsoft has an example of a DNS service that will support Active Directory networks: their own Windows 2000 DNS server, which they "Micro-centrically" call DNS Server. The following sections describe the Active Directory DNS environment. Configuring DNS, even configuring a single DNS implementation such as Microsoft DNS Server, could be the subject of a book by itself. This chapter will not attempt to derive the entire DNS system from the ground up, but will focus primarily on how Active Directory uses DNS and how to configure Windows 2000's DNS Server to support Active Directory.

It is important to note that not all networks will use Windows 2000's built-in DNS Server to support the Active Directory environment. Microsoft gives BIND 8.1.1 as an example of a DNS implementation that is compatible with Active Directory. Commercial Active Directory–compatible DNS implementations will no doubt begin to emerge as Windows 2000 begins reaching the public.

How DNS Works

As I promised, I will not attempt to describe all the options and nuances of DNS. However, it is worthwhile to pause for a brief description of what DNS is.

At its most basic level, DNS is a system for associating host names with IP addresses. Through DNS, computers and users are able to associate a computer with an easy-to-remember host name rather than with a numerical IP address. On simple networks, a computer can use a *hosts* file for host-name-to-IP-address name resolution. A hosts file is little more than a text file containing a series of host-name-to-IP-address pairs. If the computer needs to contact another computer that has the host name Ralph, it looks in its hosts file to find the entry for Ralph and retrieves the IP address for Ralph.

On larger networks, it is impractical to map all host names to IP addresses in a text file. (A good example is the Internet. Who wants to create and maintain a text file that lists all computers on the Internet?) Computers connected to the Internet or almost any other medium-to-large-sized TCP/IP network use DNS servers to resolve host names.

A DNS server offers the service of DNS name resolution for the network (see Figure 3-1). A DNS server stores several different types of DNS-related records and makes these records available to clients. These records are called *resource records*. Some common resource record types include the following:

▼ **Host record (A record)**   Associates a DNS name with an IP address.

■ **Pointer record (PTR record)**   Associates an IP address with a DNS name. PTR records are used in reverse lookup zones. See the section titled "Adding Reverse Lookup Zones," later in this chapter.

■ **Start of Authority (SOA record)**   General information on the zone, including the authoritative DNS server for the zone, the responsible person, the update serial number, and refresh and expiration parameters.

■ **Name Server (NS record)**   Primary and secondary DNS servers for the zone; delegated zones.

■ **Alias record (CNAME record)**   Lets you map additional alias host names to an A record.

■ **Service record (SRV record)**   Lets you locate network services through DNS. SRV records were infrequently used until recently, and many DNS implementations don't support them. As you'll learn in the next section, Active Directory uses DNS servers to locate Active Directory domain controllers, and, therefore, Active Directory–enabled DNS implementations must support SRV records.

▲ **Mail Exchanger (MX record)**   Used to designate mail servers for the network.

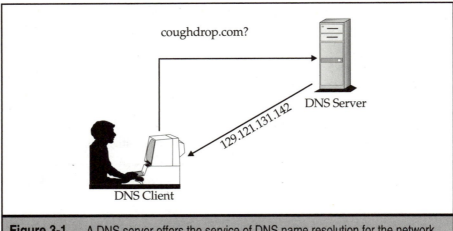

coughdrop.com?

DNS Server

129.121.131.142

DNS Client

Figure 3-1.   A DNS server offers the service of DNS name resolution for the network

In most DNS implementations, these DNS records are listed in a file on the DNS server computer. Windows 2000, however, lets you alternatively store host lookup information in the Active Directory.

You may ask what happens when the DNS server doesn't know the answer to the query. What if the query asks for an IP address that is beyond the DNS server's sphere of influence? For instance, what if a client in Kalamazoo asks for the IP address of a Web server in Katmandu? The beauty of DNS is that it is hierarchical. Multiple layers of DNS servers can work together to resolve a query. In the case of the Internet, the chain of DNS servers can reach all the way around the world.

The most common method for resolving queries beyond the local zone is known as *recursion*. An example of recursion is shown in Figure 3-2. The process is as follows:

1. A client computer in the domain shoehorn.com wants the IP address of a host named Rabbit in the west.texas.org domain. The client sends a request to its preferred DNS server.

2. The DNS server checks whether it can fulfill the request. (It checks its own zone records and its cache.)

3. If the DNS server cannot fulfill the request, it parses the domain name and sends a request to a DNS server

in the top-level domain (.org) for a DNS server in the texas.org domain.

4. The DNS server then sends a query to a DNS server in the texas.org domain for a DNS server in the west.texas.org domain.

5. The DNS server then sends a query to the west.texas.org DNS server for the address of the host *Rabbit*.

6. The DNS server replies to the client with the IP address of *Rabbit* in the west.texas.org domain.

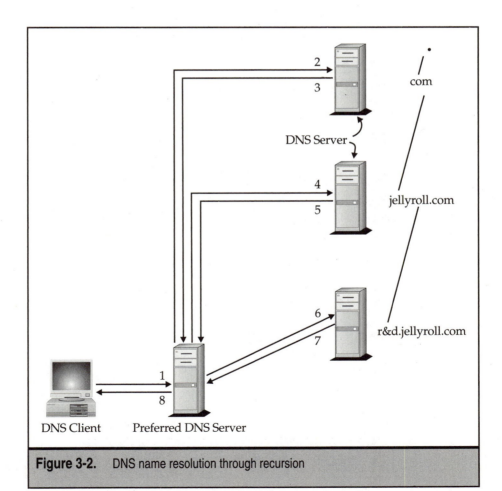

Figure 3-2. DNS name resolution through recursion

An alternative method for resolving remote queries is known as *iteration*. Iteration is used primarily in cases where either the client or the server does not support recursion. Iteration (see Figure 3-3) places the primary responsibility for resolving the query on the client. If the preferred DNS server can't resolve the query, it responds to the client with the address of another DNS server that may be closer to the queried name. The client must then contact the new DNS server and move successively through the chain of servers until it comes to a server that can resolve the query.

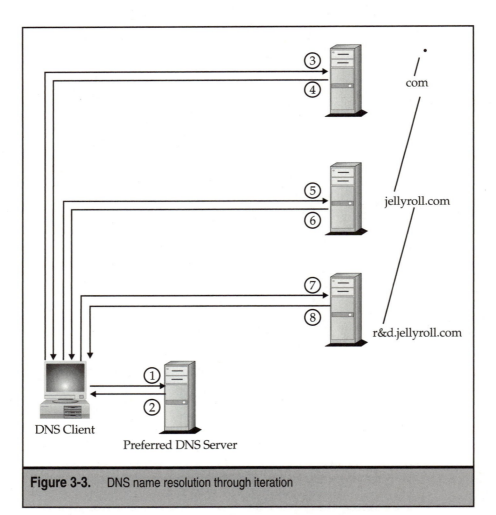

Figure 3-3. DNS name resolution through iteration

The DNS Namespace

The DNS namespace is divided into a hierarchy of names (see Figure 3-4). The highest level is always root, which is designated with a period (.). The DNS names space must have a root. If your namespace is connected to the Internet namespace, the Internet root will be the root for your namespace. If you are configuring your own local DNS namespace that won't be part of a larger namespace, you must configure root.

NOTE: If you set up DNS automatically when you install Active Directory, the Setup Wizard will configure root.

Under root are top-level domains (signifying large divisions of the namespace such as com, org, or gov), and second-level domains, typically signifying organizations. The owner of the second-level domain usually has the freedom to further subdivide its own portion of the namespace into subdomains.

At the lowest level of the tree is the host name, which typically signifies a computer. The fully qualified domain name (FQDN) for a host is a period-separated path from the host through all levels of the namespace, as shown here:

my_host.my_subdomain.my_domain.org

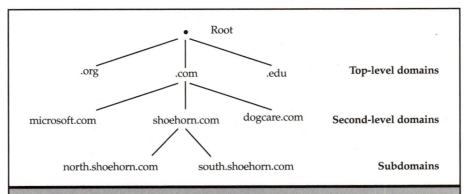

Figure 3-4.   The DNS namespace is divided into a hierarchy of names

The maximum length for a DNS name is 63 characters per label or 255 per FQDN. Internet RFC 1123 calls for DNS names to consist of numerals 0–9, capital letters A–Z, lowercase letters a–z, and the hyphen. Microsoft strongly recommends that you use these characters for DNS names. It should be noted, however, that Windows 2000's DNS implementation also supports additional ASCII and Unicode characters to promote compatibility with NetBIOS names. In Windows 2000, DNS names may include additional characters such as these: ! @ # $ % ^ & ' ( ) _ - { } ~ . Note that if you use these additional characters, you are limiting your ability to interoperate with the rest of the DNS world.

Understanding Zones

A division of the DNS database is called a *zone*. A zone might, but does not necessarily, coincide with a DNS domain. A *domain* is a division of the DNS namespace.

You can think of a zone as a range of DNS names that the DNS server will manage together. The term *zone* has also come to refer to the database of DNS-related information encompassed by the zone. If you create a zone for the DNS domain shoehorn.com, one DNS server will hold a writable master copy of the zone information. The zone is defined on this DNS server as a primary zone. It is often necessary for other DNS servers to assist with the role of resolving queries for the host names in the zone. In that case, alternate DNS servers receive a copy of the zone information from the DNS server with the primary zone. These alternate DNS servers are said to hold *secondary zones*—a copy of the primary zone information.

A DNS server with a primary zone can delegate part of the namespace within the zone to another primary zone. For instance, the DNS server that holds the primary zone for shoehorn.com can delegate primary responsibility for the subdomain north.shoehorn.com to another primary zone. Primary, secondary, and delegated zones are depicted in Figure 3-5.

Traditionally, a full copy of the primary zone was copied to the secondary zones at some predefined update interval. Recent versions of DNS, however, including the Windows 2000 DNS implementation, allow *incremental* zone transfer. Incremental zone transfer is defined

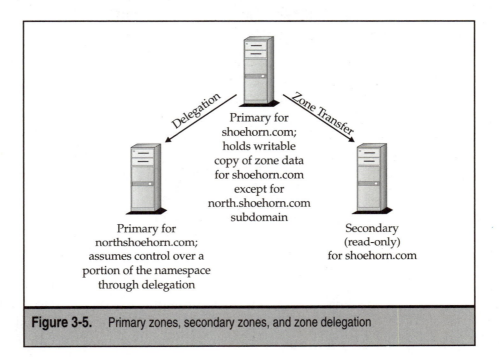

Figure 3-5.   Primary zones, secondary zones, and zone delegation

in RFC 1995. Under incremental zone transfer, the entire zone database is copied to the secondary zone when the secondary is created. After that, only changes are copied to the secondaries.

Some events that trigger a zone transfer are as follows:

▼ The end of zone refresh interval triggers an automatic transfer.

■ The primary zone server signals that it has a change.

▲ A manual zone transfer is initiated from the secondary.

A zone transfer also occurs automatically when the DNS service starts on the server that holds the secondary zone.

A DNS server can, and often does, hold multiple zones. A DNS server can be a primary for one or more zones and a secondary for other zones. Zone information is typically stored in a text file on the DNS server. On Windows 2000 Server computers, the DNS zone data file has a .dns extension and is stored in the system_root\System32\ DNS directory. Active Directory, however, adds a new twist to the process of storing and transferring zones. You'll learn about that new twist in the next section.

Active Directory—Integrated Zones

Rather than using a text file to store DNS zone data, you can elect to store zone data in Active Directory itself. You can thus leverage all the benefits of the Active Directory infrastructure for managing zone data. Some advantages of using Active Directory–integrated zones include the following:

▼ **Security**   You don't have to keep all the zone data in a text file. Active Directory includes a more secure and versatile security structure than the traditional DNS zone transfer mechanism.

■ **Efficiency**   You don't have to maintain two separate data replication systems. Active Directory transfers data faster and more efficiently than traditional DNS zone data transfer. Also, Active Directory is more attuned to the physical structure of the network and is preconfigured to compensate for slower WAN links with bandwidth-conserving intersite replication measures. (See the section titled "Sites and Subnets in Active Directory," later in this chapter.)

▲ **Fault tolerance**   The Active Directory's multimaster format allows more than one DNS server to update zone information.

An Active Directory domain controller that is acting as a DNS server can support an Active Directory–integrated zone. You can only store primary zone data in Active Directory. An Active Directory integrated zone is a primary zone. However, as a consequence of Active Directory's multimaster architecture, other DNS servers configured for the zone can write changes to the Active Directory–integrated zone database. See the later section titled "Adding Active Directory–Integrated Zones."

Dynamic Updates

Windows 2000 clients are configured to work with Windows 2000 DNS Server and the DHCP service to provide dynamic updates for A and PTR records. By default, the Windows 2000 client's DHCP client service will register dynamic DNS updates, even if the client is not receiving an IP address through DHCP.

If the client receives an IP address through DHCP and the DHCP server is configured to support dynamic updates, the client DHCP service will update the A record and the DHCP server service will update the PTR record.

To configure the DHCP service to support dynamic update, follow these steps:

1. Select Start | Programs | Administrative Tools | DHCP.

2. In the DHCP main window, right-click the server you want to configure to support dynamic update, and then choose Properties.

3. In the DHCP Server Properties dialog box, select the DNS tab.

4. In the DNS tab (see Figure 3-6), make sure Automatically Update DHCP Client Information In DNS is checked. Choose one of the following options:

   - **Update DNS Only If DHCP Client Requests**   Updates only the records the client, asks the server to update. For a Windows 2000 client in the default configuration, this will be the PTR record.

   - **Always Update DNS**   The DHCPS server updates A and PTR records whenever it assigns an address.

The Enable DNS Updates For Clients That Do Not Support Dynamic Update option lets the DHCP server update the DNS server even if the client computer does not support updates. You can use this option to support dynamic updates for pre–Windows 2000 clients, such as Windows NT 4 and Windows 95/98.

You can also configure the DNS zone for dynamic updates of zone data to secondaries. You'll learn more about configuring zones in later sections. You configure a primary zone for dynamic update through the Zone Properties General tab. The options are No, do not allow dynamic update; and Yes, allow dynamic update.

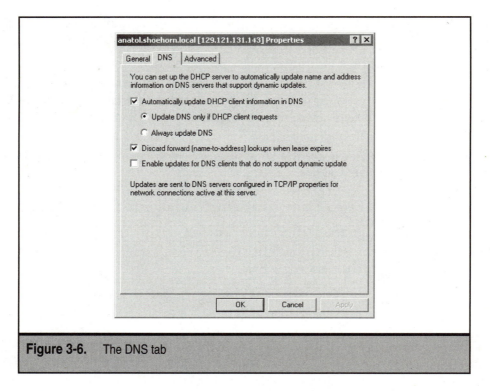

Figure 3-6.   The DNS tab

If the zone is an Active Directory–integrated zone, you'll also have an option for Only Secure Updates, which allows dynamic updates only from clients that are authorized to send dynamic updates.

How Active Directory Uses DNS

Active Directory clients use DNS servers for IP address resolution just as other network clients do. However, Active Directory clients also have special uses for DNS. The Active Directory client logon service uses DNS to locate an Active Directory domain controller. Each domain controller in the zone is registered with an SRV record in the DNS database. The SRV record provides the following information on the domain controller:

▼ The name of the host (e.g., Rabbit.west.texas.org)

■ The service offered on the host (LDAP)

▲ The port number to use for accessing the service (389 by default)

When the client starts, it queries the DNS server for a domain controller, receives the preceding contact information, and contacts the domain controller to begin the logon process.

A similar process is used for processing LDAP queries. This process is especially essential for queries to other domains in a multidomain environment. The structure of a multidomain Active Directory environment intentionally echoes the structure of the DNS namespace, and the query passes through the parallel structure of DNS domains and Active Directory domains as follows. (This process is depicted in this book's blueprint.)

1. A client in the north.shoehorn.com domain queries the DNS server for a domain controller in north.shoehorn.com. The DNS server responds with the address of a domain controller in north.shoehorn.com.

2. The client queries the domain controller for information on the user Bob, who is located in the south.shoehorn.com domain.

3. The domain controller in north.shoehorn.com responds with an LDAP referral to the domain shoehorn.com.

4. The client queries the DNS server for the address of a domain controller in shoehorn.com. The DNS server responds with the address of a domain controller in shoehorn.com. To obtain the information, the DNS server may use recursion to obtain the address from another DNS server.

5. The client queries the domain controller in shoehorn.com for information on the user Bob. The domain controller responds with an LDAP referral to the south.shoehorn.com domain.

6. The client queries the DNS server for the address of a domain controller in south.shoehorn.com. The DNS server responds with the address of a domain controller in south.shoehorn. com. The DNS server may again use recursion to obtain the address from another DNS server.

7. The client queries the domain controller in south.shoehorn.com for information on the user Bob and receives the requested information.

Installing DNS Server

If you attempt to install Active Directory on a domain controller and the network doesn't have a DNS server that supports the SRV record and dynamic update, the Active Directory Setup Wizard will ask if you wish to make the new domain controller a DNS server and will install and configure DNS if you say yes. Otherwise, you can configure DNS on a Windows 2000 Server machine using the DNS tool.

To configure the DNS service on a Windows 2000 Server, follow these steps:

1. Select Start | Programs | Administrative Tools | DNS.

2. If the DNS service is not currently configured on the server, a description of DNS will appear in the right pane of the DNS main window. To configure DNS, select the Action menu and choose Configure The Server.

3. The Configure DNS Server Wizard starts. Read the text in the first screen and choose Next.

4. The next screen asks if you wish to create a forward lookup zone. You don't have to create a zone from within the DNS Configuration Wizard. If you elect to create a zone, the steps are similar to the steps described in the following sections for adding a primary, secondary, or Active Directory–integrated zone. If you elect to create a forward lookup zone, you'll also be prompted to create a reverse lookup zone. See the later section titled "Adding Reverse Lookup Zones."

5. In the next screen, review the summary of new zone information. If everything looks right, click Finish. Otherwise, click the Back button and make the necessary corrections.

You can also configure DNS using the Configure Your Server Wizard. This wizard may pop up automatically when you install Windows 2000 Server. Otherwise, to configure DNS through the Configure Your Server Wizard, follow these steps:

1. Select Start | Programs | Administrative Tools | Configure Your Server.

2. In the Configure Your Server main screen, click Networking. Choose DNS.

3. Select Manage DNS.

Configuring DNS

The following sections will help you find your way around the Windows 2000 DNS configuration console. The DNS console, unlike many of the Microsoft Management Console snap-ins in Windows 2000, comes with fairly extensive online Help. Refer to DNS console's online Help or the Resource Kit Books Online for more on configuring Windows 2000 DNS.

Configuring DNS Zones

As Figure 3-5 shows, a big part of the task of configuring DNS is configuring DNS zones. Once you establish the zone structure, dynamic DNS servers automatically assume much of the responsibility for resolving queries and keeping the system up-to-date.

The following sections discuss

▼ Adding standard primary zones

■ Adding secondary zones

■ Adding Active Directory–integrated zones

■ Adding reverse lookup zones

■ Configuring zone properties

▲ Deleting a zone

Later sections discuss issues related to DNS servers and to interoperating Windows 2000 DNS Server with other DNS server implementations.

ADDING STANDARD PRIMARY ZONES   A primary zone is the writable master copy of the zone database. Microsoft adopted the term "standard primary" to distinguish a traditional primary zone from an Active

Directory–integrated primary zone. See the later section titled "Adding Active Directory–Integrated Zones" for more on this subject.

When you add a standard primary zone, you create a Start Of Authority (SOA) record and assign a portion of the DNS namespace to a primary DNS server. That primary server can transfer the zone to secondary servers—auxiliary servers that perform read-only resolution of DNS queries—or it can delegate part of the namespace to other primary servers.

A primary zone can either be a forward lookup zone or a reverse lookup zone. A forward lookup zone returns the IP address for a host name specified in the query. A reverse lookup zone returns the host name for an IP address specified in the query. This section describes how to configure a standard primary forward lookup zone. For information on configuring a reverse lookup zone, see the later section titled "Adding Reverse Lookup Zones."

To add a standard primary forward lookup zone to a Windows 2000 DNS Server, follow these steps:

1. Select Start | Programs | Administrative Tools | DNS.

2. In the DNS main window, click the plus sign next to the DNS server that you would like to use as the primary server for the new zone.

3. Right-click the Forward Lookup Zones icon and choose New Zone.

4. The New Zone Wizard starts. Read the text on the first screen and click Next.

5. The next screen (see Figure 3-7) asks whether you'd like to make the zone an Active Directory–integrated zone, a standard primary zone, or a standard secondary zone. Choose Standard Primary and click Next.

6. The next screen asks you to specify the domain name for the zone. Enter the domain name. Note that the domain name should be integrated with your overall DNS namespace and

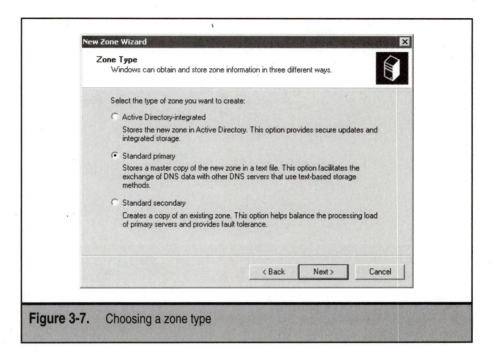

Figure 3-7.   Choosing a zone type

also with your Active Directory namespace. See the previous section titled "The DNS Namespace." Click Next.

7. The next screen (see Figure 3-8) asks if you would like to create a new file for the zone data or whether you would like to use an existing zone file. The option of using the existing file is for cases in which you are migrating DNS records to this new primary zone. See the later section titled "Migrating DNS Data to Windows 2000 DNS Server." In order to use an existing file, the file must be present in the system_root\system32\dns folder of the primary DNS server you selected in step 2. If you are not migrating records from another source, choose to create a new file (the default). Note that the default name is the zone name you chose in step 6 plus the .dns extension.

8. In the next screen, review the summary of new zone information. If everything looks right, click Finish. Otherwise, click the Back button and make the necessary corrections.

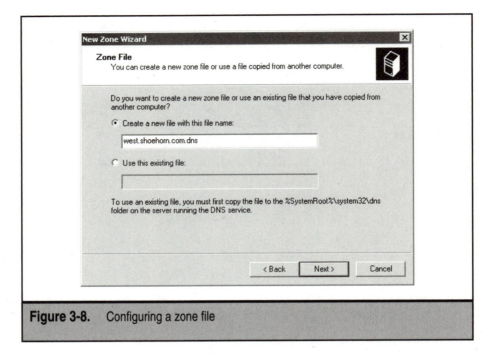

Figure 3-8. Configuring a zone file

ADDING SECONDARY FORWARD LOOKUP ZONES To add a standard secondary forward lookup zone to a Windows 2000 DNS Server, follow these steps:

1. Select Start | Programs | Administrative Tools | DNS.

2. In the DNS main window, click the plus sign next to the DNS server that you would like to use as the primary server for the new zone.

3. Right-click the Forward Lookup Zones icon and choose New Zone.

4. The New Zone Wizard starts. Read the text on the first screen and click Next.

5. The next screen (refer to Figure 3-7) asks whether you'd like to make the zone an Active Directory–integrated zone, a standard primary zone, or a standard secondary zone. Choose Standard Primary and click Next.

6. The next screen asks you to enter the DNS name of the new secondary zone. Enter the name and click Next.

7. The next screen (see Figure 3-9) asks you to enter the IP addresses of the DNS servers from which you want to copy the zone information. Enter an IP address in the IP Address box and click the Add button to add the button to the list. The list shows the order of precedence for where the secondary server should look for the zone information. If possible, the secondary should receive zone updates from the primary zone server. Use the Up and Down buttons to move the addresses up and down in the list. Click Next.

8. In the next screen, review the summary of new zone information. If everything looks right, click Finish. Otherwise, click the Back button and make the necessary corrections.

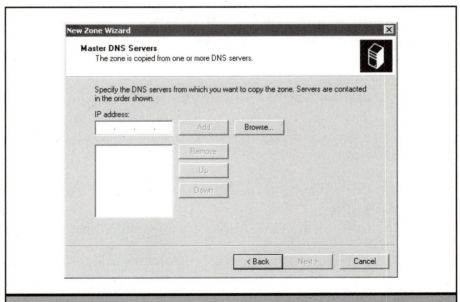

Figure 3-9. Entering the IP address for the zone transfer

After you have created the secondary zone, you must configure the primary zone to support zone transfers to the secondary.

To configure the primary zone to support zone transfers, follow these steps:

1. Select Start | Programs | Administrative Tools | DNS.

2. In the DNS main window, click the plus sign next to the DNS server that contains the zone for which you'd like to configure zone transfers.

3. Right-click the zone and choose Properties.

4. In the Zone Properties dialog box, select the Zone Transfers tab. Make sure the Allow Zone Transfers box is checked. You can elect to allow zone transfers to any server (the default), to servers listed in the Name Servers tab, or to specific servers. If you wish to configure the primary domain controller to notify the secondaries when there is a chance, click the Notify button.

5. Click OK.

ADDING ACTIVE DIRECTORY–INTEGRATED ZONES   As you learned previously in the section titled "Active Directory–Integrated Zones," you can optionally elect to place DNS zone data in Active Directory rather than in a .dns file on the DNS server. An Active Directory–integrated zone must be a primary zone. Placing zone data in Active Directory improves security and efficiency, but may add another layer of complexity if you're accustomed to text-based DNS zone data. The following procedure describes how to create an Active Directory–integrated forward lookup zone. For more on creating a reverse lookup zone, see the later section titled "Adding Reverse Lookup Zones."

To create an Active Directory–integrated zone, follow these steps:

1. Select Start | Programs | Administrative Tools | DNS.

2. In the DNS main window, click the plus sign next to an Active Directory domain controller that is configured for DNS service.

3. Right-click the Forward Lookup Zones icon and choose New Zone.

4. The New Zone Wizard starts. Read the text on the first screen and click Next.

5. The next screen (refer to Figure 3-7) asks whether you'd like to make the zone an Active Directory–integrated zone, a standard primary zone, or a standard secondary zone. Choose Active Directory–Integrated Zone and click Next.

6. The next screen asks you to specify the domain name for the zone. Enter the domain name. Note that the domain name should be integrated with your overall DNS namespace and also with your Active Directory namespace. See the previous section titled "The DNS Namespace." Click Next.

7. In the next screen, review the summary of new zone information. If everything looks right, click Finish. Otherwise, click the Back button and make the necessary corrections.

ADDING REVERSE LOOKUP ZONES   A standard primary, standard secondary, or Active Directory–integrated zone can either be a forward lookup zone or a reverse lookup zone. A forward lookup zone returns the IP address for a host name specified in the query. A reverse lookup zone returns the host name for an IP address specified in the query. This section describes how to configure reverse lookup zone.

To create a standard primary reverse lookup zone, follow these steps:

1. Select Start | Programs | Administrative Tools | DNS.

2. In the DNS main window, click the plus sign next to the DNS server that you would like to use as the primary server for the new zone.

3. Right-click the Reverse Lookup Zones icon and choose New Zone.

4. The New Zone Wizard starts. Read the text on the first screen and click Next.

5. The next screen (refer to Figure 3-7) asks whether you'd like to make the zone an Active Directory–integrated zone, a

standard primary zone, or a standard secondary zone. Choose Standard Primary and click Next.

6. The next screen (see Figure 3-10) asks you to specify the network ID or the name for the zone. The name of a reverse lookup zone consists of the network ID (with octets in reverse order) and the string *.in-addr.arpa*. You can either enter the network ID and let the wizard figure out the name or enter the name and let the wizard figure out the network ID. Note that you should not enter a zero (0) for an octet unless you want the zero to appear in the name (refer to Figure 3-10). Click Next.

7. The next screen (similar to Figure 3-8) asks if you would like to create a new file for the zone data or whether you would like to use an existing zone file. The option of using the existing file is

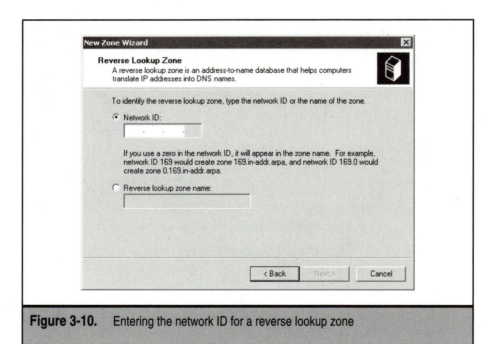

Figure 3-10. Entering the network ID for a reverse lookup zone

for cases in which you are migrating DNS records to this new primary zone. See the later section titled "Migrating DNS Data to Windows 2000 DNS Server." In order to use an existing file, the file must be present in the system_root\system32\dns folder of the primary DNS server you selected in step 2. If you are not migrating records from another source, choose to create a new file (the default). Click Next.

8. In the next screen, review the summary of new zone information. If everything looks right, click Finish. Otherwise, click the Back button and make the necessary corrections.

The steps for creating a secondary or Active Directory–integrated reverse lookup zone are similar to the steps for creating secondary or Active Directory–integrated forward lookup zones (as described in the earlier sections "Adding Secondary Forward Lookup Zones" and "Adding Active Directory–Integrated Zones"), except you launch the process from the Reverse Lookup Zones icon in the DNS main window and you enter the zone name in reverse lookup format (refer to Figure 3-10).

CONFIGURING ZONE PROPERTIES   A forward lookup zone has a Properties dialog box that lets you view and modify certain zone-related settings. To view and modify zone properties, follow these steps:

1. Select Start | Programs | Administrative Tools | DNS.

2. In the DNS main window, click the plus sign next to the DNS server that contains the zone whose properties you wish to view or modify.

3. Right-click the zone and choose Properties.

    The zone's Properties dialog box (see Figure 3-11) contains the following tabs:

    ■ **General**   Provides a summary of general information, such as the zone type. Also lets you configure dynamic

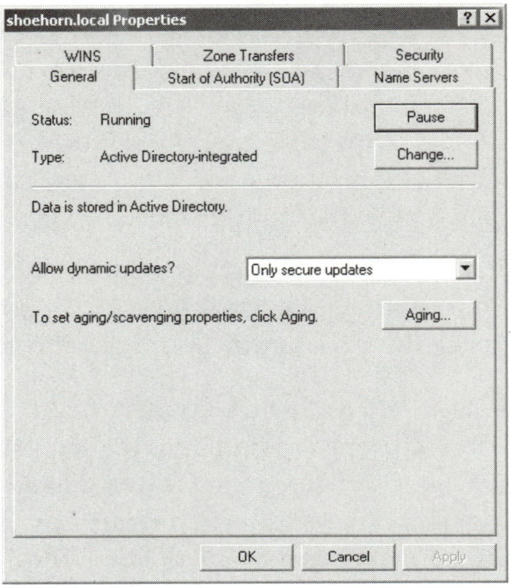

Figure 3-11. The zone's Properties dialog box

updates for the zone. The Aging button lets you configure the refresh interval and the maintenance of old (stale) records. Click the Change button to change the zone type.

- **Start of Authority (SOA)**   Lets you configure the Start of Authority record for the zone. The Start of Authority record specifies the primary server for the zone. You cannot configure this tab for secondary zones.

- **Name Servers**   Specifies known DNS servers. You can add or remove a DNS server from the list.

- **WINS**   Lets you configure WINS name resolution for unknown names within the namespace.

- **Zone Transfers**   Lets you configure zone transfer settings for the zone (see Figure 3-12).

Active Directory–integrated zones include an additional Security tab that lets you configure security settings for the zone.

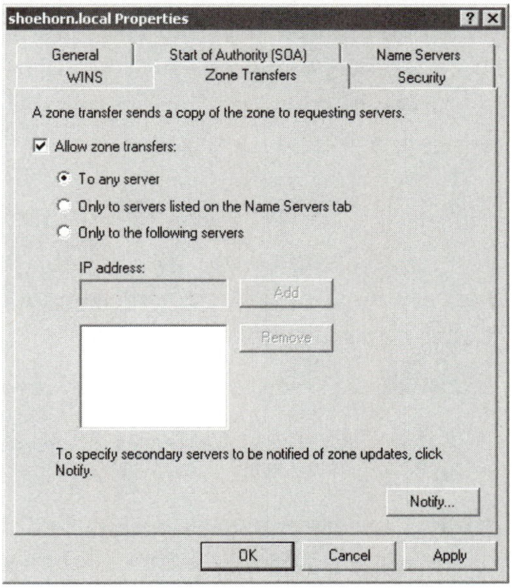

Figure 3-12.   The zone's Properties Zone Transfers tab

ADDING A DOMAIN TO AN EXISTING ZONE   You can assign a new subdomain to an existing zone. In other words, you could assign the subdomain northeast.shoehorn.com to the zone that includes the domain shoehorn.com.

   To add a domain to an existing primary zone, follow these steps:

1. Select Start | Programs | Administrative Tools | DNS.

2. In the DNS main window, click the plus sign next to the DNS server that contains the zone to which you would like to add a domain.

3. Right-click the zone and choose New Domain.

4. Type the name of the new subdomain and choose OK. The name will be prepended to the existing domain name. For example, enter **east** to add the east.shoehorn.com subdomain to the zone for the shoehorn.com domain.

5. Click OK.

DELEGATING A SUBDOMAIN   You can delegate a subdomain within an existing zone to another primary zone on the same or a different DNS server. For instance, the microsoft.com. zone could delegate the Win2000.microsoft.com. subdomain to a different primary zone.

To delegate a zone, follow these steps:

1. Select Start | Programs | Administrative Tools | DNS.

2. In the DNS main window, click the plus sign next to the DNS server that contains the zone in which you would like to delegate a subdomain.

3. Right-click the zone and choose New Delegation.

4. The New Delegation Wizard starts. Read the first screen and click Next.

5. In the next screen, enter the name of the subdomain you wish to delegate. The FQDN appears below. Click Next.

6. In the next screen, specify the DNS server that is the host of the delegated zone. (A primary zone for the delegated namespace must be configured on the host that is receiving the delegation.) To add a server, click the Add button. Click Next.

7. Read the summary of information and click Finish.

DELETING A ZONE   To delete a zone, follow these steps:

1. Right-click the zone you wish to delete in the DNS main window.

2. Select Delete.

ADDING RECORDS MANUALLY   If your configuration supports dynamic update for DNS clients (as described earlier, in the section "Dynamic Updates"), host (A) records and pointer (PTR) records will be updated automatically. Other records, such as SOA records, are created through the DNS Server console when you create and configure a zone. Windows 2000's DNS Server lets you carry out much of the DNS configuration without worrying about manually configuring individual resource records. However, you may occasionally wish to add individual resource records to the zone configuration.

To add a resource record manually, follow these steps:

1. Select Start | Programs | Administrative Tools | DNS.

2. In the DNS main window, click the plus sign next to the DNS server that contains the zone to which you would like to add a record.

3. Right-click the zone. The context menu offers options for adding a new host (A record), a new alias (CNAME record), or a new mail exchanger (MX record). Selecting New Host gives you the option of also creating a new pointer (PTR record). You can also choose Other New Records for a complete list of record types.

4. Enter the requested information.

Managing Servers in the DNS Console

Having multiple DNS servers is a good idea for reasons of efficiency and fault tolerance. Some of the features discussed earlier in this chapter, such as secondary zones and zone delegation, are intended for cases in which multiple DNS servers are operating on the network. The following sections discuss issues related to administering the following:

▼ Adding or removing a server from the DNS console

■ Changing a server's host name

▲ Changing the domain name

Microsoft recommends you have at least one DNS server on each routed network segment and provide a means for clients on that segment to reach another server if the local server is down.

TIP: Windows 2000's DNS Server offers several options for configuring forwarders, monitoring, logging, and multiple network interfaces for a DNS server. See the online Help in the Windows 2000 DNS utility.

By default, the management console that appears when you open the DNS utility (Start | Programs | Administrative Tools | DNS) displays the local DNS configuration. You can add additional DNS servers to the DNS console. Or, you can create your own Microsoft Management Console containing multiple DNS servers. You may wish to create a management console containing all the DNS servers on your network to create a central management point. To add a server to the management console, the DNS service must already be configured on the server. See the previous section titled "Installing DNS Server."

To add a DNS server to the management console, follow these steps:

1. Select Start | Programs | Administrative Tools | DNS.

2. In the DNS main window, right-click the DNS icon. Select Connect To Computer.

3. In the Select Target Computer dialog box, click the radio button labeled The Following Computer and enter the name of the computer to which you'd like to connect. Click OK.

To remove a server from the management console, follow these steps:

1. Select Start | Programs | Administrative Tools | DNS.

2. In the DNS main window, right-click the icon for the server you wish to remove from the console. Select Delete.

3. A dialog box asks if you really want to remove the server. Click OK.

Removing a server from the DNS management console does not remove the DNS service from the server.

Once a server is installed in the management console, you can access a number of server configuration options through the right-click context menu (see Figure 3-13) or through the server's Properties dialog box.

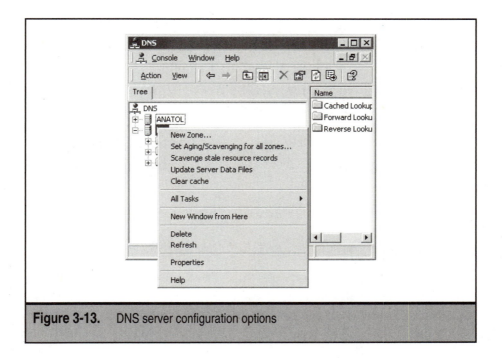

Figure 3-13.   DNS server configuration options

Migrating DNS Data to Windows 2000 DNS Server

Because DNS data is typically stored in a text file, it usually isn't difficult to migrate DNS data to a Windows 2000 DNS Server. If you wish to upgrade a Windows NT 4 DNS Server to Windows 2000, you don't have to do anything. Just upgrade the server. According to Microsoft, the Installation Wizard will take care of any conversion issues.

If you wish to migrate data from another DNS implementation, such as a BIND implementation, you have two principal options:

▼   *Move the DNS data files to the Windows 2000 DNS directory and rename them so Windows 2000 will know what they are.* Files should be placed in the system_root\system32\dns directory of the DNS server. Note that the names of the files should be changed so Microsoft DNS Server will recognize them. The forward lookup zone file should be the name of the domain followed by the .dns extension: mydomain.dns. The reverse lookup zone file should have the name of the reverse lookup zone followed by the .dns extension.

▲ *Configure the Windows 2000 DNS Server as a secondary server for the zone.* The Windows 2000 DNS Server will then receive the zone through a zone transfer operation. You can then convert the zone type for the Windows 2000 DNS Server from secondary to standard primary or Active Directory–integrated. To change the zone type, click the Change button in the General tab of the Zone Properties dialog box.

Interoperating with Other DNS Servers

According to Microsoft, the following considerations are important if you wish to use a different DNS service with Active Directory:

▼ The DNS implementation must support SRV records.

▲ The DNS implementation should (but doesn't absolutely have to) support dynamic update.

Microsoft claims to have tested Active Directory successfully with BIND versions 4.9.7, 8.1.2, and 8.2. You can also use Active Directory with Windows NT 4's DNS Server if you upgrade to Service Pak 4.

If you attempt to use Active Directory with a server that does not support dynamic update, you'll have to perform additional manual configuration. It is especially important to ensure that SRV records, which point to Active Directory domain controllers, are kept current. See the DNS utility online Help.

TIP: Microsoft points out that some later DNS implementations (including Windows 2000 DNS Server) use a compression-based fast transfer method for zone transfers. Other DNS implementations (such as BIND versions prior to version 4.9.4) do not support fast transfer. If you're interoperating with a DNS implementation that doesn't support fast zone transfer, you better turn off fast zone transfer for the Windows 2000 server. To do so, go to the Advanced tab of the Properties dialog box for the DNS server and deselect BIND Secondaries.

SITES AND SUBNETS IN ACTIVE DIRECTORY

As Chapter 1, "The Active Directory Environment," mentioned, the concept of a *site* figures prominently into Active Directory. A site is a well-connected network—a system of computers, routers, and other devices that are connected with fast (LAN-speed) connection. This site configuration is a structure that reflects the design of the physical network and is wholly separate from the security structure reflected in the Active Directory domain system. A single Active Directory domain can contain multiple sites, or a single site can contain multiple Active Directory domains.

The reasons for dividing your network into sites are twofold:

▼ To identify slow WAN links to the Active Directory domain controllers so that they can build an efficient topology for replicating the Active Directory. (You'll learn about replication topologies in Chapter 4.)

▲ To define a collection of computer resources in a single location for the purpose of applying site-based group policy. (You'll learn more about group policy in Chapter 6.)

As you'll learn in Chapter 4, the Active Directory replication process is an important consideration in the design of an Active Directory network. The process of replicating Active Directory changes can consume large amounts of bandwidth. Thus, there is a constant tension between the desire for more consistent and up-to-date Active Directory replicas (requiring frequent replication) and the desire to minimize the effect of replication on network performance (requiring minimal replication). The ideal level of replication is, therefore, dependent on the speed of the network wires. Higher-bandwidth connections can support a higher level of replication without adversely affecting performance.

Microsoft designed Active Directory so that directory replication could occur invisibly and automatically, and Microsoft soon came to the conclusion that the system would work best if there were some way of configuring the network to be aware of which connections were fast, LAN-based connections and which were slow, WAN-based connections. This realization gave rise to the concept of the site. You'll learn more about intrasite vs. intersite replication in Chapter 4.

This chapter introduces the Active Directory site feature, discusses how to create a site and how to add a server to a site, and describes the relationship between sites and IP subnets.

The Active Directory Sites and Services utility is the principal tool for managing sites, subnets, and site connections. Active Directory Sites and Services is a Microsoft Management Console snap-in that appears in the Administrative Tools group (Start | Programs | Administrative Tools) when you first install Active Directory. (See Chapter 7 for more on installing Active Directory.) You can also add Active Directory Sites and Services to a custom management console.

Subnets and Sites

When you install Active Directory on the first domain controller in the forest, a default site called Default-First-Site-Name is created. Unless you say otherwise, Active Directory assumes additional domain controllers (and the entire network, for that matter) are part of this original default site. If your network is all on one well-connected LAN, you don't have to do anything with the site design. In that case, it is perfectly acceptable to let the entire network fall within this default site. (You may, however, wish to change the name of this default site from Default-First-Site-Name to something else.)

TIP: To change the name of a site, open Active Directory Sites and Services. Click the plus sign next to the folder labeled Sites. Right-click the site name and choose Rename.

If your Active Directory network consists of multiple sites connected with WAN links, you should configure those sites through Active Directory Sites and Services. The task of configuring a site in Active Directory Sites and Services includes the following steps:

1. Create a site object.

2. Define Active Directory subnets and associate them with the site.

3. Place Active Directory domain controllers in the site.

4. Create site links, site link bridges, and connection objects.

Chapter 4 discusses how to create site links, site link bridges, and connection objects. This chapter describes how to define subnets and sites and how to place domain controllers in sites.

By default, all network addresses are considered part of the default site. To configure an alternative site, you must first define the subnets that will be part of that site and then associate those subnets with the site definition. It is important to remember that your TCP/IP network will operate with or without an Active Directory site configuration. The TCP/IP stack of Windows 2000 computers and other TCP/IP-enabled computers is capable of delivering messages across routers and to different subnets, whether or not those subnets are configured in Active Directory Sites and Services. The site definition features are a means for optimizing Active Directory replication, not a means of configuring TCP/IP.

NOTE: You could divide a single well-connected LAN into multiple sites if you really wanted to. Although this typically isn't the preferred configuration, it may occasionally have advantages for application of group policy (see Chapter 6) or for the use of special search features such as the printer locator (see Chapter 8). You could also encompass WAN links within a single site, although there would be little reason to force intrasite replication over a slow WAN link. In some cases, WAN bandwidth may be sufficient to support intrasite replication. In that case, placing multiple locations in the same site would reduce latency for Active Directory updates. See Chapter 4 for more on directory replication.

Configuring Active Directory Sites

The task of defining a site in Active Directory Sites and Services creates a site object in Active Directory. The site is of no particular use to the network until you assign subnets and domain controllers to the site. This section describes how to create a site. Later sections describe how to create subnets and place domain controllers in sites.

To create a new Active Directory site, follow these steps:

1. Select Start | Programs | Administrative Tools | Active Directory Sites and Services. Or, open Active Directory Sites and Services from a custom management console.

2. Right-click the Sites folder and choose New Site.

3. In the New Object - Site Link dialog box (see Figure 3-14), enter a new name for the site and choose a site link object for the site. A site link object defines a pathway for intersite replication and an accompanying set of replication-related settings. If you're setting up the first new site, choose the default (...). You can add or modify site link settings later. See Chapter 4 for more on site links in Active Directory.

4. A dialog box appears and lets you know that you are about to create a site. It tells you to finish the site configuration once the site is created and lets you know that you still need to verify the site link structure, add subnets to the site, and add domain controllers to the site. You can also add a licensing computer to the site. Click OK.

After you have created the site, you should associate subnets with the site, as described in the next section "Defining Active Directory Subnets."

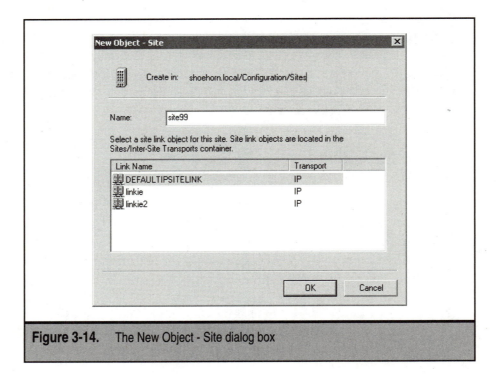

Figure 3-14.   The New Object - Site dialog box

Like other Active Directory objects, a site has a Properties dialog box that you can use to view and modify site configuration settings. To configure site properties, follow these steps:

1. Select Start | Programs | Administrative Tools | Active Directory Sites and Services. Or, open Active Directory Sites and Services from a custom management console.

2. Click the plus sign next to the Sites folder.

3. Right-click the site whose properties you wish to view or modify, and choose Properties.

4. The Site Properties dialog box appears (see Figure 3-15).

   The Site Properties dialog box has the following tabs:

   ■ **Site**   Gives the name of the site and lets you enter an optional description.

   ■ **Location**   Lets you enter an optional string defining the site's location. Microsoft recommends a standard notation

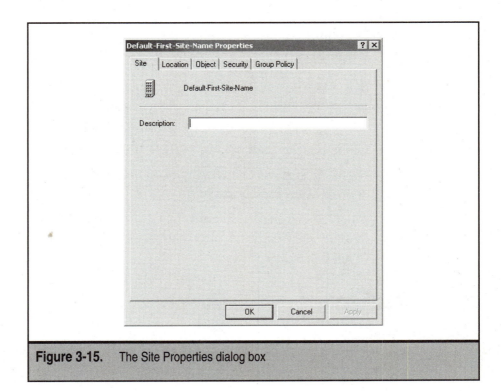

Figure 3-15.   The Site Properties dialog box

for defining the location setting. See the discussion of printer location tracking in Chapter 8. The location setting can be used to determine the location of an object in Active Directory searches.

- **Object**   Site object information.

- **Security**   Security settings for access to the site object. See Chapter 5, "Users and Groups." The Security tab is a common feature of Active Directory objects.

- **Group Policy**   Lets you assign group policy objects to the site. Group policy is one of the most powerful and important features of the Active Directory environment. See Chapter 6 for more on group policy.

You can also delegate control of a site to a particular set of users or groups. Delegation of control is another one of the innovations of the Active Directory environment. Delegation of control is a good way of giving a user administrator-like control of a particular object without giving the user administrator status for the rest of the domain. See Chapter 5 for more on delegation of control. In this case, delegating control of a site assigns control of the site object.

To delegate control of a site, follow these steps:

1. Select Start | Programs | Administrative Tools | Active Directory Sites and Services. Or, open Active Directory Sites and Services from a custom management console.

2. Click the plus sign next to the Sites folder.

3. Right-click the site to which you'd like to delegate control and choose Delegate Control.

4. The Delegation of Control Wizard starts. Click Next, and provide the necessary information. See Chapter 5 for more on delegation of control.

Defining Active Directory Subnets

Active Directory thinks of a site as a collection of subnets, and you must associate subnets with a site in order for the site to be useful to

Active Directory. The exception to this rule is the default site (Default-First-Site-Name—unless you rename it). IP addresses are considered to be part of the default site unless you associate the subnet that contains those addresses with a different site.

To add a subnet object, follow these steps:

1. Select Start | Programs | Administrative Tools | Active Directory Sites and Services. Or, open Active Directory Sites and Services from a custom management console.

2. Click the plus sign next to the Sites folder.

3. Right-click the Subnets folder and choose New Subnet.

4. The New Object - Subnet dialog box appears (see Figure 3-16). Enter the network address and mask for the subnet. Choose the site to which you'd like the subnet to belong.

5. Click OK.

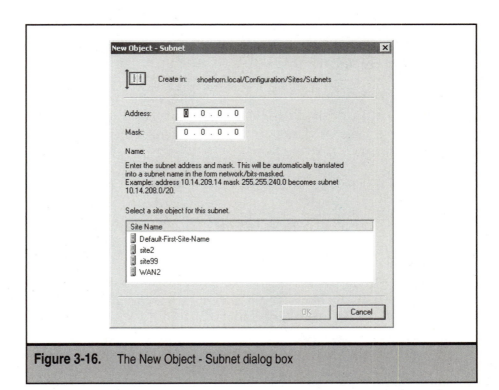

Figure 3-16.   The New Object - Subnet dialog box

Placing Servers in Sites

Active Directory clients are automatically associated with the site to which the subnet of the client's IP address belongs. Active Directory domain controllers, however, must be placed within the Servers container for the site. As you'll learn in Chapter 4, Active Directory uses the site membership information to generate replication topologies. You can also place a server that is not a domain controller in a site.

When you first install Active Directory on a domain controller, a server object for the domain controller is created in Active Directory Sites and Services. This icon corresponds to an Active Directory object with site-related information about the domain controller. At the time the server object is created, it is placed in the site associated with the domain controller's IP address. If you have not yet configured additional sites for the network, the server object will be placed in the default site. If you create a site structure after the Active Directory domain controller is installed, you may need to move the domain controller to a new site.

To move a server to a new site in Active Directory Sites and Services, follow these steps:

1. Select Start | Programs | Administrative Tools | Active Directory Sites and Services. Or, open Active Directory Sites and Services from a custom management console.

2. Click the plus sign next to the Sites folder.

3. Click the plus sign next to the site that contains the server object.

4. Click the plus sign next to the Servers folder for the site.

5. Right-click the server whose properties you wish to move and choose Move.

6. In the Move Server dialog box, choose the new site to which the server will belong.

7. Click OK.

As this chapter mentioned, if you install a new domain controller at a later date, a server object for the domain controller will initially be placed in the site that contains the subnet associated with the domain controller's IP address. It is also possible to create a new server object from scratch and associate that object with an existing computer. This is not the preferred way to do it, but it is an option that may be useful in some situations.

To add a new server object to a site, follow these steps:

1. Select Start | Programs | Administrative Tools | Active Directory Sites and Services. Or, open Active Directory Sites and Services from a custom management console.

2. Click the plus sign next to the Sites folder.

3. Click the plus sign next to the site to which you would like to add the server object.

4. Right-click the Servers folder for the site and select New | Server.

5. In the New Object - Server dialog box, enter the name of the new server object. Note that this object is located in the domain_name/Configuration/Sites/site_name/Servers container. It is not the same as a domain controller object created in Active Directory Users and Computers.

6. Click OK.

After you have created the new server object, you can associate that object with a computer through the object's Properties dialog box:

1. Select Start | Programs | Administrative Tools | Active Directory Sites and Services. Or, open Active Directory Sites and Services from a custom management console.

2. Click the plus sign next to the Sites folder.

3. Click the plus sign next to the site that contains the server object you wish to configure.

4. Click the plus sign next to the Servers folder for the site.

5. Right-click the server object whose properties you wish to configure and choose Properties.

6. The server object's Properties dialog box appears (see Figure 3-17). Click the Change button at the bottom of the Server tab to associate a computer with the server object.

7. Click OK.

NOTE: See Chapter 4 for more on the other settings in the Server Properties Server tab, such as intersite transport and bridgehead server properties (refer to Figure 3-17).

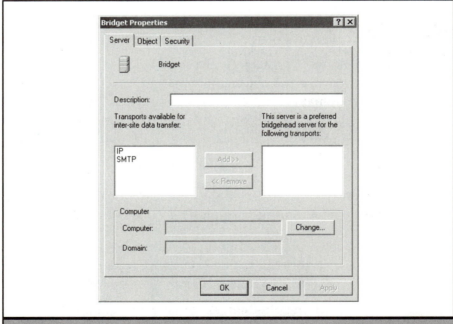

Figure 3-17. The Active Directory sites and services server object Properties dialog box

SUMMARY

This chapter gives some of the background you'll need to understand how Active Directory works with TCP/IP. The object of this chapter was not to provide a complete primer on TCP/IP or DNS, but to highlight the important TCP/IP networking concepts and procedures that a network administrator will need to configure a network for Active Directory. You learned how Active Directory uses DNS and how to configure Active Directory–enabled DNS zones. This chapter also discussed how to create and configure Active Directory sites and how to associate sites with IP subnets. Sites are an important component of Active Directory replication. In fact, this discussion of sites in Active Directory is not complete without a discussion of the Active Directory replication process and how Windows 2000 works through site links, site link bridges, and connection objects to replicate the Active Directory. You'll learn more about that process in the next chapter.

CHAPTER 4

Understanding Replication

On Active Directory networks, the domain controllers automatically update themselves to ensure that each has an up-to-date copy of the directory. Because Active Directory is a multimaster environment, all domain controllers receive and process directory changes. In this chapter, you'll learn the details of Active Directory replication.

REPLICATION AND ACTIVE DIRECTORY

Changes to the Active Directory are made directly through the user interface of an Active Directory–enabled workstation, server, or domain controller. The interface tool that makes the change (such as Active Directory Users And Computers or Active Directory Domains And Trusts) transmits the change to a domain controller somewhere in the domain. Once a change has been made to the directory database of one domain controller, the change must be propagated to all other domain controllers so that all remain in equilibrium. Microsoft calls this process *replication.*

Each domain controller does not necessarily propagate its changes to all other domain controllers, but, instead, changes follow a pathway known as a *replication topology.* Active Directory's Knowledge Consistency Checker (KCC) service automatically generates a replication topology for the network. You'll learn more about the KCC and how it works later in this chapter in the section titled "Replication and the KCC."

The goal of the replication process is to transmit a directory change made on one domain controller to the other domain controllers on the network. That simple goal is greatly complicated by the necessity for version control and conflict resolution in a multimaster environment. The network must be capable of passing changes among the domain controllers automatically and, at the same time, resolving conflicts that occur when a single value is changed twice from different locations. Active Directory replication includes its own built-in bookkeeping processes designed to ensure that all changes are reliably propagated with the minimum expense of bandwidth.

In a simple replication topology, each domain controller may propagate changes to two other domain controllers, and each of the receiving domain controllers may pass those changes to two other domain controllers, and so forth, until the change filters through all the system (see Figure 4-1). One can envision a busy network in a constant state of replicating changes. Only occasionally (in the middle of the night, perhaps) is the database at equilibrium—with all domain controllers holding an identical copy of the directory. At other times, the database replicas are out of equilibrium but

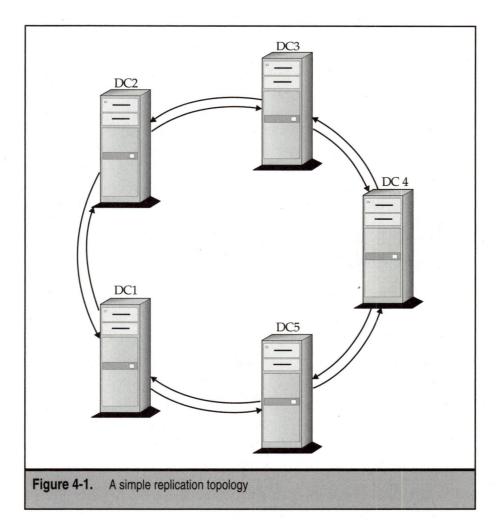

Figure 4-1. A simple replication topology

attempting to converge—initiating changes and receiving changes as the directory (and the organization) evolves.

One of Microsoft's goals for the replication process was to make sure that this replication occurred as efficiently as possible. It would, of course, be possible to keep the directory current by simply copying the entire database to every domain controller every time one domain controller made a change, but that solution would be hugely wasteful and time consuming, and it would consume much or all of the network's bandwidth. Microsoft knew it needed to devise a replication environment that would transmit changes reliably and also minimize the number of changes to preserve network bandwidth.

The replication scheme would also have to lead to convergence (in other words, to all domain controllers holding an identical copy of the changed attribute value). You may wonder what happens when two domain controllers change the same setting at about the same time and both new values are propagating through the network at once (see Figure 4-2). How do you prevent the possibility that the domain controller will receive the later change first and then (incorrectly) update the later change with the earlier change?

The first thing to remember about Active Directory replication is that only *changes* are replicated. The complete directory is not copied across the network unless a new domain controller is installed.

According to Microsoft, directory replication consists of the following types of changes:

▼ **Add** A new object is added to the directory—for instance, a printer, a computer, or a new user.

■ **Delete** An object is deleted from the directory.

■ **Modify** An attribute associated with an existing directory object is modified—for instance, a user's password is changed.

▲ **ModifyDN** An object's name is changed or the object is moved to a different container.

To understand how these changes are propagated throughout the network, you must first understand that Active Directory makes a

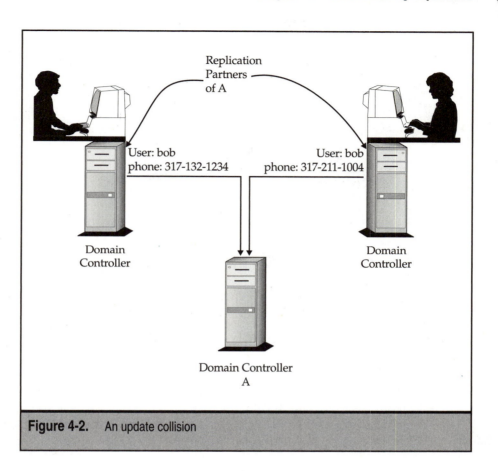

Figure 4-2.   An update collision

distinction between an *originating update* (the update that first registers a change to the directory) and a *replicated update,* an update that results from a domain controller replicating the change to another domain controller (see Figure 4-3).

Each update received at a domain controller is assigned an *update sequence number* (USN). Every domain controller keeps its own list of USNs. In other words, every domain controller has an independent USN sequence. This means that Active Directory does not have to expend resources maintaining a single, authoritative version number for each change that occurs anywhere in the forest. It is important to note, however, that because each domain controller has an

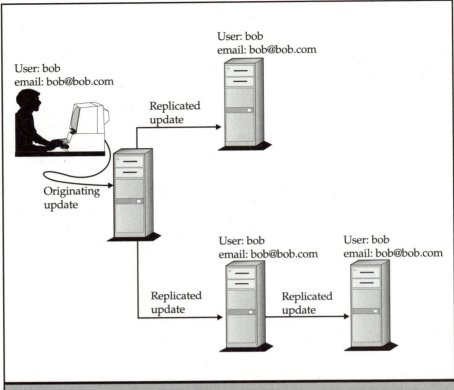

Figure 4-3.   An originating update comes from the domain controller that first registered the change

independent sequence of USNs, a USN is meaningful only if it is associated with the GUID of the domain controller that assigned it. Each domain controller transmits a number of important USN values with an Active Directory update:

▼   **Local USN**   The local USN value

■   **usnChanged**   The highest local USN of all attributes associated with the object

▲   **originating USN**   The USN of the update on the domain controller that originated the update

Each domain controller stores a pair of important settings associated with each of the other domain controllers:

▼ **high watermark**   The highest usnChanged value received from each replication partner

▲ **up-to-date vector**   A series of GUID/value pairs showing the highest originating USN associated with every domain controller that has originated an update

Table 4-1 shows an example of the high watermark settings stored on domain controller DC5. Note that the USN values shown in the table are chosen for illustration purposes only. When a domain controller requests a change from an upstream replication partner, it sends the high watermark setting associated with the upstream partner. The upstream replication partner transmits only changes that have a usnChanged value higher than the high watermark received from the downstream domain controller. The downstream domain controller also sends its up-to-date vector along with the request (see Table 4-2). The upstream partner checks the up-to-date vector received from the downstream domain controller to ensure that the update it is about to transmit has an originating USN value higher than the value associated with the originating domain controller in the up-to-date vector.

Domain Controller	High Watermark (highest usnChanged value) received from
DC1	121
DC2	160
DC3	92
DC4	135

Table 4-1.   High Watermark Table for Domain Controller DC5

Domain Controller	Highest originating USN for an update originating from
DC1	113
DC2	42
DC3	92
DC4	128

Table 4-2. Up-to-Date Vector for DC5

The replication process follows:

1. A domain controller (say, DC4) announces to another domain controller for which it is a replication partner (say, DC5) that it has been informed of updates.

2. The downstream domain controller DC5 requests an update, sending its high watermark for DC4 and a copy of its up-to-date vector.

    The upstream replication partner DC4 prepares to send DC5 all updates that have a usnChanged value greater than the high watermark it received from DC5. Before transmitting an update, DC4 checks the originating USN number associated with the update against the up-to-date vector received from DC5 to ensure that DC5 has not already received the update from another source. It then transmits any necessary updates to the downstream domain controller.

Figure 4-4 shows the path of an update as it travels through the network. Note that the local USN value of the update changes at each stop in the replication path to reflect the USN of the update on the transmitting computer, but the originating USN (which gives the USN of the originating update) never changes.

One can imagine situations in which even both the high watermark and the up-to-date vector are insufficient to ensure the

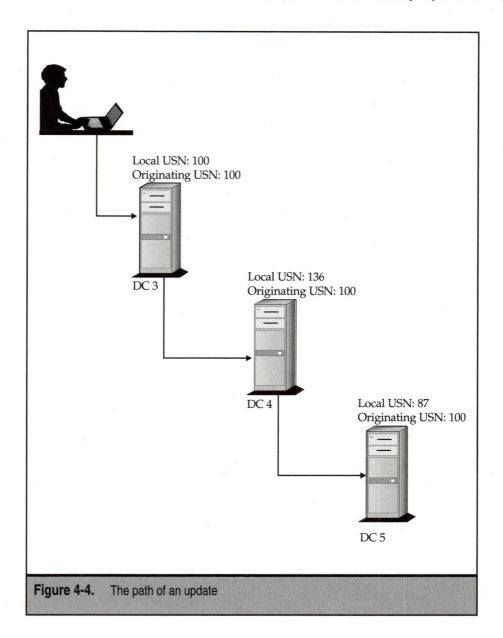

Local USN: 100
Originating USN: 100

DC 3

Local USN: 136
Originating USN: 100

DC 4

Local USN: 87
Originating USN: 100

DC 5

Figure 4-4. The path of an update

replicated value is the current setting. For instance, the same setting may have been changed on two different domain controllers at approximately the same time. Active Directory also transmits a *stamp* along with the update that provides the additional information necessary for conflict resolution. The stamp includes three parts:

▼ **version**   The version number for the change. The version number changes with each originating write to an attribute setting. Note that the version number is associated with the attribute itself (as opposed to the USN, which is associated with a domain controller).

■ **originating time**   The time of the original update. Active Directory tries to operate without a lot of emphasis on system time, but it does synchronize clocks on domain controllers and uses the originating time (to the nearest second) for rare tie-breaker situations.

▲ **originating DSA**   The GUID of the originating domain controller.

If a conflict occurs, Active Directory accepts the update with the later version number. If the conflicting version numbers are the same, Active Directory accepts the update with the later originating time. If the times are the same (and we're growing ever more hypothetical), Active Directory accepts the update with the higher originating DSA value.

NOTE: There is no particular justice in accepting the update that originated from the domain controller with the numerically higher GUID (keep in mind that this will probably never happen). This rule is basically equivalent to a rule that says, "If you don't know who to believe, believe the person whose last name begins with a letter that is later in the alphabet." However, this rule provides a good example of an underlying principle of Active Directory and all other multimaster directory systems: "When you can't have perfection, settle for consistency." Each domain controller is processing updates independently. Even if it can't determine which value is correct, the directory system must provide some means of ensuring that all replicas hold the same information.

Replication Topology

As you have already learned, a replication topology is a logical structure describing the replication pathways through the network. The Knowledge Consistency Checker (KCC) service automatically creates a replication pathway. The KCC uses several factors when determining a replication scheme. The most important of these is information on the sites within the networks. As you learned in Chapter 3, "Active Directory with TCP/IP and DNS," an Active Directory network can be divided into LAN-based sites (with fast internal network speeds) connected by WAN links (with slower speeds). The replication scheme for domain controllers within a site is totally different from the scheme for replication across slower WAN links. Chapter 3 describes how to configure Active Directory sites. This chapter describes how to manage intrasite, as well as intersite, replication.

The KCC also uses other criteria for defining replication pathways. The default replication topology is based on the following:

▼ The KCC attempts to organize the domain controllers into a two-directional ring.

▲ The number of hops an update makes should be three or fewer.

Recall that the Active Directory database is actually divided into three partitions:

▼ Schema partition (replicated throughout the forest)

■ Configuration partition (replicated throughout the forest)

▲ Domain partition (replicated throughout the domain)

The forestwide directory partitions require a forestwide replication topology. Replication topology is, therefore, specific to the directory partition rather than to the directory as a whole. In most cases, a single, forestwide replication topology will provide for replication of the schema and configuration partitions, and each domain will have a replication topology for its domain partition.

NOTE: You may recall that global catalog servers replicate a partial domain partition for each domain in the forest. In multidomain environments, you can think of global catalog servers as having their own replication topology. A global catalog server can replicate partial domain partitions of other domains to other global catalog servers. Because a global catalog server is a functioning domain controller, it participates in the process of replicating the full domain partition within its own domain.

If the update passes through three hops within the local (intrasite) replication topology, and the intrasite replication interval is 5 minutes, a change should propagate through the site in an average of 15 minutes.

Replication among different sites is much more complicated. You'll learn more about intersite replication later in this chapter in the section titled "Intersite Replication."

Replication and the KCC

As you may have guessed, the KCC is the key to the Active Directory replication process. The first thing to understand about the KCC is that there is no such thing as *the* KCC for the entire network. The KCC is a process running on each Active Directory domain controller. Because all KCCs behave the same way, and because the domain controllers on a given network have the same information about network conditions, the KCCs (theoretically) act in harmony. *The KCC for the network* (as the term is commonly used) is really the combined behavior of a community of KCC processes within the community of domain controllers.

NOTE: As you will learn later in this chapter, replication between sites is a bit more complex. A single domain controller in each site (called the Intersite Topology Generator) defines the intersite replication topology for the site.

According to Microsoft, the KCC process falls into two phases:

▼ Evaluation of current replication topology and generation of new connection objects

▲ Translation of connections into the *connection agreements* used internally by the domain controllers to share information

By default, the KCC checks the replication topology 300 seconds (5 minutes) after the domain controller starts and at 900-second (15-minute) intervals thereafter. You can specify alternative REG_WORD values for these settings in the Registry key

HKEY_LOCAL_MACHINE\SYSTEM\CurrentControlSet\ Services\NTDS\Parameters

with the entries:

▼ **Repl topology update delay (secs)**   For the startup interval

▲ **Repl topology update period**   For the time between topology checks

You'll learn more about intrasite and intersite replication topology later in this chapter in the sections titled "Managing Intrasite Replication" and "Intersite Replication."

Connection Objects

Active Directory, as you may have learned by now, is built from objects and attributes, and the replication topology is no exception. Microsoft uses an object called a *collection object* to define a potential direct replication pathway among Active Directory domain controllers.

A connection object is, basically, a potential connection that KCC may use as a link in the replication topology. Connection objects are *one-way*. In other words, a connection object points from the receiving domain controller to the upstream source.

MANAGING INTRASITE REPLICATION

Intrasite replication is directory replication that takes place among domain controllers in the same site. Intrasite replication is managed differently from replication among sites (intersite replication). Domain controllers within a site are assumed to be connected through a high-speed, LAN-based network medium, and intrasite replication is therefore designed to deliver updates quickly and thereby minimize latency.

Within a site, the KCCs use an algorithm to determine the replication topology for the site. Because all domain controllers share the same information, the KCCs on all the domain controllers should arrive at the same topology. The KCC on each domain controller then creates the necessary connection objects so that the domain controller can receive updates through the topology ring. In other words, each domain controller creates connections to itself from upstream domain controllers, and the sum total of all the connection objects created for the site *is* the replication topology. The goal of the KCC is to ensure that all replication updates can pass through the site in three hops. The strategy the KCCs use for achieving this goal depends on the number of domain controllers in the site. If the site has seven or fewer domain controllers, the KCCs will arrive at what is called a *simplified ring* topology (refer to Figure 4-1). Note that, with seven domain controllers, an update originating anywhere in the ring can pass to all domain controllers in three or fewer hops. The bidirectional nature of the topology ring ensures that if a connection fails somewhere in the ring, the replication process will still succeed in passing updates to all domain controllers (though if a failure occurs, the path may require more than three hops).

NOTE: The full directory partition, as you learned earlier, is replicated only within a domain. If the site shown in Figure 4-1 included more than one domain, the replication topology for the directory partition within each of the domains would be a smaller ring encompassing only the domain controllers within that domain. Global catalog servers, on the other hand, hold partial domain partitions of all domains. The global catalog servers or the forest replicate the partial domain partitions among themselves and, therefore, have their own topology.

If the number of domain controllers in the site exceeds seven, the simplified ring topology will not be able to update all domain controllers in three or fewer hops. In this case, the KCCs add additional connection objects as required to achieve the three-hop limit. This is known as the *expanded ring topology* (see Figure 4-5).

If a server does not respond, the KCCs declare the server unavailable. By default, for immediate neighbors (that is, neighbors within the basic site topology ring) a domain controller will wait 2 hours after a failed replication request before declaring a server unavailable. For connections created as part of an expanded ring topology to keep the hop limit at three hops (Microsoft calls these *optimizing connections*), the domain controller waits for 12 hours after the second failed request. You can specify alternative values for these defaults through REG_WORD Registry entries in the Registry key

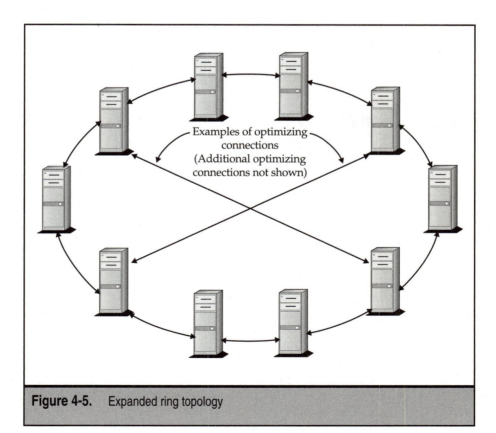

Figure 4-5.   Expanded ring topology

HKEY_LOCAL_MACHINE\SYSTEM\CurrentControlSet\Services\NTDS\Parameters:

▼ **CriticalLinkFailuresAllowed** Failures allowed for immediate neighbors

■ **MaxFailureTimeForCriticalLink** Time interval after failure for immediate neighbors

■ **NonCriticalLinkFailuresAllowed** Failures allowed for optimizing connections

▲ **MaxFailureTimeForNonCriticalLink** Time interval after failure for optimizing connections

In the following sections, you'll learn how to:

▼ View connection objects and connection object properties

■ Create a new connection object

■ Check the replication topology

▲ Force replication manually

Viewing Connection Objects and Properties

As an earlier section mentioned, the KCC creates a scheme (called a replication topology) for transmitting directory updates. That replication topology is implemented through *connections objects*. A connection object is a link from a domain controller sending the update to a domain controller receiving the update. The KCC automatically creates the connection objects it needs to implement a replication topology within the site.

To view the connection objects and or edit connection object properties, follow these steps:

1. Click the Start button and choose Programs | Administrative Tools | Active Directory Sites And Services.

2. In the Active Directory Sites And Services tree, click the plus sign next to the Sites icon to view the sites associated with your network.

3. Click the plus sign next to the site that contains the server whose connection objects you wish to view. Then click the plus sign next to the Servers folder.

4. Double-click the computer ID for the domain controller whose connections you wish to view.

5. Select the NTDS Settings icon under the computer ID.

    The connection objects associated with the server you chose in step 3 appear in the right pane.

6. To view the properties of a connection, right-click the connection in the right pane and choose Properties.

7. The Properties dialog box appears with the Active Directory Connection tab in the foreground (see Figure 4-6). In the Active Directory Connection tab, you can choose the transport

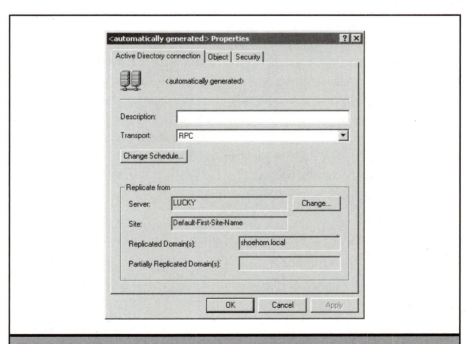

Figure 4-6.   The connection object Properties dialog box

you wish to use for the connection. Options include IP, RPC, or SMTP.

8. Click the Change Schedule button to change the replication schedule.

9. View the name of the server and the site location of the server that will be replicating to the local server through this connection in the section labeled Replicate From at the bottom of the tab. To change the Server, click the Change button.

The Replicated Domains box gives the name of the domain whose domain partition will be replicated. If your network includes multiple domains, a partial domain partition is replicated to global catalog servers. The Partially Replicated Domains box is used for connections to global catalog servers that receive the partial domain partition.

Creating a New Connection Object

You can create your own connection objects to link two domain controllers for direct replication. In most situations, you won't need to create your own connection objects. The KCC automatically generates a topology that will ensure that updates reach all domain controllers. In some cases, however, you may wish to create a connection object to reduce the time it takes for updates from one domain controller to reach another domain controller.

If you do create your own connection object, the KCC works around the new object and builds it into the replication topology. According to Microsoft:

▼ If a manually created connection object is in place, the KCC will not create a duplicate connection object for the same connection.

▲ The KCC won't delete a manually created connection object.

A manually created connection object can speed up replication to a part of the network, but it is important to remember that it also requires additional processing time and network bandwidth.

To create a new connection object:

1. Click the Start button and choose Programs | Administrative Tools | Active Directory Sites And Services.

2. In the Active Directory Sites And Services tree, click the plus sign next to the Sites icon to view the sites associated with your network.

3. Click the plus sign next to the site that contains the domain controller for which you wish to create the connection object. Then click the plus sign next to the Servers folder.

4. Click the computer ID of the domain controller for which you wish to create the connection.

5. Right-click the NTDS Settings icon under the computer ID. In the context menu, select New Active Directory Connection.

6. The Find Domain Controllers window appears (see Figure 4-7). Select the domain controller that will replicate updates to the computer you chose in step 4. Click OK.

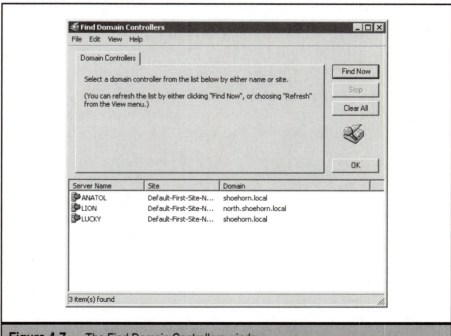

Figure 4-7.   The Find Domain Controllers window

7. The New Object dialog box asks you to choose a name for the new connection object. The default name is the name of the domain controller you chose in step 6. Click OK.

The new connection appears under NTDS Settings for the domain controller you chose in step 4.

Checking the Replication Topology

You can use the KCC to manually check the replication topology for the site. Checking the replication topology is sometimes a good troubleshooting step if replication is not occurring properly. Note that, in theory, the KCC is supposed to adapt to network conditions and create new connection objects automatically, if necessary. However, if you want immediate information on the readiness of the network for replication, you can manually check the replication topology.

To check the replication topology, follow these steps:

1. Click the Start button and choose Programs | Administrative Tools | Active Directory Sites And Services.

2. In the Active Directory Sites and Services tree, click the plus sign next to the Sites icon to view the sites associated with your network.

3. Click the plus sign next to the site that contains the domain controller for which you wish to check the replication topology. Then click the plus sign next to the folder labeled Servers.

4. Double-click the computer ID of the domain controller for which you wish to check the replication topology.

5. Right-click the NTDS Settings icon under the computer ID. In the context menu, select All Tasks, then choose Check Replication Topology. A dialog box appears, telling you that Active Directory has checked the replication topology. Click OK.

Forcing Replication Manually

If you make a change at a domain controller, you may wish to replicate that change immediately to other domain controllers rather than waiting for the replication cycle to distribute the change into the network. You can use Active Directory Sites And Services to force Active Directory replication. Note that the manual replication feature acts over a single connection. By using this feature, you cause immediate directory replication over the link defined by the connection object. This single connection is only part of the replication topology, and replicating over the connection *does not* distribute the change to all other domain controllers on the network. (The change will, of course, eventually pass to other domain controllers through the normal replication process.)

It is also worth mentioning that the connection object is listed in AD Sites And Services under the domain controller that will *receive* the update. This can sometimes cause confusion when it comes to the manual replication feature. If you make a change on domain controller A and you wish to replicate that change to domain controller B, you must locate the connection to A stored under domain controller B's NTDS settings.

To force replication manually, follow these steps:

1. Click the Start button and choose Programs | Administrative Tools | Active Directory Sites And Services.

2. In the Active Directory Sites And Services tree, click the plus sign next to the Sites icon to view the sites associated with your network.

3. Click the plus sign next to the site that contains the domain controller that will receive the manual replication. Then click the plus sign next to the folder labeled Servers.

4. Double-click the computer ID of the domain controller that will receive the manual replication.

5. Click the NTDS Settings icon under the computer ID. The connections associated with the domain controller appear in the right pane.

6. Right-click the icon for the connection over which you wish to manually replicate. Select Replicate Now (see Figure 4-8).

INTERSITE REPLICATION

In Active Directory, *intersite* replication (replication among sites) is treated in a totally different way from *intrasite* replication. In fact, one of the principal reasons for Active Directory's site structure is to allow for a separate replication process designed for slower, WAN-based network connections. The following sections discuss some issues you'll need to understand to implement intersite replication. If your network does not have multiple sites, you will never face many of the issues described in this section.

Microsoft says that the intersite replication topology is designed to connect sites in a tree structure, which means that sites connect outward from the center rather than roundabout in a ring. Intersite

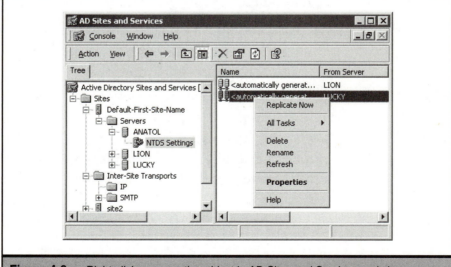

Figure 4-8.   Right-click a connection object in AD Sites and Services and choose Replicate Now to force replication over the connection

replication is optimized to minimize bandwidth, and, therefore, replication updates are compressed to 10 to 15 percent of their original size.

The process for defining and implementing a replication topology among sites is totally different from the process for implementing the topology within a site. Instead of all domain controllers participating as equals in the replication process, a few domain controllers (called *bridgehead* servers) replicate directory data across site links. One domain controller for the entire site (called the Intersite Topology Generator) creates the inbound connection objects necessary for supporting replication to bridgehead servers. The intersite topology, in contrast to the intrasite topology, is created and managed for the site by the Intersite Topology Generator and is not the result of collective action. The first domain controller in the site automatically becomes the Intersite Topology Generator. Active Directory automatically chooses a new Intersite Topology Generator if the current one is offline. It is not possible for a human to change the Intersite Topology Generator role.

To determine the Intersite Topology Generator for the site, follow these steps:

1. In Active Directory Sites and Services, expand the Sites folder and select the icon for a site.

2. In the right panel, right-click NTDS Settings and choose Properties.

    The name of the current Intersite Topology Generator appears in the Site Settings tab of the NTDS Settings Properties dialog box.

By default, replication updates are transmitted over the network using a remote procedure call (RPC) over IP. However, for intersite updates, you also have the option of transmitting intersite updates using Simple Mail Transfer Protocol (SMTP). The SMTP option uses Internet Information Server (IIS)'s SMTP feature to transfer replication data in an e-mail message format using the Collaborative Data Objects (CDO) interface. This SMTP method does not support the File Replication Service and therefore cannot replicate the full domain partition. It therefore cannot be used for connections within the same domain and is used, instead, to replicate the schema and configuration partitions when the site boundary corresponds to a domain boundary. The SMTP option *can* be used to replicate the partial domain partition to a global catalog server.

The primary difference between RPC and SMTP replication is that RPC replication is *synchronous* and SMTP replication is *asynchronous*. SMTP replication is provided for low-speed (or low-quality) WAN connections that cannot reliably transmit the synchronous signals required for RPC.

Active Directory uses a domain controller within a site to act as a bridgehead to other sites. The bridgehead server replicates the directory across site links. Other domain controllers replicate within the site only.

After you've added a second site to your network, you'll need to configure intersite replication. The following sections discuss

▼ Configuring site links

■ Configuring site link bridges

▲ Configuring preferred bridgehead servers

CONFIGURING SITE LINKS

Replication among sites occurs via a site link. A *site link* is an intersite replication pathway. When you create a new site, Windows 2000 asks you to specify a site link that will link the site to the rest of the network. A default IP site link called DEFAULTIPSITELINK is created when you set up multiple sites. You can add additional sites links at any time.

A site link may sound a lot like a connection object, but, in fact, a site link is very different. In the first place, a site link doesn't apply to a specific connection between servers but is, instead, a link between sites. One site link can connect more than two sites. A site link is more like a bundle of properties that govern intersite replication. Specifically, a site link defines the following:

▼ **A transport** The transport that will be used for replication across the site link. Options include IP (actually RPC over IP) and SMTP.

■ **A collection of member sites** The sites that will use the site link. A link that connects more than two sites may sound strange. Microsoft says this multisite capability is intended for situations such as an ATM backbone connecting several sites.

■ **The *cost* of replication over the site link** The replication cost parameter is not intended to represent an actual price but rather a relative measure of the cost-effectiveness of the link. You'll learn more about replication cost later in this section.

■ **A replication interval** The interval at which changes will be replicated over the link. The upstream replication partner will save changes for an interval before replicating to downstream partners. This replication interval prevents the replicating domain controllers from tying up access to the line.

▲ **A replication schedule** The schedule is hours of the day during which replication will take place. Note that this is different from the interval. The interval may specify that replication takes place every 15 minutes. The schedule could then specify that these replications (at 15-minute intervals) take place only between 11:30 P.M. and 11:30 A.M.

A site link is intended to represent a network medium that connects two or more LANs. If a network contains several sites, multiple pathways may exist for carrying data through the chain of sites. The KCC must, therefore, choose one of several replication paths. Active Directory's replication cost factor is intended as a measure of the relative desirability of a site link representing a network medium. For instance, a site link over a T1 line passes data more efficiently than a site link that uses a 56K modem. You can assign a lower cost to the site link using the T1, and the KCC will give preference to the T1 link when forming the replication topology. See the procedure on viewing and modifying site link properties (the second procedure in this section) for a description of how to assign a cost to a site link.

To create a new site link, follow these steps:

1. Click the Start button and choose Programs | Administrative Tools | Active Directory Sites And Services.

2. In the Active Directory Sites And Services tree, click the plus sign next to the Sites icon.

3. Click the plus sign next to the folder labeled Inter-Site Transports. (This procedure assumes you have configured two or more sites. To create a new site, see Chapter 3.)

4. You'll see a folder labeled IP and a folder labeled SMTP. Decide whether you would like the site link to use RPC over IP (the IP option) or SMTP. See the discussion earlier in this chapter. Right-click the transport you wish to use. In the context menu, choose New Site Link.

5. In the New Object dialog box (Figure 4-9), enter a name for the new site link. Click an available site in the box on the left and click the Add button to add the site to the list of sites associated with the site link. Add at least one more site. The site link must contain at least two sites.

6. Click OK.

Figure 4-9.   The New Object – Site Link dialog box

To view and modify site link properties, follow these steps:

1. Click the Start button and choose Programs | Administrative Tools | Active Directory Sites And Services.

2. In the Active Directory Sites And Services tree, click the plus sign next to the Sites icon.

3. Click the plus sign next to the Inter-Site Transports folder. (This procedure assumes you have configured two or more sites. To create a new site, see Chapter 3.)

4. Click the folder for the transport of the site link you wish to modify (IP or SMTP).

5. A list of site links appears in the right pane. Right-click the site link whose properties you wish to view or modify. Choose Properties.

6. In the site link Properties dialog box (see Figure 4-10), enter a description for the site link. Select a site and click the Add or

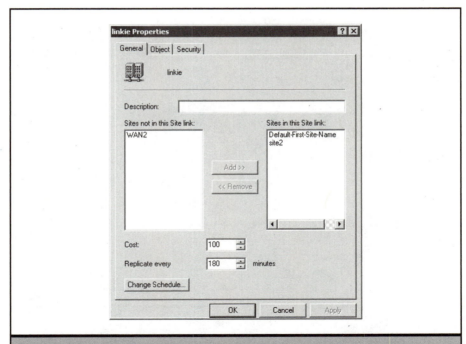

Figure 4-10.   The site link Properties dialog box

Remove button to add or remove the site from the list of sites associated with the site link.

7. Enter a cost value for the link.

    As described earlier in this section, the cost value is an indication of how much you want Active Directory to use this link. The higher the cost, the less desirable this link is compared to other options.

8. Enter a replication interval for the site link in the Replicate Every box. The replication interval tells Active Directory how frequently it should replicate changes across the link.

9. To view or modify the time window in which replication will take place, click the Change Schedule button. The subsequent Schedule dialog box (Figure 4-11) lets you choose blocks of time during which replication will or will not be available.

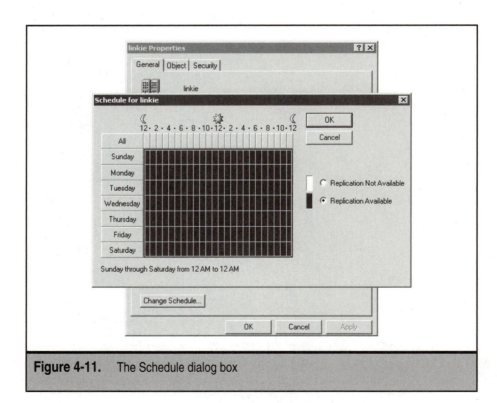

Figure 4-11. The Schedule dialog box

10. When you are finished modifying the site link properties, click OK. Remember that it will take time for this change to replicate to all domain controllers on the network. You can replicate the changes immediately to other specific domain controllers using Active Directory Sites and Service's manual replication feature (described earlier in this chapter) or using Replication Monitor (described later in this chapter).

Note that the Change Schedule option in the Schedule dialog box (see step 9 of the preceding procedure) does not actually schedule replication but instead defines a time window in which replication will occur. Within that time window, replication will occur according to the replication interval (see step 8 of the preceding procedure). The Schedule option is available only for links using the RPC transport.

Configuring Site Link Bridges

By default, all site links for a given transport are transitive. In other words (see Figure 4-12), if Link 1 joins Site A and Site B and Link 2 joins Sites B and C, the KCC recognizes that Sites A and C are joined through the Link 1/Link 2 pathway as well as through Link 3. Microsoft calls these links *bridged* links. You can deselect this default bridging feature and thereby make the links intransitive. If you turn off the Bridge All Site Links feature, the KCC will not assume that a replication update beginning in site A will be able to reach site C through the link 1/link 2 pathway.

In some cases, you may wish for some links to be transitive and for some to be *intransitive*. In other words (see Figure 4-13), for whatever reasons relating to the WAN links on your network, you

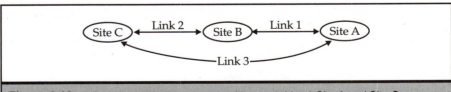

Figure 4-12. By default, site links are transitive, or *bridged*; Site A and Site C can communicate even without the direct link Link3

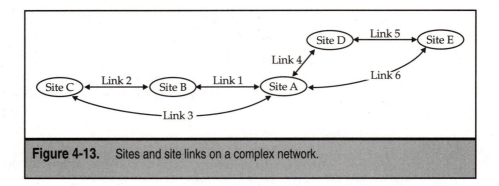

Figure 4-13. Sites and site links on a complex network.

may wish to configure your network so that the link 1/link 2 pathway is considered transitive and the link 4/link 5 pathway is considered intransitive. In that case, you should

1. Turn off the Bridge All Site Links setting.

2. Create a site link bridge to bridge any links you wish to specifically consider as transitive.

A *site link bridge* is a user-specified collection of fully routable site links. The collection of pathways between the sites in a site link bridge is considered transitive or bridged.

To turn on or off the Bridge All Site Links option, follow these steps:

1. Click the Start button and choose Programs | Administrative Tools | Active Directory Sites And Services.

2. In the Active Directory Sites And Services tree, click the plus sign next to the Sites icon.

3. Click the plus sign next to the Inter-Site Transports folder.

4. Right-click the folder for the transport of the site link you wish to modify (IP or SMTP) and then choose Properties.

5. In the subsequent Properties dialog box (see Figure 4-14), select (or deselect) Bridge All Site Links. Than click OK.

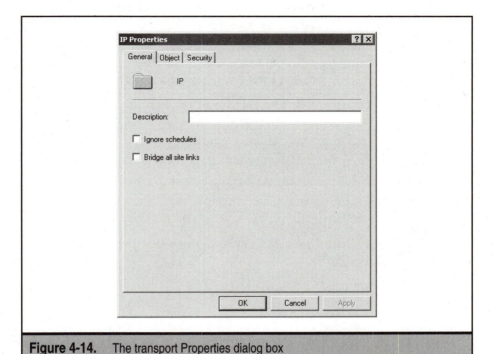

Figure 4-14.   The transport Properties dialog box

NOTE: A site link bridge is unnecessary unless you turn off the Bridge All Site Links option for the transport. The default Bridge All Site Links option essentially creates a single site link bridge for all links.

To configure a site link bridge, follow these steps:

1. Click the Start button and choose Programs | Administrative Tools | Active Directory Sites And Services.

2. In the Active Directory Sites And Services tree, click the plus sign next to the Sites icon.

3. Click the plus sign next to the Inter-Site Transports folder. (This procedure assumes you have configured two or more sites. To create a new site, see Chapter 3.)

4. You'll see a folder labeled IP and a folder labeled SMTP. Decide whether you would like the site link bridge to apply to RPC over IP (the IP option) or SMTP. Right-click the transport you wish to use. In the context menu, choose New Site Link Bridge.

5. In the New Object – Site Link Bridge dialog box (see Figure 4-15), the links listed in the box on the left are not part of the site link bridge, and the links listed on the right are part of the site link bridge. Select a site link in the box on the left and click the Add button to add it to the box on the right. Select a link in the box on the right and click the Remove button to remove the link from the site link bridge.

6. In the Name box, enter a name for the site link bridge. Then click OK.

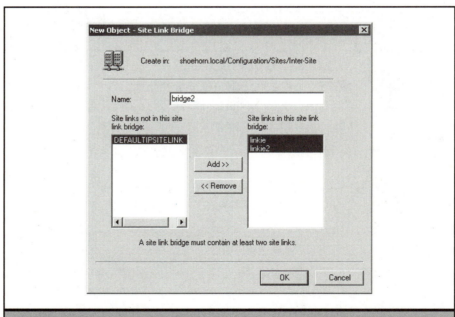

Figure 4-15. Enter a name for the site link bridge

Configuring a Preferred Bridgehead Server

To minimize replication traffic across WAN connections, Active Directory designates a single domain controller, called a *bridgehead server*, to perform intersite replication for the site. The bridgehead server replicates across site links to other sites. Typically, the same bridgehead server is used for all its site's intersite replication under a given transport. In some cases, the site may require multiple bridgehead servers because of differing topologies for different directory partitions.

It is important to note that the bridgehead server may not be the same as the Intersite Topology Generator. The Intersite Topology Generator (described earlier in this chapter) generates the intersite replication topology for the site. The bridgehead server participates in that replication topology by replicating across site links.

Active Directory will automatically assign the bridgehead server role. However, in some cases, you may wish to specifically designate a bridgehead server. The bridgehead server typically participates in a greater share of replication, so you may wish to assign a particularly well-equipped (or underused) domain controller to the bridgehead server role. You can designate one of the domain controllers in the site as a preferred bridgehead server. Active Directory will assign the bridgehead role to the preferred bridgehead server. If you specify more than one preferred bridgehead server, Active Directory chooses one to act as the preferred bridgehead server for the site.

If you let Active Directory choose the bridgehead server and that bridgehead server fails, Active Directory will automatically choose another bridgehead server. If, on the other hand, you specify one or more preferred bridgehead servers, Active Directory will use only one of the preferred bridgehead servers you specify. If preferred bridgehead servers are specified but no preferred bridgehead server is available, intersite replication will fail.

To designate a preferred bridgehead server, follow these steps:

1. Click the Start button and choose Programs | Administrative Tools | Active Directory Sites And Services.

2. In the Active Directory Sites And Services tree, click the plus sign next to the Sites icon.

3. Click the plus sign next to the site that contains the domain controller you wish to designate as a bridgehead server.

4. Click the plus sign next to the Servers folder.

5. Right-click the computer ID of the computer you wish to designate as a bridgehead server. In the Properties dialog box (Figure 4-16), select a transport in the left column that you wish to assign to the bridgehead server. The bridgehead server will be used for replication through site links.

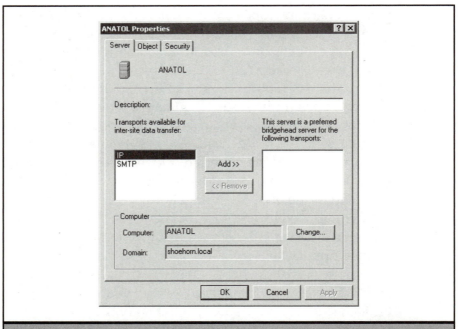

Figure 4-16. The AD Sites and Services Server Properties dialog box

MANAGING AND MONITORING REPLICATION

Microsoft provides some useful tools for managing and monitoring replication on an Active Directory network. Two of these tools are new with Windows 2000; others are familiar Windows NT tools. This section describes the following:

▼ Repadmin

■ Replication Monitor

■ Performance Monitor

▲ Network Monitor

Repadmin is a command-line support tool that lets you manage the replication process. Replication Monitor is designed specifically to administer intrasite replication. Performance Monitor and Network Monitor are general monitoring tools that can be used to monitor replication as well as other services and processes.

Repadmin

Repadmin.exe is a command-line utility that lets you manage and monitor the replication process. Repadmin is located in the Windows 2000 Support Tool package. Once you have installed Windows 2000 Support Tools, you can go to the command prompt and type **repadmin ?** for a summary of repadmin syntax. Or consult Windows 2000 Support Tools Help for a complete look at repadmin syntax and examples.

NOTE: To install the Windows 2000 Support Tools (including Replication Monitor), insert the Windows 2000 Server CD, open the Support folder, and then open the Reskit folder. Double-click the Setup icon. The Windows 2000 Resource Kit Setup Wizard will prompt you for additional information.

The general format of a repadmin command is:

repadmin *commands/arguments [/U:user /pw:password]*

▼ *commands/arguments* is the specific repadmin command you're using and any options or arguments that accompany that command

■ *user* is the username of the user account you wish to perform the command under. Precede the username with the domain name if the account is in a different domain: domainA\user1. The user must have administrative privileges.

▲ *password* is the password of the user account you wish to perform the command under

NOTE: The username and password are optional. If they aren't specified, the current user's account name and password will be used.

Repadmin has several options that perform a range of useful functions (see Table 4-3). See Windows 2000 Support Tools Help for more on repadmin.

Command	Arguments	Description
/sync	Distinguished name of directory partition Source domain controller Destination domain controller	Starts replication for specified directory partition for specified source and destination domain controllers
/showvector	Distinguished name of directory partition Domain controller	Shows up-to-date vector for the specified directory partition

Table 4-3. Some Repadmin Commands and Arguments

Command	Arguments	Description
/showreps	Distinguished name of directory partition Domain controller	Shows replication partners of the specified domain controllers and the specified directory partition
/showmeta	Distinguished name of object	Displays replication metadata such as local USN, originating USN, version number, etc. for specified object

Table 4-3.   Some Repadmin Commands and Arguments *(continued)*

Replication Monitor

Replication Monitor is a many-featured tool included with the Windows 2000 Support Tools. The Windows 2000 Support Tools, which are included on the Windows 2000 Server CD, are a subset of the tools found in the Windows 2000 Resource Kit. (See the preceding section, "Repadmin," for a note on how to install the Windows 2000 Support Tools.)

The purpose of Replication Monitor is to monitor the status of individual domain controllers with regard to the replication process. Replication Monitor lets you:

▼ Monitor the replication status of directory partitions on individual domain controllers.

■ Synchronize a domain controller with all its replication partners.

■ Generate a replication status report and configure status logging.

■ View which domain controllers are direct, indirect, or bridgehead replication partners of a given domain controller.

■ Check whether a domain controller has directory changes that haven't yet been replicated through the network.

▲ View the replication tables (so-called Attribute Meta-Data Tables) that the domain controller uses to provide version control for updates (this process was discussed earlier in the chapter).

To view replication information with Replication Monitor, follow these steps:

1. After you've installed the Windows 2000 support tools (see preceding note), start Replication Monitor by clicking the Start menu and choosing Programs | Windows 2000 Support Tools | Tools | Active Directory Replication Monitor.

2. When you first start Replication Monitor, the left pane will display an icon labeled Monitored Servers. To monitor the replication status of a computer on your network, right-click the Monitored Server icon and select Add Monitored Server.

3. In the Add Monitored Server Wizard (Figure 4-17), select either Add The Server Explicitly By Name or Search The Directory For The Server To Add. If you elect to search the directory (which really should say *Browse* the directory, since that's more like what you do), the domain name will appear in the text box. If you have more than one domain, click the down arrow beside the text box and choose the domain on which the domain controller is located. Click Next.

NOTE: Throughout the NT 4 era, Microsoft was always careful not to routinely use the word "server" to refer to a domain controller, since the term could refer to a member server, a print server, or any other kind of server. The company has abandoned that practice in Windows 2000. Get used to seeing the word "server" for domain controllers.

4. If you chose to search the directory in step 3, the next screen asks you to select the domain controller. Click a site and browse for the domain controller you wish to monitor. Click Finish.

The domain controller you selected will appear in the left pane of the Replication Monitor main window beneath an icon for the site to which the domain controller belongs.

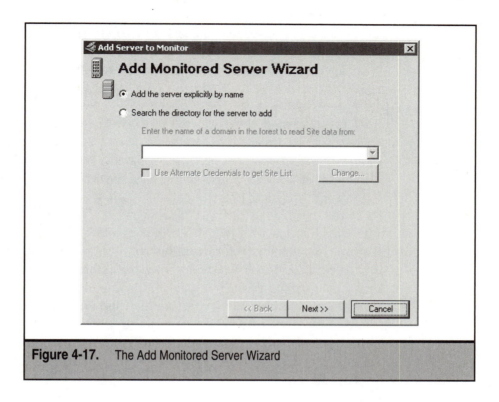

Figure 4-17.   The Add Monitored Server Wizard

5. To monitor additional domain controllers, right-click the
   Monitored Servers icon and select Add Monitored Server.
   Repeat steps 3–4.

6. Click the plus sign next to a domain controller. Three icons
   appear representing the three partitions of the Active Directory
   (Schema, Configuration, and Domain). Recall from earlier in this
   chapter that the forest-based replication partitions (the schema
   and configuration partitions) may have a different replication
   topology and hence a different combination of replication
   partners. If the domain controller you chose in step 3 is a global
   catalog server, you'll also see an icon representing the partial
   domain partition for each additional domain.

7. Click the plus sign next to one of the partitions. You'll see a list
   of icons representing direct and transitive replication partners.
   Note that the Transitive Replication Partner icon is a little
   computer with a blue monitor (a blue screen?). The Direct

Replication Partner icon consists of two little gray computers attached to a network backbone. If your network has multiple sites, you may notice a third icon for a bridgehead server.

NOTE: A domain controller lists itself as a transitive replication partner. You may wonder if a domain controller acting as its own replication partner would lead to some form of infinite loop. It doesn't, because the version control rules (discussed earlier in this chapter) mean that a domain controller will not accept an update it has already received.

After you click one of the replication partners listed under a directory partition, a log of replications from that partner appears in the right pane. The log shows the time, update status, and current property update USN for each log cycle. If some attribute within the partition is replicated to the server, the qualified name, attribute name, and USN of the update are recorded in the log. The display shown in Replication Monitor is a little tidier than the actual log file. A sample from a replication log file is shown in the listing a little later in this chapter.

The Update Automatically button above the right pane of the Replication Monitor main window (see Figure 4-18) lets you allow the log view in the right pane to automatically update itself. You must specify the update interval. When you start the automatic update, the label on the button will change to Cancel Auto Update. Click Cancel Auto Update to stop the automatic updating of the log file.

Right-clicking a Replication Partner icon under a directory partition yields the following options:

▼ **Synchronize With This Replication Partner**   Causes Replication Monitor to request that the partition be synchronized with the replication partner you selected. Note that Replication Monitor cannot actually perform the synchronization. It requests that the replication service perform the update.

■ **Check Current USN And Unreplicated Objects**   Checks to see whether the replication partner has any updates that have

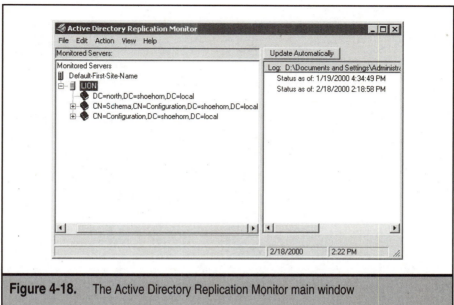

Figure 4-18.   The Active Directory Replication Monitor main window

not yet been replicated to the partition you selected.
Replication Monitor prompts you to supply credentials to
access the replication partner. The default is to use the current
credentials, which usually works if you have administrator
privileges on a domain-based security system. You can also
elect to supply alternate credentials.

■ **Clear Log**   Clears the Replication Monitor log file for the
partition you selected.

▲ **Properties**   Opens the Replication Partner Properties dialog
box, which provides a useful summary of information on the
replication partner (Figure 4-19).

Here's an excerpt from a sample replication log file:

```
"DateTime","10/13/1999 1:35:01 PM"
"PartnerType",">> Direct Replication Partner Data <<"
"RepsFromUSN","Property Update USN: 9138"
"RepsFromSuccess","The last replication attempt was successful.
This took place at: 10/13/1999 12:55:14 PM (local)"
```

```
"DateTime","10/13/1999 2:55:33 PM"
"USNData","9277"
"AttributeChangeObject","DN: DC=143,DC=131.121.129.in-addr.arpa,
CN=MicrosoftDNS,CN=System,DC=mass,DC=local"
"AttributeChangeDetail","Attribute: dnsRecord"
"AttributeChangeDetail","Remote USN: 9224"
"DateTime","10/13/1999 2:55:33 PM"
"PartnerType",">> Direct Replication Partner Data <<"
"RepsFromUSN","Property Update USN: 9260"
"RepsFromSuccess","The last replication attempt was successful.
This took place at: 10/13/1999 2:55:17 PM (local)"
"DateTime","10/13/1999 3:01:54 PM"
"USNData","9277"
"DateTime","10/13/1999 3:01:54 PM"
"PartnerType",">> Direct Replication Partner Data <<"
"RepsFromUSN","Property Update USN: 9260"
"RepsFromSuccess","The last replication attempt was successful.
This took place at:  10/13/1999 2:55:17 PM (local)"
"DateTime","10/13/1999 3:07:56 PM"
"USNData","9277"
"DateTime","10/13/1999 3:07:56 PM"
"PartnerType",">> Direct Replication Partner Data <<"
"RepsFromUSN","Property Update USN: 9260"
"RepsFromSuccess","The last replication attempt was successful.
This took place at:  10/13/1999 2:55:17 PM (local)"
"DateTime","10/13/1999 3:14:01 PM"
"USNData","9295"
"AttributeChangeObject","DN:
DC=143,DC=131.121.129.in-addr.arpa,CN=MicrosoftDNS,CN=System,DC=ma
ss,DC=local"
"AttributeChangeDetail","Attribute: dnsRecord"
"AttributeChangeDetail","Remote USN:  9292"
"DateTime","10/13/1999 3:14:01 PM"
"PartnerType",">> Direct Replication Partner Data <<"
"RepsFromUSN","Property Update USN: 9292"
"RepsFromSuccess","The last replication attempt was successful.
This took place at:  10/13/1999 3:10:06 PM (local)"
```

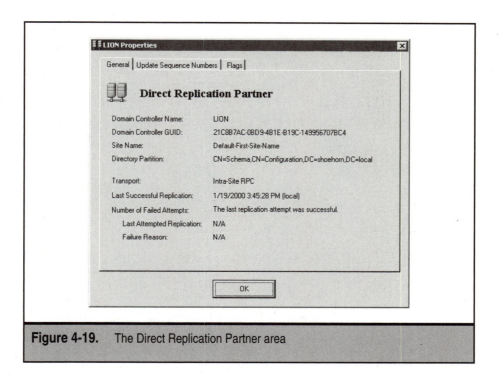

Figure 4-19. The Direct Replication Partner area

Replication Monitor provides several options for controlling the contents of its log files. To access these options, choose Options from the View menu. The General tab of the Replication Monitor Options dialog box is shown in Figure 4-20. Some of the more interesting options are as follows:

▼ **Notification Options**   You can configure Replication Monitor to an e-mail message or write an event to the application event log after a given number of failed replications.

■ **Log Files**   By default, Replication Monitor log files are stored in the Resource Kit directory, which is typically in the Program Files folder of the Windows 2000 partition. Use these options to specify a path for the replication log files.

▲ **Enable Debug Logging**   You can enable debug logging and write debug information to the event log or to a log file using these options.

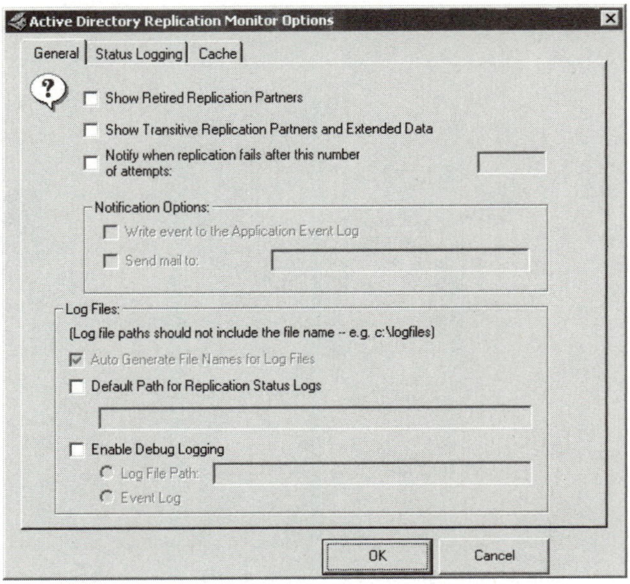

Figure 4-20. General tab of the Replication Monitor Options dialog box

The Status Logging tab of the Options dialog box (Figure 4-21) also offers some interesting options. One of the most interesting is the Performance Statistics option, which lets you log Performance Monitor counters to the replication log. To add a counter to the replication log, check the Performance Statistics checkbox and click the Add button. You'll be asked to specify the *object\counter* pair you wish to add (see Figure 4-22). (See "Performance Monitor" later in this chapter.)

Replication Monitor must query the domain controllers for any information it receives. In some cases, Replication Monitor caches query results for data that changes infrequently. To flush the cache, select Options from the View menu, choose the Cache tab in the Options dialog box, and then click the Reset button.

If you right-click the name of a server in Replication Monitor (see Figure 4-23), you'll see several useful choices. Many of these choices are self-explanatory and request certain display options (such as a list of domain controllers in the domain or a summary of group policy object information).

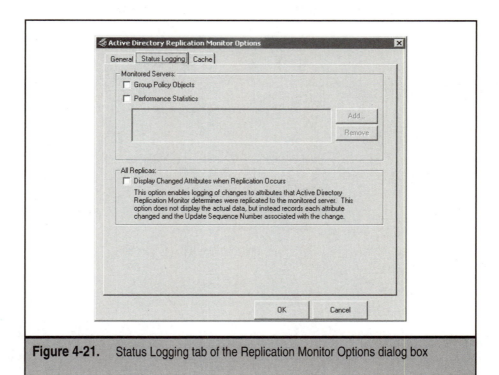

Figure 4-21.   Status Logging tab of the Replication Monitor Options dialog box

Synchronize Each Directory Partition with All Servers

Choosing the Synchronize Each Directory Partition With All Servers option produces the forbidding dialog box shown in Figure 4-24. This powerful feature actually causes all replication partners of the server you selected to replicate their directory changes to the server. This, of course, may take some time, depending on the size of your network. The synchronization options in Figure 4-24 are designed to reduce or

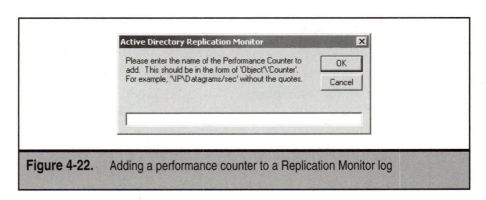

Figure 4-22.   Adding a performance counter to a Replication Monitor log

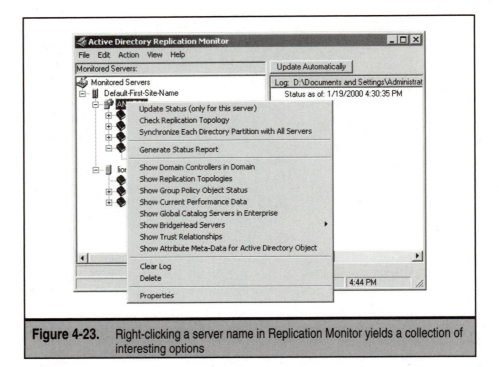

Figure 4-23. Right-clicking a server name in Replication Monitor yields a collection of interesting options

expand this synchronization process. Some of the notable options are as follows:

▼ **Disables Transitive Replication** By default, changes will replicate from all replication partners, both transitive and direct. If you enable this option, only direct (adjacent) partners will replicate their changes to the server during this synchronization.

■ **Push Mode** Push mode pushes changes out from the server you selected to the replication partners. Note that this is backward from the usual direction of replication, and, in some cases, the replication partners must be reached through transitive replication. Recall that connection objects are one-way. Just because computer A directly replicates changes to computer B, it doesn't mean computer B directly replicates to computer A (although, in some cases, it may). The replication service knows the topology and will make sure all partners receive the change.

▲ **Cross Site Boundaries**   Synchronizes with partners on other sites. (By default, the synchronization command only works within a site.) Note that intersite replication must use the IP (which is actually RPC over IP) transport for this option to work.

If you click the OK button in the synch options dialog box (shown in Figure 4-24), Replication Monitor asks you to confirm that you want to proceed and warns you that this process may take some time if you have several domain controllers. Replication Monitor will be unavailable until the synchronization is complete.

Show Attribute Meta-Data for Active Directory Object

Choosing Show Attribute Meta-Data For Active Directory Object (refer to Figure 4-23) starts an interesting option that helps to illustrate the replication version control system described earlier in this chapter. You can use this option to track updates received by the server for any object. Recall from an earlier section that replication updates are sent by attribute and that a collection of additional data (which Microsoft calls *meta-data*) is sent with the update. This

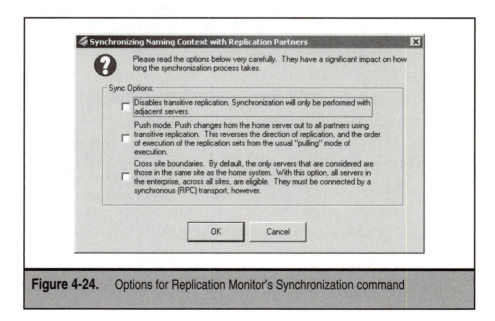

Figure 4-24.   Options for Replication Monitor's Synchronization command

meta-data includes the originating server, the USN on the originating server, and the version number. The Show Attribute Meta-Data option lets you view the meta-data for all attributes associated with an object you specify.

To display attribute meta-data for an object, follow these steps:

1. After you've installed the Windows 2000 support tools, click the Start menu and choose Programs | Windows 2000 Support Tools | Tools | Active Directory Replication Monitor.

2. In the Replication Monitor main window, right-click the Monitored Servers icon and add the domain controller whose replication meta-data table you'd like to check.

3. Right-click the icon for the domain controller and choose Show Attribute Meta-Data For Active Directory Object.

4. Replication Monitor prompts you to specify the necessary credentials to access the server. The default is to use credentials already supplied for the server. If your network is a single domain and you are operating with domain admin privileges, you should be OK. Otherwise, choose Use Alternative Credentials.

5. In the View Meta-Data for Object dialog box shown in the following illustration, specify the distinguished name of the object with the attributes whose meta-data you wish to view. Click OK.

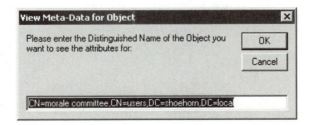

A table will appear showing the meta-data for all attributes associated with the object you chose (see Figure 4-25). Note that you can view the attribute name, local USN, originating server, USN on originating server, and version number.

It is important to remember that the attribute meta-data displayed through the Show Attribute Meta-Data For Active Directory Object command is the data stored *on the server you selected* at the time you perform the command. This data may or may not be current with the latest change to the attribute, depending on whether the update has reached the server.

Performance Monitor

The Performance Monitor utility survived its run as a tuning and diagnostic tool of the NT era and lives on in Windows 2000. Performance Monitor charts, graphs, and logs a vast array of performance statistics. For a complete discussion of how to use Performance Monitor, consult a Windows 2000 or Windows NT text. For purposes of this chapter, it is worth noting that

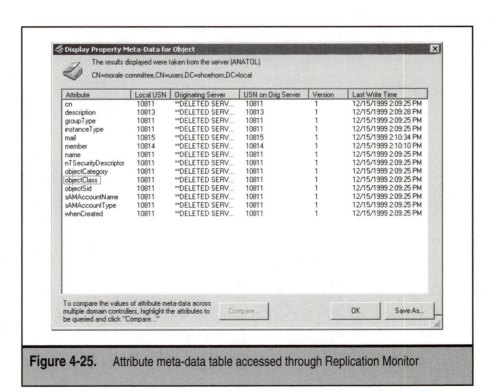

Figure 4-25.   Attribute meta-data table accessed through Replication Monitor

Microsoft includes a number of performance counters that measure replication activity.

Performance Monitor's replication-related counters are primarily located in the NTDS performance object (NT Directory Replication object), which contains many counters related to directory service activities. Counters beginning with the initials DRA specifically measure replication processes.

To view replication-related performance counters, follow these steps:

1. Click the Start menu and choose Programs | Administrative Tools | Performance.

2. In the Performance Monitor main window, click the plus sign (+) button in the right pane.

3. In the Add Counters dialog box, choose the computer you wish to monitor from the drop-down list. Click on the arrow to the right of the Performance Object box and choose NTDS.

   A list of Active Directory counters appears in the box in the lower left. Browse through the list. The counters whose names begin with DRA relate specifically to replication. Note that some of the counters refer to whether or not the data is compressed. Recall that intersite replication is typically compressed, whereas intrasite replication typically is not. The presence of compression is a handy way to check for intersite (as opposed to intrasite) replication.

4. To track a counter, select the counter in the list and click the Add button. You can track multiple counters simultaneously. When you are finished choosing counters, click Close.

   Performance Monitor graphs real-time activity of the counters you chose in step 4 in the right pane of the Performance Monitor main window. Statistics appear at the bottom of the screen. In the left pane, click Performance Logs And Alerts to create logs and to configure an automatic alert when a counter reaches a predefined threshold.

NOTE: As already described, you can also write Performance Monitor counter statistics directly to the Replication Monitor log. This useful feature lets you view replication events and the accompanying replication performance statistics at once. See the earlier section entitled "Replication Monitor."

Network Monitor

The Network Monitor utility, another holdover from the NT era, is best described as a built-in packet sniffer. The Network Monitor included with NT 4 was a scaled-down version of the Network Monitor utility included with the BackOffice SMS package. Network Monitor is also included with Windows 2000 Server, and the version included with Windows 2000 is similar to the NT Network Monitor.

Network Monitor can be used to measure packets coming and going from a network interface, and you can therefore use it to measure replication. Microsoft suggests that you do the following:

1. Start Network Monitor and set it up to capture.

2. Force replication using the Active Directory Sites and Services manual replication (Replicate Now) feature—described earlier in this chapter.

3. When replication is complete, stop the capture.

Next you can analyze the network data captured by Network Monitor.

One problem with this approach is that replication that occurs through the RPC transport uses a dynamic port number, so it isn't easy to tell what part of the captured data is actually replication traffic. Microsoft has noticed this shortcoming, and has suggested that if you really want to isolate all replication traffic captured by Network Monitor, the easiest way to do it is to set a static port number for replication using the following Registry key:

HKEY_LOCAL_MACHINE\CurrentControlSet\Services\ NTDS\Parameters\TCP/IP Port

Network Monitor can then filter the captured traffic by port number and isolate the replication traffic. Whether this method is as effortless as Microsoft suggests is a matter of some speculation. Before doing this, it is also worth considering whether the information you wish to obtain could alternatively be obtained through Replication Monitor or Performance Monitor coupled with a Network Monitor capture of general traffic.

If you are measuring replication that uses the SMTP transport, you can filter the captured data for the SMTP static port 25. This will, of course, also capture nonreplication SMTP traffic, but at least you can filter out much of the irrelevant traffic.

SUMMARY

This chapter examined how the directory is replicated to domain controllers throughout the network. The directory replication process is necessary because all domain controllers have a writable copy of the Active Directory, and it has no equivalent in the architecture of Windows 2000's NT predecessors.

This chapter looked at how updates occur and how to configure the replication infrastructure for intrasite and intersite replication. The chapter also examined how to manage and monitor replication using Windows 2000 utilities such as Active Directory Sites and Services, Replication Monitor, Performance Monitor, and Network Monitor. For more on defining Active Directory's site structure, see Chapter 3. For more on objects, attributes, and the Active Directory schema, see Chapter 10, "Active Directory Schema."

CHAPTER 5

Users and Groups

Beneath the surface, Active Directory's user and group structure may be similar to Windows NT's. The Active Directory architecture, however, creates some opportunities for enhanced user and group functionality. Active Directory also adds some new concepts and provides a more systematic integration of group structures in a multidomain environment. This chapter discusses Active Directory users and groups.

A QUICK LOOK AT WINDOWS NT AND WINDOWS 2000 SECURITY

When a user logs on to a Windows 2000 network, the user is assigned an *access token.* An access token is a binary bundle of data describing the user's access privileges and the groups to which the user belongs.

Each resource in Windows 2000 is associated with a *security descriptor.* The security descriptor includes an access control list (ACL) that describes which users or groups have permission to access the resource and the nature of that permission. Before a user can access a resource, Windows 2000 compares the user's access token to the resource's access control list to see if the user or any groups to which the user belongs have permission to access the resource.

When you assign permissions to a resource in Windows 2000/ Active Directory, you are configuring the access control list for the resource object.

You can assign permissions for a resource to either users or *security groups.* A security group is basically a container of users with an accompanying set of rights and access permissions. Any user in the group has all the permissions granted to the group (except in the case of the No Access permission, which overrides other permissions and locks the user out of the resource).

Although it is possible to directly assign a user permission to a resource, , Microsoft usually recommends that you assign permissions for a resource through group membership and grant access to the user by placing the user in a group that has the appropriate permissions. In other words, rather than giving user Bill permission to access to the Financial Records folder, give the members of the

Finance group access to the folder and then place Bill in the Finance group (see Figure 5-1).

There are, of course, different types of permissions and different types of groups. You'll learn more about user and group permissions later in this chapter.

UNDERSTANDING GROUPS

Active Directory provides two types of groups:

▼ **Security groups**   Used to assign privileges and permissions to users.

▲ **Distribution groups**   Used to distribute electronic mail to a group of users.

The distribution group is a new concept with Windows 2000. What was called a *group* in Windows NT is called a *security group* in Windows 2000. Security groups are an essential component of the network. The following section introduces Active Directory's distribution groups. The rest of the chapter focuses primarily on security groups.

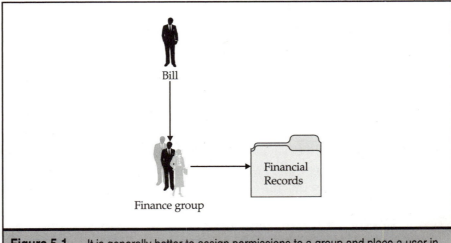

Figure 5-1.   It is generally better to assign permissions to a group and place a user in the group rather than to assign permissions directly to a user

Distribution Groups

A *distribution group* is a collection of users that has no relation at all to the security infrastructure. A distribution group does not assign any rights or permissions to its members. Distribution groups are used primarily to distribute information. Applications such as e-mail clients can use distribution groups to send a message to group members. In addition, Active Directory's Send Mail option, described later in this chapter in the description of the User Properties General tab, can send a message directly to a distribution group.

Distribution groups appear with security groups in the Active Directory Users And Computers utility (described later in this chapter). If your Active Directory network is operating in native mode, you can change a security group to a distribution group (and vice versa).

To change the group type, follow these steps:

1. Right-click a group in Active Directory Users And Computers.

2. Select Properties in the context menu.

3. In the Group Properties General tab, change the Group Type radio button to the new group type (Security or Distribution).

4. Click Apply or OK.

CAUTION: Your network must be in native mode before you can change the Group Type setting.

Security Groups

As described earlier in the chapter, every object has an access control list, which contains a list of users and groups, and permissions associated with those users and groups. It is therefore possible to assign permissions for a specific resource directly to a user, but in most cases, the recommended practice is to assign permissions through group membership and to provide access to the user by making sure the user is placed in the appropriate group(s). Granting permissions through groups has the following advantages:

▼ **Fewer permissions**   Since each group includes multiple users, permission needs to be granted only once for the group rather than separately for each user.

▲ **Fewer changes to ACLs**   If a user quits or is transferred, the administrator needs only to remove the user from the group. Access control lists (ACLs) for individual resources do not have to change.

Active Directory supports the following types of groups:

▼ **Computer local groups**   Groups administered through the local account database on an NT/2000 workstation or member server. Controls permission for resources on the local machine. Can contain computer local users or domain local users and groups.

■ **Domain local groups**   Can contain user accounts, global groups, and universal groups from any domain. Can be used to assign permissions only to objects in the domain in which the group exists.

■ **Global groups**   Can contain global groups and user accounts from the domain in which the group resides. Can be used to assign permissions for all domains.

▲ **Universal groups**   Can contain accounts, global groups, and universal groups from all domains. Can assign permissions to all domains.

These group types are almost always introduced together, and the implication is that they are somehow parallel or equally important. Each group type, though, has a different role to play.

The attribute that describes whether a group is domain local, global, or universal is called the group's *scope.* You define the scope attribute when the group is created, and, if your Active Directory network is operating in native mode, you can change the scope of an existing group.

To view and modify a group's scope, follow these steps:

1. From the Start menu, choose Programs | Administrative Tools | Active Directory Users And Computers.
   Or
   Choose Active Directory Users And Computers from the Microsoft Management Console.

2. Expand the tree for the domain that contains the group.

3. Open the folder for the container or organizational unit that contains the group. (If you don't know, try Users.)

4. Right-click the group's icon and choose Properties.

5. In the Group Properties dialog box, check the Group Scope section for the current scope of the group. If your network is operating in native mode, you can select a different scope. Then click OK.

Planning and Implementing Active Directory Groups

Active Directory comes with a collection of built-in global and domain local groups. You can also add your own groups, as you'll learn in a later section. Each built-in group comes with a predefined set of privileges, and each is designed for a different type of user. Network administrators typically create their own group accounts for well-defined groups of users who need similar access permissions and privileges. It is a good idea to give the group a descriptive name so that it is easily identified.

Microsoft's recommended strategy for assigning permissions to groups, called the *A G DL P strategy* (Figure 5-2), is as follows:

1. User accounts (A) are assigned to global groups (G).

2. Resource permissions (P) are assigned to domain local groups (DL).

3. To provide users with access to resources, global groups are placed within domain local groups.

Note that this preferred strategy does not mention the use of universal groups. *Universal groups* do not fit neatly into the chain of

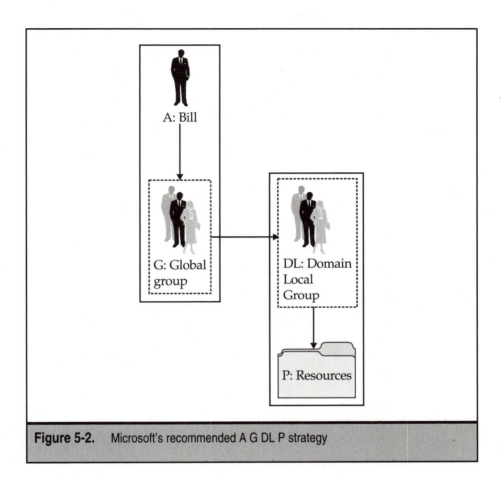

Figure 5-2.   Microsoft's recommended A G DL P strategy

security defined in Figure 5-2. Also, because membership lists for universal groups must reside on global catalog servers, access to resources through universal groups may be slower, and unnecessary universal groups add unnecessary data manipulation and replication traffic to global catalog servers. Universal groups are primarily for special situations, but if you feel your network configurations warrant the use of one or more universal groups, the best strategy is still to place users in global groups and then add the global group(s) to the universal group (see Figure 5-3).

CAUTION: Your network must be in native mode if you plan to use universal security groups.

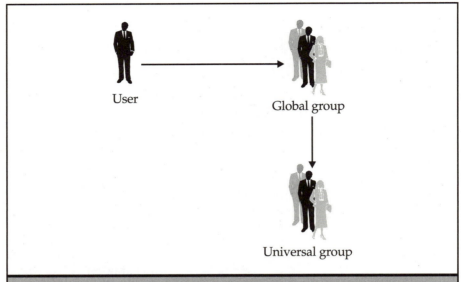

Figure 5-3.   For performance reasons, the best way to assign users to universal groups is to place the users in a global group and then place the global group in the universal group

PREDEFINED AND BUILT-IN GROUPS

Active Directory comes with several ready-made groups that fall into two types:

▼ **Built-in groups**   Domain Local groups located (by default) in the Active Directory Users And Computers Builtin folder for the domain.

▲ **Predefined groups**   Global groups located (by default) in the Active Directory Users And Computers Users folder for the domain.

You may wonder why Microsoft has chosen to create two different classifications for ready-made groups and to place the groups in two different locations. Actually, this choice is understandable in the context of Microsoft's A G DL P strategy. The implication is that the domain local built-in groups will receive permissions necessary for the various activities that must take place within the domain. The global predefined groups serve as containers for users (hence the location—the Users folder). The global predefined groups can then be placed within the built-in groups to assign users rights and permissions within the domain. Table 5-1 shows the default user rights for some of Active Directory's built-in groups.

Group	Description	Rights
Administrators	The powerful Administrators group is for users who perform critical system administration and configuration tasks	Access this computer from the network; back up files and file folders; change the system time; create a pagefile; debug programs; force a shutdown from a remote system; increase scheduling priority; load and unload device drivers; log on locally; manage auditing and security log; modify firmware environment variables; profile single process; profile system performance; restore files and file folders; shut down the system; take ownership of files or other objects
Users	Everyday users	Log on locally; shut down the system
Guests	Temporary users	None
Backup Operators	Users authorized to perform backups	Back up files and file folders; log on locally; restore files and file folders; shut down the system

Table 5-1. Default Rights for Some Important Built-In Groups

MANAGING USERS AND GROUPS

You can perform most User and Group management tasks through the Active Directory Users And Computers utility. The following sections discuss some common management tasks related to users and groups, including the following:

▼ Creating new users

■ Adding users to groups

■ Removing users from groups

■ Viewing and modifying user properties

■ Moving users

■ Deleting users

■ Creating groups

■ Adding groups to other groups

■ Removing groups from other groups

■ Viewing and modifying group properties

■ Moving groups

▲ Deleting groups

In the Active Directory environment, users and groups are managed through the Active Directory Users And Computers utility (see Figure 5-4). To access Active Directory Users And Computers, choose Start | Programs | Administrative Tools | Active Directory Users And Computers.

NOTE: The Active Directory Users And Computers option will not be available unless you have installed Active Directory (on a domain controller) or installed Active Directory management tools (on a workstation or member server).

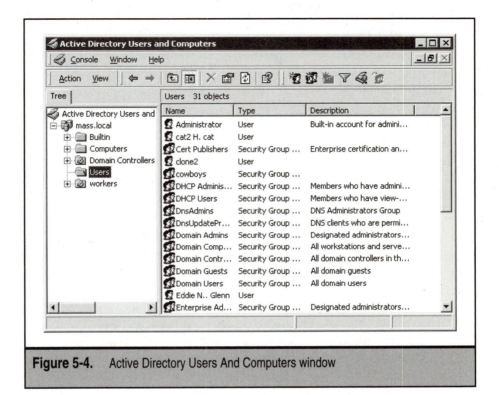

Figure 5-4.   Active Directory Users And Computers window

Creating New Users

Creating new users is a routine administration task. The Active Directory Users And Computers utility makes it easy to create new user accounts. By default, new users are members of the Domain Users group for the domain in which they were created.

To create a new user account, follow these steps:

1. From the Start menu, choose Programs | Administrative Tools | Active Directory Users And Computers.
   Or
   In Microsoft Management Console, select Active Directory Users And Computers.

2. Expand the tree for the domain to which you wish to add the user.

3. Right-click the organizational unit that will own the account. In the context menu, choose New | User.

4. In the New Object-User dialog box, enter the user's First Name, Initials, Last Name, Full Name, and User Logon Name (see Figure 5-5).

The Full Name value must be unique within the organizational unit. The drop-down box after the User Logon Name value (refer to Figure 5-5) specifies the UPN suffix the account will use. The UPN suffix is an alternative suffix that will accompany the logon name at logon. In other words, if user bob belonged to a domain called long.longer.muchlonger.domain.name.com, an administrator could create a UPN suffix called long.com so that rather than typing bob@long.longer.muchlonger. domain.name.com, bob could type bob@long.com. See the later section "Creating or Deleting a User Principal Name (UPN) Suffix" for more information.

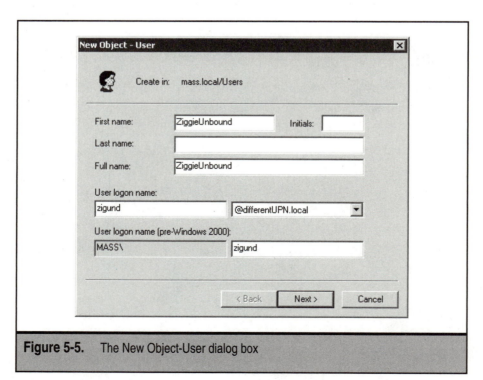

Figure 5-5.   The New Object-User dialog box

5. Note that the New Object-User dialog box lets you enter an alternative logon name for pre–Windows 2000 logon. The pre-2000 logon name must be unique for the domain. Click Next.

6. In the next New Object-User dialog box, enter a password for the user in the Password field and enter it again in the Confirm Password field. Then click Next. You can also select any of the following options:

   ■ User Must Change Password At Next Logon

   ■ User Cannot Change Password

   ■ Password Never Expires

   ■ Account Is Disabled

7. In the final dialog box, review the Full Name and User Logon Name for the account. If you wish to make any changes, click Back. Otherwise, click Finish.

Active Directory creates the new user account. The account will first be created on the domain controller where you entered the information. Or, if you entered the information from a Windows 2000 workstation or member server, the account will be created on the originating domain controller. From there, the new account will replicate through the network via directory updates.

The Active Directory User object contains many different attributes, and the values that you enter when you create an account are only a small subset of the possible settings. After you create the account, you may wish to get in the habit of immediately opening the Properties dialog box for the account and entering additional account settings. These additional settings are initially left blank or set to a default value. See "Viewing and Modifying User Properties," later in this chapter.

To create a new account that is similar to an existing account without having to configure these many additional settings, use the Active Directory Users And Computers Copy feature:

1. From the Start menu, choose Programs | Administrative Tools | Active Directory Users And Computers.
   Or

Select Active Directory Users And Computers in the Microsoft Management Console.

2. Expand the tree for the domain of the user account you wish to copy.

3. Select the container or organizational unit that contains the user account you wish to copy. (This will likely be Users.)

4. Right-click the user account you wish to copy, and then click Copy.

5. A dialog box similar to the one shown in Figure 5-5 appears. Refer to steps 4–6 of the preceding procedure for creating a new user account.

When you finish the setup dialogs, Windows 2000 will create the account and copy some of the properties from the account you selected in step 4 to the new account. Note that this account feature copies only *some* of the account properties. Other properties must be set directly in the new account. Settings that are copied to the new account include these:

▼ Address information

■ Account information such as logon hours and logon servers

■ User profile and logon script paths

■ Organization information (except not the user's title)

▲ Group memberships

NOTE: See the section entitled "Viewing and Modifying User Properties" for more on user account settings.

Adding or Removing Users from Groups

You can add or remove a user from a group through either the user's Properties dialog box or the group's Properties dialog box. As discussed earlier in this chapter, Microsoft recommends adding users to global groups and then placing the global groups in either domain local groups or universal groups if necessary. Although

Microsoft does not state so, this recommendation is most relevant to multidomain networks.

To add a user to a group through the group's Properties dialog box, follow these steps:

1. From the Start menu, choose Programs | Administrative Tools | Active Directory Users And Computers.
   Or
   Select Active Directory Users And Computers in the Microsoft Management Console.

2. Expand the tree for the domain that contains the group to which you wish to add or remove a user.

3. Click the organizational unit that contains the group to which you wish to add or remove a user.

4. Right-click the group to which you wish to add or remove a user and then click Properties.

5. In the Group Properties dialog box, click the Members tab.

6. To remove a user, select the user in the members list and click Remove. Click OK.

7. To add a user, click Add in the Members tab. The Select Users, Contacts, Or Computers dialog box appears (see Figure 5-6). In the dialog box, select the user account you wish to add in the upper panel and click Add. The user account appears in the lower panel. To add additional users, select additional accounts and click Add. When you are finished, click OK.

8. The users you added in step 7 will appear in the Members tab. Click Apply to add the users immediately, or click OK to add the users and close the Group Properties dialog box.

Here's how you can add or remove a user to/from a group through the user's Properties dialog box:

1. From the Start menu, choose Programs | Administrative Tools | Active Directory Users And Computers.
   Or

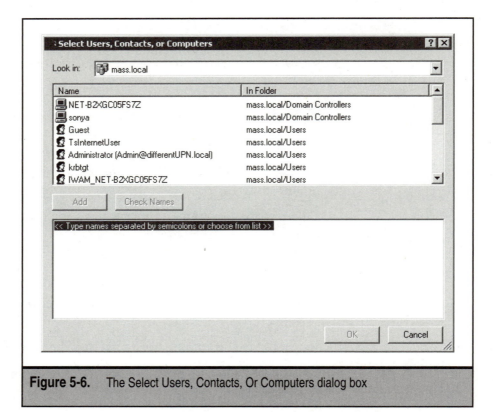

Figure 5-6. The Select Users, Contacts, Or Computers dialog box

Select Active Directory Users And Computers in the Microsoft Management Console.

2. Expand the tree for the domain that contains the user you wish to add or remove from a group.

3. Click the container or organizational unit that contains the user you wish to add or remove from a group.

4. Right-click the user you wish to add or remove from the group and click Properties.

5. In the user's Properties dialog box, select the Member Of tab. (You may need to use the scroll arrows to the right of the tab headers to scroll to the Member Of tab.)

6. To remove the user from a group, select the group in the Member Of list and click Remove. Click OK.

7. To add a user, click Add in the Member Of tab. The Select Groups dialog box appears (similar to Figure 5-6). In the Select Groups dialog box, select the group to which you wish to add the user in the upper panel and click Add. The group appears in the lower panel. To add the user to additional groups, select each group and click Add. When you are finished, click OK.

8. The groups to which the user belongs appear in the Member Of tab. Click Apply to add the user to the group or click OK to add the user to the group and close the Group Properties dialog box.

Active Directory also provides a shortcut for adding a user to a single group:

1. From the Start menu, choose Programs | Administrative Tools | Active Directory Users And Computers.
   Or
   Select Active Directory Users And Computers in Microsoft Management Console.

2. Expand the tree for the domain that contains the user you wish to add to a group.

3. Click the organizational unit that contains the user you wish to add to a group.

4. Right-click the user you wish to add to a group and click Add Members To A Group.

5. In the Select Group dialog box, select the group in which you would like the user to belong. Click OK.

Viewing and Modifying User Properties

The user Properties dialog box provides a large assortment of configuration settings. Some of those settings relate directly to the management of the account, and other settings have nothing to do with the account itself but are, instead, a reflection of Active Directory's role as a big database (phone numbers, fax numbers, company name). Many of these user settings are written to the global catalog servers so that they will be available for fast, network-wide searches. Other settings reside only in the full directory, but even if an attribute is not part of the global catalog, you can still search the directory for the attribute.

NOTE: Chapter 10 describes how you can add an attribute to the global catalog if it is not there already.

It is not necessary to set all the values in the user Properties dialog box. In fact, when the account is first created, most of the user account settings are simply left blank. (Otherwise, it would take 20 minutes to set up a single user.)

To access the user Properties dialog box, follow these steps:

1. From the Start menu, choose Programs | Administrative Tools | Active Directory Users And Computers.
   Or
   Select Active Directory Users And Computers in Microsoft Management Console).

2. Expand the tree for the domain that contains the user account.

3. Click the organizational unit that contains the user account.

4. Right-click the User Account icon and click Properties.

The user Properties dialog box is shown in Figure 5-7. You may see a scroll bar to the right of the tab heads that lets you scroll through the dialog box's many tabs:

▼ **General**   General account information, such as the account name and description.

■ **Address**   User address information.

■ **Account**   Settings governing the user's access to the account, such as account expiration, logon hours, and password settings.

■ **Profile**   User profile, logon script, and home folder settings.

■ **Telephones**   Settings for various phone numbers (home phone, pager, mobile phone, fax, IP phone).

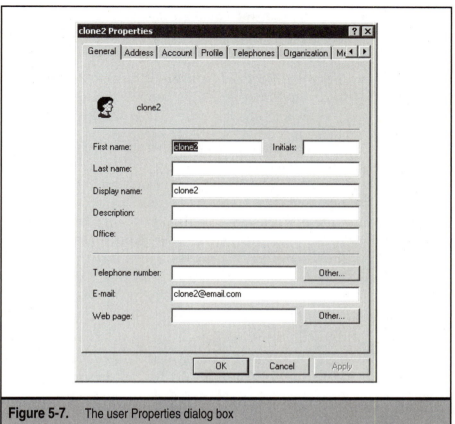

Figure 5-7.   The user Properties dialog box

- **Organization**   Informational settings describing the organization and the user's role within it.

- **Member Of**   The user account's group memberships. See the previous section entitled "Adding or Removing Users from Groups."

- **Dial-in**   Remote Access Service (RAS) settings for the user account.

- **Environment**   Terminal services startup settings.

- **Sessions**   Terminal Services timeout and reconnect settings.

- ■ **Remote Control**   Settings that govern the account's access to Windows 2000's remote control feature, which lets remote users control or observe a user's session.

- ▲ **Terminal Services Profile**   Settings that govern the account's access to Windows 2000's Terminal Server service. Settings include a terminal service profile and home directory.

Many of these tabs provide information that does not pertain directly to Active Directory and thus will not be covered here in detail. However, a few settings are worth noting.

In the General tab (refer to Figure 5-7), the E-mail and Web Page settings provide relevant data for a pair of Active Directory's niftier admin tricks. If you right-click a user account icon in Active Directory Users And Computers, the context menu includes options for Open Home Page (which opens the user Web page specified in the General tab) and Send Mail (which sends an e-mail message to the E-mail address specified in the General tab).

 NOTE: Like other user property settings, the user's e-mail and Web page settings are eligible for Active Directory searches. A search for a user's e-mail address is a common scenario.

The Account tab contains some important settings that play a role in defining the user's Active Directory configuration (see Figure 5-8). The User Logon Name, pre-Windows 2000 logon name, and UPN suffix settings (at the top of the screen) were entered automatically when the account was created, but you can change these from this tab. The UPN suffix is the box to the right of the User Logon Name. Click the arrow next to the UPN suffix box to display a list of alternative UPN suffix names. (See the section entitled "Creating or Deleting a User Principal Name (UPN) Suffix," later in this chapter).

The Logon Hours button lets you specify the hours during which the user will be permitted to access the account. Clicking the Logon Hours button invokes the Logon Hours dialog box (see Figure 5-9). The default setting is 24-hour, seven-day access to the account. To

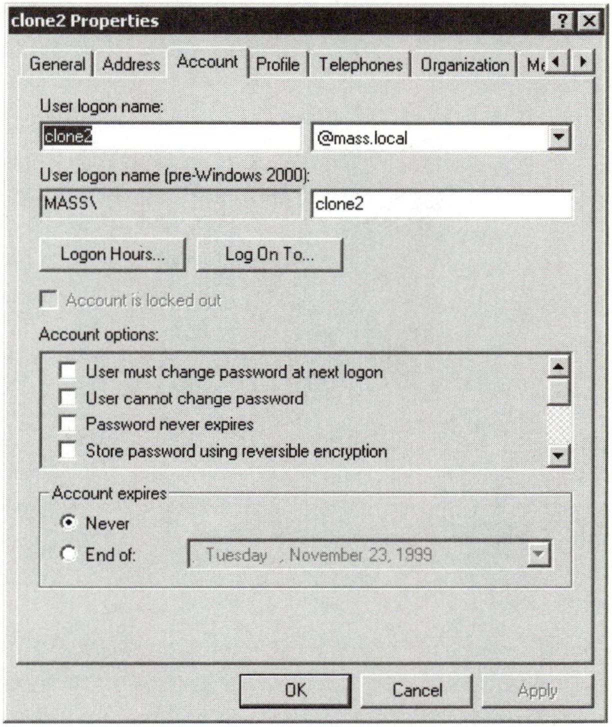

Figure 5-8.   The Account tab

limit the user's access to the account, click a point in the grid and drag the cursor to select a portion of the schedule. Click the Logon Denied button to deny access for the times you selected.

The Log On To button (see Figure 5-8) lets you specify which workstations the user can log on from. This option is a holdover from a similar option in Windows NT Server's User Manager For Domains utility, and Microsoft has not gone to much trouble to update it for the Windows 2000 environment. The Log On To option is NetBIOS-based and requires the use of the pre–Windows 2000 computer name (specified in the General tab—refer to Figure 5-7).

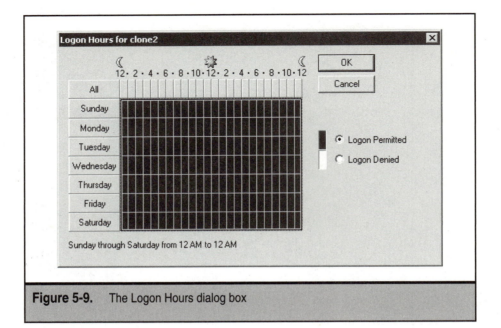

Figure 5-9. The Logon Hours dialog box

The Account Options checkboxes in the Account tab are password options and other security settings. Some of these password settings are reminiscent of the Windows NT Password Policy settings. Other account options are related directly to Active Directory security.

Moving Users

Windows 2000 makes it convenient to move a user to a different organizational unit or even to a different domain. If a user transfers to a different department or branch office, you can move the user's account to the new location.

NOTE: Why move a user account within the same domain? In the Active Directory environment, moving an object such as a user account to a different organizational unit can change the delegation of authority or group policy settings for the account. If an administrator has authority over an organizational unit, moving the user into that organizational unit will give the administrator authority over the account.

To move a user account, follow these steps:

1. From the Start menu, choose Programs | Administrative
   Tools | Active Directory Users And Computers.
   Or
   Select Active Directory Users And Computers in Microsoft
   Management Console.

2. Expand the tree for the domain that contains the user account
   you wish to move.

3. Click the organizational unit that contains the user account
   you wish to move.

4. Right-click the user account you wish to move and click Move.

5. In the Move dialog box (see Figure 5-10), select a new
   container for the object and click OK.

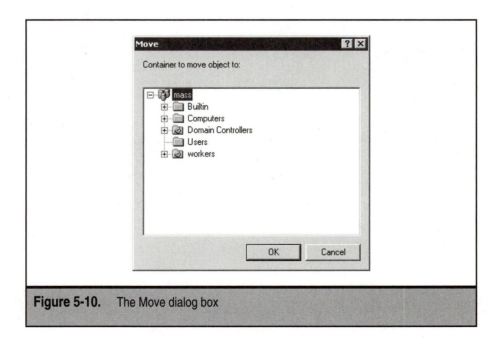

Figure 5-10. The Move dialog box

Deleting, Disabling, and Renaming User Accounts

If a user leaves your organization, you have three primary options for what to do with the user's account:

▼ **Delete**   Deleting an account removes the account from the Active Directory.

■ **Disable**   Disabling an account renders the account unusable until someone reenables it. If you think there is any chance the employee will be back, or if you haven't decided what to do with the account yet, disabling the account is a good option.

▲ **Rename**   When you delete an account, the account's ownerships, group memberships, and resource permissions all disappear. In some environments, the web of relationships surrounding a user's account is difficult to document or re-create. And in many cases, when a user quits, a new user with an identical job description takes over. Active Directory therefore provides the option of renaming an existing user account.

CAUTION: If a new user takes over an existing account, it is a good idea to immediately reset the account password and change other personal account settings such as a home phone number.

To delete, disable, or rename a user account, follow these steps:

1. From the Start menu, choose Programs | Administrative Tools | Active Directory Users And Computers.
   Or
   Select Active Directory Users And Computers in the Microsoft Management Console.

2. Expand the tree for the domain that contains the user account you wish to delete, disable, or rename.

3. Click the organizational unit that contains the user account you wish to delete, disable, or rename.

4. Right-click the user account. In the context menu, do one or more of the following:

- Select Delete to delete the account. Windows 2000 will ask if you're sure you want to go through with it. Click Yes if you're sure.

- Select Disable Account to disable the account. The icon for the disabled account will appear with a red X. To reenable the account, right-click the account and click Enable Account.

- Select Rename to rename the account. The account name will suddenly appear as part of a text box. Type the new name or place the cursor inside the text box to edit the existing name. Press ENTER. If you are renaming the account because a different person will be using it, right-click the account and click Reset Password. Then go to the account Properties dialog box and change any personal settings (such as a home phone number).

Creating or Deleting a User Principal Name (UPN) Suffix

As Chapter 2 describes, the user principal name (UPN) is a name that identifies the user if the logon requires pass-through authentication to another domain.

The default form of the UPN is

```
logon_name@domain_name
```

where `logon_name` is the user logon name specified when the account was created and given in the Account tab of the user's Properties dialog box (refer to Figure 5-8). The `domain_name` portion is the name of the domain on which the account is stored (e.g., freebird.com, automation.creation.org, or borderline.local).

This formulation of the UPN is only a default, though. You can specify a different suffix for the UPN and Active Directory will still be able to find the account. (The suffix is the portion of the name that follows the @ sign.)

If the account has a long or difficult-to-remember domain name (such as *this.long.domain.qwertyuiop.com*), you can specify another UPN suffix (such as *qwert*), so that instead of having to type mattie@this.long.domain.qwertyuiop.com the user can type mattie@qwert.

In addition to providing convenience, an alternative UPN can also provide a measure of additional security, because it allows you to give the user a logon name that doesn't reveal anything about the domain structure.

It is interesting to note that this alternative UPN suffix is independent of the domain. It is *not* another way of saying the domain name and, as you'll learn in the following procedure, is entered into the Active Directory without any reference to any particular domain. Instead, the alternative UPN suffix is simply an attribute assigned to the user object.

To specify an alternative UPN suffix, follow these steps:

1. From the Start menu, choose Programs | Administrative Tools | Active Directory Domains And Trusts.
   Or
   Select Active Directory Domains And Trusts in Microsoft Management Console.

2. In the left pane of the Active Directory Domains And Trusts main window, right-click the icon labeled Active Directory Domains And Trusts and click Properties.

3. The UPN Suffixes tab appears (see Figure 5-11). Enter an alternative suffix and click Add. The new suffix will appear in the list. You can type in additional suffixes and click Add to add each suffix to the list. When you are finished, click OK.

NOTE: You can also remove a suffix from the Alternative UPN Suffixes list using the UPN Suffixes tab. To do so, select a suffix and then click Remove.

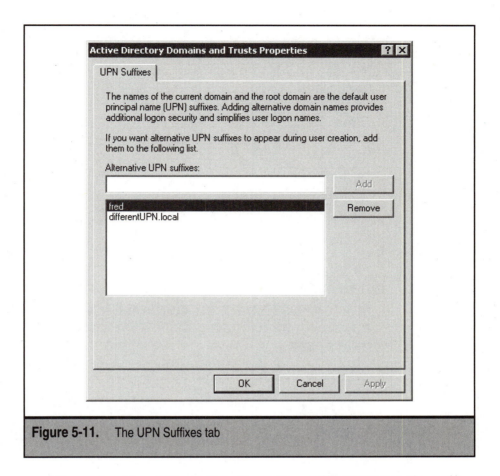

Figure 5-11.   The UPN Suffixes tab

After you add a suffix to the alternative suffix UPN list, the suffix will become a logon name suffix option when you create a new user or view user properties. Click the arrow by the box to the right of the User Logon Name box in the New Object-User dialog box (refer to Figure 5-5). The alternative UPN will appear in the drop-down list.

Creating Groups

The Active Directory built-in groups are designed to cover a range of common network roles. In most cases, however, you will occasionally need to create your own groups—to collect users with a common description into a single administrative unit, or to assign permissions for a collection of common resources, or both. To create a new group, follow these steps:

1. From the Start menu, choose Programs | Administrative Tools | Active Directory Users And Computers.
   Or
   Select Active Directory Users And Computers in Microsoft Management Console.

2. Expand the tree for the domain that will contain the new group.

3. Right-click the organizational unit that will contain the new group and choose New | Group.

4. In the New Object-Group dialog box (see Figure 5-12), enter a group name. The new group name will become the default pre–Windows 2000 group name. Enter a different pre-2000 group name if you wish.

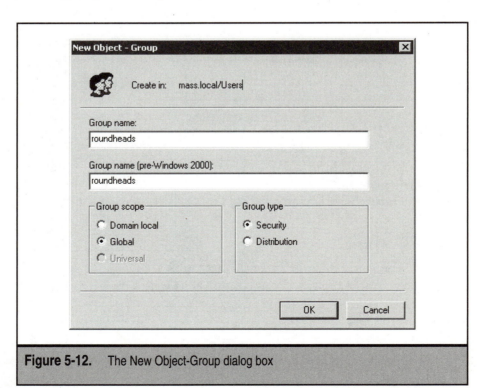

Figure 5-12.   The New Object-Group dialog box

5. Select a group scope (Domain Local, Global, or Universal) and a group type (Security or Distribution). Click OK.

NOTE: Although global and universal groups have cross-domain applications, they are still created within a domain. Global and universal groups still *belong* to a domain, even though they can be used in other domains.

Adding or Removing Groups from Other Groups

In mixed mode or native mode, you can add global groups to a domain local group. In native mode, you can add domain groups to other domain groups (this is called *nesting*). Universal groups cannot even exist unless you are operating in native mode. In native mode, you can add universal groups to domain local groups. In native mode, you can also add global groups or universal groups to other universal groups. These relationships are depicted in Table 5-2.

To add or remove a group from another group, follow these steps:

1. From the Start menu, choose Programs | Administrative Tools | Active Directory Users And Computers.
    Or
    Select Active Directory Users And Computers in Microsoft Management Console.

	Groups of this Scope can contain		
Mode	**Domain Local**	**Global**	**Universal**
Mixed mode	User accounts; global groups	User accounts	N/A
Native mode	User accounts; global groups; universal groups	User accounts; global groups	User accounts; global groups; universal groups

Table 5-2.   Allowable Contents for Active Directory Groups by Scope

2. Expand the tree for the domain that contains the group you wish to add or remove from a group.

3. Click the organizational unit that contains the group you wish to add or remove from a group.

4. Right-click the group you wish to add or remove from a group and click Properties.

5. In the group Properties dialog box, select the Member Of tab. (You may need to use the scroll arrows to the right of the tab headers to scroll to the Member Of tab.)

6. To remove the group, select the group in the Member Of list and click Remove. Click OK.

7. To add the group to another group, click Add in the Member Of tab. The Select Groups dialog box appears (similar to Figure 5-6). In the Select Groups dialog box, select the group to which you wish to add the group and click Add. The name of the group you're adding to appears in the lower panel. Click OK.

8. The groups to which the current group belongs appear in the Member Of tab. Click Apply to add the group to the new group or click OK to add the group and close the group Properties dialog box.

Viewing and Modifying Group Properties

The group Properties dialog box lets you view and modify the group scope, the group type (security or distribution), the list of members for the group, the list of groups of which this group is a member, and the group's managing authority.

To access the group Properties dialog box, follow these steps:

1. From the Start menu, choose Programs | Administrative Tools | Active Directory Users And Computers.
Or
Select Active Directory Users And Computers in Microsoft Management Console).

2. Expand the tree for the domain that contains the group.

3. Click the organizational unit that contains the group.
   (If you don't know, try the Users container.)

4. Right-click the group's icon. In the context menu, click
   Properties.

Moving Groups

To move a group to a different container, follow these steps:

1. From the Start menu, choose Programs | Administrative
   Tools | Active Directory Users And Computers.
   Or
   Select Active Directory Users And Computers in Microsoft
   Management Console.

2. Expand the tree for the domain that contains the group you
   wish to move.

3. Click the organizational unit that contains the group you wish
   to move. (If you don't know, try the Users container.)

4. Right-click the group's icon. In the context menu, click Move.

5. The Move dialog box asks you to choose a new container for
   the group. Select a new container and click OK.

Deleting Groups

Deleting a group removes the group from the Active Directory. If
you delete a group, users and groups who are members of the group
remain in the Active Directory and are not deleted. However, if a
user received access to any network resource through the account
that was deleted, the user will no longer have access to the resource.

To delete a group, follow these steps:

1. From the Start menu, choose Programs | Administrative
   Tools | Active Directory Users And Computers.
   Or

Select Active Directory Users And Computers in Microsoft
Management Console.

2. Expand the tree for the domain that contains the group you
   wish to delete.

3. Click the organizational unit that contains the group you wish
   to delete. (If you don't know, try the Users container.)

4. Right-click the group's icon. In the context menu, select
   Delete. Windows 2000 will ask whether you are sure you wish
   to delete the account. Click Yes.

ASSIGNING PERMISSIONS

As mentioned earlier in the chapter, every Windows 2000 object
has a security descriptor that defines which users or groups have
permissions to access the object. You can set permissions for many
types of directory objects, including users, groups, OUs, and domains,
as well as for physical resources such as printers, network shares,
and computers. The NTFS file system lets you set permissions for
directories and files. The Properties dialog box for most types of
objects includes a Security tab where you can set permissions for
the object.

NOTE: Right-click an object in Active Directory Users And Computers and
click Properties. In the Properties dialog box, look for the Security tab. If you
don't see the Security tab, open the View menu in the Active Directory Users
And Computers main window and choose Advanced Features. Then try again.

The Security tab in the object's Properties dialog box (see
Figure 5-13) defines which types of permissions for the object are
assigned to which users or groups. The permissions in the list may
depend on the type of object.

Following are some common permissions:

▼ **Full control**   Full control over the object, including the
   power to read, write, take ownership, execute, and change
   permissions.

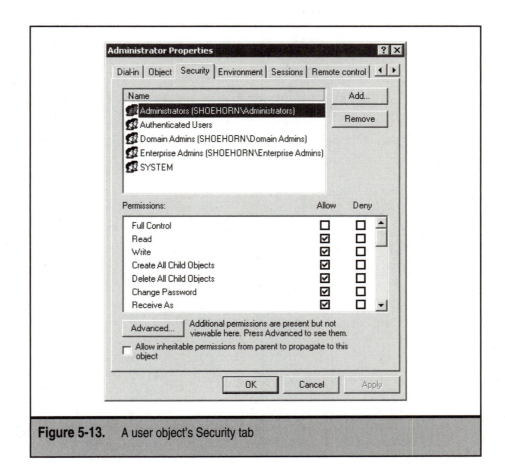

Figure 5-13.   A user object's Security tab

- **Read**   View the object and object attributes such as permissions and ownership.

- **Read & Execute**   View the object and object attributes and also execute the object if it is an executable file.

- **Write**   Save changes to the object.

- **Read Phone and Mail Options**   Read phone and mail information pertaining to the object (applies to users and group objects).

- **Write Phone and Mail Options**   Write phone and mail information pertaining to the object (applies to user and group objects).

■ **Create All Child Objects**   Create objects within the current object (applies to OUs, domains, and similar container objects).

■ **Delete All Child Objects**   Delete objects within the current objects (applies to OUs, domains, and similar container objects).

▲ **Manage Replication Topology**   Manage the replication topology (applies to domains).

In the Active Directory environment, you can Allow or Deny a permission attribute or you can leave that permission attribute unconfigured. Permissions are *cumulative*, which means that a user's effective permissions for a resource are the total of all user and group permissions for the resource from all sources (user permissions and group permissions for all groups to which the user belongs). However, a Deny permission takes precedence over any Allow permissions. For instance, suppose user Bill belongs to the Marketing group and the Fishtasters group. Bill's user account allows Read access to the *freshcatch* folder. The Fishtasters group also allows Read access to the *freshcatch* folder. The Marketing group, however, explicitly denies Read access to the *freshcatch* folder. Bill will not be able to access *freshcatch*.

To configure access permissions for an object, follow these steps:

1. Right-click an object in a management utility such as Active Directory Users And Computers, Active Directory Sites And Services, or Windows Explorer. If you are using Active Directory Users and Computers, make sure Advanced Features has a checkmark beside it in the View menu. (If not, select Advanced Features.) Choose Properties from the object's context menu. Note that you can't set permissions for files and folders on FAT partitions.

2. In the object Properties dialog box, open the Security tab. In the Security tab (refer to Figure 5-13), select the user or group for which you wish to view access permissions. Permissions assigned to that user or group appear in the Permissions list in the lower portion of the tab. To configure permissions for a user or group that doesn't appear in the list, click the Add

button. To remove a user or group from the list, click the
Remove button.

Note that the Permissions list in the Security tab shows only a
selection of standard permission attributes. For a complete list of
permissions, click Advanced and then click the View/Edit button in
the Access Control Settings Permissions tab.

NOTE: You can assign permissions to certain types of objects by
delegating control of the object. See the section "Delegation of Control,"
later in this chapter.

Ownership

A Windows 2000 resource also has an *owner*. The owner of an object
has the power to grant permissions for the object. By default, the user
who creates an object is the owner. Certain Active Directory objects
are owned by built-in groups, such as the Administrator's group.

Members of the Administrator's group have the right to *take
ownership* of an object; in other words, to become the object's owner.
This right is provided in case the original object owner leaves the
organization or in case the administrator needs to access the resource
in an emergency. It is important to note that the owner of an object
can't transfer that ownership to someone else. In other words, once
an administrator takes ownership of an object, the administrator
must keep ownership of the object until another administrator takes
it away. This feature is provided for security reasons. Windows NT
was designed for secure environments in which even administrators
might not necessarily be trusted. By taking ownership, an
administrator can gain access to the resource, but he or she cannot
cover the tracks by passing the ownership to someone else.

To take ownership of an object, follow these steps:

1. Right-click an object in a management utility such as Active
    Directory Users And Computers, Active Directory Sites And
    Services, or Windows Explorer. If you are using Active
    Directory Users And Computers, make sure Advanced

Features is checked in the View menu. (If not, select Advanced
Features.) Choose Properties in the object's context menu.
Note that you can't set permissions or take ownership of files
and folders on FAT partitions.

2. In the object Properties dialog box, select the Security tab
    (refer to Figure 5-13). Click the Advanced button.

3. In the Access Control Settings dialog box, click the Owner tab.
    The current owner of the resource is listed at the top of the
    dialog box. Other users or groups who are eligible to become
    owners are listed below. Select a new owner and choose Apply.

TIP: If you're locked out of a file or directory and can't change the
permissions to gain access, take ownership of the file and then change the
permissions.

Setting Inheritance

In the Windows 2000 environment, you can decide whether you want
permissions for a container object to be *inherited* by child objects
within that container. You can also override inheritance by canceling
the propagation of inherited permissions to the child object.

To configure a child object to receive or not receive inherited
permissions, follow these steps:

1. Right-click an object in a management utility, such as Active
    Directory Users And Computers, Active Directory Sites And
    Services, or Windows Explorer. (If you are using Active
    Directory Users And Computers, make sure Advanced Features
    is checked in the View menu.) Choose Properties. Note that you
    can't set permissions for files and folders on FAT partitions.

2. In the object Properties dialog box, select the Security tab
    (refer to Figure 5-13). To allow inheritable permissions, check
    the box labeled Allow Inheritable Permissions From Parent
    To Propagate To This Object. To disallow inheritance, clear
    the checkbox.

If you clear the checkbox, you are asked whether you want to copy any currently inherited permissions to the object (so that the effective permissions will remain unchanged) or to simply remove all inherited permissions.

To configure a container object to propagate permissions to child objects, follow these steps:

1. Right-click an object in a management utility such as Active Directory Users And Computers, Active Directory Sites And Services, or Windows Explorer. If you are using Active Directory Users And Computers, make sure Advanced Features is selected in the View menu. Choose Properties. Note that you can't set permissions for files and folders on FAT partitions.

2. In the Properties dialog box, choose the Security tab (refer to Figure 5-13). In the Security tab, click the Advanced button. In the Access Control Settings dialog box, select the permission for which you would like to establish inheritance and click the View/Edit button.

3. In the Permission Entry dialog box (see to Figure 5-14) check the box labeled Apply These Permissions To Objects And/Or Containers Within This Object Only.

4. Also, note the text box at the top of the Permission Entry dialog box labeled Apply Onto. Click the down arrow next to the Apply Onto box for a list of options. The options may depend on the type of object. For a folder object, for instance, you can elect to apply the permissions to the folder only, the folder and subfolders, the folder, subfolders, and files, etc.

5. When you are finished, click OK in the Permission Entry dialog box and click OK in the Access Control Settings dialog box. Click OK or Apply in the object Properties dialog box.

TIP: If the permissions for an object aren't what you expect them to be, check to see if the object is receiving permissions through inheritance.

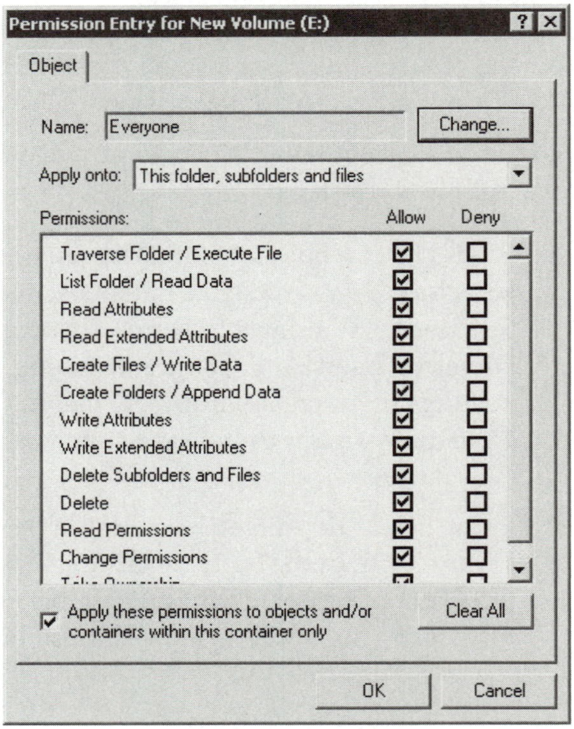

Figure 5-14.   The Permission Entry dialog box

Delegation of Control

Active Directory lets an administrator delegate control of a container object to a user or group. This feature is typically used to place a user in charge of a container (such as an organizational unit) and objects within it. For instance, the container may represent a small subnet (containing computers, users, printers, etc.) within a larger network. An administrator can delegate control over the objects in the subnet container to a user who provides tech support for the subnet without giving that user administrative control over other objects elsewhere in the network.

The Delegation of Control feature is one of the key components of the Active Directory environment, and Microsoft intends for the delegation of control to be a regular part of the security strategy.

To delegate control over a container object, follow these steps:

1. Right-click a container (such as a domain or OU) in Active Directory Users And Computers, or right-click a site in Active Directory Sites And Services.

2. In the context menu, click Delegate Control. (Note that you can't delegate control for the Builtin folder in Active Directory Users And Computers.)

3. The Delegation Of Control Wizard starts. In the first screen, click Next.

4. The Delegation Of Control Wizard asks you to specify the users or groups to whom you would like to delegate control of the object. Click the Add button to add users and groups.

5. In the Select Users, Computers, or Groups dialog box, select a user or group to which you would like to delegate control and click Add. Add additional users or groups as desired. When you are finished, click OK. The user(s) or group(s) you selected will appear in the Delegation Of Control Wizard's users or group list. Click Next.

6. Depending on the object you selected, you may be presented with a list of specific tasks. If you wish to grant these specific rights and permissions, check the appropriate boxes. Or, click Create A Custom Task To Delegate if you wish to delegate a different combination of rights and permissions.

7. In the next screen, choose to select the default (Delegate Control Of This Folder, Existing Objects In This Folder, And Creation Of New Objects In This Folder) or select the radio button labeled Only The Following Objects In The Folder and select the objects for which you wish to delegate control. Click Next.

8. In the Permissions screen (see Figure 5-15), select the permissions you wish to grant to the user(s) or group(s) you selected in Step 5.

9. The last screen presents a summary of information provided in previous screens. If the information is correct, click Finish.

SUMMARY

This chapter discussed Active Directory's user and group security and described how to configure users and groups. You also learned about delegation. It is wise to consider how you will organize users and groups on your network before you design your Active Directory infrastructure. The next chapter discusses Active Directory's powerful group policy features.

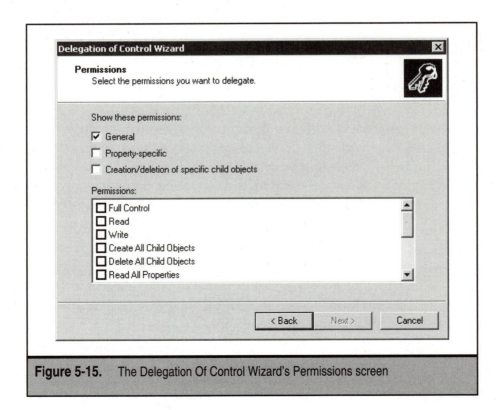

Figure 5-15.   The Delegation Of Control Wizard's Permissions screen

CHAPTER 6

Group Policy

Group policy is one of the more interesting developments associated with Active Directory. It is an extremely powerful feature that, unfortunately, may prove to be so bewilderingly complicated that it never achieves its true potential on the average network. Still, almost any network has *something* to gain from some form of group policy implementation. This chapter begins our discussion of this important feature. You'll continue to learn about group policy in future chapters.

WHAT IS GROUP POLICY?

Windows 2000 *group policy* is a means of imposing configuration settings on collections of users or computers. You can use group policy to control the following:

▼ Security (see Chapter 11, "Active Directory and Windows 2000 Security")

■ Registry settings (see Chapter 8, "Managing Active Directory")

■ Software installation (see Chapter 8)

■ Logon scripts (see Chapter 12, "Scripting Active Directory")

■ Logon policy (see Chapter 12)

■ Folder redirection (see Chapter 8)

■ Windows components such as Internet Explorer and Task Scheduler

▲ The desktop environment

To explain what group policy *is*, I'll begin by explaining what it *is not*:

▼ *Group policy is not a characteristic of a group.* It is unfortunate that Microsoft chose to use the term "group policy." A group policy can apply to a local computer or to users or computers within a site, domain, or organizational unit (OU)—whether or not those users are in the same group. (You can, however, filter group policy so that it affects the users in only one group.)

▲ *Group policy is not a renamed version of the Windows NT 4 system policy feature.* Some group policy settings bear a resemblance to Windows NT system policy settings, but the way group policy works and the way it is applied are different from the system policy of NT days.

You implement group policy by associating a *group policy object* (GPO) with a site, domain, organizational unit, or computer (see Figure 6-1). Like other Active Directory objects, a group policy object is a collection of attribute settings. The settings associated with a group policy object are settings that govern a user's or computer's configuration. These settings override any settings a user might try to make while logged on. A vast collection of settings is available for a GPO, and you'll learn about some of them later in this chapter and in later chapters on security, scripting, and administration.

The primary purpose of group policy is to reduce administrati on cost by letting network administrators manage large numbers of users and computers in an orderly fashion. Group policy can affect many aspects of Windows 2000 configuration, and consequently, you'll be hearing about it throughout this book. This chapter offers an introduction to group policy and a description of some of the tools you'll need to manage it on your network.

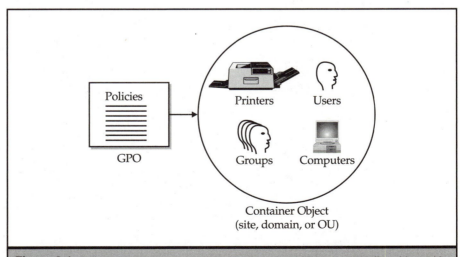

Figure 6-1.   To implement group policy, you must associate a group policy object with a site, domain, or organizational unit

A LOOK AT POLICY IN ACTIVE DIRECTORY

A *policy* is a predefined setting that applies to a user or computer regardless of the contents of the Registry. The Active Directory environment offers several avenues for imposing policy settings (see Figure 6-2). These policy-related features provide a similar interface and, in many cases, identical settings that interact differently depending on how you configure them.

You'll learn more about these policy types later in this chapter. Briefly, you can set group policies through the following:

▼ **Local policy** Every Windows 2000 computer has a local computer policy. Local policy is considered a group policy variant and is configured through the Group Policy Object Wizard. The local policy is processed before, and therefore overridden by, site, domain, and OU policies.

■ **Default policy** Windows 2000 comes with a default domain policy and a default domain controller policy. You can configure these default policies directly to change default settings.

■ **Group policy objects** A group policy object (GPO) is a collection of policy settings. You can create GPOs and then associate them with sites, domains, and OUs.

▲ **NT system policy** Windows NT and Windows 95/98 clients cannot process group policies, so the NT-style system policies still have a role in Active Directory networks. You can also set system policies for Windows 2000 clients.

The following sections discuss these policy types in the Active Directory environment.

Local Policy

A local group policy is stored on each Windows 2000 computer. The local policy is overridden by site, domain, and OU policies. You'll find the Windows 2000 local computer policy in the directory system_root\System32\GroupPolicy.

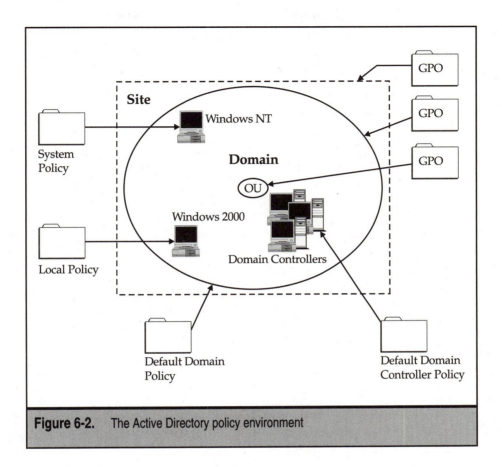

Figure 6-2.   The Active Directory policy environment

To view and manage the local computer policy, follow these steps:

1. From the Start menu, choose Run.

2. In the Run dialog box, enter **mmc** and click OK (mmc stands for Microsoft Management Console).

3. From the Microsoft Management Console main window's Console menu, choose Add/Remove Snap-In.

4. In the Add/Remove Snap-In dialog box, click the Add button.

5. In the Add Standalone Snap-In dialog box, choose Group Policy and then click Add.

6. A Select Group Policy Object Wizard starts. The Group Policy Object text box should contain the words *Local Computer*. Click Finish to add a snap-in for the local computer policy. See the later section entitled "Setting Up Group Policy" for more on editing group policy from a Microsoft Management Console snap-in.

In a network environment, it is usually inefficient to control group policy by defining a local policy independently for each computer. Local policy can be used effectively, however, for stand-alone systems, including laptop systems that are sometimes attached to the network and sometimes used off the network.

The Local Security Policy tool in the Administrative Tools folder opens the Security Settings tree of the local computer policy. To access local computer security policy from the Start menu, choose Programs | Administrative Tools | Local Security Policy.

See Chapter 11 for more on group policy security settings.

Default Policy

Active Directory automatically applies the following default policies:

▼ **Default domain policy**   Policy settings that apply by default to the domain

▲ **Default domain controller policy**   Policy settings that apply to domain controllers within the domain

You can access these default policies and edit them as you would any group policy object.

To access the default domain policy, follow these steps:

1. Right-click the name of the domain in Active Directory Users And Computers. Choose Properties.

2. In the domain Properties dialog box, choose the Group Policy tab.

3. In the Group Policy tab, choose Default Domain Policy and click the Edit button. (You'll learn more about editing group policy later in this chapter.)

To access the default domain controller policy, follow these steps:

1. Right-click the Domain Controllers container in Active Directory Users And Computers. Choose Properties.

2. In the Domain Controller Properties dialog box, choose the Group Policy tab.

3. In the Group Policy tab, choose Default Domain Controller Policy and click the Edit button. You'll learn more about editing group policy later in this chapter.

The Domain Security Policy tool in the `Administrative Tools` folder provides a shortcut to the Security Settings section of the Default Domain Policy. The Domain Controller Security Policy tool, also in the `Administrative Tools` folder, is a shortcut to the Security Settings section of the default domain controller policy.

NOTE: See Chapter 11 for more on group policy security settings.

Group Policy Objects

Group policy objects are policy filters that you create and apply selectively to sites, domains, and organizational units. Group policy objects provide a number of configuration options, including security and software installation, folder redirection, and component configuration.

Most of the power of group policy comes from how you customize and configure your group policy objects. You can apply more than one group policy object to a single site, domain, or OU. You can also link multiple containers to a single group policy object. See "Setting Up Group Policy," later in this chapter, for more on creating and editing group policy objects.

System Policy

Pre–Windows 2000 computers such as Windows NT 4 and Windows 95/98 computers cannot use Active Directory group policies. You must use the pre–Windows 2000 system policies feature to apply policy settings to pre–Windows 2000 computers on your network. Windows NT system policies can also apply to Windows 2000 client computers.

Use the System Policy Editor (`poledit.exe`) to configure system policies for pre–Windows 2000 computers. `Poledit.exe` is included with Windows 2000 Server and is located in the Windows 2000 `root` directory.

See a Windows NT text for a discussion on creating and implementing system policies.

The basic idea behind System Policies is that you use System Policy Editor to create a policy file (called `NTConfig.pol` for Windows NT computers or `config.pol` for Windows 95/98 computers) and place the policy file in the Netlogon share of the primary domain controller. In the Active Directory environment, place the `NTConfig.pol` and/or `Config.pol` policy files in the Netlogon share of an Active Directory domain controller. In Windows 2000, the Netlogon share is the folder `SYSVOL\sysvol\`*domain_name*`\scripts`.

The familiar template files you used to create policy files in the NT environment—`winnt.adm`, `windows.adm`, and `common.adm`—are also included with Windows 2000. You'll find these files in the `system_root\inf` directory (the `\inf` subdirectory of the Windows 2000 `root` directory).

SETTING UP GROUP POLICY

To set group policy, you must have read and write permission to the SysVol folder for an Active Directory domain controller as well as permission to modify the Active Directory container to which the policy applies.

To get a look at the types of settings you can apply to the Windows 2000 environment through group policy, view the group policy tree. The easiest way to view the tree is through the Group Policy tab of the site's, domain's, or OU's Properties dialog box.

To access the Group Policy tab for a domain, follow these steps:

1. Choose Programs | Administrative Tools | Active Directory Users And Computers

2. Right-click a domain name. In the context menu, choose
   Properties.

3. Select the domain Properties dialog box, and choose the
   Group Policy tab.

   The Group Policy tab shows a list of all group policy objects
   that have been applied to the domain (see Figure 6-3).

4. To associate an existing GPO with the container, click Add.
   To create a new GPO, click New.

   You'll see an icon with a text box containing the words New
   Group Policy Object in the Group Policy Object Links list.

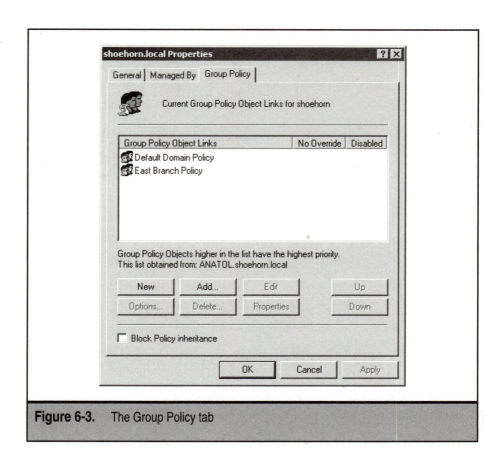

Figure 6-3.   The Group Policy tab

5. Enter a name for the new GPO by typing it in the text box. Then select the new GPO in the list and click Edit.

When you select a GPO and click the Edit button, the Group Policy window opens, showing the policy tree for the policy you selected. Browsing through this policy tree is a good way to get an idea of the uses for group policy.

The next section describes some of the basic policy folders and policies. When you first open the Group Policy window for a new GPO (see Figure 6-4), all of the policies are marked as Not Configured. You must *turn on* any policies you wish to activate for this new GPO. To configure a policy for the GPO, double-click a policy icon in the right pane. The policy Properties dialog box

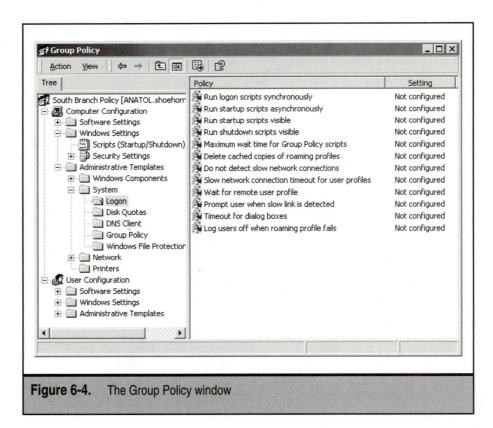

Figure 6-4. The Group Policy window

appears. In the Policy tab of the Properties dialog box (see Figure 6-5), you can set the following options:

▼ **Not Configured**   Active Directory ignores the policy setting

■ **Enabled**   The policy is enforced

▲ **Disabled**   The policy is not enforced, and it is actively turned off if it was previously enabled in another GPO

Some settings may require additional input, such as the name of a script or a file, or a choice from a drop-down menu related to the setting.

In the Explain tab, you'll see a brief description of the policy. To turn on a policy for this group policy object, select the Enabled option and then click Apply or OK. You can activate as many policies in the

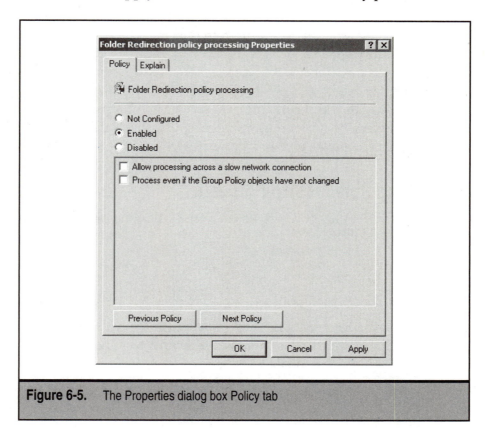

Figure 6-5.   The Properties dialog box Policy tab

GPO as you wish. Or, you can edit the GPO later and make changes to your original settings.

NOTE: You'll learn more about how to set specific group policies, such as security policies, Windows component policies, and logon script policies, in later chapters.

The instructions for associating a group policy object with an organizational unit or a site are similar, except that you access the site Properties dialog box from the Active Directory Sites And Services utility.

If you create a GPO through the Properties dialog box of a site, domain, or OU (as in the preceding procedure), the GPO is automatically associated with the object for which it was created. Once the policy object is created, you can associate it with other objects using the Add button in the Group Policy tab (refer to Figure 6-3).

As described in the later section, "How Group Policies Interact," multiple GPOs can be applied to the same container object, and a user within that container can receive GPOs from several sources. The result is the complex interplay of policies that gives this group policy feature much of its power.

How Group Policies Are Processed

Group policies are processed in the following order:

1. Local policies.

2. Site policies.

3. Domain policies.

4. Organizational unit policies. (In the case of nested OUs, the parent OU is processed first and the innermost child OU is processed last.)

Group policies are processed as follows when the system starts and a user logs on:

1. The computer starts.

2. The system comes online with the network and obtains a list of group policy objects that pertain to the computer (see the following section "How Group Policies Interact").

3. Computer policies are applied as follows: local policy, site policy, domain policy, OU policy, child OU policy.

4. Computer startup scripts (defined through the group policy objects) execute invisibly.

5. A user logs on.

6. The user profile is loaded. (See Windows 2000 online Help or a Windows 2000 reference for more on user profiles in Windows 2000.)

7. The system obtains a list of group policy objects that pertain to the user.

8. User policies are applied as follows: local policy, site policy, domain policy, OU policy, child OU policy.

9. User logon scripts run. Scripts defined through group policies run first. The last script to run is the logon script specified for the user in the Profile tab of the user Properties dialog box.

By default, Windows 2000 waits for computer policies to process before it displays the Logon dialog box and waits for user policies to process before giving the user access to the computer. Microsoft calls this *synchronous processing*. The group policy settings Apply Group Policy For Computers Synchronously During Startup and Apply Group Policy For Users Synchronously During Startup allow you to modify this default behavior so that the logon can proceed without waiting for the policies to finish. See the later section on "Setting Group Policies that Control Group Policy." Microsoft does not recommend asynchronous processing in most cases and warns that it can cause "unpredictable side effects."

Once the user is logged on, computer group policies are periodically checked and refreshed. By default, computer group policy is updated every 5 minutes for domain controllers. On other computers, computer group policy is updated every 90 minutes with a 0–30 minute random offset. User policy is updated every 90 minutes with a 0–30 minute random offset. You can change these refresh intervals using group policy settings in the Administrative `Templates\System\Group Policy` folder of the group policy computer configuration or user configuration subtree.

Where Group Policies Are Stored

When you create a site, domain, or OU-based GPO, a folder for the GPO is created in the `Sysvol` directory on Windows 2000 domain controllers. This folder is known as the `Group Policy Template (GPT)` folder—another unfortunate terminology collision, since the folder contains more than templates. The `GPT` folder bears the name of the GPO's globally unique identifier (GUID). You specify the location of the `Sysvol` directory when you install Active Directory on a Windows 2000 Server machine. The default location for a `GPT` folder is

```
system_root\Sysvol\Sysvol\domain_name\Policies\GUID_of_GPO
C:\winnt\sysvol\sysvol\shop.com\Policies\{31B2F340-016D-...}
```

The `GPT` folder contains items such as administrative-template-based policies, security settings, and script files. The `gpt.ini` file, located in the `GPT` directory, contains information about the policy. For Active Directory GPOs, the `gpt.ini` file contains the version number of the policy.

The `GPT` directory also contains the following subdirectories:

▼ **Adm** All `.adm` template files for this policy. See the later section, "Templates."

■ **Scripts** Scripts used with this policy.

■ **User** Files and folders related to user configuration policies. This includes a file called `Registry.pol` with user policy Registry-related settings.

▲ **Machine** Files and folders related to computer configuration policies. This includes a `Registry.pol` file with computer policy Registry-related settings.

Within the Active Directory, group policy object properties are stored in a group policy container (GPC). The GPC contains information on the version number (which must be synchronized with the GPT version number), the components that have settings within the GPO, and the state of the GPO (enabled or disabled).

How Group Policies Interact

It is possible to apply several GPOs to the same site, domain, or OU object. The Group Policy Object Links list in the object Properties dialog's Group Policy tab (refer to Figure 6-3) lists all GPOs associated with the object. The list appears in order of decreasing priority (the first GPO in the list has the highest priority). The Up and Down buttons let you change the order of the GPOs in the list.

NOTE: Microsoft claims that policies are processed "from the farthest from the computer to the closest." Note that this rule of thumb ignores the local policy (which is processed first but is actually closest to the computer). Also, note that this rule assumes the site is more distant in the hierarchy than the domain. This is sometimes true, but not always.

Any number of site, domain, or OU policies may affect a user's or computer's configuration. Windows 2000 also provides the following settings, which you can use to structure the effect of group policy interacting policies:

▼ **Options**   Group policy Link Options provide a No Override option, which keeps other policies from overriding policies set in the current GPO. The Disabled option prevents the GPO from being applied. To access the group policy link options, select a GPO in the Group Policy tab (refer to Figure 6-3) and click the Options button.

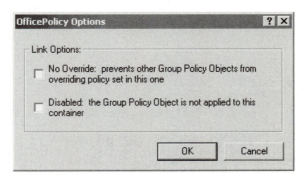

▲ **Block Policy Inheritance**   Prevents the inheritance of group policies from parent containers (see Figure 6-3). In other words, this option eliminates the influence of GPOs applied through parent containers. For instance, if Block Policy Inheritance is set in a child OU, policies set in the parent OU will not be inherited by the child.

You can set the No Override option for any domain-based GPO. If more than one GPO applied to the same object is marked for No Override, the policy that is highest in the list (in the Group Policy tab) takes precedence.

The Block Policy Inheritance setting does not apply to policies that have been marked No Override.

CREATING A GROUP POLICY SNAP-IN

Each of the trees you see in the Group Policy Editor (Figure 6-4) is an extension to the Group Policy snap-in. Some group policy extensions are shown in the following table. You can create a custom Management Console snap-in for a GPO and add or remove any extensions you don't wish to use.

Group policy extensions DLLs are located in the \system32 subdirectory of the Windows 2000 root directory.

Extension	File
Administrative templates	gptext.dll
Security settings	wsecedit.dll
Scripts	gptext.dll
Software installation	appmgr.dll
Folder redirection	fde.dll

To create a custom Group Policy snap-in:

1. From the Start menu, choose Run.

2. In the Run dialog box, enter **mmc**.

3. In the Microsoft Management Console window's Console menu, choose Add/Remove Snap-In.

4. In the Standalone tab of the Add/Remove Snap-In dialog box, click the Add button.

5. In the Add Standalone Snap-In dialog box, choose Group Policy and click the Add button.

   The Select Group Policy Object Wizard starts. By default, the Local Computer policy should appear in the Group Policy Object box.

6. To select the Local Computer policy, click Finish. To select a group policy object, click the Browse button.

7. If you clicked the Browse button in step 6, the Browse For A Group Policy Object dialog box appears (see Figure 6-6). Select the policy you wish to add to the console. Note the separate tabs for domain/OU policies, site policies, and computer policies. In the Computers tab (see Figure 6-7), you can choose whether to select the computer policy for the local computer or for another computer. When you have selected a policy, click OK.

8. Click Finish in the Select Group Policy Object Wizard.

9. In the Add Standalone Snap-In dialog box, click Close.

   The group policy object you chose in step 7 should appear in the Standalone tab of the Add/Remove Snap-In dialog box.

10. Select the Extensions tab in the Add/Remove Snap-in dialog box (see Figure 6-8).

11. In the Extensions tab, notice that the Add All Extensions check box is selected by default. Deselect the Add All Extensions check box. Browse through the list of available extensions and select or deselect the extensions you wish to include or exclude in the snap-in. When you are finished, click OK.

12. In the Management Console window, browse through the policy tree to make sure the settings you wish to include are present. To save the custom console, pull down the Console menu and choose Save As. Enter a name and a directory location for the custom group policy console.

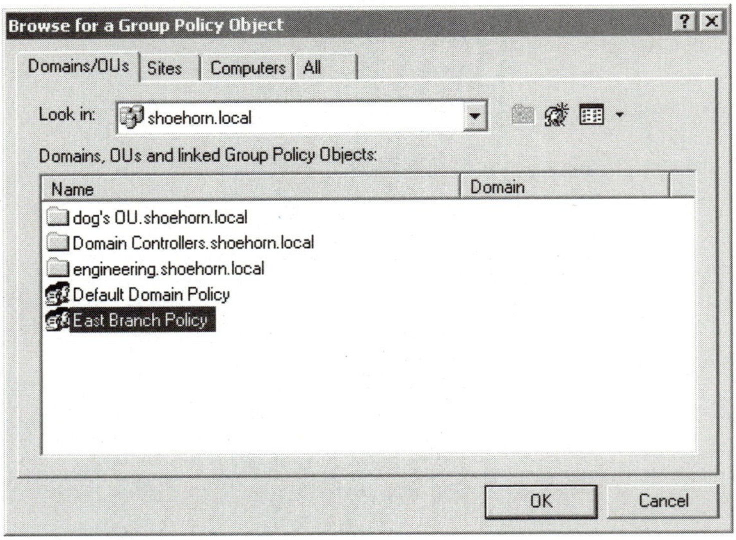

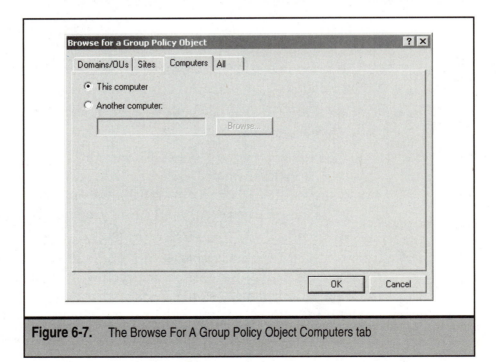

Figure 6-6. The Browse For A Group Policy Object dialog box

Figure 6-7. The Browse For A Group Policy Object Computers tab

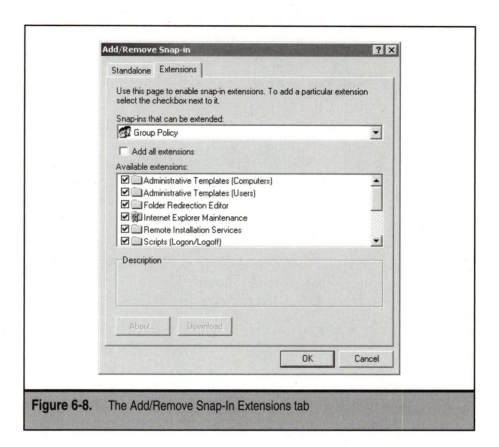

Figure 6-8. The Add/Remove Snap-In Extensions tab

UNDERSTANDING GROUP POLICY OPTIONS

Group policy settings affect either a *user* or a *computer*. The Group Policy window (refer to Figure 6-4) has a separate subtree for the computer configuration and the user configuration.

NOTE: Whether a GPO applies to any particular user or computer depends on whether the user or computer resides in a container with which the GPO is associated and on various other influences that may affect the application of group policy. See the earlier section entitled "How Group Policies Interact."

The user configuration and computer configuration subtrees are similar in structure. Each have the following subfolders:

▼ **Software Settings**   Software installation policy settings.

■ **Windows Settings**   Windows settings let you designate scripts (startup/shutdown and logon/logoff scripts) and security settings. See Chapter 12, for more about scripts in Active Directory. The security policies come from one or more *security template*s configured for the GPO. User configuration Windows settings also include folder redirection and other Windows-related options.

▲ **Administrative templates**   Various administrative settings used to shape the desktop environment. The Administrative templates typically provide Registry settings that will be saved to `Registry.pol` files in the `GPT` directory.

A vast array of browsable group policy configuration options are added to the Group Policy windows through either *security templates* or *administrative templates*. A template is a predefined set of policy attributes. When you load a template into a group policy object, the policies associated with that template become part of the policy tree visible in the Group Policy window. At any time, several policy templates may be included in a GPO.

Templates

The settings you see in the Group Policy Object Editor come from group policy templates. The Administrative templates included with Windows 2000 are shown in Table 6-1. By default, a newly created GPO includes the `system.adm`, `inetres.adm`, and `conf.adm` templates.

To add or remove an administrative template:

1. Right-click the user or computer configuration Administrative Templates folder in the Group icy window (refer to Figure 6-4) and choose Add/Remove Templates.

2. In the Add/Remove Templates dialog box, select a template and choose Remove to remove the template. To add a new template to the GPO, click the Add button. A list of available administrative templates in the `system_root\INF` folder will appear.

3. Choose one of the available templates or browse for another administrative template. Click Add.

4. In the Add/Remove Templates dialog, click Close.

Windows 2000's administrative templates are similar in character to the policy templates provided with Windows NT 4. In fact, as you can see in Table 6-1, legacy policy templates `winnt.adm`, `common.adm`, and `windows.adm` are even included with Windows 2000.

Template	Description
common.adm	Common NT 4 and Windows 95/98 policies
conf.adm	NetMeeting policies
inetcorp.adm	Internet Explorer policies
Inetres.adm	Internet Explorer settings
Inetset.adm	Internet Explorer settings
System.adm	Windows 2000 policies
Windows.adm	Windows 95/98 policies
winnt.adm	Windows NT 4 policies
wmp.adm	Windows Media Player settings

Table 6-1.   Administrative Templates Available Through Active Directory

The procedure for importing a security template is similar:

1. Right-click the user or computer `Windows Settings\ Security Settings` folder in the Group Policy window (refer to Figure 6-4) and choose Import Policy.

2. In the Import Policy From dialog box, choose the security template you wish to import. A list of available security templates in the `system_root\security\templates` folder will appear. Choose one of the available templates or browse for another security template. Click Open.

NOTE: You'll learn more about security policy in Chapter 11.

Links

As the section "Setting Up Group Policy" described, you can link an existing GPO to a container object (site, domain, or OU) by using the Add button in the object properties Group Policy tab (refer to Figure 6-3). A single GPO may thus be linked to multiple objects.

GPOs reside within a domain and are not replicated across domains. However, you can link to a GPO in a different domain. When you click the Add button in the Group Policy tab, the Add A Group Policy Object Link dialog box (Figure 6-9) lets you browse for a GPO in any available domain. Right-click the arrow beside the box labeled Look In to choose a domain. Browse for a GPO in the box below.

To view all the links associated with a GPO, follow these steps:

1. Open the Group Policy window for the GPO by selecting the GPO in the object properties Group Policy tab (refer to Figure 6-3) and clicking Edit.
    or
    Open the Microsoft Management Console Group Policy snap-in and select the GPO in the Startup Wizard (as described earlier in the section "Creating a Group Policy Snap-In").

2. In the Group Policy window, right-click the icon for the group policy object (the `root` node in the group policy tree) and choose Properties.

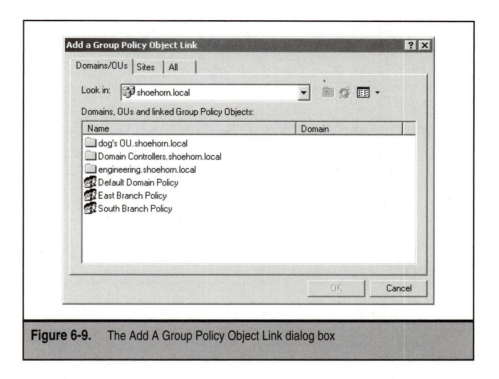

Figure 6-9.   The Add A Group Policy Object Link dialog box

3. In the Group Policy Object Properties dialog box, open the Links tab.

4. In the Links tab, select the domain in which you'd like to search for links to the GPO and click Find Now. All the links associated with the GPO are displayed.

Filtering Group Policy

A group policy object includes an Apply Group Policy permission, which you can use to selectively apply or remove the policy for a particular group.

To *turn off* a GPO and then activate it for a particular group, follow these steps:

1. From the Group Policy tab, right-click a GPO and choose Properties.

2. In the GPO Properties dialog box, open the Security tab (Figure 6-10).

3. By default, the Authenticated Users group has Read and Apply Group Policy permissions. To turn off the policy for all authenticated users, select the Authenticated Users group and choose Deny for the Read and Apply Group Policy permissions.

4. To apply the GPO to a particular group, click the Add button to add the group to the list at the top of the Security tab, and then select the group.
   Or
   Select the group in the list, and then apply the Read and Apply Group Policy permissions to the group you selected.

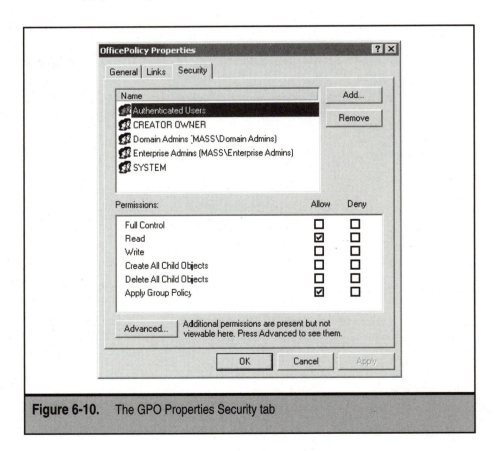

Figure 6-10.   The GPO Properties Security tab

The Apply Group Policy permission can be used to selectively apply group policy to the users in a particular group. For instance, suppose an administrator who manages an organizational unit containing managers and technicians wants to use one GPO for the managers and another GPO for the technicians. The administrator could take the following actions:

1. Create a Managers GPO and apply the Managers GPO to the organizational unit. In the Security tab of the Managers GPO Properties dialog box, remove the Read and Apply Group Policy permissions for the Authenticated Users group. Add the Read and Apply Group Policy permissions for the Managers group.

2. Create a Technicians GPO and apply the Technicians GPO to the organizational unit. In the Security tab of the Technicians GPO Properties dialog box, remove the Read and Apply Group Policy permissions for the Authenticated Users group. Add the Read and Apply Group Policy permissions for the Technicians group.

In some cases, additional steps may be necessary to ensure that the Manager and Technician policies take effect. If this doesn't work, make sure other policies aren't overriding or blocking inheritance.

Setting Group Policies that Control Group Policy

The user configuration or computer configuration `Administrative Templates\System\Group Policy` folder contains a number of other group-policy-related group policies (see Table 6-2).

Specifying a Domain Controller

Active Directory's multimaster architecture can create confusion when it comes to writing changes to group policies. To avoid data loss caused by different versions of a policy replicating through the network, the default behavior is for all GPO changes to be

Location	Policy	Description
`Computer Configuration\ Administrative Templates\ System\Group Policy`	Disable background refresh of group policy	Stops group policy from being refreshed during a user session.
	Apply group policy for computers asynchronously during startup	Asynchronous processing lets the system proceed with the logon prompt while the group policies are processed in the background.
	Apply group policy for users asynchronously during startup	Asynchronous processing lets the system proceed with the logon prompt while the group policies are processed in the background.
	Group policy refresh interval for computers	Lets you configure the refresh interval for computer policy.
	Group policy refresh interval for domain controllers	Lets you configure the refresh interval for domain controllers.
	User group policy loopback processing mode	Checks for specific, alternative user policies designed to be used with a specific computer. When a user logs on, the computer's local group policy object determines which policies to apply.
	Group policy slow link detection	Defines the transmission speed that constitutes a slow link.
	Registry policy processing	Defines whether Registry-based policy settings will be updated in the background.

Table 6-2.   Group Policies

Location	Policy	Description
	Internet Explorer maintenance policy processing	Update configuration for Internet Explorer maintenance policies.
	Software installation policy processing	Configuration settings for software installation policy (see Chapter 8).
	Folder redirection policy processing	Configuration settings for folder redirection.
	Scripts policy processing	Configuration settings for policy scripts (see Chapter 12).
	Security policy processing	Configuration settings for Security policy (see Chapter 11).
	IP security policy processing	Configuration settings for IP security policy (see Chapter 11).
	EFS recovery policy processing	Configuration setting for encryption policy.
	Disk quota policy processing	Configuration settings for disk quota policy.
`User Configuration\ Administrative Templates\System\ Group Policy`	Group policy refresh interval for users	Refresh interval for user configuration policy.
	Group policy slow link detection	Defines the transmission speed that constitutes a slow link for user configuration policy.
	Group policy domain controller selection	Specifies the domain controller used by the Group policy snap-in.
	Create new group policy object links disabled by default	Specifies that group policy object links are disabled by default.

Table 6-2.   Group Policies *(continued)*

Location	Policy	Description
	Enforce show policies only	Forces the group policy interface to display only "true policies" (policies using the `Software\ Policies` or `Software\ Microsoft\ Windows\ CurrentVersion\ Policies` Registry keys.
	Disable automatic update of .adm files	Prevents update of .adm files through the group policy interface. The .adm files must be updated manually.

Table 6-2.   Group Policies *(continued)*

written to the PDC emulator. It is possible, however, to change that default behavior or to restore the default behavior after it has been changed.

To specify a domain controller, follow these steps:

1. In the Group Policy Editor window (see Figure 6-4) choose View | DC Options. The Options For Domain Controller Selection dialog box appears.

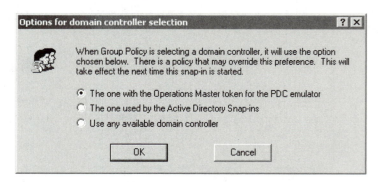

2. Select one of the following options:

   ■ **The One With The Operations Master Token For The PDC Emulator**   Writes GPO changes to the PDC emulator.

■ **The One Used By The Active Directory Snap-Ins**   Writes changes to whatever domain controller the snap-in is connected to. (For example, if you are using Active Directory Users and Computers, you can right-click the top-level icon labeled Active Directory User And Computers, choose Connect To Domain Controller, and select a domain controller to which you want to connect.)

■ **Use Any Available Domain Controller**   Writes changes to any available domain controller.

3. Click OK when you're finished.

CAUTION: Microsoft recommends against choosing the Use Any Available Domain Controller option. For most situations, Microsoft recommends writing group policy changes to the PDC Emulator (the default setting).

The Group Policy Domain Controller Selection setting in User Configuration/Administrative Templates/System/Group Policy (see the section, "Setting Group Policies that Control Group Policy") overrides the DC Options setting. The Group Policy Domain Controller Selection options are the same as the DC Options options (PDC, current snap-in, or any available). If you choose one of these options through the Group Policy Domain Controller Selection setting, the alternatives will be unavailable in the Options For Domain Controller Selection dialog box.

GROUP POLICY STRATEGIES

Group policy objects take time to process, so from a performance standpoint, fewer is better. There is, however, a conflicting interest in keeping GPOs clear and specific to a particular user environment so that they can be delegated more efficiently (see the example of the Managers and Technicians groups in "Filtering Group Policy" earlier in the chapter).

Microsoft recommends that you limit the use of override options such as the link options and the Block Inheritance check box.

Microsoft also recommends that you disable the parts of a GPO that are not being used. You can elect to disable either the computer configuration settings or the user configuration settings for a GPO. Disabling the subtree lets Windows 2000 ignore that subtree rather than checking each value for a configured setting.

To disable the computer configuration or user configuration subtree for a GPO, follow these steps:

1. Choose a GPO in the object properties Group Policy tab (refer to Figure 6-3).

2. Click the Properties button.

3. In the General tab of the Default Domain Policy Properties dialog box (Figure 6-11), select Disable Computer Configuration Settings or Disable User Configuration Settings. Then click OK.

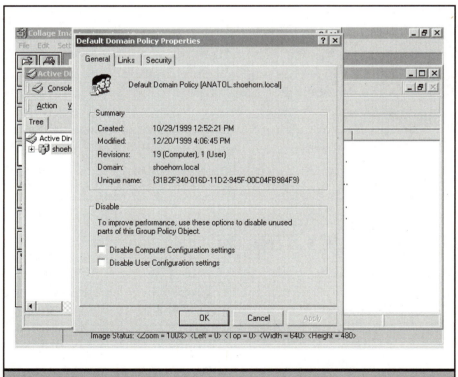

Figure 6-11.   The Default Domain Policy Properties General tab

Error Message: Failed to Open GPO

A common error message in the Active Directory environment is "Failed to Open Group Policy Object." Because the message mentions group policy and this chapter, obviously, covers group policy, you may have visited this chapter in hopes of discovering the source of the problem. In fact, Microsoft states that the most common reason for this message is a DNS problem. If you see this message, Microsoft recommends that you do the following:

▼ Check for stale DNS entries.

▲ Resolve local DNS server and ISP DNS server entries.

The problem sometimes occurs on computers that are configured for both a local DNS server and a second (remote) DNS server such as an ISP DNS server. If this is the case, try removing the second DNS server from the IP address information and adding it instead to the list of forwarders for the local DNS server.

SUMMARY

This chapter described Active Directory's powerful group policy feature. Group policy is designed to serve as an integral part of the Active Directory environment. You can apply group policy to sites, domains, OUs, and computers. This chapter described how to create and manage group policy objects.

Group policy settings allow you to manage security, software installation, scripts, and the desktop environments. You'll learn more about specific group policy options in later chapters:

▼ See Chapter 8 for more on group policy settings related to software installation and the desktop environment.

■ See Chapter 11 for more on group policy settings related to security.

▲ See Chapter 12 for more on group policy scripts.

It is worth your time to study group policy and to plan carefully how you'll implement it on your Active Directory network. Many of the benefits of Active Directory come from careful and well-considered application of this important feature.

CHAPTER 7

Setting Up
Active Directory

Discussions of deployment strategies are often fraught with excruciating details about assessing management goals and determining how to staff the test lab. Microsoft, in particular, is as interested in management as it is in operating systems, and nowhere is this more apparent than in its lengthy discussions of the deployment process. Most of it is good advice. You really do need to think seriously about how you will deploy Windows 2000 in your own environment.

This chapter describes the deployment process, highlights some important deployment considerations, and describes and investigates several procedures you'll need for setting up your Windows 2000 network.

NOTE: The Windows 2000 Support Tools kit includes a useful HTML Help file called the Deployment Planning Guide, with information on how to plan and deploy Windows 2000 and Active Directory. (See the later section titled "Installing the Windows 2000 Support Tools" for a discussion of how to install the Windows 2000 Support Tools.) The Deployment Planning Guide is the deployment section of the Windows 2000 Resource Kit's Books Online.

THE DEPLOYMENT PROCESS

Ultimately, your organization must design a deployment plan for its own unique needs, customs, and personnel. If your network is big enough to need Active Directory, it is big enough to require a careful and methodical deployment. Most deployments consist of variations of the following steps:

1. Determine whether you need Active Directory.

2. Plan and set up a test site. Determine whether Active Directory does what you need it to do and get some experience working with it.

3. Plan and set up a pilot installation on a small part of your production network. Find out how Active Directory works in a production environment.

4. Plan your Active Directory network.

5. Plan your Active Directory rollout.

6. Execute your rollout.

These steps build upon one another, and, presumably, feedback from one step helps to formulate later steps. For instance, input from pilot-site users and administrators should be systematically incorporated into the eventual rollout and network design. The brevity of this list conceals the formidable complexity of each of these tasks.

This chapter describes some specific Active Directory issues as they relate to the deployment process. The chapter does not attempt to re-create the many site-specific management and logistical issues you'll face as you migrate to Active Directory. It is also worth noting that there is much to Windows 2000 besides Active Directory, and your plans for deploying an Active Directory network may depend in part on non-Active Directory topics, such as Remote Access Server (RAS), Internet Information Server (IIS), and the various services of the BackOffice suite.

The following sections offer some thoughts on the phases of the rollout process.

Do You Really Need Active Directory?

The question of whether you need Active Directory may seem obvious at a glance. If you didn't need it, you wouldn't have bought the book. It is clear, though, that Active Directory is not for every network.

Active Directory is designed for

▼   Large networks

■   Networks with complex divisions of authority—different people responsible for different resources

■   Multisite networks

■   Networks that benefit from a central, integrated database of directory information

▲   Networks using software that requires Active Directory. (Eventually, software vendors—including Microsoft—may cease to support older Windows versions.)

Chapter 1, "The Active Directory Environment," describes some of the shortcomings of Windows NT networks and how those shortcomings were addressed through Active Directory. If Windows NT is coming up short on your network, and if Active Directory addresses some of your concerns about the NT environment, then your organization may make good use of Active Directory.

If you have a NetWare 4.*x* network, and you'd like to migrate to a Microsoft networking environment without giving up all the benefits of NDS, your network might benefit from Active Directory.

The reasons for migrating to Active Directory are many—you'll have to read this whole book to learn even one author's view of them all. But you don't *have to* upgrade if Active Directory does not provide some benefit to your network. Learn about Active Directory, study it, and then decide if it is what need. A very small network, for instance, with only one site, two domain controllers, and one network administrator, probably does not need Active Directory.

A few points worth remembering:

▼ **DNS integration**   Microsoft's goal of eliminating NetBIOS is in *the company's* interest in the long term, but it is not necessarily in *your* interest now. NetBIOS name resolution works fairly efficiently on NT networks with Microsoft clients. (And NetBIOS continues to work efficiently in Windows 2000.) Active Directory's DNS integration is an advantage for heterogeneous networks with non-Microsoft servers and clients or for networks that allow direct access to resources from the Internet. Windows NT 4.0 actually has its own form of DNS/NetBIOS integration, which isn't as elegant as Active Directory's but still provides access to NetBIOS resources through DNS. On the other hand, the dynamic DNS package provided with Windows 2000 offers features that weren't available through Windows NT's DNS.

■ **Directory database**   Much will be made of Active Directory's database search capabilities. Windows NT has no equivalent to the capability of querying the operating system for a user's e-mail address. However, before you use this feature in a memo as a justification for upgrading to Active Directory, keep in mind that Microsoft does not recommend using the Active

Directory as the master copy of records such as employee data records. You still need to keep a master record of personnel data somewhere. On the other hand, the Active Directory *is* the master copy of network-related data, such as which printers are currently available. In environments where users move around a lot, it is very useful to be able to query the database for locations of printers and other network devices.

▲ **NT support**   How long will Microsoft support NT? Upcoming versions of the BackOffice products (such as Microsoft Exchange) are designed for the Windows 2000 environment. Sooner or later, you may need to upgrade in order to stay current with new software. It is very possible, however, that this moment won't come as quickly as Microsoft would like. If the world doesn't rush to Windows 2000, Microsoft may need to slow down NT's planned obsolescence.

The observations of this section should warn but not alarm. There are many good reasons for migrating to Active Directory. But you need to go through the steps of seeing whether those reasons apply to your network.

Planning and Implementing a Test Site

The Windows 2000 Support Tools Deployment Planning Guide (described earlier in this chapter) includes a lengthy section on how to set up a lab for testing Windows 2000 and Active Directory. The discussion ranges from management theory, to risk-management theory, to plain common sense.

The basic point is that you should first set up Active Directory in a nonproduction environment and systematically test it. The goals of the testing process are as follows:

▼ To ensure that your Active Directory network will be compatible with all software and hardware that may need to run on it, including home-grown and third-party applications and legacy hardware systems

■ To give your IT staff some experience using Active Directory

■ To evaluate the many configuration options so that you'll arrive at a configuration that works best for your network

■ To identify in advance any potential problems and develop solutions and workarounds

▲ To gather information on Active Directory: comments, insights, and warnings that will be used in developing a final design for your network

The best way to accomplish these goals is for your lab network to include as many of the key features of your production network as possible.

If you have an existing network that you plan to upgrade to Active Directory, remember that you must actually test two things: your Active Directory network configuration and your deployment plan. Make sure that all the key steps in the deployment process have been thoroughly tested in conditions that are as close to the actual conditions as possible, including all types of hardware, software, key network services, domain structures, and network media. The testing should also address any interoperability issues you'll face in the production environment, including other operating systems, other DNS implementations, and firewall or proxy server issues.

The test lab is also the place to test any techniques you'll need to carry out your Windows 2000 installation and rollout. Your deployment testing should include the following:

▼ Upgrading the network DNS implementation to an Active Directory–compatible DNS

■ Upgrading the Windows NT PDC to Active Directory

■ Migrating other Windows NT domain controllers

■ Installing new domain controllers

■ Migrating clients and member servers to the Active Directory environment

■ Transitioning from mixed mode to native mode

▲ Procedures necessary for supporting or migrating other operating systems such as NetWare or UNIX servers

If you plan to use network-based installation or any of the Windows 2000 deployment tools, these features should also be part of your testing process.

You should also make an effort to model the site structure of your production network so that you can test intersite and intrasite replication and (if necessary) site link bridges or other site-related features. If you want a really smooth transition, make sure to test the actual inheritance and group policy configuration of your final network, including logon scripts and effective rights and permissions.

Your test network (like any Active Directory network) must include an Active Directory–compatible DNS server. The Active Directory installation program will install a DNS server if you don't have one on the network; however, it is important that you make an effort to simulate the actual DNS environment of the production network. In particular, if you plan to use a third-party DNS system on a network that uses DHCP, Microsoft recommends that you verify that the DNS functions properly with Windows 2000 DHCP. Dynamic DNS depends on close interaction between the DNS and DHCP services. It is also important to include any Microsoft BackOffice products or any other third-party networking products that you will use on your network in your test environment.

Planning and Implementing a Pilot Site

The information on developing a pilot is even more amorphous than the information on developing a test lab. Yet, the pilot is still a crucial step in the deployment. The pilot site is your last chance to perfect your configuration and improve your understanding of Active Directory before your rollout on the full network.

The basic point of the pilot is to try out Windows 2000 and Active Directory on a small part of your production network. Microsoft is very serious about the pilot phase and, in fact, states, "To minimize your risk during deployment, plan on having several pilots. For example, you might have one pilot for your namespace design, another one for your standard desktop configuration and security model, and still another one for deploying applications remotely." (See the Windows 2000 Support Tools Deployment Planning Guide.)

Of course, the size and complexity of your pilot phase will depend on the size and complexity of your network. But the fact that Microsoft suggests several pilot sites within your network is an indication of the fact that Active Directory was created to support *large* networks.

It is theoretically possible to make the pilot site the initial step of the rollout and then build out from the pilot to encompass the entire network, but this is generally not what Microsoft means by a pilot. Also, the fact that Active Directory domain controllers cannot be renamed or moved to different domains makes it difficult to incorporate the pilot into the final production network.

Planning Your Active Directory Network

Take the time to carefully plan your Active Directory network. Chapters 1 through 6 of this book discuss concepts you'll need to understand for your deployment to succeed, such as domains and OUs, TCP/IP, DNS, LDAP, replication, groups, and group policy. Be familiar with the material of these chapters before you design your network. You may also want to refer to Chapter 9, "Active Directory Clients," and Chapter 11, "Active Directory and Windows 2000 Security," before you begin your design.

At some point in the design process, make a point of incorporating input from users and administrators of the test and pilot sites. In one sense, the design phase must span all the other phases of the deployment process. You must have some idea of the design in order to *test* that design in the testing lab, but the testing lab serves no purpose unless you allow the results of the testing process to have an effect on the eventual design.

There is no secret formula for designing the network. Start with the big questions and move to the smaller ones. A first look at a network design typically begins with questions of

▼ **Domain structure**   One domain or multiple domains? Tree or forest? Trust relationships between domains?

▲ **Organizational unit structure**   How will the organizational units be structured within a domain? Which groups or users will have authority over which OUs?

Once you've addressed these issues, you can start to address issues relating to users, groups, and group policy, and you can start to think about where to locate network resources.

NOTE: If your network uses the Microsoft BackOffice suite of server products, you'll need to carefully consider how to integrate Active Directory with BackOffice applications. Microsoft Exchange Server, in particular, can be integrated with the Active Directory environment. See Chapter 13, "Interoperating Windows 2000," for a discussion of how to integrate Exchange with Active Directory.

The following list shows rules for locating some of the basic components you'll find on an Active Directory network. The following sections describe some additional rules and tips that will help you see your way through the many configuration choices.

▼   **Domain controllers (Total)**   *Required:* One per domain (not recommended); two minimum in root domain. *Recommended minimum:* Two per site. *Considerations:* One per site is sometimes acceptable with failover authentication across the WAN link. Note that, with one per site, the same domain controller must field all authentication traffic and also serve as global catalog server. The optimum number of domain controllers varies depending on hardware, workload, and network configuration. If you have only one domain controller in the root domain of a multidomain network and that domain controller fails, you won't be able create a new domain controller in the root domain.

■   **RID master, PDC Emulator**   *Required:* One per domain (exactly). On most domains, the same domain controller should be RID master and PDC emulator. On very large domains, or in a mixed environment when the PDC emulator receives heavy traffic, use separate domain controllers.

■   **Infrastructure master**   *Required:* One per forest (exactly). Infrastructure master should be a domain controller that isn't a global catalog server but is on the same site as a global catalog server.

- **Schema master, domain naming master**   *Required:* One per forest (exactly). The same domain controller should serve as both schema master and domain naming master. Locate on the same site with the users or groups who are most likely to create a domain or alter the schema.

- **Global catalog servers**   *Required:* One per domain. *Recommended minimum:* One per domain or one per site if the domain spans multiple sites. Global catalog servers support cross-domain authentication, universal groups, and directory searches. Optimum number varies depending on hardware, workload, and network configuration.

- **DNS servers**   *Required:* Accessibility to DNS server for all computers. *Recommended minimum:* One DNS server per site authoritative for locator records within the site. Optimum number varies depending on hardware, workload, and network configuration.

- **WINS servers**   *Required:* None for native-mode networks with no legacy clients. *Recommended:* If you're using WINS to support legacy systems or applications, one WINS server per site recommended or two (min) for fault tolerance. Microsoft likes to say that WINS is not necessary for a fully compliant Active Directory network in native mode. But it also likes to point out that, before you take away WINS, you'd better be sure you have everything you need. Window 95/98, Windows NT, or WfW systems require NetBIOS name resolution through a WINS server, an LMHOST S file, or broadcast. Even Windows 2000 clients use WINS as a backup if DNS name resolution is unsuccessful.

CAUTION: In multidomain networks, the domain controller processing a user logon contacts a global catalog server for information on the user's universal group memberships. If a global catalog server is not available to process the request, the user will not be able to log on.

Axioms, Tips, and Best Practices

The following sections summarize some considerations to keep in mind when planning an Active Directory network. These considerations fall into the following topics:

▼ Domains

■ OUs

■ Sites

■ Mixed vs. native mode

■ Groups

■ Group policy

▲ Replication

Every network, of course, contains infinite variations of elements. You will have the joy of applying these rules to your own situation.

Domains

You need at least one Windows domain for an Active Directory network. Active Directory's group structures, DNS integration, and directory replication system make it well suited for multidomain environments. But Active Directory's organizational units (OUs) make it unnecessary to create multiple domains as a means of assigning authority for resources.

Microsoft recommends that you start by considering one domain for your network, and consider a multidomain configuration only if a single domain is unworkable or if you have a good justification for incurring the added complexity and overhead of additional domains. Some reasons for adopting a multidomain configuration are as follows:

▼ **Politics**   Or, that is, *administrative reasons*. Some organizations have well-defined administrative boundaries that lend themselves to well-defined domain boundaries.

■ **Continuity**   You may wish to maintain multiple Windows 2000/Active Directory domains because your network had multiple Windows NT domains. Although the NT-style resource domains are not necessary in Active Directory, some NT networks had multiple domains for other reasons, such as PDC availability and SAM size limit. For whatever reason, you may wish to simplify your upgrade by not worrying about reorganizing the domain structure and just converting an existing NT multidomain environment.

■ **Security**   One part of an organization may wish to maintain an entirely separate security structure. Or, two subgroups within an organization may have completely different domain-based security policies, such as password policies.

▲ **Efficiency**   (This only applies to big networks.) In a single-domain environment, the complete domain partition must replicate to all domain controllers throughout the domain. If the domain is divided into smaller domains, each domain partition is relatively smaller in size and takes less time to replicate through a smaller domain. (A partial domain partition must, of course, replicate to global catalog servers in other domains.)

A single domain can hold approximately 100,000 objects in the Active Directory. The 100,000-object limit compares to about 40,000 objects for a Windows NT domain. The Active Directory domain is more complex and, therefore, *needs* more objects, but Microsoft nevertheless maintains that an Active Directory domain can be considerably bigger than a Windows NT domain.

Organizational Units

You can use OUs simply as a tool for organizing the objects in the Active Directory Users and Computers utility. Or, you can use OUs as an integral part of your security and group policy system.

Delegation of authority for an OU to an OU administrator group essentially eliminates the need for Windows NT–style resource domains and is a central feature of the Active Directory environment.

OUs should be organized the way your network services team is organized. In other words, if your organization places an individual in charge of all objects in a specific room or region within a larger network, an OU should be created for that room or region. If your organization places one individual in charge of printers and another individual in charge of users, OUs should be organized according to object type.

Microsoft advocates a security scheme in which the number of domain administrators is kept to a minimum and management of resources occurs primarily at the OU level (see Figure 7-1). This scheme simplifies administration and limits the power of IT support staff beyond their assigned region. Microsoft also recommends that you take advantage of the inheritance feature whenever possible to ensure that objects within the group will inherit attributes of the container.

It is possible to place an OU inside of other OUs. This *nesting* of OUs may look elegant on corporate flowcharts, but don't nest your OUs just for the sake of elegance. Nesting OUs makes the Active

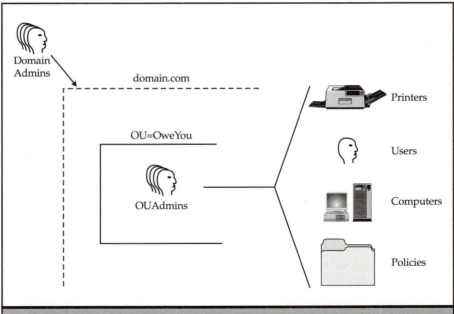

Figure 7-1.   A good approach for many networks is to manage resources at the OU level and minimize the number of domain administrators

Directory work harder to find an object, and it makes the user work harder to type in the LDAP distinguished name. It also adds a layer of complexity to inheritance, delegations, and group policy. There are, however, some cases in which nested OUs are an appropriate solution. A large OU, for instance, may have some internal division of authority that lends itself to hierarchies of sub-OUs (see Figure 7-2). In the case of nested OUs, Microsoft's recommendation is to assign control at the highest OU level wherever possible and let permissions pass down through inheritance.

Sites

The decision of where and how to divide a network into sites is almost always based on conditions of the physical network. If your network consists of one LAN, you only need one site. If your network consists of two or more LANs connected with WAN-type slow network connections, each LAN should be a separate site.

I cannot think of any good reasons for tampering with this simple strategy, although it should be noted that you *don't have* to have a WAN link to implement multiple sites. See Chapter 3, "Active Directory with TCP/IP and DNS," for a discussion of creating sites,

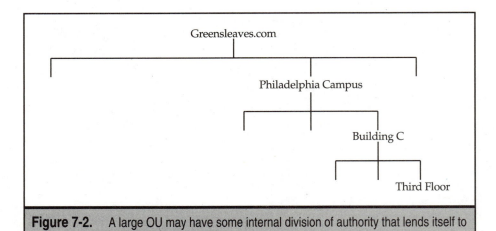

Figure 7-2.   A large OU may have some internal division of authority that lends itself to hierarchies of sub-OUs

and Chapter 4, "Understanding Replication," for a discussion of configuring intersite and intrasite replication.

> **NOTE:**   A site (which is bounded by slow WAN links) should not be confused with a network segment, which is bounded by connectivity devices such as routers. The well-connected LAN that makes up a site may include multiple network segments and routers.

One of the only subtleties you may face when deciding whether to configure multiple sites is the case where you are lucky enough to have a WAN link that isn't a *slow* WAN link. Microsoft, for instance, reportedly connects several locations in the Puget Sound area through a high-performance SONET network, and the connections between these locations are fast enough for the locations all to be in one site.

Mixed Mode vs. Native Mode

Active Directory's mixed mode is designed to support Windows 2000 and also Windows NT domain controllers. If you're upgrading an existing Windows NT network, you'll need to keep the network in mixed mode while you upgrade your domain controllers. Here are a few points to remember about mixed mode and native mode:

▼   Native mode offers a full range of Active Directory features, but does not support Windows NT 4 domain controllers.

■   Mixed mode does not offer all Active Directory features, but lets you operate the network with a mix of Windows 2000 and Windows NT 4 domain controllers.

▲   Native mode can support Windows 95/98 clients and Windows NT clients and member servers, even though it cannot support NT domain controllers.

Mixed mode is designed to facilitate the migration process. You can keep running Active Directory in mixed mode indefinitely, but once you switch to native mode, you can't switch back.

Shortcomings of Mixed Mode

As stated in Chapter 2, "Active Directory Concepts," the principal shortcomings of mixed mode are as follows:

▼ Mixed mode does not support universal groups. (A universal group can include members from any domain in the forest and provide access to resources on any domain in the forest.)

■ Mixed mode does not support nested groups.

■ Mixed mode does not provide the full range of management options for Windows NT 4 domain controllers through the Windows 2000 management tools.

■ Mixed mode does not permit you to control remote access through Windows 2000's access-by-policy administrative model.

■ Mixed mode does not automatically provide password filtering on all domain controllers—you have to configure password filtering separately.

▲ Mixed-mode domains have the same size limitations as NT 4 domains. The total number of computers, groups, and users for a mixed-mode domain should not exceed 40,000.

Users and Groups

Recall Microsoft's A G DL P strategy, described in Chapter 5, "Users and Groups":

1. User accounts (A) are assigned to global groups (G).

2. Resource permissions (P) are assigned to domain local groups (DL).

To provide users with access to resources, global groups are placed within domain local groups. Because membership lists for universal groups must reside on global catalog servers, access to resources through universal groups may be slower. If you think your network warrants the use of one or more universal groups, place users in global groups and then add the global group(s) to the universal group.

Rename the Administrator account. Renaming the Administrator account forces an attacker to guess the username as well as the password. Microsoft recommends that you not tinker with user rights unless you must.

Group Policy

Group policy is a huge issue in Active Directory. Much of the task of configuring an Active Directory network consists of configuring the network's group policy settings. See Chapter 6, "Group Policy," for a discussion of group policy in Active Directory.

Here are a few simple tips for sorting through the endless possibilities of group policy interaction:

1. Let group policy flow down through inheritance. Avoid block inheritance and No Override options unless they are necessary. Overriding inheritance makes policy assignments less uniform and makes it difficult to predict which policies are assigned to a particular user.

2. Use site policy only for settings related to the site configuration (such as replication settings)—except, if multiple domains are on the site, set common policies for all domains through site policy. (Certain security-related policies, such as password policies, must be set at the domain level.)

3. Set domain-wide policy at the domain level.

4. Let OU administrators control other settings at the OU level.

You may wish to amend these rules for your network. It's important that you have a short, simple list of logical rules for how policy should be applied. Rule 1 is important no matter what strategy you use: it is best to avoid excessive use of policy blocks and no-overrides.

Replication

Windows NT Server networks used directory replication through the LMRepl service to replicate files and directories throughout the network. Directory replication was typically used to replicate logon scripts and other files that the network administrator wanted to update automatically from a single export point.

Windows NT's directory replication feature is not supported in Windows 2000. Windows 2000 instead uses the File Replication Service (FRS) to replicate files. Use Windows 2000's Distributed File Service (DFS) to replicate files and folders. Move logon scripts to a domain controller's SysVol folder. Changes to the SysVol folder are replicated to other domain controllers' SysVol folders through Active Directory's multimaster replication. If you are upgrading a Windows NT network to Active Directory, your deployment plan should include a plan for converting from Windows NT directory replication to FRS replication.

Planning Your Active Directory Rollout

Once you have determined how your Active Directory network will look, the next step is to chart a course for how to get there. This section describes some of the installation and upgrade options.

I will begin by clarifying one important fact. Installing Active Directory is a different process from installing Windows 2000. The initial, out-of-the-box state of Windows 2000 after you install will not include Active Directory. The non–Active Directory Windows 2000 is instead designed for a network system similar to Windows NT 4. This may seem confusing, since Active Directory networks and Windows NT 4 networks are fundamentally different. (Adding Active Directory is *way* more drastic than adding the media player or a new network service.) But in some ways, this two-tiered installation is conceptually simpler because it boils down the Active Directory setup to only those elements that pertain directly to Active Directory.

Think of the Windows 2000 setup as a basic operating system installation or upgrade. It isn't even all that related to Active Directory, and for that reason you won't find much coverage of Windows 2000 setup in this chapter (although this chapter does provide a brief procedure for installing Windows 2000.

It is only in the second phase—when you install Active Directory on the Windows 2000 computer—that you transform the computer to an Active Directory domain controller and unlock all the secrets described in this book.

The dcpromo.exe utility performs the task of promoting a Windows 2000 Server computer to an Active Directory domain controller. When you run dcpromo, it asks if you would like to place the domain controller in

▼ A new root domain of a new tree in a new forest

■ An existing Windows 2000 domain

■ A new child domain in an existing tree

▲ A new root domain of a new tree in an existing forest

If you elect to create a new domain, dcpromo creates the domain automatically and places the new Active Directory domain controller in it.

This choice of where to place the new domain controller allows you to create the domain structure of a new Active Directory network or totally reform the structure of an existing Windows NT network through the upgrade process. Keep this choice in mind when you study the following sections, which provide schematic descriptions of the following topics:

▼ Installing a new Active Directory network

■ Upgrading a Windows NT network to Active Directory

▲ Migrating a NetWare network to Active Directory

All of these procedures are variations of the basic process of creating a domain structure and then populating the domain(s) with domain controllers, users, and groups. Your deployment plan will contain a combination of procedures such as these using methods and tools described in later sections. Your own deployment plan will be much more detailed than the schematic procedures described in the following sections. For instance, you'll need to preplan your DNS hierarchy and have a DNS name for each computer. You'll need to know how the installation will take place (Unattended? From which server?) and which applications or functions you'd like to assign to each machine.

As this chapter has already stated, before you get around to implementing installation procedures such as those described in the following sections, you should test them thoroughly.

NOTE: The dcpromo utility is described in greater detail later in this chapter in the section titled "Installing Windows 2000."

Installing a New Active Directory Network

One of the cleanest and easiest ways to install Active Directory is to start a whole new domain structure that is independent of any preexisting domains. This is, of course, the only option if you're building a new network from scratch. However, as you'll learn in the next section, even if you're upgrading an existing Windows NT network, you may wish to proceed by creating an entirely separate Windows 2000 domain structure and leave the existing NT network in operation as you move ahead with the rollout.

To create a New Windows 2000 environment, follow these steps:

1. Install Windows 2000 on a computer.

2. Promote the computer to an Active Directory domain controller using the dcpromo.exe utility. When dcpromo asks where to place the domain controller, say you would like to place it in a root domain of a new forest.

3. Install Windows 2000 on additional computers that you wish to make domain controllers on the domain you created in step 2. Run dcpromo on each computer and, when prompted, say you wish to add the domain controller to an existing domain. Give the name of the domain you created in step 2.

4. To create a child domain, run dcpromo on a Windows 2000 Server computer and, when prompted, say you'd like to place the domain controller in a new child domain. Give the name of the parent domain and the name of the new child domain. Add additional domain controllers to the child domain as described in step 3.

5. To create a new domain tree, run dcpromo on a Windows 2000 Server computer and, when prompted, say you'd like to place the domain controller in a new root domain of an existing forest. Add additional domain controllers to the new domain as described in step 3, or add child domains to the new domain as described in step 4.

The actual procedure for running dcpromo is described later in the section titled "Installing Windows 2000."

The first domain controller you install automatically assumes all operations master roles. The first domain controller in any additional domain assumes the domain-based operations master roles (RID master and PDC emulator) for the new domain. Some of the operations master roles can be reassigned later to other domain controllers, if necessary. See Chapter 8, "Managing Active Directory."

When you promote the first domain controller to Active Directory, Windows 2000 will make sure there is a DNS server running on your network that is compatible with Active Directory. (See Chapter 3.) If Windows 2000 can't find a DNS server, it asks if you would like to set up a DNS server and, if you say OK, sets up Windows 2000 DNS automatically. For all but the simplest networks, it is really worth setting up your DNS service beforehand rather than letting Windows 2000 set up the default DNS configuration on one of your first domain controllers. See Chapter 3 for more on DNS.

Migrating a Windows NT Network to Active Directory

Microsoft provides two different ways of migrating a Windows NT network to Windows 2000. The first is an actual upgrade:

1. A domain is officially considered a Windows NT 4.0 domain until the Primary Domain Controller (PDC) is upgraded to Active Directory. The migration begins with upgrading your Windows NT PDC to Windows 2000 and then installing Active Directory using dcpromo. The dcpromo utility migrates accounts (including computer accounts) and groups to Active Directory.

2. Once the PDC is upgraded and Active Directory is installed, the domain becomes a mixed-mode domain. In mixed mode,

Windows NT 4 Backup Domain Controllers (BDCs) continue to function as before.

3. While the domain operates in mixed mode, gradually upgrade the BDCs to Windows 2000.

4. Once all domain controllers have been upgraded to Windows 2000 Active Directory domain controllers, you can switch the operating mode to native mode using the Active Directory Users and Computers utility (as described later in this chapter in the section titled "Switching to Native Mode").

The other way to upgrade a Windows NT network to Active Directory is to create a new Active Directory environment (as described in the preceding section) with the desired domain structure and then migrate accounts, groups, and resources to the new domain using the special deployment tools in the Windows 2000 Support Tools set:

1. Create a new Active Directory environment, as described in the preceding section.

2. Use the Netdom tool (described later in this chapter in the section titled "Useful Deployment Utilities") to create any necessary trusts to ensure that the new domain has access to resources in the existing Windows NT domain system.

3. Use the ClonePrincipal tool (described later in this chapter in the section titled "Useful Deployment Utilities") to clone global groups from the existing NT domain to the new Active Directory environment.

4. Use ClonePrincipal to clone users from the existing NT domain to the new Active Directory environment.

5. Test the new configuration to ensure that users can log into the Active Directory environment and access resources.

6. When all users and groups have migrated to the new Active Directory environment and you're sure everything is working, turn off the domain controllers of the old NT network beginning with the BDCs. Turn the PDC off last.

Microsoft recommends that you store the PDC in case you need it for disaster recovery.

TIP: The migration procedures discussed in this chapter use the Netdom and ClonePrincipal tools included with the Windows 2000 support tools set. The Active Directory Migration Tool, which Microsoft recently licensed and distributes free at its Web site, offers similar migration services and provides some additional enhancements. See the later section titled "Active Directory Migration Tool."

Windows NT environments often consist of multiple domains in a single-master or multimaster configuration (see Figure 7-3). Logons are processed from the master *account* domains, and resources are managed from *resource* domains. Resource domains are not necessary in Active Directory networks because OUs can

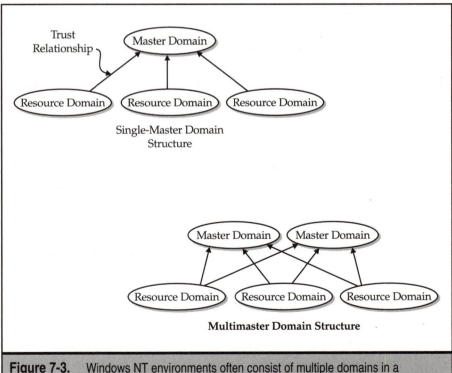

Figure 7-3.   Windows NT environments often consist of multiple domains in a single-master or multimaster configuration

serve the same role with more flexibility and efficiency. Often, one of the tasks when upgrading a Windows NT network to Active Directory is consolidating existing unnecessary resource domains into larger domain structures of the Active Directory environment.

To consolidate a resource domain, follow these steps:

1. Create an Active Directory networking environment, as described in the earlier section titled "Installing a new Active Directory Network."

2. Use the Netdom utility (described later in this chapter in the section titled "Useful Deployment Utilities") to establish trusts from the target Active Directory domain to the account domains that the resource domain trusts (see Figure 7-4).

3. Use ClonePrincipal (described later in this chapter in the section titled "Useful Deployment Utilities") to clone shared local groups of the resource domain to the target domain.

4. In the resource domain, upgrade the PDC to Windows 2000 and install Active Directory.

5. In the resource domain, upgrade the BDCs to Windows 2000 and run dcpromo. When prompted by dcpromo, elect to make each BDC into a member server.

6. Move clients and member servers from the resource domain to the target Active Directory domain. Note that the resource domain is still operational at this point because the PDC is still functioning on the resource domain.

7. Use dcpromo to promote any Windows 2000 member servers moved to the target domain to the domain controllers, if desired.

8. When all resources have migrated to the new Active Directory environment and you're sure everything is working, turn off the domain controllers of the old NT domain beginning with any remaining BDCs. Turn off the PDC last.

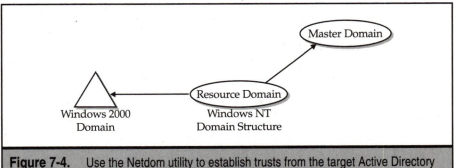

Figure 7-4. Use the Netdom utility to establish trusts from the target Active Directory domain to the account domains that the resource domain trusts

Migrating a NetWare Network to Active Directory

Active Directory includes several features that allow it to coexist with a working NetWare environment; but, if you want to migrate from NetWare to Active Directory, you can do that, too. Windows 2000 includes the Directory Service Migration Tool, which lets you migrate accounts, group permissions, and files from either an NDS environment or a bindery environment to the Active Directory.

To migrate from a NetWare environment to Active Directory, follow these steps:

1. Create a new Active Directory networking environment, as described in the earlier section titled "Installing a New Active Directory Network."

2. Use the Directory Service Migration Tool to migrate NetWare permissions, groups, accounts, and resources to Active Directory.

3. Configure and upgrade clients as necessary to access the Active Directory network. See Chapter 9 for more on client configuration.

NOTE: See Chapter 13 for more on NetWare interoperability issues.

Executing Your Active Directory Rollout

If you implement a pilot site and carefully plan and test your deployment, as Microsoft describes in the Windows 2000 Support Tools Deployment Planning Guide, the chances are that your rollout will go smoothly.

If you are upgrading an existing Windows NT network to Active Directory, you can progress gradually with the upgrade, since Active Directory's mixed mode essentially lets Windows NT and Active Directory coexist in the same environment.

In a production environment with several domain controllers and many clients, you'll very likely decide to use network installation techniques for some or all of the installations. Of course, before you install Active Directory, you must install Windows 2000. Although this book does not attempt to provide complete coverage of general Windows 2000 topics, the basic steps of Windows 2000 installation are so fundamental that this chapter will describe them. Later sections describe how to install Windows 2000 and Active Directory from the CD and over the network. Topics include the following:

▼ Active Directory system requirements

■ Installing Windows 2000

■ Creating Active Directory domain controllers

■ Installing over the network

■ Troubleshooting installation

■ Useful deployment utilities

▲ Important setup procedures

If you have a large network, the task of migrating to Active Directory could keep you busy for months; but, if you proceed carefully, you should be able to continue to use the network without interruption.

Active Directory System Requirements

The minimum system requirements for installing Windows 2000 Server on an Intel-based system are as follows:

▼ **CPU**   Pentium-class 133MHz or higher (higher is better—133MHz is slow for an Active Directory domain controller). Maximum of four CPUs per computer.

■ **Memory**   128MB RAM minimum supported. 256MB RAM recommended minimum. 4GB maximum.

▲ **Disk Space**   685MB on the partition with the system files (1GB recommended). Disk space requirement may depend upon installation method. Microsoft notes that FAT partitions require and additional 100–200MB of disk space. Also, network installations require an additional 100–200MB.

CAUTION: Microsoft also notes that an upgrade can require *more* disk space than a new installation because the existing account database may increase in size by a factor of ten during the conversion to Active Directory. If the computer will be an Active Directory domain controller, you must also have at least one NTFS partition to hold the SysVol folder.

Microsoft originally intended to provide a version of Windows 2000 for the Compaq Alpha chip; but sometime in the beta testing phase, Compaq decided not to support Windows 2000. The Alpha processor is not supported in the release version of Windows 2000.

Upgrade Paths

Keep the following options in mind as you upgrade:

▼ You can upgrade a Windows 3.51 or Windows 4.0 domain controller to a Windows 2000 domain controller and install Active Directory.

- You can upgrade a Windows 3.51 or Windows 4.0 member server to a Windows 2000 member server and then upgrade it to an Active Directory domain controller.

▲ You must first upgrade a Windows 3.1 or Windows 3.5 server to Windows 3.51 or Windows 4.0, and then upgrade it to Windows 2000. Once you have installed Windows 2000, you can upgrade the computer to an Active Directory domain controller. Note that Windows 2000's hardware requirements are way higher (off the chart) than requirements from the Windows 3.1/3.5 era. If you're upgrading a legacy server, make sure you have the necessary hardware.

Synchronizing Clocks

Although Windows 2000 prides itself in not requiring the tight time synchronization necessary for NetWare and some other networking systems, you do have to at least try. The Active Directory Installation Wizard checks the system clock of the domain controller you're upgrading and compares it to the time on the existing Active Directory domain controllers. If the time is too far off from the time on other domain controllers, you won't be able to install Active Directory. Before you install Active Directory, synchronize the time with the Active Directory domain controllers. If your network is functioning properly, Active Directory should keep the domain controllers in synch.

CAUTION: It seems odd to have to mention it, but if you have any problems, it is worth checking to make sure that your *time zones* are synchronized. Some prerelease versions of Windows 2000 switched the time zone unexpectedly at installation. If the time zones are not the same, the time is not synchronized even though the same numbers may be appearing on the clock.

Installing Windows 2000

Before you install Active Directory, you must install Windows 2000. You'll find many discussions about how to install Windows 2000 in

Microsoft Help sources and also in Windows 2000 books. The
following short summary is included for your convenience.

1. Boot to the current operating system. If you are installing onto
    a new or newly formatted PC, boot to a bootable floppy disk
    or, if your system supports CD boot, you can boot directly to
    the Windows 2000 CD. Insert the Windows 2000 CD in the CD
    ROM drive. A dialog box appears, asking if you want to
    install Windows 2000. Click Yes.

2. If the setup program doesn't support an upgrade from your
    present operating system, you'll receive a message saying
    that upgrade is not supported. You'll have to perform a full
    installation. Click OK.

3. The Windows 2000 Setup Wizard asks if you'd like to perform
    an upgrade or a new installation. (If you received the step 2
    warning stating that the upgrade option is not available, you
    won't be able to choose Upgrade. Choose Upgrade or Install
    and click Next.

4. The License agreement appears. Read through the agreement
    and click I Accept to accept the agreement. You must accept
    the agreement in order to proceed. Click Next.

5. In the Select Special Options screen, click Language Options,
    Accessibility Options, or Advanced Options for the
    appropriate option dialog boxes:

    ■ **Language Options**   Lets you choose a language for the
       Windows 2000 user interface.

    ■ **Accessibility Options**   Offers options for the vision
       impaired. You can choose Magnifier (displays an enlarged
       portion of the screen in a separate window) or Narrator
       (a narrator reads the contents of the screen.)

    ■ **Advanced Options**   Lets you specify the following:

       ■ The location of the Windows 2000 files. This option
          provides for convenient network installation. The
          default location is the CD-ROM drive.

■ The name of the Windows installation folder (the Windows 2000 root folder).

■ Copy all Setup files from the Setup CD to the hard drive. This option liberates the CD so you can use it somewhere else. The default is No (unchecked).

■ I want to choose the installation partition during setup.

The next screen asks if you'd like to view the online directory of Windows 2000–compatible and certified applications. This list is available at the Microsoft Web site. It is a good idea to look through the list to see whether crucial applications on your network are Windows 2000 compatible. Your applications still might be compatible even if they aren't on the list, but you'll want to be extra careful to thoroughly test any applications that aren't on the list on your Active Directory test network. You'll need a working Internet connection to access the online list during setup. For more on Active Directory hardware and software compatibility, see http://www.microsoft.com/windows 2000/compatible.

6. A dialog box tells you that Setup is copying files. Setup then restarts your PC. Your system restarts in the text-based Windows 2000 Server setup mode. A prompt asks whether you'd like to set up Windows 2000, repair a Windows 2000 installation, or quit Setup. Press ENTER to install Windows 2000.

7. Choose the partition onto which you'd like to install Windows 2000. Press ENTER.

8. If you are installing Windows 2000 onto a FAT partition, Setup asks if you'd like to convert the partition to NTFS. If you plan to install Active Directory, you'll need a working NTFS partition on your network to store the Active Directory. The Windows 2000 system files do not have to go on an NTFS partition, but for security and performance reasons, it is a good idea to use NTFS. Note that only Windows NT and Windows 2000 systems can read an NTFS partition. (In fact, you can only access Windows 2000 NTFS from NT 4 if you're using one of the later Windows NT 4 service packs.) If you're planning to dual boot with NT 4, make sure your NT system

has the most current NT service pack. If you are planning to dual boot with an OS such as Windows 95 or Windows 98, make sure any files you need for the alternative boot configuration remain on a FAT partition.

Setup copies files to the Windows 2000 installation folders. The system then reboots and the Windows 2000 graphic interface appears. If you elected to convert the partition to NTFS, Setup coverts the partition. The system reboots again.

The Windows 2000 Setup Wizard appears and announces that it will be collecting information. Setup searches your system and installs devices. (This takes a while.)

9. The Setup Wizard asks if you would like to customize Windows 2000 for different regions and languages. Click the locale or keyboard Customize button for customization options. Click Next.

10. Enter your name and the name of your organization.

11. Enter the licensing mode you'd like to use for the Windows 2000 system. This system is similar to the Windows NT Server licensing system. See Windows 2000 documentation for a complete discussion of per server and per seat licensing. They are briefly explained here:

   ■ **Per server**   You license the server to support a maximum number of concurrent client connections. You must specify the number.

   ■ **Per seat**   Client licenses are applied to each client. The server itself does not limit the number of connections.

12. Specify a NetBIOS computer name and a password for the Administrator account on the Windows 2000 Server.

13. Choose which Windows 2000 components you'd like to include with the installation. Browse through the options. Consult a Windows 2000 reference for additional details.

14. Set the time and time zone. Click Next. Setup installs various components and performs final setup tasks. (This takes a while.)

> ## Some Useful URLs
> ▼ **www.microsoft.com/Windows2000** Windows 2000 home page
>
> ■ **windowsupdate.microsoft.com** Windows update Web site
>
> ■ **www.microsoft.com/windows2000/compatible** Hardware and software compatibility information
>
> ■ **www.microsoft.com/hcl** Hardware compatibility list
>
> ▲ **support.microsoft.com/support** Microsoft tech support site

Installing Over the Network

Windows 2000's network installation options are similar to Windows NT's. The basic process is this:

1. Make the Windows 2000 installation files available on a network share, either from a shared CD-ROM drive or by copying the CD to a hard disk. If you have several installations ahead, it may be worth it to copy the files to a hard disk rather than the slower CD-ROM drive.

2. Start the computer you'd like to install Windows 2000 on using an operating system with suitable network client software and connect to the network share with the installation files.

3. Execute one of the following Windows 2000 Setup files. These files are located in the I386 directory for Intel systems:

   ■ **Winnt32.exe** For Windows NT and Windows 2000 upgrades

   ■ **Winnt.exe** For all other installations

   Each file offers several optional switches. For a list of command-line options, type the path and command at the command prompt and specify the /? Option. For example: e:/I386/winnt.exe /?.

Creating Active Directory Domain Controllers

Dcpromo.exe is a tool that installs, configures, and removes Active Directory from Windows 2000 Servers. If you forget the name, think *dc* (domain controller) *promo* (promotion). Actually, you might not need to remember the name. The main task of dcpromo is to start and run the Active Directory Installation Wizard.

The Active Directory Installation Wizard promotes and demotes domain controllers and even creates domains. But it does not create sites. If your computer contains multiple sites, you must either set the site up before you install the domain controller or, if the new site is in the same domain, you can create the site later and move the domain controller to the new site. See Chapters 3 and 4 for more on Active Directory sites.

When you install Windows 2000 Server (as described in the preceding section) and reboot your computer, you'll see the Windows 2000 Configure Your Server screen (see Figure 7-5). To install Active Directory, click Active Directory in the left-hand column. The next screen provides you with some warnings about Active Directory and the Active Directory Installation Wizard. Scroll to the bottom of the screen and click Start to start the Active Directory Installation Wizard.

Alternatively, you can start the Installation wizard at any time by clicking the Start button, choosing Run, and typing **dcpromo** in the Run dialog box.

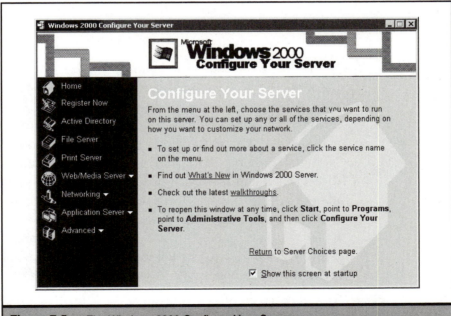

Figure 7-5.   The Windows 2000 Configure Your Server screen

The Active Directory Installation Wizard proceeds as follows:

1. The first screen welcomes.

2. The second screen asks you to choose whether the computer will be a domain controller for a new domain or a domain controller on an existing domain. Note that if you choose to make it a domain controller on an existing domain, you'll lose all local accounts when the computer assumes domain controller status.

3. If you chose to create a new domain in step 2, you'll be asked to specify whether this will be a new domain tree or a child domain of an existing tree. If you choose to create a new domain tree, a subsequent screen asks whether you'd like to create a new forest or place the new domain tree in an existing forest.

4. The next screen asks you to supply the username, password, and domain of the administrator-level account you wish to use for this operation. (You won't see this screen if you're creating a new forest.)

5. Enter the full DNS name of the domain that the computer will join (e.g., chips.com or child.parent.org). Click the Browse button to browse for available domains. Click Next.

6. In the next screen, specify the location of the Active Directory database file. The database can grow to be very large, so make sure it is on a disk with enough room. Microsoft recommends as much as 1GB free space for production environments. The actual size will vary depending on the size of your network. Note that the default location is the Windows 2000 root directory. If you are concerned about performance, it is a good idea to put the database on a separate disk and controller from the operating system files. The wizard also asks for the location of the Active Directory log. As the wizard mentions, it also a good idea to put the log on a different disk from the database. Click Next.

7. The next screen asks for the location of the SysVol folder. The SysVol folder holds this domain controller's copy of public

files such as domain-based policies and scripts. The SysVol folder must be on an NTFS partition. Click Next.

8. In the next screen, specify a password that will be used to recover the directory in Directory Services restore mode (see Chapter 8). You'd better remember this password. You'll need it to restore the Active Directory. Confirm the password. Click Next.

9. The Active Directory Installation Wizard provides a summary of the information you input in previous screens. Make sure the information is correct. If you need to, click the Back button to go backward through the wizard and change any incorrect settings. When you have finished, click Next.

After you click the last Next, the Active Directory Installation Wizard will reconfigure the computer as an Active Directory domain controller. If this computer is not the first domain controller, the wizard will copy the Active Directory database over the network to the computer. (This could take a while.) If this computer is the first domain controller in a domain, the wizard will automatically create the domain.

If the new domain controller is being added to an existing domain, the wizard creates a computer account in the domain. There is a delay between when the account is first created and when the account is written to the Active Directory database, so you may receive a message that a computer account wasn't found. Wait a few minutes and try again. Take the time to check the Network Identification tab in the System control panel to ensure that the domain name and full computer name of the computer are correct.

If your network has multiple sites and the setup information has to pass across a WAN link before it is available for authentication, it may take additional time before you can complete the setup process.

Troubleshooting Installation

Many of the problems you'll encounter with the installation and upgrade process are Windows 2000 configuration problems that do not pertain specifically to Active Directory. You can expect some problems with hardware compatibility. Windows 2000 is still new, and the Windows 2000 Server CD does not contain all the drivers for every device that could theoretically run under Windows 2000. It is best to explore as many hardware issues as you can in the testing phase. You won't want unattended installations hanging up over driver compatibility issues during your rollout.

You can check the latest version of the Windows 2000 Hardware Compatibility List (HCL) to see which devices have been tested for Windows 2000 compatibility. The HCL is available at the Microsoft Web site at http://www.microsoft.comhcl. Microsoft also has a Web site devoted specifically to Windows 2000 compatibility information at www.microsoft.com/windows 2000/compatible.

A device might still work if it isn't on the list. If necessary, check the vendor's Web site and download Windows 2000 drivers for the device.

Windows 2000 has many of the same troubleshooting tools found in previous versions of Windows:

▼ **Device Manager**   Displays information on system devices and device drivers. To reach Device Manager, right-click the My Computer icon. Choose Properties. Then click the Hardware tab and click the Device Manager button. Browse for the device that you think may be malfunctioning.

■ **System Information utility**—provides information on hardware resources, drivers, environment variables, ports, and devices. To reach System Information utility, choose Start | Programs | Accessories | System Tools | System Information.

▲ **Event Viewer**   Event Viewer reads the event log—a log of system, security, and application errors; warning; and information. To reach the Event Viewer, choose Start | Programs | Administrative Tools | EventViewer.

Windows 2000 assembles a collection of management utilities (including the preceding three utilities) into the Computer Management utility (see Figure 7-6), which offers a handy tree view of system tools. To reach the Computer Management utility, choose Start | Programs | Administrative Tools | Computer Management.

If you think your problem is related to a driver, start with Device Manager and Event Viewer. Download a new driver, if necessary, and install it through Device Manager.

Windows 2000 also offers several *troubleshooters*—souped-up Help topics designed to help you isolate a problem interactively. To reach

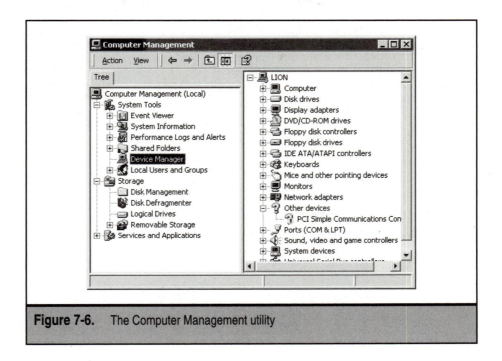

Figure 7-6. The Computer Management utility

the troubleshooters, go to Windows 2000 Help and search the index for one of the following topics, or else search for the word *troubleshooters*. You'll find troubleshooters for the following:

▼ Client Services for NetWare
■ DHCP
■ Display
■ Group policy and Active Directory
■ Domain Name System
■ Hardware
■ Internet connection
■ Modem
■ MS-DOS programs
■ Multimedia games
■ Networking
■ Print
■ Routing and remote access
■ Remote installation services
■ Sound
■ Startup and shutdown
■ Stop errors
■ System setup
■ Server management
■ Windows 3.*x* programs
▲ WINS

The relationship of Windows 2000 with DNS is still rather mysterious and, unfortunately, unpredictable in some cases. The Event Viewer reports most common DNS errors. You can also use the DNS troubleshooter, or any of the standard TCP/IP command-line utilities such as ping or nslookup.

If you are trying to check your TCP/IP configuration, don't look for the Network control panel. The TCP/IP configuration is found in the Properties dialog box of the Local Area Connection icon in the Network and Dial-Up Connections control panel. The fastest way to reach it is to choose Start | Settings | Network and Dial-Up Connections, then right-click Local Area Connection and choose Properties. Then select TCP/IP and click Properties (see Figure 7-7).

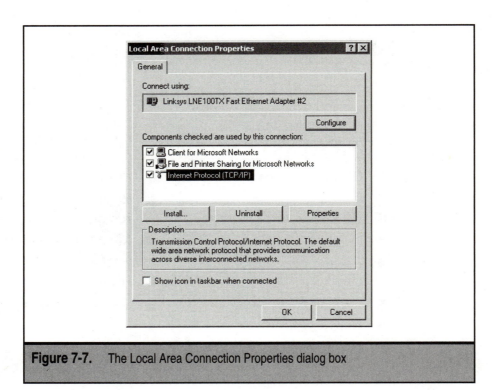

Figure 7-7. The Local Area Connection Properties dialog box

TIP: Windows 2000 Server sometimes has trouble installing Active Directory if a network connection is not available. In other words, even if you are installing Active Directory locally on a single system for testing and evaluation purposes, you may need to ensure that an adapter is installed and the computer is connected to a network.

Microsoft offers the following tips if a computer is unable to connect to a domain controller after installation:

▼ Verify the domain name.

■ Verify that a domain controller and a DNS server are both online.

■ Verify that the protocol and network adapter settings are correct.

▲ If you are reinstalling Windows 2000 and you are using the same computer name you used before, delete the computer account on the domain and re-create it.

Of course, the troubleshooters and the Windows 2000 utilities will not help you if you can't install Windows 2000 or can't log on. Consult a Windows 2000 reference for more on the full range of troubleshooting topics, such as the System Recovery console, the emergency repair disk, and the boot log.

AUTHORIZING DHCP   DHCP must be authorized in Active Directory before you can use it. If the DHCP server is not authorized, it will not respond to client requests. If you upgrade a Windows NT DHCP server to Windows 2000/Active Directory and the DHCP service isn't working, make sure the DHCP server is authorized. To authorize a DHCP server:

1. Select Start | Programs | Administrative Tools | DHCP.

2. In the DHCP console, right-click the DHCP icon and choose Manage Authorized Servers.

3. In the Manage Authorized Servers dialog box, click the Authorize button.

4. Enter the name or IP address of the DHCP server you wish to authorize. Click OK.

5. Click OK in the Manage Authorized Servers dialog box.

Microsoft also states that the DHCP authorization process won't work correctly unless the first DHCP server on the network is aware of Active Directory (in other words, is either a Windows 2000 member server or an Active Directory domain controller). See Windows 2000 Server Help for more on DHCP authorization.

Useful Deployment Utilities

The Windows 2000 Support Tools package provides a number of useful tools that assist with the process of migrating to Active Directory. Keep these tools in mind when you're planning your Active Directory migration:

▼ **Clonepr.dll (ClonePrincipal)**   Migrates groups and users by *cloning* existing groups and accounts to the new domain. ClonePrincipal can consolidate several groups to one new group.

■ **Netdom.exe (Windows 2000 Domain Manager)**   Creates and manages trust relationships between Windows 2000 domains and NT domains. NetDom enables Windows 2000 computers to join NT domains.

■ **Movetree.exe**   Lets you move objects such as users and OUs between domains.

▲ **Msicuu.exe (Windows Installer Cleanup utility)**   Cleans up after a failed Windows 2000 installation. The Windows Installer Cleanup Utility removes installer settings and registry entries. The command-line version is msizap.exe.

See Windows 2000 Support Tools Help for more on these important deployment tools. These tools were part of Microsoft's original vision for the domain migration process and are included in some of the migration procedures described earlier in this chapter.

(See the earlier section titled "Migrating a Windows NT Network to Active Directory.") Microsoft later decided to license the powerful Active Directory Migration Tool (ADMT) to assist with the migration process. ADMT is discussed in the next section. ADMT may prove to be a better option for many migration tasks originally intended for the deployment utilities discussed in this section.

Active Directory Migration Tool

Sometime during the Windows 2000 beta process (at Beta 3, to be exact), Microsoft received word from beta testers that the company's developers needed to work on a way to simplify the domain migration process. In particular, testers said they wanted help with upgrading Windows NT domains, migrating users and computers, and consolidating NT multidomain networks to Windows 2000 networks. Microsoft quickly cut a deal with Mission Critical, Inc., to license Mission Critical's promising suite of Active Directory domain migration tools. The result of this union is Active Directory Migration Tool (ADMT). At this writing, ADMT is available for download from the Microsoft Web site at www.microsoft.com/Windows2000/ guide/server/solutions/admt.asp. ADMT may eventually be integrated into the Windows 2000 distribution.

If you are planning to migrate a Windows NT network to Active Directory, it is definitely worth your time to download ADMT and see what it offers. The command-line tools discussed in the previous section are nice and compact, but the fact is, command-line tools work best for routine tasks that you execute every day. Domain migration is something you do only once in a while, and the process is so complex that you may wish you had a wizard. ADMT provides several wizards that greatly simplify the migration process. ADMT also includes options not available with the built-in tools, such as better rollback and reporting support.

ADMT provides the following wizards:

▼ User Migration Wizard

■ Group Migration Wizard

■ Computer Migration Wizard

■ Security Translation Wizard

- Reporting Wizard
- Service Account Migration Wizard
- Exchange Directory Migration Wizard
- Trust Migration Wizard
- ▲ Group Mapping and Merging Wizard

Despite the fact that ADMT isn't presently included on the Windows 2000 CD, it may emerge as the tool of choice for managing Active Directory migrations. Stay tuned to Microsoft for further developments.

Configuring Trusts

Microsoft uses the word *trust* for a relationship between domains. If domain A trusts domain B, users in domain B can be assigned access to domain A resources. Users with accounts in domain B can log in from domain A workstations and the login request will *pass through* to domain B for validation.

In Windows NT, trust relationships were one-way, intransitive, and explicit. In other words, you had to manually create trust relationships, and just because domain A trusted domain B didn't mean domain B trusted domain A or domain A trusted any other domains trusted by B.

One of the goals of Windows 2000 was to simplify the tangle of trust relationships that often resulted from a complex multidomain Windows NT network. The use of organizational units, in the first place, reduces the need for multidomain networks in the Active Directory environment. If you decide to implement a multidomain Active Directory network, the trust relationships necessary for linking all domains in the forest are created automatically.

In the Active Directory environment, the trusts created automatically as part of the forest domain structure are two-way and transitive. A trust relationship between domains A and B implies that A trusts B and B trusts A. Furthermore, because the trusts are transitive, if domain A trusts domain B and domain B trusts domain C, then domain A trusts domain C.

Root domains in an Active Directory forest are automatically linked with a transitive, two-way *tree-root trust* relationship. The domains within a single domain tree are linked with a transitive, two-way *parent-child* trust relationship. The system of tree-root trusts and parent-child trusts means that all Active Directory domains in the forest will trust all other Active Directory domains.

You can also manually link domains through trust relationships. Trust relationships that you create yourself are known as *explicit* trusts. You might ask why it would be necessary to create trust relationships when all domains in the forest trust each other automatically.

In the Active Directory environment, explicit trusts fall into two categories:

▼ Shortcut trusts

▲ External trusts

These explicit trust types are discussed in the following sections. A special kind of external trust, called a *non–Windows Kerberos realm trust,* connects an Active Directory domain with a Kerberos realm. See the later section titled "Creating Explicit Trusts" for more on the non–Windows Kerberos realm trust.

SHORTCUT TRUSTS   A *shortcut trust* (sometimes called a *cross-link trust*) is an explicit trust you create within an Active Directory forest for optimization purposes. The default structure of trust relationships in an Active Directory forest means that, if you are in the child domain of one tree and you wish to log into a child domain of another tree in the forest, the authentication must pass up through the chain of parent-child trusts linking the domains in your current tree, across the tree-root trust at the root domain to the other tree, and down through the chain of parent-child trusts in the other tree. (The system of trust relationship through which an authentication request passes is known as a *trust path*.) A shortcut trust lets you create your own trust path directly linking two domains that are otherwise connected only implicitly through the tree structure. A shortcut trust does not provide any functionality you didn't have already, but it improves performance by shortening the trust path. Any two Active Directory domains in a forest can participate in a shortcut trust. A shortcut trust must be transitive; however, like other explicit trusts, a shortcut trust is a one-way trust. If you want to create the effect of a two-way shortcut trust, you must create two, one-way trusts.

EXTERNAL TRUSTS   An *external trust* is a one-way, nontransitive trust that links a domain in the forest with another domain outside the forest. External trusts are most often used for the following purposes:

▼ To link domains in two different Active Directory forests

▲ To link an Active Directory domain with a Windows NT domain

Another use for an external trust is to connect an Active Directory domain with a non–Windows Kerberos realm. A non–Windows Kerberos realm trust is a special type of trust used to facilitate the interoperability of Windows 2000 Kerberos with other Kerberos systems. See the later section titled "Creating Explicit Trusts" for more on creating a non–Windows Kerberos realm trust.

The intransitive, one-way nature of an external trust is reminiscent of a Windows NT domain trust. Because an external trust is nontransitive, you can't depend on the system of parent-child and tree-root relationships to pass an authentication request through the forest after it crosses the external trust.

External trusts with NT domains sometimes play an important role in the migration process. See the earlier section titled "Migrating a Windows NT Network to Active Directory."

NOTE: Microsoft states that if you intend to operate your network in mixed mode, external trust relationship in which a Windows 2000 domain trusts a Windows NT domain should be deleted.

CREATING EXPLICIT TRUSTS   You must create explicit trusts manually. The Active Directory Domains and Trusts tool lets you create explicit trusts for Active Directory domains and manage and monitor Active Directory trust relationships. You must configure the trust relationship twice: once for the trusting domain and once for the trusted domain. If you are configuring an external trust with a

Windows NT domain, the other side of the trust must be configured from Windows NT.

To create an explicit trust relationship for an Active Directory domain:

1. Select Start | Programs | Administrative Tools | Active Directory Domains And Trusts.

2. In the Active Directory Domains And Trusts console, right-click the domain to which you would like to add the trust relationship and select Properties.

3. In the domain properties dialog box, select the Trusts tab.

4. The Trusts tab lets you add trust relationships for the domain. The trust tab includes two lists: Domains Trusted By This Domain and Domains That Trust This Domain. Depending on which end of the one-way trust relationship you're configuring, click the upper or the lower Add button to add a trust relationship for the current domain. You'll be asked to enter the name of the domain and a password for the trust. The password you enter for the trusted domain must match the password you enter for the trusting domain.

5. Click OK in the domain Properties dialog box.

6. Repeat the procedure to configure the domain on the other side of the trust relationship.

You can also use the versatile Netdom utility to create trust relationships. Netdom in one of the Windows 2000 support tools. See "Installing the Windows 2000 Support Tools," later in this chapter. The netdom trust command lets you create a trust relationship:

netdom trust trusting_domain /D:trusted_domain /Add

Provide user account names and passwords directly using the following switches:

/Ud: *user account in trusted domain*
   (in domain_name\account_name format)
/Pd: *password in the trusted domain*
/Uo: *account name in the trusting domain*
/Po: *password in the trusting domain*

TIP: Use the /REMOVE switch with the netdom trust command to remove a trust.

You can use the Netdom /Realm switch to create a trust relationship with a non–Windows Kerberos realm. As with other netdom trust commands, the /D: switch signifies the trusted domain (or realm) and the trusting domain (or realm) is given as a command object without a switch.

To create a non–Windows Kerberos Realm trust with the Active Directory domain as the trusting domain:

    netdom trust /d:realm_name trusting_domain /ADD
    /PT:realmpassword /REALM

To create a non–Windows Kerberos Realm trust with the Kerberos realm as the trusting domain:

    netdom trust /d:trusted_domain realm_name /ADD /REALM

Use the /TWOWAY switch to make the non–Windows Kerberos realm trust a two-way trust. You can change an existing non–Windows Kerberos realm trust to a two-way trust using the /TRANS:yes switch.

NOTE: See Windows 2000 support tools help for more on using Netdom.

IMPORTANT SETUP PROCEDURES

The following sections briefly cover some procedures you'll probably need when you're configuring your Active Directory network.

Installing the Windows 2000 Support Tools

The Windows 2000 Support Tools is a collection of tools and documents from the Windows 2000 Resource Kit. The Windows 2000 Supports Tools package includes several tools discussed in this chapter and also the Windows 2000 Deployment Planning Guide.

To install the Windows 2000 Support Tools, follow these steps:

1. Choose Start | Settings | Control Panel.

2. Open the Add/Remove Programs control panel.

3. In the Add/Remove Programs control panel, click Add New Programs.

4. In the next screen, click the button labeled CD or Floppy. The wizard then asks you to insert a floppy or CD. Insert the Windows 2000 CD and click Next.

5. Click the Browse button and browse to the SUPPORT/TOOLS directory of the CD.

6. Select Setup and click Open.

7. In the Run Installation Program screen, click Finish.

8. The Windows 2000 Support Tools Setup Wizard starts. Follow the wizard instructions to install the Windows 2000 Support Tools.

TIP: For any professional deployment of Windows 2000, you should also obtain the full Windows 2000 Resource Kit. See the Windows 2000 Web site: www.microsoft.com/windows 2000.

Switching to Native Mode

The task of switching your domain from mixed mode to native mode is not difficult once you're finally ready to make the change. Remember, though, once you switch your domain to native mode, you can't change back to mixed mode. See the previous section on "Mixed Mode vs. Native Mode."

To switch your domain to native mode:

1. Select Start | Programs | Administrative Tools | Active Directory Users And Computers.

2. In the Active Directory Users And Computers console, right-click the domain you wish to switch to native mode and choose Properties.

3. In the General tab of the domain properties dialog box, click the Change Mode button.

4. A warning dialog asks if you'd really like to go through with the change. Choose Yes.

5. Click OK.

Configuring Global Catalog Servers

To configure a computer as a global catalog server, follow these steps:

1. Open the Active Directory Sites and Services utility by choosing Start | Programs | Administrative Tools | Active Directory Sites and Services.

2. Click the plus sign by the Sites folder. Click the plus sign for the site that contains the domain controller you wish to make into a global catalog server. Click the plus sign by the folder labeled Servers. Select the domain controller.

3. In the right pane, right-click NTDS Settings and choose Properties.

4. In the NTDS settings General tab, check the box labeled Global Catalog to make the domain controller into a global catalog server. If the domain controller is already a global catalog server and you wish to stop it from being one, uncheck the Global Catalog check box. Click OK or Apply.

Creating an OU

To create a new organizational unit, follow these steps:

1. Open the Active Directory Users and Computers utility by choosing Start | Programs | Administrative Tools | Active Directory Users and Computers.

2. In the Active Directory Users and Computers tree view, right-click the domain on which you'd like to create the new OU.

3. In the context menu, choose New; then choose Organizational Unit.

4. Enter a name of the new OU.

Delegating Control of an OU

To delegate control of an OU to a user or group, follow these steps:

1. Open the Active Directory Users and Computers utility by choosing Start | Programs | Administrative Tools | Active Directory Users and Computers.

2. In the Active Directory Users and Computers tree view, click the plus sign next to the domain that contains the OU. Right-click the OU for which you wish to delegate control.

3. Right-click the OU for which you wish to delegate control and choose Delegate Control.

4. The Delegation of Control Wizard starts. Click Next in the first screen.

5. In the Users and Groups screen, click the Add button. Select the users or groups to whom you would like to delegate control of the OU. Click Next.

6. In the Tasks to Delegate screen, choose the tasks you'd like to delegate to the user(s) or group(s) you select in step 5. Click Next. Or, choose Create A Custom task to delegate for additional choices. Click Next.

7. A final summary screen lists the choices you made in the wizard. Click Finish to complete the delegation.

See Chapter 5 for more on delegation of the authority and the Delegation of Control Wizard.

NOTE: The steps for delegating control of a domain are similar. Right-click the domain in Active Directory Users and Computers and choose Delegate Control. In Active Directory Sites and Servers, right-click a site and choose Delegate Control to delegate control of the site.

Moving Objects

Windows 2000 makes it easy to move objects between OUs or sites. You can even move some objects between domains. (You can't move domain controllers to other domains!)

To move an object to a different container in the Active Directory Users and Computers or Active Directory Sites and Services utility, follow these steps:

1. Right-click the object. Choose Move in the context menu.

2. In the Move dialog box, choose a new container for the object. Click OK.

NOTE: The MoveTree utility, in the Windows 2000 Support Tools, lets you move OUs between domains.

Demoting a Domain Controller

If you run dcpromo on a computer that is already an Active Directory domain controller, you can demote the domain controller to a member server. To demote a domain controller, follow these steps:

1. On the Active Directory domain controller you wish to demote, click the Start button, and choose Run. In the Run dialog box, enter **dcpromo**.

2. The Active Directory Installation Wizard welcomes you and announces that if you continue, you will demote this domain controller to a member server. Click Next.

3. The wizard asks if the domain controller is the last domain controller in the domain. (If so, the wizard will delete the whole domain as well as demoting the domain controller. If this is the last domain controller, check the box provided. Click Next.

4. Enter the password for the server's Administrator account. Confirm the password.

5. The wizard tells you it is about to demote the domain controller and gives you a last chance to change your mind. Click Next if you wish to continue. The computer is demoted to a member server.

SUMMARY

This chapter assembled and highlighted some of the important factors you'll need to consider when you plan your Active Directory network. The planning, testing, and pilot phases are very important for a successful migration to Active Directory. As you plan and test your own network, you'll build on the information in this chapter to create a custom plan for deploying Active Directory in your own environment.

CHAPTER 8

Managing
Active Directory

BACKING UP AND RESTORING THE ACTIVE DIRECTORY

The backup plan for your network should include a plan for backing up your Active Directory database files. Windows 2000 backs up the necessary directory files (and other files essential for recovering the current configuration, such as Registry files) into what Microsoft calls the System State. When you perform a system backup using Windows 2000's Backup utility, select the System State option to back up the Active Directory and related components.

The contents of a System State backup are as follows:

▼ System startup files

■ Registry

■ COM class registrations

■ DNS data

■ Cluster service data

■ Certificate service data

■ File replication service data (including the SysVol directory)

■ Active Directory files:

   ■ **Ntds.dit**   The Active Directory database file

   ■ **Edb.chk**   Checkpoint file

   ■ **Edb*.log**   Transaction logs

   ■ **Res1.log and Res2.log**   Reserved transaction logs

The Backup utility included with Windows 2000 is capable of performing live backups. In other words, you can back up Active Directory when the directory is online. However, Windows 2000's Backup utility supports only local backup. A Windows 2000 domain controller using the built-in Backup utility can back up only its own directory replica. It can back the data up to a network share, but the backup itself must be run locally.

You can back up the Active Directory through a normal backup only. In other words, the Backup utility backs up the entire backup collection (including the entire Active Directory) and the archive attribute is cleared. You cannot back up the System State in an incremental backup.

NOTE: If the NT experience is any indication, third-party backup utilities will emerge that address the shortcomings of the built-in Backup tool, such as the lack of support for network backup of the Active Directory.

Microsoft identifies the following primary methods for restoring the Active Directory. These methods are discussed in later sections.

▼ **Replication restore**   Reinstall Windows 2000 and Active Directory and put the domain controller back online. The normal replication process (described in Chapter 4 "Understanding Replication," will update the directory to the current state.

■ **Nonauthoritative restore**   Restore the directory from a System State backup. The normal replication process (as described in Chapter 4) will update the local directory with all changes that have occurred since the time of the backup.

▲ **Authoritative restore**   Restore the directory from a System State backup. Mark directory settings from the backup set that you wish to protect from directory replication overwrites. The normal replication process (as described in Chapter 4) will update the local directory, except that any settings you marked in the restored local directory will not be overwritten by updates.

To back up Active Directory, you must be an administrator or a member of the Backup Operators group. To restore Active Directory on a Windows 2000 computer, you must be a member of the local Administrators group for the Windows 2000 computer.

If you are restoring Active Directory from backup media (a nonauthoritative or authoritative restore), you must boot Windows 2000 into directory services restore mode (as described in the later section titled "Nonauthoritative Restore"). Directory services restore mode prevents replication and keeps the directory inaccessible to the network. When you are certain the directory is restored successfully, reboot the domain controller in normal mode to resume normal operation.

The process of restoring from backup media is roughly as follows:

1. If necessary, re-create the disk configuration of the domain controller. (The restore operation attempts to put the Active Directory in the same directory where it was before.)

2. Boot the computer to Directory Services Restore mode.

3. Perform a restore operation (as described in the later section titled "Nonauthoritative Restore").

4. Perform additional operations if you are performing an authoritative restore. Those operations may include marking directory attributes for protection from replication updates or restoring the directory a second time to an alternative location (for authoritative restore of the SysVol folder). See the later section titled "Authoritative Backup."

5. Reboot in normal mode to resume operation.

NOTE: The System State restore operation automatically causes the domain controller to receive a new GUID. This is necessary to ensure an orderly transition of the replication process (described in Chapter 4) to include the domain controller. Otherwise, the USN sequencing process, which is used to impose version control on the replication process, may produce discontinuities that could lead to loss of data.

Backing Up System State Data

To perform a System State backup (which includes a backup of the Active Directory), follow these steps:

1. Select Start | Programs | Accessories | System Tools | Backup.

2. In the Backup utility, select the Backup tab.

Active Directory
Blueprints

Table of Contents

Active Directory Referral 2

Replication and Directory Partitions 4

Kerberos Authentication 6

Group Policy Process 8

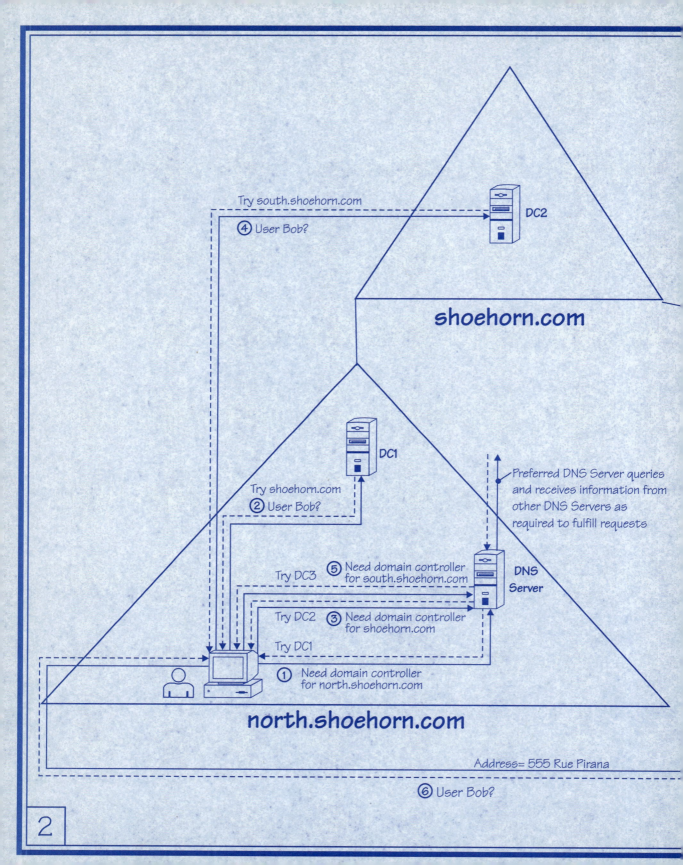

Try south.shoehorn.com

④ User Bob?

DC2

shoehorn.com

DC1

Try shoehorn.com

② User Bob?

Preferred DNS Server queries
and receives information from
other DNS Servers as
required to fulfill requests

⑤ Need domain controller
for south.shoehorn.com

Try DC3

DNS
Server

Try DC2   ③ Need domain controller
for shoehorn.com

Try DC1

① Need domain controller
for north.shoehorn.com

north.shoehorn.com

Address= 555 Rue Pirana

⑥ User Bob?

2

Active Directory
Referral Process

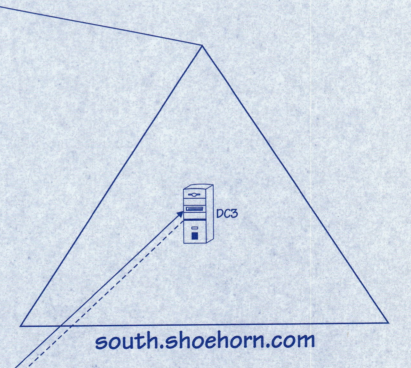

DC3

south.shoehorn.com

Intrasite Replication

- All domain controllers participate

Domain A   Domain B

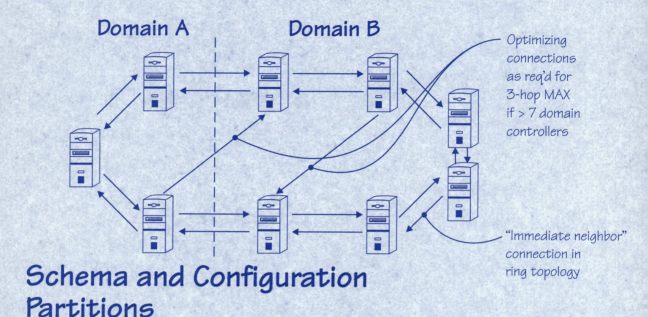

Optimizing connections as req'd for 3-hop MAX if > 7 domain controllers

"Immediate neighbor" connection in ring topology

Schema and Configuration Partitions

Domain A   Domain B

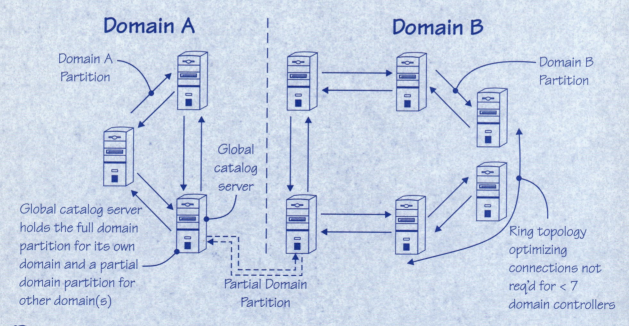

Domain A Partition

Domain B Partition

Global catalog server

Global catalog server holds the full domain partition for its own domain and a partial domain partition for other domain(s)

Partial Domain Partition

Ring topology optimizing connections not req'd for < 7 domain controllers

Domain Partition

Directory Partitions

- **Schema Partition**. Defines the structure of the Active Directory database. Replicated throughout forest.

- **Configuration Partition**. Defines the structure of the network (domains, sites, domain controllers, and services). Replicated throughout forest.

- **Domain Partition** (one per domain). Provides domain object data. Replicated within the domain only.

- **Partial Domain Partition** (one per domain). Provides a subset of domain object data for global catalog lookups. Replicated to all global catalog servers in the forest.

Intersite Replication

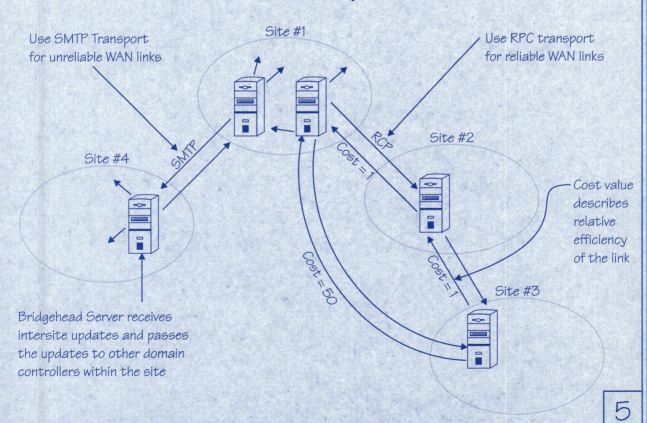

Use SMTP Transport for unreliable WAN links

Use RPC transport for reliable WAN links

Site #1

Site #2

Site #3

Site #4

SMTP

RCP

Cost = 1

Cost = 50

Cost = 1

Cost value describes relative efficiency of the link

Bridgehead Server receives intersite updates and passes the updates to other domain controllers within the site

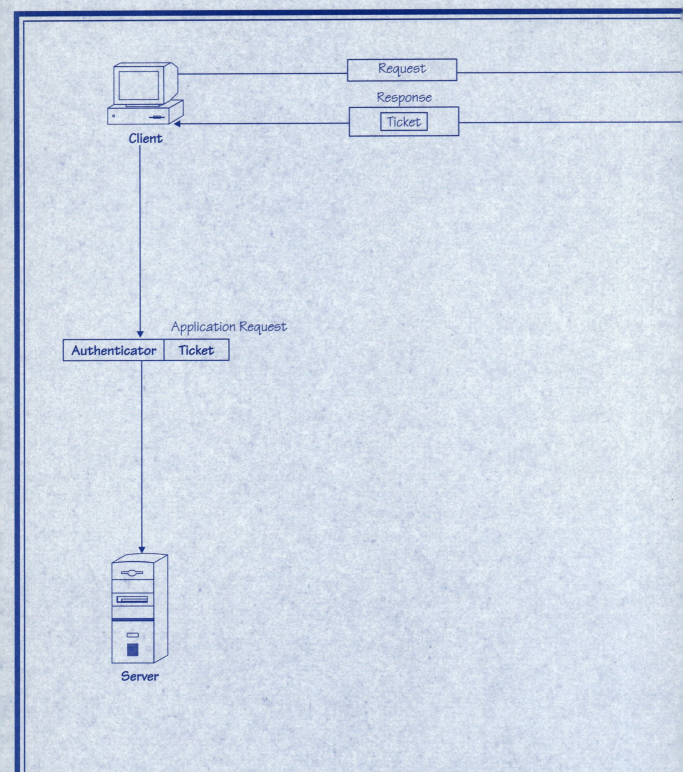

Request

Response

Ticket

Client

Application Request

Authenticator	Ticket

Server

6

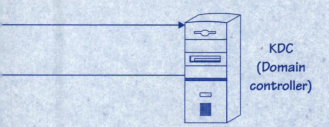

KDC
(Domain
controller)

Kerboros
Authentication

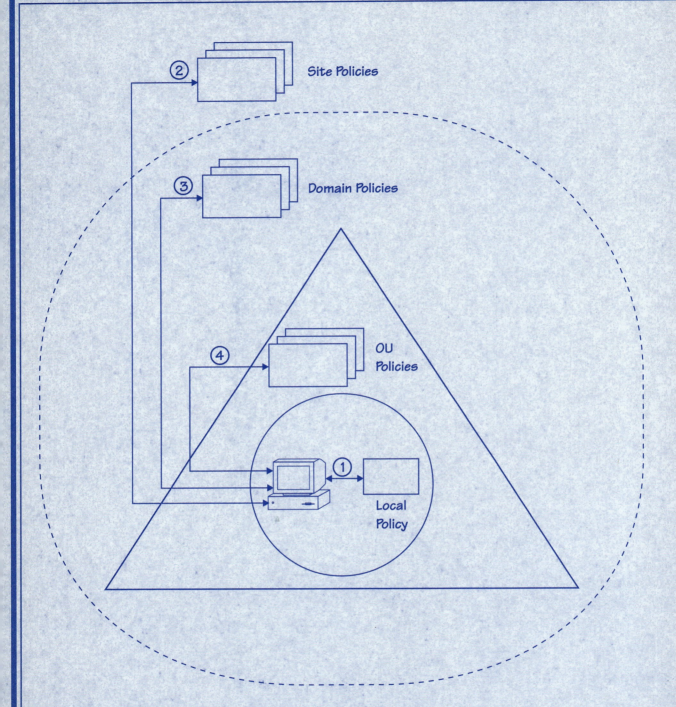

② Site Policies

③ Domain Policies

④ OU Policies

① Local Policy

Group Policy Process

Local policy is processed first, and
then policies for the site, domain, and OU

3. In the Backup tab (see Figure 8-1), check the box beneath the My Computer icon labeled System State.

4. Add additional files and directories if desired.

5. Select the backup media or filename.

6. Click Start Backup to begin the backup operation.

Replication Restore

Because the Active Directory replication ring is itself a fault-tolerant system, it is possible to restore the Active Directory by simply letting replication run its course. If a domain controller experiences a catastrophic failure, you can simply reinstall Windows 2000 and Active Directory and place the domain controller back online. The directory replication process will bring the domain controller's directory to the current state. This may, however, cause quite a lot

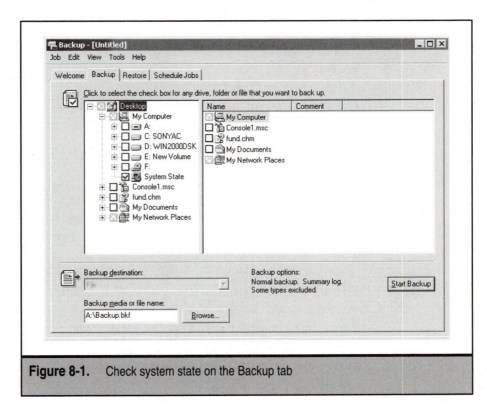

Figure 8-1. Check system state on the Backup tab

of replication and may take some time. This method also does not preserve other System State data (such as Registry data and DNS service information).

Nonauthoritative Restore

A nonauthoritative restore restores the Active Directory files and other System State data from backup media and then lets the replication process update the local database with any changes that have occurred since the backup.

To restore the directory from backup media, follow these steps:

1. Start the domain controller.

2. When the boot menu asks you to choose an operating system, press F8.

3. In the next menu, choose Directory Services Restore mode. Press ENTER.

4. Log on to an administrative account that is stored on the local SAM database. You may recall that when you first installed Active Directory on the domain controller, you were asked to specify a password for recovering the directory in Directory Services Restore mode. Specify that password now.

5. Choose Start | Run. In the Run dialog box, type **ntbackup**.

6. In the Tools menu, select Restore Wizard.

7. Follow the instructions in the Restore Wizard. Be sure the backup media is online. Select the backup set you wish to restore. When prompted, choose to restore the System State.

NOTE: The restore operation places the system data in its original place in the Windows 2000 directory by default. You can change the restore directory for some components of the System State backup using the Advanced option in the last screen of the Restore Wizard. This alternative restore location option does not work for restoring Active Directory itself or for restores of COM registrations or certificate services.

Microsoft recommends that you verify the nonauthoritative restore operation by checking whether the applicable services (Active Directory, certificate services, and so forth) are functioning properly. You can also perform what Microsoft calls an *advanced* verification of the Active Directory by checking to see if a value is set for the RestoreInProgress entry in the Registry subtree HKEY_LOCAL_MACHINE\SYSTEM\CurrentControlSet\Services\NTDS.

You need to look for this entry before you reboot the domain controller to normal mode. The RestoreInProgress setting is set after a restore operation, and the setting is removed when the operation completes on reboot to normal mode.

TIP: The Ntdsutil utility (described in the next section) also provides the option of displaying information on the success of a restore operation.

The preceding procedure performs a nonauthoritative restore. It restores the directory to the state that it was in at the time of the backup. Once the domain controller is back online, the replication process will update the domain controller with changes that have happened since the backup. Sometimes, however, you may not *want* to update the domain controller with all the changes that have happened since the backup. (For instance, you may be restoring the directory because a network administrator inadvertently deleted 400 users and you wouldn't want the replication process to update the domain controller with the change that deleted the 400 users.) Microsoft provides an option for an authoritative restore, which lets you protect specific attributes so they won't be overwritten in the subsequent replication update process.

TIP: The restore process works best when you're restoring to the original computer. If you are restoring Active Directory to a different computer, make sure the disk drive configuration is the same. Microsoft also states that if you suspect the new computer has different hardware from the original computer (especially, a new video adapter or network adapter), uninstall the hardware before restoring Active Directory. When you reboot, the components will be reinstalled through plug and play. See the Windows 2000 Resource Kit Books Online.

Authoritative Restore

When a restore operation completes, the Active Directory replication process brings the local directory replica up-to-date with the current state of the directory. In some cases, though, this may not be what you want to do. If, for instance, some important Active Directory component was deleted and that is why you're performing the restoration, letting the local directory reach equilibrium with the current network state would have the effect of deleting the component all over again and making the restoration completely pointless. (It would be interesting to know the details of the moment in which Microsoft first discovered this phenomenon.)

Microsoft lets you mark specific Active Directory attributes so that they will not be overridden by the directory updates that follow a restore operation. This is known as an authoritative restore.

To perform an authoritative restore, follow these steps:

1. Perform a nonauthoritative restore (as described in the preceding section "Nonauthoritative Restore").

2. When the domain controller is still in directory services mode, go to the command prompt and type **ntdsutil**.

3. Ntdsutil starts. At the ntdsutil: prompt, type **authoritative restore**.

4. If you wish to perform an authoritative restore of the whole directory, type **restore database**. If you want only one subtree of the directory to be marked for authoritative restore, type **restore subtree** and enter the distinguished name of the subtree you wish to mark for authoritative restore.

5. Mark additional subtrees as necessary. When you are finished with ntdsutil, type **quit**.

TIP: The ntdsutil's *restore database* and *restore subtree* commands support an optional verinc option that lets you specify an increase value for attribute version numbers: restore database verinc <increase#>. If you don't specify a version number increase, ntdsutil applies an increase automatically.

Note that the preceding process lets you mark only items that are in Active Directory. Active Directory also uses the SysVol folder to hold group policy objects and directory-related files. The SysVol folder is itself subject to the replication process, so if you want to perform an authoritative restore of SysVol, you must do the following:

1. Perform a nonauthoritative restore.

2. Perform a nonauthoritative restore a second time to a different location.

3. Mark any directory objects you wish to select for authoritative restore.

4. Reboot into normal mode.

5. Once the SysVol folder is published on the domain controller, copy the SysVol folder (or any specific files, such as policy files, that you wish to make authoritative) from the alternative location to the domain controller's SysVol share.

Microsoft points out that if you're performing an authoritative restore on objects that are accompanied by passwords, the password will be reset to the older value. The user is, therefore, forced to remember his or her old password. Also, however, there may be more subtle effects of resetting passwords in the directory. Network connections and other features that use passwords stored on the user's workstation may suddenly be inoperable. Kerberos authentication and domain trust relationships may also be affected.

TIP: The ntdsutil utility also performs a number of other directory maintenance functions. For additional ntdsutil commands, type **ntdsutil /?** at the command prompt.

Modifying the Directory

The easiest way to modify an Active Directory object is to make a change to the object through one of the Active Directory management tools (such as Active Directory Users and Computers or Active Directory

Domains and Trusts). You'll learn about these tools throughout this book. Windows 2000 includes a few special tools that are designed for viewing and modifying directory contents. These tools include the following:

▼ ADSI Editor

■ LDP

■ CSVDE

▲ LDIFDE

You'll learn about these directory management tools in the following sections.

ADSI Editor

ADSI Editor is a tool that lets you browse the partitions of the Active Directory and directly edit Active Directory objects. You can use ADSI Editor to edit attribute settings for Active Directory objects.

ADSI Editor provides a uniform, hierarchical means of viewing and modifying Active Directory settings. However, you shouldn't use ADSI Editor for routine changes to the Active Directory, such as a new user account or new trust relationship. Management tools such as Active Directory Users and Computers and Active Directory Domains and Trusts offer a simpler and more fail-safe method for updating routine directory settings. However, the Active Directory management tools do not necessarily provide you with access to *all* directory settings. Also, the management tools are designed to operate closer to the human side of the interface. You don't always know the name or syntax of the attribute you're configuring. The ADSI Editor is much more like an actual window into the Active Directory. You get a very uncluttered view of the directory contents. ADSI Editor is designed for configuring attribute settings that aren't accessible from other user interface tools. The Windows 2000 online help occasionally makes reference to settings that can be configured through ADSI Editor.

NOTE: As the Windows 2000 world develops, it is possible that ADSI Editor will serve a role similar to the Registry Editor: you'll use it to change very specific, obscure settings that you heard about in a tip from Microsoft.

ADSI Editor is part of the Windows 2000 support tools set. See Chapter 7, "Setting Up Active Directory," for more on how to install the Windows 2000 Support Tools. Once you have installed the Windows 2000 support tools, you can reach ADSI Editor by selecting Start I Programs I Windows 2000 Support Tools I Tools I ADSI Edit.

To add ADSI Editor to Microsoft Management Console, follow these steps:

1. Choose Start I Run.

2. Type **mmc** in the Run dialog box and click OK.

3. In the Microsoft Management Console main window, select the Console menu and choose Add/Remove Snap-In.

4. In the Add/Remove Snap-In dialog box, click the Add button.

5. In the Add Standalone Snap-In dialog box, select ADSI Edit and click the Add button. Then click the Close button.

6. ADSI Edit should appear in the Add/Remove Snap-In dialog box. Click OK.

7. ADSI Edit should appear in the Microsoft Management Console main window. To save the console, select the Console menu, choose Save As, and enter a name for the console.

TIP: You can also add ADSI Editor to an existing Microsoft Management Console instance.

ADSI Editor reflects the internal organization of the directory. To find an object, browse through the container hierarchy as it appears in a distinguished name. At the highest level are the directory partitions. Beneath the partitions are containers and OUs. You can add a specific directory partition to the ADSI Editor console so that it is available automatically the next time you open the console. You can also add a container or OU to the console for direct access from the ADSI Editor (so you don't have to browse for it). To make a partition, container, or OU available in ADSI Editor, you connect to it. If you access the ADSI Editor from the Start menu via the Windows 2000 support tools program group (Start | Programs | Windows 2000 Support Tools | Tools | ADSI Edit), the three directory partitions will appear automatically. If you access ADSI Editor through the Microsoft Management Console, you'll need to connect to the partitions you wish to view or edit. The following procedure assumes you're using the Management Console. The rules for using the ADSI Edit utility in the Windows 2000 Support Tools group are similar.

To view or modify attribute settings for an Active Directory object in ADSI Editor, follow these steps:

1. Click the ADSI Editor icon in Microsoft Management Console to see whether the partition or container you need is already installed in the ADSI Editor interface. If not, right-click the ADSI Edit icon and choose Connect To.

2. In the Connection dialog box (see Figure 8-2), enter the connection point and the domain or server to which you'd like to connect. The connecting point is the top-level subtree that will appear below the ADSI Editor icon in the console. Note that the radio button labeled Naming Context is selected by default. The naming context, in this case, is the Active Directory partition. Click the down arrow to select the domain, configuration, or schema partition. Alternatively, you can enter the distinguished name of a partition, container, or OU. The Select Or Type A Domain Or Server box lets you choose a different domain or domain controller from which to obtain the directory information. The Advanced button invokes the Advanced dialog box (see Figure 8-3), which lets you enter logon credentials and protocol access information for connecting to another server. Click OK when you have finished configuring the Connection dialog box.

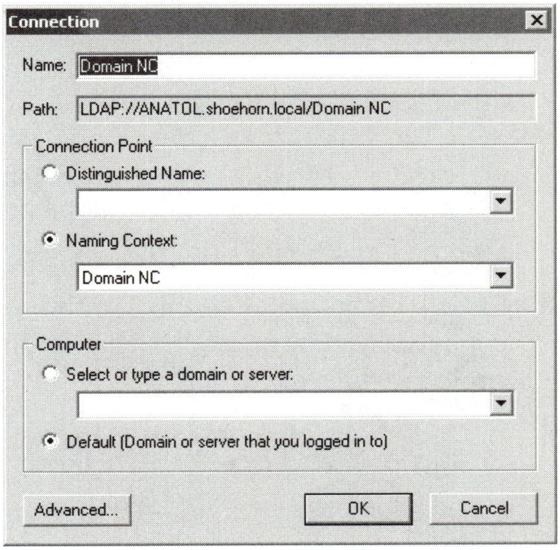

Figure 8-2. Enter connection point and domain in the Connection dialog box

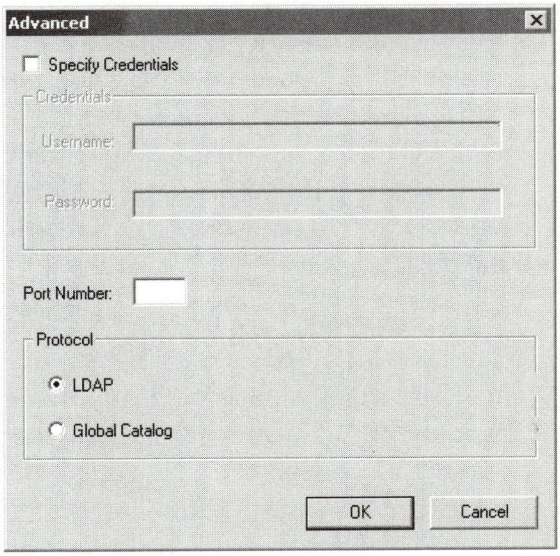

Figure 8-3. Enter logon credentials and protocol access information in the Advanced dialog box

3. The partition or container you select in step 2 appears below the ADSI Edit icon in the ADSI Editor console. Click the plus sign next to the partition to reveal a folder showing the distinguished name of the partition. Click the plus sign next to the Partition folder to reveal any containers or OUs within the partition. (If you choose the domain partition, the tree of containers and OUs is similar to the tree you see within Active Directory Users and Computers.)

4. Browse to the container that has the object whose properties you wish to view or modify. The contents of the container appear in the right pane.

5. Right-click the object whose properties you wish to view or modify. Select Properties. For example, to modify the attribute settings for a user account in the Users container, select the Users container and then right-click the account in the right pane and choose Properties.

6. The Object Properties dialog box appears. As far as ADSI Editor is concerned, the properties of an object are the values assigned to attributes associated with the object. (See Chapter 10, "Active Directory Schema," for more on Active Directory attributes and attribute syntax.) In the Object Properties Attributes tab (see Figure 8-4), click the arrow next to the Select Which Properties To View box to choose whether to view mandatory attributes, optional attributes, or both. Choose Both to have access to all attributes associated with the object.

7. The option you chose in step 6 (Mandatory, Optional, or Both) defines which attributes will appear in the drop-down list accessed from the Select A Property To View box. Choose an attribute from the drop-down list. The syntax of the attribute and the value assigned to the attribute for this object appear in the Attribute Values section (refer to Figure 8-4). To change the value, enter a new value in the Edit Attribute box and click the Set button.

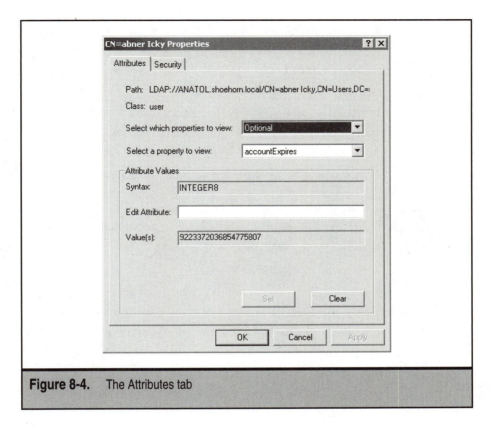

Figure 8-4.   The Attributes tab

8. Selecting the Security tab lets you configure security for the directory object.

9. When you have finished viewing or configuring the object's attribute settings, click OK.

To add an object using ADSI Editor, follow these steps:

1. In ADSI Editor, browse to the container or OU in which you will add the object. (If the partition or container doesn't appear, see steps 1 and 2 of the preceding procedure.)

2. Right-click the container for the icon and choose New | Object.

3. A wizard starts and asks you to choose a class for the object. Select the object class and choose Next. (See Chapter 10 for more on classes and attributes.)

4. Subsequent wizard screens ask you to enter values for any attributes associated with the class.

To delete an object in ADSI Editor, follow these steps:

1. In ADSI Editor, browse to the object you wish to delete. (If the partition or container that contains the object doesn't appear, see steps 1 and 2 of the preceding procedure.)

2. Right-click the object you wish to delete and choose Delete.

NOTE: For information on editing the Active Directory schema using ADSI Editor, see Chapter 10.

LDP

Ldp.exe is an even lower-level LDAP tool than ADSI Editor. Ldp is designed to perform LDAP protocol operations. You can use Ldp to search for, modify, and delete LDAP records, including Active Directory records. However, you'd better be comfortable working with distinguished names if you're going to use Ldp. Most options require you to enter the distinguished name of the object you wish to find or modify. Ldp gives every indication of being a generic LDAP editor. You could forget you're working in Windows, except that it does offer the option of viewing object security descriptors and replication meta-data.

Ldp is one of the Windows 2000 support tools. (See Chapter 7 for a discussion of how to install Windows 2000 support tools.) Once you have installed the support tools, you can start Ldp from the command prompt (type **ldp**). You can also start Ldp from the Run dialog box (Start | Run, then enter **ldp** in the Run dialog box).The Ldp main window is shown in Figure 8-5. Ldp uses generic RFC-based terminology for LDAP operations.

Here's a short summary of important terms:

▼ **Connect** An operation that connects to an LDAP database. In the case of Active Directory, you are connecting to a domain controller. You can connect only to one database

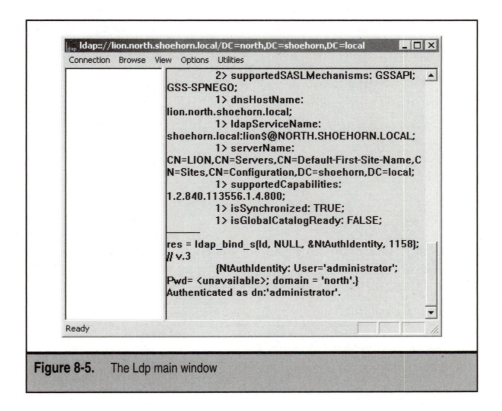

Figure 8-5. The Ldp main window

at a time. To connect to a database, choose Connect from the
Connection menu. Ldp will prompt for the name of the server.
Note that you can enter a port for the connect request. Port
389 is the default LDAP port. The default port for the Active
Directory global catalog is 3268.

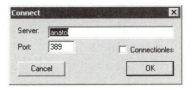

■ **Disconnect** An operation that terminates an LDAP
connection. In Ldp, you must disconnect from the current
connection before you can form a new connection. To
disconnect, choose Disconnect from the Connection menu.

▲ **Bind** An LDAP bind operation is basically an authentication. Select Bind from the Ldp Connection menu to send credentials for a connection to another domain. If the username and password are left blank in the Bind dialog box, the current credentials are used for the connection.

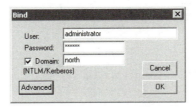

Once you have established a connection, the most common LDAP operations are accessible from the Browse menu. Table 8-1 shows the options of the LDP Browse menu and their meaning.

Command	Description
Add	Lets you add an object to the directory. Be ready to enter the distinguished name for the new object and any attribute values (see Figure 8-8). Type in an attribute name and attribute value, then press ENTER to add the value to the entry list. You can also edit or remove existing attribute values. See Chapter 10 for more on attributes in Active Directory.
Delete	Lets you delete an object. You must enter the full distinguished name. If the object is a container, the Recursive option deletes child objects and containers.
Modify	Lets you modify values assigned to an existing object. The options are similar to those in the Add dialog box (see Figure 8-6).

Table 8-1. Ldp Browse Menu Commands

Command	Description
ModifyRdn	Deleting the relative distinguished name (RDN) of an object requires a special operation in LDAP. Use this option to rename an object or to move an object to a new container.
Search	Lets you search for an object. You must use a valid LDAP filter. The search base defines the container that you are searching.
Compare	Lets you check the value of an attribute for an object. You enter the distinguished name of the object, the attribute, and the value to which the setting will be compared. The operation returns True (if the value you enter is the same as the attribute setting) or False.
Extend Op	Lets you submit an extended LDAP operation.
Security	Lets you view the security descriptor for an object.
Replication	Displays replication meta-data for the object. See Chapter 4.
Process Pending	Lets you view, execute, remove, or abandon pending processes.

Table 8-1.   Ldp Browse Menu Commands *(continued)*

LDIFDE

The LDIFDE tool lets you export Active Directory objects to an export file and import Active Directory objects from an import file. (LDIFDE stands for LDAP Data Interchange Format Data Exchange.) LDIFDE is designed for batch directory import and export operations and is therefore a good choice for situations in which you must move multiple objects at once.

Since LDIFDE's export operation is really just a form of file-based output, LDIFDE is actually a very powerful tool for searching and

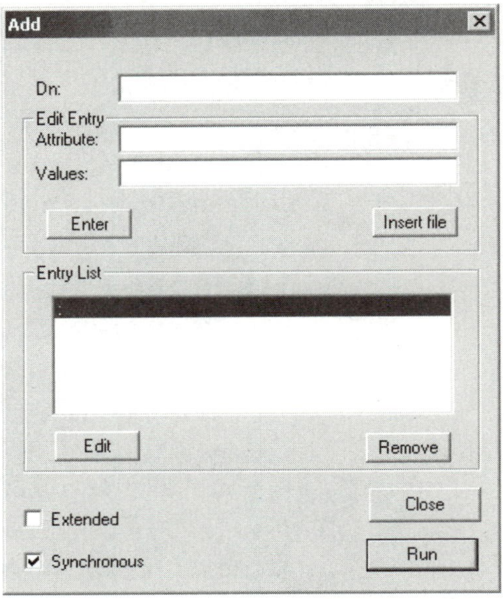

Figure 8-6. LDP Add dialog box

filtering Active Directory object data. You can use LDIFDE, for instance, to output a list of the phone numbers for all users in a specific container or to find all object settings for a user named *Smith*. On a large scale, you can use LDIFDE to export a large number of users from one domain and import them into another. The –c option even lets you convert the distinguished name of the object as it is imported to the new location.

LDIFDE runs from the command prompt. Each command imports or exports to a text file in LDIF format. The command syntax is

LDIFDE *option1 option1_data option2 option2_data...*

The options are nothing more than DOS-like command switches, as described in Table 8-2. The long list of command line options makes it appear that LDIFDE is vastly complicated, but it isn't too bad. Most of the switches are optional. You do need to specify a filename (with the –f options) and, for exports, you'll most likely need to specify the distinguished name of the search base with the –d option.

Category	Option	Description
General Options	-i	Specifies the import mode (otherwise, export mode is used).
	-f	Filename of the file to which the data will be exported or from which the data will be imported.
	-s	Server name of domain controller to use for the operation.
	-c	Changes the distinguished name; followed by the old distinguished name and the new distinguished name.
	-t	Port number (the default is default LDAP port 389).
	-v	Verbose mode.
	-?	Help.
Export Options	-d	Distinguished name of the search base (the container to which the search will apply).
	-g	No paged search. If not specified, searches will be paged.
	-j	Location of log file (default is the current directory).
	-l	Attribute list. Specifies which attributes to return. If omitted, the search will return all attributes for the found object.
	-m	Omits attributes that apply only to Active Directory objects (as opposed to other LDAP directories)— for instance, objectGUID, objectSID, samAccountType.
	-n	Omits binary values.

Table 8-2.   LDIFDE Command Options

Category	Option	Description
	-o	Omits a list of attributes (this is the opposite of the –l option).
	-p	Sets the scope of the search (values are Base, OneLevel, or SubTree—SubTree is the default).
	-r	Specifies an LDAP filter.
	-u	Enables Unicode.
	-y	Enables lazy commit to the directory.
Import Option	-k	Causes LDIFDE to skip error messages.
Security-Related Options	-a	Lets you specify a username and password for the command to run under. The username should be a user-distinguished name in quotes. Use the * option to hide the password (default is for the command to run under the current user's credentials).
	-b	Lets you specify a username and password for the command to run under. Use username domain password format. Use * to hide the password.

Table 8-2.   LDIFDE Command Options *(continued)*

TIP: When you type in a distinguished name, you may be tempted to place a leading blank after a comma. Don't do it; the command won't work.

Some LDIF examples are as follows:

```
ldifde -f output.out
```

outputs the current domain to the file output.out.

```
ldifde -i -f input.in
```

inputs the file input.in

```
ldifde -f exp.ldf -d cn=users,dc=shoehorn,dc=local
```

exports the users container for the domain shoehorn.local to the file exp.ldf. By default, subcontainers are included. To exclude subcontainers, use the –p Base option.

```
ldifde -f exp.ldf -d cn=users,dc=shoehorn,dc=local -l
-homedirectory,telephoneNumber-
```

exports the homedirectory and telephoneNumber attributes for objects in the users container of the domain shoehorn.local. The object's distinguished name will also be listed with the homedirectory and telephoneNumber attributes.

NOTE: Data is imported and exported to an LDIF file. LDIF is a generic text file format used in other LDAP implementations as well as Active Directory. LDIF format consists of the object's distinguished name followed by a series of attribute/value pairs. In some LDAP implementations, it is common to create LDIF files from scratch and then import them directly into the database. It's also possible to create LDIF files manually in the Active Directory environment, but most common Active Directory object types include mandatory security attributes, such as the object's security identifier (SID). Most of the attributes associated with a user, for instance, are fairly easy to reproduce in text file format, but you'd still need some way of generating an objectGUID and object SID.

CSVDE

Despite the interoperability of Windows 2000, Microsoft is still reluctant to give up its parallel universe. As you might expect, Microsoft uses a modified version of LDIF format for exporting to applications such as Excel. Comma-Separated Value file format (CSV) can be read by many applications, but it isn't as readily written or read by non-Microsoft LDAP servers. CVS uses a comma-separated data format.

The CSVDE tool imports from and exports to CVS files. CVSDE is a command-line tool. The command options for CVSDE are the same as those for LDIFDE (see Table 8-2). CSVDE is a useful tool if you would like to export Active Directory data into an application such as an Excel spreadsheet for sorting or processing.

MANAGING FILES AND FOLDERS IN ACTIVE DIRECTORY

The Active Directory environment offers many options and tools for managing file resources. Many of these options, such as configuring security, compression, and file sharing, have little to do with Active Directory and are primarily basic Windows administration tasks. The following sections discuss a few file management tricks related to Active Directory, including the following:

▼ Folder publication

▲ File-related group policies

Publishing Folders

Not all Windows 2000 objects are Active Directory objects. Shared folders, for example, are not automatically placed in the Active Directory. However, it is possible to create an entry in the Active Directory for a shared resource such as a shared folder. This is called *publishing* the resource. Publishing a shared folder makes the folder appear in Active Directory searches. Information on the resource is replicated across the network through Active Directory replication, and LDAP clients can retrieve information on the resource. Also, you can manage the resource through Active Directory interface tools such as Active Directory Users and Computers.

To publish a folder in the Active Directory, follow these steps:

1. Make sure the folder is shared on the network. (Right-click the folder in Windows Explorer or My Computer and choose Sharing.)

2. Select Start | Programs | Administrative Tools | Active Directory Users and Computers.

3. Right-click the domain, container, or OU where you would like to place the Active Directory object representing the shared resource and choose New | Shared Folder.

4. In the New Object dialog box (see Figure 8-7), enter the name for the folder as you would like to see it appear in the Active Directory. Enter the UNC path to the folder. Click OK.

5. An icon for the published folder object appears in the container you chose in step 3. To configure additional settings, right-click the Published Folder icon and choose Properties.

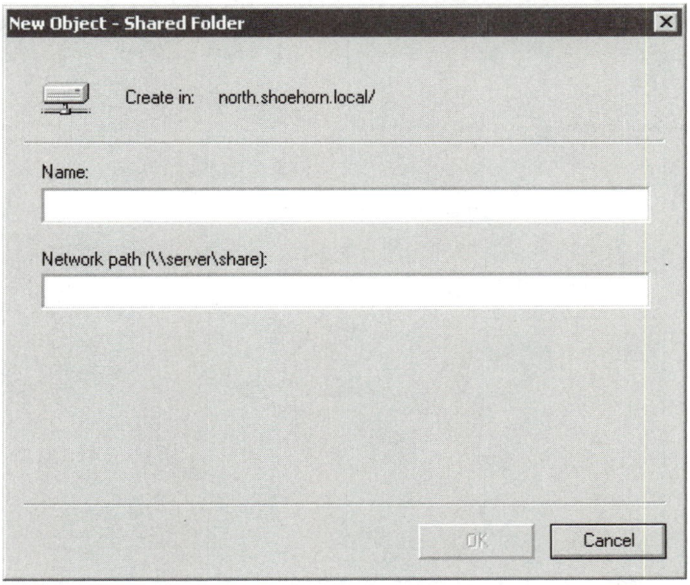

Figure 8-7.   The New Object dialog box

The Properties dialog box is shown in Figure 8-8. Note that you can click the Keywords button to enter keywords that will be associated with the folder for keyword-based directory searches.

Once you have published a folder in Active Directory, you can search for and manage the folder through Active Directory User and Computers.

To find a published folder, follow these steps:

1. Select Start | Programs | Administrative Tools | Active Directory Users And Computers.

2. In the Active Directory Users And Computers main window, right-click a domain, container, or OU and choose Find.

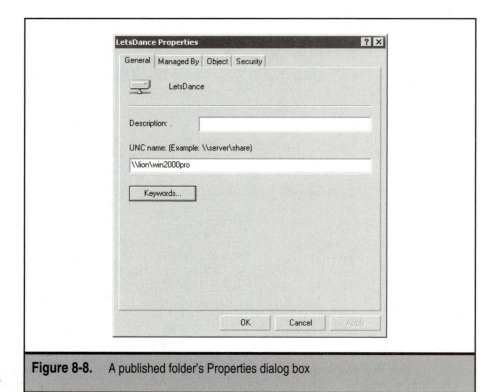

Figure 8-8. A published folder's Properties dialog box

3. In the Find Shared Folders dialog box (see Figure 8-9), click the arrow next to the Find box and select Shared Folders. The container you selected in step 2 should appear in the In box. To search the whole domain, a different domain, or the entire directory, click the down arrow and choose the desired search option. Click the Browse button to choose another Active Directory container OU.

4. In the Named box (refer to Figure 8-9) enter the Active Directory name of the shared folder. Alternatively, enter one or more keywords associated with the shared folder. (Now see step 5 of the preceding procedure.)

5. To begin the search, click Find Now.

Managing Files and Folders through Group Policy

Active Directory lets you extend some of Windows 2000's file management features through the application of group policy. Those features include the following:

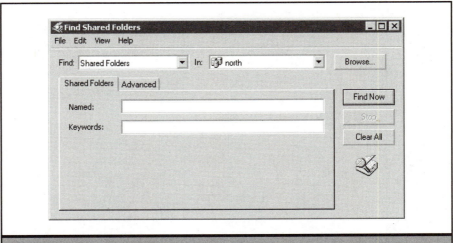

Figure 8-9.   The Find Shared Folders dialog box

▼ **Offline Files** A feature that lets you continue to work with network files even when you are disconnected from the network.

■ **Disk Quotas** A feature that manages disk space usage for NTFS volumes.

▲ **Windows File Protection** A feature that monitors attempts to overwrite Windows system files, checks the signature of the new file version, and acts accordingly to protect the system files if necessary.

These features are built into Windows 2000 and are not Active Directory features. However, you can use Active Directory group policies to manage these features on your network. See Windows 2000 help for additional information on offline files, disks, quotas, and Windows file protection. Offline file policy settings are available through the Group Policy Editor in Computer Configuration\ Administrative Templates\Network\Offline Files and User Configuration\Administrative Templates\Network\Offline files. Disk quota and Windows file protection policies are available through Computer Configuration\Administrative Templates\System. Table 8-3 shows group policy settings related to disk quotas and Windows file protection.

Location	Policy	Description
Computer Configuration\Administrative Templates\System\Disk Quotas	Enable disk quotas	Enables disk quota management for NTFS volumes. Prevents users from disabling disk quota management.
	Enforce disk quota limit	Enables enforcement of disk quota limits.
	Default quota limit and warning level	Lets you set a default disk quota limit.

Table 8-3. Group Policy Settings for Disk Quotas and Windows File Protection

Location	Policy	Description
	Log event when quota limit is exceeded	Specifies that an event will be logged to the local application log when a user reaches a quota limit.
	Log event when quota warning level is exceeded	Specifies that an event will be logged to the local application log when a user reaches a quota warning level.
	Apply policy to removable media	Specifies that disk quota policies will apply to removable media as well as permanent media.
Computer Configuration\Administrative Templates\System\Windows File Protection	Set Windows file protection scanning	Lets you set a scanning frequency for scanning Windows system files.
	Hide the file Scan Progress window	Hides the Scan Progress window during scan.
	Limit file protection cache size	Sets the maximum disk space for the cache used by Windows file protection.
	Specify Windows file protection cache location	Specifies the location of the Windows file protection cache.

Table 8-3.   Group Policy Settings for Disk Quotas and Windows File Protection
(continued)

NOTE: See Chapter 6, "Group Policy," for more on using group policy in the Active Directory environment.

MANAGING PRINTERS IN ACTIVE DIRECTORY

Printers, like folders, can be published in the Active Directory and located through Active Directory search features. Windows 2000 computers use Active Directory to maintain the printer list and locate printers. Pre–Windows 2000 print browse master features are used to support pre–Windows 2000 clients. Active Directory domain controllers check periodically to ensure that published printers are online and, if not, remove the printers from the active list. This process is known as *pruning*.

To publish a Windows 2000 printer in the Active Directory:

1. Select Start | Settings | Printers.

2. In the Printers window, right-click the printer you wish to publish in the Active Directory and choose Sharing.

3. The Printer Properties dialog box appears with the Sharing tab in the foreground. If the printer is not already shared on the network, click Share As and enter a share name for the printer. Check the List In The Directory box.

To publish a pre–Windows 2000 printer in the Active Directory:

1. Select Start | Programs | Administrative Tools | Active Directory Users And Computers.

2. Right-click the domain, container, or OU where you would like to place the Active Directory object representing the shared resource and choose New | Printer.

3. In the New Object dialog box, enter the UNC path to the pre–Windows 2000 printer. Click OK.

You can manage several printer configuration settings through group policy. Printer-related group policy settings are shown in Table 8-4. Note that some of these settings apply specifically to printer publication. If you are not able to publish printers, or if printers are getting published automatically when you don't expect them to, check the chain of group policy objects to ensure that policy settings are not interfering with your desired configuration.

Location	Policy	Description
Computer Configuration\Administrative Templates\Printers	Allow printers to be published	Printers can be published in Active Directory unless you disable this option.
	Automatically publish new printers in Active Directory	Windows 2000 Server publishes shared printers automatically unless you disable this option.
	Allow pruning of published printers	Domain controllers can delete the published printer from Active Directory if the host computer does not respond unless this option is disabled.
	Printer browsing	Specifies whether the printer will be listed with print browse masters.
	Prune printers that are not automatically republished	Pre–Windows 2000 computers do not know how to republish their printers when they come back online. This policy configures a method for pruning pre–Windows 2000 printers.
	Directory pruning interval	Specifies interval for checking whether printers are online and pruning those that aren't.
	Directory pruning retry	Specifies how many times to try to contact the printer server computer before pruning the printer.
	Directory pruning priority	Lets you configure the system priority for printer pruning processes.
	Check published state	Specifies a time interval for checking to see whether published printers are online.

Table 8-4.   Printer-Related Group Policy Settings

Location	Policy	Description
Computer Configuration\Administrative Templates\Printers	Web-based printing	Enables Internet printing.
	Custom support URL in the Printers folder's left pane	Gives link title and URL for printer support.
	Computer location	Overrides value used with Windows 2000 Printer Location Tracking feature.
	Prepopulate printer search location text	Enables printer location tracking.

Table 8-4.   Printer-Related Group Policy Settings *(continued)*

NOTE: By default, the Windows 2000 Server's Add Printer Wizard shares a new printer and adds it to the Active Directory unless you choose Do Not Share This Printer in the Add Printer Wizard. Windows 2000 Professional does not automatically share and publish printers.

Printer location tracking (refer to Table 8-4) is a useful feature of Windows 2000 that estimates the nearest printer for the user performing a search at a specific location. Printer location tracking is an example of a technology that shows what Microsoft is trying to do with Active Directory. The user can (basically) ask Windows 2000 to find the closest printer. You must enable printer location tracking using the Pre-Populate Printer Search Location Text Policy setting.

The basic idea behind printer location tracking is that you create a site for each location (say, each floor of a building) and associate a subnet with each site. You then create a standard naming convention for all the sites. If you plan to use printer location tracking, the location names should consist of one or more levels separated with

the slash (/) character—for instance, Europe/Spain/Madrid/Casa1.
Enter the location name in the Properties dialog box for the site in
Active Directory Sites and Services. Then enter the location name
for each printer in the Printer Properties dialog box. If printer location
tracking is enabled, you should be able to search for printers by location.

To search for a printer from a Windows 2000 computer, follow
these steps:

1. Select Start | Search | For Printers.

    The Find Printers window appears. Note that you can search for
    a printer by location. If you're using printer location tracking,
    enter the slash-separated location name for your present location.
    You can also search for a printer by name or model.

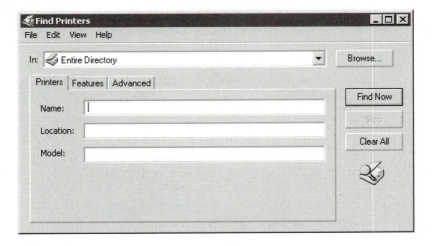

2. When you have entered the search criteria, click Find Now.

MANAGING SOFTWARE IN ACTIVE DIRECTORY

For many organizations, a large share of computer technology resources
is devoted to paying network administrators to walk around the
office installing software. The Active Directory environment lets you
deploy software from a central location through group policy. Like
other group policies, the software deployment policies can be applied

through group policy objects assigned to sites, domains, and OUs. You can therefore tailor the group policy interactions to meet your own preferences and the requirements of your network. (See Chapter 6 for more on how to create and apply group policies to sites, domains, and OUs.)

Active Directory's software deployment capabilities are the result of the interaction of group policy with Microsoft's Windows Installer feature. Microsoft intends to make versions of Windows Installer available to Windows NT and Windows 95/98 computers; however, since pre–Windows 2000 computers are not capable of using group policy, the range of automated deployment features described in this section is available only to computers using Windows 2000.

You can assign software installation policies through either the computer configuration or the user configuration. Software installation policies are located in the Computer Configuration\Software Settings\ Software Installation and User Configuration\Software Settings\ Software Installation policy containers. To deploy an application through a software installation policy, you must have a *package file* for the application. A package file is an installation file specially created to be used with the Windows Installer feature. Package files have an .msi extension. (A form of the package file designed to apply modifications to the .msi file has an .mst extension.) Many software packages come with (or will come with) Windows package files. Microsoft, for instance, includes several package files on the Windows 2000 Server CD, such as the .msi file used to install the Windows 2000 support tools (described in Chapter 7). Commercial applications are also available for creating packages. And you can also use a text file called a .zap file to deploy software if a package file is not available. See the later section titled "Creating a .zap File."

Microsoft defines the following classifications for deploying new software:

▼ **Assigning** Assigning an application places the application directly on the computer affected by the policy. If the application is assigned through computer policy, the application is installed automatically the next time the computer restarts. If the application is assigned through user policy, an icon for the application is placed on the desktop and in the Start menu.

The application appears to be installed, but it does not actually install until the user accesses the icon. If the user attempts to delete an assigned application after it is installed, the application will reinstall the next time the computer restarts or the user logs on.

▲ **Publishing**   Publishing an application makes the application available for the user to install but does not automatically advertise the application with desktop and Start menu icons. The user must deliberately open the Add/Remove Programs Control Panel to install the application.

You can assign an application through either computer or user policy, but you can publish an application only through the User Configuration Group Policy tree. Software installation policy also offers a number of other deployment options, such as upgrade, redeployment, and removal. You'll learn more about the following software deployment topics in upcoming sections:

▼ Assigning software

■ Publishing software

■ Creating a .zap file

▲ Configuring software installation file properties

See Chapter 6 for more on how to integrate these options into an overall group policy strategy.

Assigning Software

Assigning an application effectively places the application directly on the computer. You can assign software through either computer policy or user policy. If you assign the application through user policy, an icon for the application is placed on the desktop and in the Start menu, but the application does not actually install until a user attempts to access it for the first time. By waiting to install the application until the user attempts to access it, the installer minimizes the strain on network traffic and ensures that the user will not have to wait through the installation unless he or she actually needs to use the application. If you assign an application through computer policy, the application installs automatically the next time the computer starts.

TIP: The computer configuration assignment and user configuration assignment are each designed for different situations. If you want the application to be permanently available to all users on a computer, use computer configuration assignment. If you plan on deploying an application broadly across many computers, user configuration assignment may be more efficient because the application doesn't actually install unless a user needs it.

To assign a software package to a computer or user through group policy, follow these steps:

1. Open the group policy object to which you would like to add the software installation policy (see Chapter 6 for more on opening a group policy object and using Group Policy Editor).

2. In the Group Policy tree, browse to Computer Configuration\ Software Settings\Software Installation or User Configuration\ Software Settings\Software Installation (depending on whether you wish to assign the application through computer policy or group policy—as discussed earlier in this chapter).

3. Right-click the Software Installation icon and select New | Package.

4. In the Open dialog box, browse for the software package file you would like to assign. Typically, the package file will have an .msi extension. (You may not see the .msi extension, however, if the folder is configured to hide file extensions.) Select the file and click Open.

5. The Deploy Software dialog box asks you to choose a deployment method (Published, Assigned, or Advanced Published Or Assigned). If you chose the Computer Configuration tree in step 2, the Published option will be disabled. Click Assigned. The Advanced Published Or Assigned option opens the Software Policy Properties dialog box and lets you configure additional property settings, such as placing the application in an Add/Remove Programs category or adding modification (.mst) files.

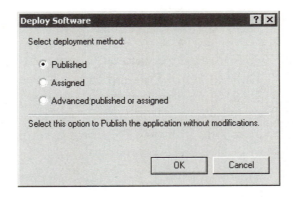

6. An icon for the software package appears in the right pane. Double-click the icon to view and modify policy property settings.

Publishing Software

When you publish an application through group policy, the application becomes available in the Add/Remove Programs Control Panel of the user to which the policy applies. The user must then install the application manually through the Add/Remove Programs Control Panel (Start | Settings | Control Panel | Add/Remove Programs).

To publish a software package through user configuration group policy, follow these steps:

1. Open the group policy object to which you would like to add the software installation policy (see Chapter 6 for more on opening a group policy object and using Group Policy Editor).

2. In the Group Policy tree, browse to User Configuration\ Software Settings\Software Installation.

3. Right-click the Software Installation icon and select New | Package.

4. In the Open dialog box, browse for the software package file you would like to publish. Typically, the package file will have an .msi extension. (You may not see the .msi extension, however, if the folder is configured to hide file extensions.) Select the file and click Open.

5. The Deploy Software dialog box (see Figure 8-10) asks you to choose a deployment method (Published, Assigned, or Advanced Published Or Assigned). Click Published. The Advanced Published Or Assigned option opens the Software Policy Properties dialog box and lets you configure additional property settings, such as placing the application in an Add/Remove Programs category or adding modification (.mst) files.

6. An icon for the software package appears in the right pane. Double-click the icon to view and modify policy property settings.

Creating a .zap File

A .zap file is a homegrown version of an installation package file. Software installation group policy can process a .zap file as it would an .msi file for purposes of publishing an application. You cannot use a .zap file to assign an application. Microsoft provides a few other caveats for using a .zap file with software installation group policy:

▼ .zap files typically aren't as automated. They usually just run the software's basic setup program and therefore require additional input from the user.

■ .zap files run under the user's security context (as opposed to other package files, which are able to run under the context of the Windows Installer).

▲ .zap files are not able to monitor and repair the software installation. If the application doesn't start, the whole installation is rerun.

If you wish to publish an application and you don't have a package file, however, a .zap file is a simple solution. A .zap file is a simple text file that merely points the installer to the setup file and provides a few additional configuration settings. The format is reminiscent of the classic .ini file format. The .zap file consists of a mandatory [Application] section and an optional [Ext] section. The [Application] section has the following format:

```
[Application]
FriendlyName =Application_name
SetupCommand =\\path\file.exe /options...
DisplayVersion = (version number)
Publisher = application_vendor
URL = (url with information about the application)
```

The [Ext] section lists file extensions that are mapped to the application. You can associate more than one file extension with the application. An example is as follows:

```
[Ext]
DIX=
PIX=
NIX=
```

Configuring Software Installation Policy Properties

Once you have created a software installation policy object (as described in the previous sections, "Assigning Software" and "Publishing Software," you can configure additional settings through the policy's Properties dialog box.

To access the Software Installation Properties dialog box, follow these steps:

1. Select the Software Installation icon in the group policy object's Computer Configuration\Software Settings or User Configuration\Software Settings container.

2. Current software installation policies appear in the right pane. Right-click the desired policy and select Properties.

3. The policy's Properties dialog box appears (see Figure 8-10). The Properties dialog box has the following tabs:

   - **General** Product name and general information on the product (see Figure 8-10).

   - **Deployment** Various deployment options.

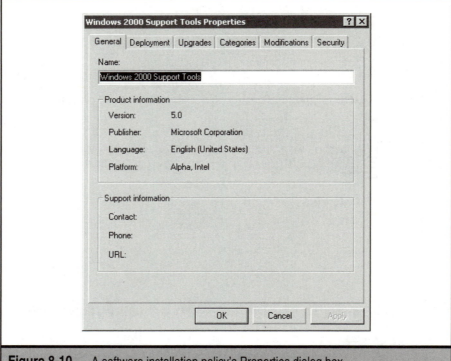

Figure 8-10. A software installation policy's Properties dialog box

- **Upgrades** Instructs the installer to replace an old version of the application with a new version. Windows 2000–ready installation package files can automatically detect old versions of the program for upgrade. For other package files, you must manually enter the names of the packages that will be upgraded. You can elect to require the upgrade or to make it optional.

- **Categories** Lets you place the application in one of the program categories listed in the Add/Remove Programs Control Panel.

- **Modifications** Lets you add customized .mst package files to the installation. Consult the application vendor.

- **Security** Security settings for the software installation policy object.

4. Choose the desired options and click Apply or OK.

MANAGING THE USER DESKTOP THROUGH GROUP POLICY

You can also group policies to manage the user's desktop. The desktop configuration policies are the group policies that are perhaps most reminiscent of Windows NT system policies, and their purpose is similar. The primary goals of the assorted desktop configuration policies are to increase security and to lower total cost of ownership by limiting the end user's configuration options. (The philosophy is that you can't break what you can't see. Also, you can't be confused by what isn't there. By simplifying the desktop interface through group policy, you make it easier for end users to figure out what they are supposed to be doing.) Windows 2000 also offers some additional desktop configuration features that weren't available in Windows NT, such as the handy Folder Redirection feature, which lets you specify an alternative location for user folders such as the My Documents folder. You'll learn more about folder redirection in a later section titled "Folder Redirection."

Most of the desktop configuration policy options are located in the User Configuration\Administrative Templates container or a group policy object. The options are numerous, and the best way to learn about them is to browse through the User Configuration\Administrative Templates container. Some useful desktop-related policy containers include the following:

▼ **Desktop (User Configuration\Administrative Templates\Desktop)**   Settings that configure the desktop. You can hide all desktop icons or remove individual icons such as My Documents, My Network Places, or Internet Explorer. You can also elect not to save the current desktop settings at exit.

■ **Start Menu and Taskbar (User Configuration\Administrative Templates\Start Menu & Taskbar)**   A myriad of options for configuring the Start menu and taskbar. You can remove Start menu options, disable logoff or shutdown, configure document history, and more.

■ **Control Panel (User Configuration\Administrative Templates\Control Panel)**   The default administrative template lets you configure settings for the Add/Remove

Programs, Display, Printers, and Regional Options
Control Panels.

▲ **System (User Configuration\Administrative Templates\
System)**   The System container offers some of the most
powerful desktop configuration options. You can specify
Windows applications that will be the only applications that
can run on the computer (or Windows applications that *won't*
run on the computer). You can disable Registry editing tools
or the command prompt. You can even enter an alternative
user interface (instead of the Windows interface Explorer.exe).

If you remember a desktop policy from Windows NT, look
around for it. You may find it somewhere in the Windows 2000
group policy object.

NOTE: Configuring user desktops is, of course, only a small part of
managing users in the Active Directory environment. See Chapter 5, "Users
and Groups," and Chapter 6 for additional information on configuring and
managing group policies and user accounts.

Folder Redirection

The folder redirection policy lets you redirect special user interface
folders to a network location. You can apply folder redirection to any
of the following folders:

▼ Application Data

■ Desktop

■ My Documents

■ My Documents\My Pictures

▲ Start Menu

In some environments, it is useful to be able to place special
folders, such as My Documents, on the network. This conserves disk
space on the client computer and provides for easier backup of folder
contents. Because of the Windows 2000 Offline Files feature, users
can access these folders even when the network isn't working.

To configure folder redirection for a group policy object, follow these steps:

1. Open the group policy object to which you would like to configure folder redirection (see Chapter 6 for more on opening a group policy object and using Group Policy Editor).

2. In the Group Policy tree, browse to User Configuration\ Windows Settings\Folder Redirection.

3. Subcontainers appear below the Folder Redirection container labeled Application Data, Desktop, My Documents, and Start Menu. The My Documents container has its own subcontainer for My Pictures. Right-click the folder for which you would like to configure folder redirection and select Properties.

4. In the Target tab of the Properties dialog box (see Figure 8-11), choose whether you'd like to redirect the folder of all users to

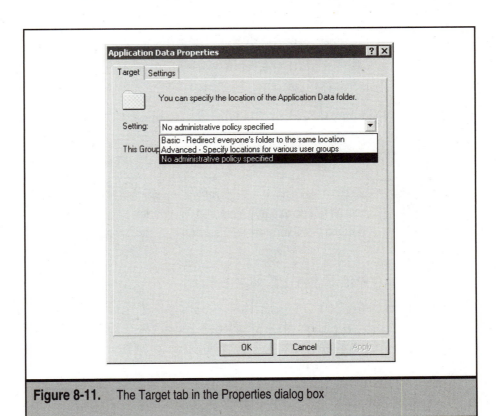

Figure 8-11.   The Target tab in the Properties dialog box

whom the policy applies or whether you wish to specify different folder locations for different user groups. In the box that appears below, enter the path(s) for the network-based folder.

5. Click the Settings tab to configure additional options.

6. When you are finished, click Apply or OK.

MANAGING OPERATIONS MASTERS

In the best case, you won't have to do a lot of tinkering with the operations master roles once they're established. Chapter 7 describes tips on the best practices for locating operations masters. However, occasionally an operations master role must be reassigned. The following sections discuss:

▼ Reassigning the schema master

■ Reassigning the domain naming master

▲ Reassigning the relative identifier (RID) master, PDC emulator, or infrastructure master

See Chapter 2, "Active Directory Concepts," and Chapter 7 for more on operations masters in the Active Directory environment.

NOTE Reassigning an operations master role is a very invasive act. Consult Windows 2000 Help and the Windows 2000 Web site for up-to-date, best-practice information on seizing operations master roles.

Reassigning the Schema Master

According to Microsoft, the schema master role should not be reassigned unless absolutely necessary. Temporary unavailability of the schema master is usually not a big concern unless an administrator or a program tries to modify the schema. Once the schema master role is reassigned, the old schema master *must not* be placed back on the network.

Reassign the schema master role (if you really have to) through the Active Directory Schema Snap-In. Active Directory Schema is described in greater detail in Chapter 10.

1. Install the Active Directory Schema Microsoft Management Console Snap-In (see Chapter 10).

2. Right-click the Active Directory Schema icon in Microsoft Management Console.

3. Select Change Domain Controller in the Context menu. In the Change Domain Controller dialog box, select the Specify Name radio button and enter the name of the computer that you would like to make the schema master. You cannot change the schema master from the current schema master. Click OK.

4. Right-click the Active Directory Schema icon in Active Directory Schema. Select Operations Master.

5. The Change Schema Master dialog box appears. Make sure the lower box shows the name of the computer you'd like to make the schema master. Click Change.

6. A Warning dialog box asks if you really want to go through with the change. Click OK.

Reassigning the Domain Naming Master

Temporary loss of the domain naming master is usually not a problem, since the domain naming master is used only when a domain is added or removed. Changing the domain naming master is a drastic step (according to Microsoft) that should be taken only when you are certain the old domain naming master has failed permanently.

To change the domain naming master, you must first connect to the new domain naming master in Active Directory Domains and Trusts:

1. Select Start | Programs | Administrative Tools | Active Directory Domains and Trusts.

2. In the Active Directory Domains and Trusts main window, right-click the Active Directory Domains and Trusts icon and choose Connect To Domain Controller. Browse to the domain controller to which you'd like to assign the domain naming

master role. Note that you can select Any Writable Domain Controller to let Active Directory decide which domain controller to connect to.

3. In the Active Directory Domains and Trusts main window, right-click the Active Directory Domains and Trusts icon and choose Operations Master.

4. In the Change Operations Master dialog box, make sure the domain controller you wish to make the new domain naming master is in the lower box. Click Change.

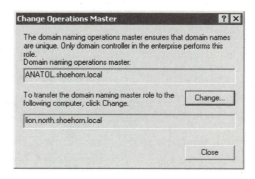

5. Click Close.

Reassigning the RID Master, PDC Emulator, or Infrastructure Master

The RID master, PDC emulator, or infrastructure master role is assigned for each domain. Microsoft classifies changing the RID master as "drastic" and warns that this course should be taken only when the failure of the old RID master is considered permanent. Microsoft is less emphatic on the perils of changing the PDC emulator and infrastructure master roles, but you're still better off leaving them alone unless you're sure you have a good reason for changing them. It is especially important to seize the PDC emulator role if you need to, since the PDC emulator is used for authentication of pre–Windows 2000 systems and thus is necessary for efficient functioning of the network. You can reassign these roles through Active Directory Users and Computers.

Before reassigning an operations master role, make sure the current operations master is off the network. To reassign the RID master, PDC emulator, or infrastructure master role, follow these steps:

1. Select Start | Programs | Administrative Tools | Active Directory Users And Computers.

2. In the Active Directory Users And Computers main window, right-click the Active Directory Users And Computers icon and choose Connect To Domain Controller. Browse to the domain controller to which you'd like to assign the operations master role. Note that you can select Any Writable Domain Controller to let Active Directory decide which domain controller to connect to.

3. In the Active Directory Users And Computers main window, right-click Active Directory Users And Computers and choose Operations Masters.

4. In the Operations Master dialog box, select the appropriate tab (RID, PDC, or Infrastructure). Make sure the domain controller you wish to make the new operations master is in the lower box. Click Change.

5. Click OK.

SUMMARY

This chapter toured through a number of management features that are closely related to Active Directory. One of the most fundamental Active Directory–related management problems is managing the directory itself. This chapter described how to back up and restore the Active Directory and how to view and modify the Active Directory using ADSI Editor and other directory management tools. You also learned about some important management capabilities built into the Active Directory Group Policy feature. This chapter discussed Active Directory–based file publication, printer publication, and software publication, as well as group-policy–based desktop management settings. Lastly, you learned how to reassign operations master roles if one of the Active Directory operations masters fails.

Management is another of those big topics that could truly be the subject of a book by itself. There are, of course, many other aspects of managing a Windows 2000 system that couldn't be covered in this chapter. See Windows 2000 Online Help or the Windows 2000 Resource Kit's Books Online. Other facets of Active Directory management appear throughout this book. You may wish to pay particular attention to Chapter 4 and Chapter 6 for pertinent information on managing directory replication and the implementing of Active Directory's important Group Policy feature.

CHAPTER 9

Active Directory
Clients

Microsoft is very clear about what it considers the best way to support clients in Active Directory: upgrade all clients to Windows 2000 Professional. The company is, however, also clear about the fact that not all client systems have the hardware necessary to run Windows 2000. And though Microsoft always leads with the upgrade option, it would also tell you that, depending on your requirements for the client system, an upgrade to Windows 2000 may not be necessary. This chapter unravels the various client options and describes some of the tasks associated with supporting clients in the Active Directory environment.

UNDERSTANDING CLIENT OPTIONS

If your network is functioning perfectly well as a Windows NT domain, you can rest assured that your clients' systems will continue to function under Windows 2000. Windows NT and Windows 95/98 clients will still be able to access file shares and print to network printers. However, pre–Windows 2000 systems will not be able to participate fully in all Active Directory's features.

Your pre–Windows 2000 clients won't know about Active Directory and will, essentially, operate much as they did before you installed Active Directory. What do they miss out on? The following three features, for instance, are three of the principal reasons for installing Windows 2000 Professional on network clients:

▼ **Directory searches**   LDAP searches on the Active Directory.

■ **Group policy**   Active Directory's elaborate group policy structure (see Chapter 6, "Group Policy") provides an efficient system for managing and securing the network.

▲ **Kerberos**   Kerberos provides integrated network logon security in a heterogeneous environment. See Chapter 11, "Active Directory and Windows 2000 Security."

Windows 95/98 and Windows NT clients (and other legacy Microsoft clients) will not be able to use these important features. As you'll learn later in this chapter, Microsoft provides tools that enable certain Active Directory features for certain clients. For instance, the ldp.exe utility (included with the Active Directory support tools) lets a Windows 98 or Windows NT 4 client search the Active Directory. The Directory Services Client application lets Windows 95 or Windows 98 search the Active Directory and also provides some other features, such as the ability to use Windows 2000's Distributed File System (DFS).

The lack of support for group policy, though, means that your older Windows systems will never be truly integrated into the Active Directory environment. Group policy (see Chapter 6) is a huge consideration in the design and management of your Active Directory network, and it plays a role in such important Active Directory tasks as:

▼ Security (see Chapter 11)

■ Logon scripts (see Chapter 12, "Scripting Active Directory")

■ Folder redirection (see Chapter 8, "Managing Active Directory")

▲ Software publishing (see Chapter 8)

It is currently impossible to implement group policy on any computer that isn't running some version of Windows 2000. Instead (as you learned in Chapter 6), Windows NT and Windows 95/98 must use a separate structure of system policies to provide policy support. In fact, as you may remember from NT days, Windows NT and Windows 95/98 policies are not even compatible, so if you plan to support a mix of Windows 2000, Windows NT, and Windows 95/98 clients, you'll need separate policies for Windows NT and Windows 95/98 clients in addition to the many-tiered group policy structure used on Windows 2000 systems. Because group policy is specifically envisioned as a system, with several levels and policies *flowing* from higher levels toward the client, it is particularly problematic for some computers within the network to be completely independent of that system.

The lack of group policy support may be part of the reason why Microsoft always begins any discussion of client issues with the upgrade option. (Of course, sales would be another good reason why Microsoft likes the upgrade option.) If you want a client computer to be able to use group policy, Kerberos for cross-domain logon, and other features such as DFS, you'll need to upgrade it to Windows 2000 Professional.

If you're content with your client computers acting as they do now on a Windows NT network without all the additional features, you don't have to upgrade them. But then, if you're happy with the NT environment, it is also worth considering whether you need to install Active Directory on your network at all.

Some older systems do not have the hardware necessary for supporting Windows 2000. The following sections discuss some critical upgrade issues and describe how to get the most functionality from a Windows NT or Windows 95/98 client on an Active Directory network.

TIP: It is important to remember that the components and utilities discussed in this chapter are only those provided by Microsoft. As Windows 2000 becomes the focus of public attention, you'll begin to see additional third-party Active Directory client options. The lack of an Active Directory client for Windows NT is particularly curious. It seems that, if a client can be written for Windows 95/98, it ought to be possible to write one for Windows NT. One wonders if the absence of an NT client is part of Microsoft's effort to encourage the upgrade of client systems to Windows 2000. In any case, you can expect to see third-party NT client options in the near future.

Windows 2000 Professional Hardware Requirements

Before you make plans to upgrade, you'd better make sure your client computers have the horsepower to support Windows 2000. Microsoft specifies the following system requirements for Windows 2000 computers:

▼ Processor: 133MHz Pentium class

■ RAM: 32MB minimum, 64MB recommended

▲ Disk: 2GB disk with 1GB free space (or more if installing over the network)

TIP: Some experienced Windows 2000 users believe that Microsoft's recommendations for RAM and processor speed are on the low side—especially if you're running expansive Windows applications such as the Microsoft Office applications. If you really want Windows 2000 Professional to be at home, put it on a Pentium-class 333MHz processor with 128MB of RAM.

Some other more subtle hardware issues are also worth mentioning. Windows 2000 supports the *Advanced Configuration and Power Management Interface* (ACPI). ACPI provides power management features (designed primarily for laptops) that let the computer enter a sleep state when no one is using it. ACPI interacts with the system BIOS. Some systems do not have a BIOS that fully supports ACPI, so those systems will not be able to fully support Windows 2000 power management. Also, at the time of the Windows 2000 release, all necessary drivers for all possible computer systems were not available for inclusion on the Windows 2000 CD.

Microsoft set up a Web site that prompts users to provide hardware upgrade details for a specific system. Enter the make and model of your computer and you are linked automatically to a site that provides downloadable drivers and BIOS upgrade software to make the system Windows 2000–ready. This Windows 2000 hardware update site is located at www.hardwareupdate.com.

You may also wish to consult the Windows 2000 Hardware Compatibility List (HCL) and other Microsoft Web resources (see Chapter 7, "Setting Up Active Directory").

TIP: You can find the Windows 2000 hardware update site at www.hardwareupdate.com. You can also find the Windows 2000 Readiness Analyzer tool at www.microsoft.com/Windows2000/upgrade/compat.

If you need to install multiple computers, you may wish to use the Windows 2000 Readiness Analyzer tool. You'll find the Readiness Analyzer at the Windows 2000 Home Page under Check Hardware and Software Compatibility. Or, you can find it directly at www.microsoft.com/Windows2000/upgrade/compat.

The Windows 2000 Readiness Analyzer is sometimes referred to by its real name: chkupgrd.exe. The chkupgrd.exe utility extracts itself and then checks the local system for Windows 2000 compatibility. chkupgrd.exe is a stand-alone version of the routine that checks for system compatibility during the Windows 2000 installation process, although Microsoft warns that results of the Windows 2000 installation check may vary slightly from results of chkupgrd.exe.

Chkupgrd.exe analyzes the local system and looks for any hardware or software compatibility issues (see Figure 9-1). Click the Details button or click Save As to save a text file with a brief description of each compatibility problem discovered by chkupgrd.exe. If you plan on deploying Windows 2000 Professional on several clients throughout the network and you have any doubts about the compatibility of the systems, you may wish to run chkupgrd.exe on each system. You can then generate a text file with compatibility information for the system by clicking the Save As option. Next, as you edit the text file, make any notations necessary for you to associate this file with the local computer (for example, host name or a description). You can then print or collect the files and develop an overall strategy for addressing the upgrade issues prior to installation.

Often, the most useful information you'll get from chkupgrd.exe is a report on any hardware for which the Windows 2000 CD does not have a built-in driver. Consult the driver vendor's Web site for Windows 2000–compatible drivers.

An alternative to the chkupgrd.exe utility is to run the Windows 2000 setup program winnt32.exe with the /checkupgradeonly option. Typing the following command at the system prompt performs a system compatibility check using the compatibility checker built into winnt32.exe:

```
yepwinnt32.exe /checkupgradeonly
```

On Windows 95 or 98 computers, the compatibility report is saved to the file upgrade.txt in the Windows Installation folder. On Windows NT 3.51 or Windows NT 4 computers, the compatibility report is saved to the file winnt32.log in the Installation folder.

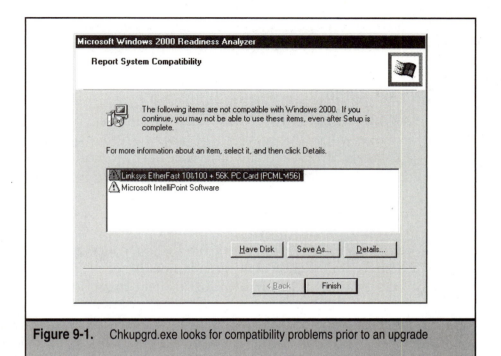

Figure 9-1.   Chkupgrd.exe looks for compatibility problems prior to an upgrade

Windows 2000 Clients

Windows 2000 Professional is specifically designed to serve as a client in the Active Directory environment. You can perform Active Directory functions from Windows 2000 Professional computers just as you can from Windows 2000 Server computers. Windows 2000 Professional computers can be managed from Active Directory–based tools such as Active Directory Users and Computers. Active Directory computers are subject to group policies.

By default, Windows 2000 Professional does not contain all the Active Directory management tools described in this book. However, you can install the Windows 2000 Administrative Tools onto a Windows 2000 Professional client. The Windows 2000 Administrative Tools include management tools such as Active Directory Users and Computers, Active Directory Domains and Trusts, Active Directory

Sites and Services, and Active Directory Schema. See the section "Managing the Network from Clients," later in this chapter.

Windows NT Clients

A Windows NT 3.51 or Windows NT 4 client computer participates in the network security system. (It works directly with access tokens and access control lists and has a computer account within the domain.) Windows NT clients appear in the Computers folder of Active Directory Users and Computers. However, according to Microsoft, a Windows NT client is *not* an Active Directory client. Microsoft does not provide a Windows NT Active Directory client comparable to the Windows 95/98 Directory Services Client component described in the next section.

A Windows NT computer can do all the things it used to do on a Windows NT network; however, it does not have access to the Active Directory or to Active Directory–based features. An exception to this is a Windows NT 4 computer with Internet Explorer 5 installed: this computer can search the Active Directory using the Address Book search feature, as described later in the section titled "Address Book."

Windows 95/98 Clients

Windows 95 and Windows 98 computers participate in the network much as they did under Windows NT. However, as you may recall from Windows NT days, the participation of Windows 95 and Windows 98 in the domain was fairly limited. A user may log on to the network *from* a Windows 95/98 computer, but the computer itself is not fully capable of participating in the domain security system.

If you want your Windows 95/98 computer to have access to group policy and other Windows 2000 innovations, you must upgrade it. However, you can enable some Windows 2000 features by installing the Directory Services Client component included on the Windows 2000 Server CD. The Directory Services Client lets a Windows 95 or Windows 98 computer perform the following tasks:

▼ Search the Active Directory

■ Use DFS

▲ Change passwords on domain controllers

To install Directory Services Client on a Windows 95/98 computer, follow these steps:

1. Click the Start button and select Run.

2. Insert the Windows 2000 Server CD in the CD-ROM drive. In the Run dialog box, browse to the \Clients\Win9x folder of the Windows 2000 Server CD. Alternatively, if a copy of the Windows 2000 Server CD is present on your network, browse to the network copy of the \Clients\Win9x folder.

3. Double-click the DSClient icon to start the Directory Services Client Wizard.

4. Click Next.

5. Read the license agreement. If you accept it, click I Accept This Agreement. If you don't accept it, you won't be able to install.

6. When the next screen asks you to confirm that you want to install Directory Services client, click Finish.

7. Click OK at the prompt, and then click Yes to restart your computer.

Note that, as mentioned previously in the section "Understanding Client Options," the Windows 95/98 Directory Services client does not let the Windows 95/98 computer participate in group policy and other features that are part of group policy (such as group-policy–based scripts, service advertisement, software installation, and security).

Windows 98 computers can gain some Active Directory capabilities (such as the ability to search the Active Directory) if you install the Windows 2000 Server support tools. See the section "Managing the Network from Clients" later in this chapter.

Clients from Other Networking Systems

Chapter 13, "Interoperating Active Directory," discusses Windows 2000's and Active Directory's support for other network systems, including support for clients from those other systems accessing Windows 2000 resources. Some of Windows 2000's support for other clients is inherited from Windows NT Server. However, Windows 2000 adds several useful new features, especially for Macintosh and UNIX-based client support.

Windows 2000 provides file services, print services, and gateway capabilities for the following network systems:

▼ NetWare

■ Macintosh

▲ UNIX and UNIX-based

Windows 2000's enhanced support for TCP/IP-related utilities, such as Telnet and FTP, provide additional integration for clients running other operating systems.

Of course, access to file and print services is not the same as access to the Active Directory. Microsoft does not provide a client package that will allow a NetWare, Macintosh, or UNIX client to search the Active Directory. However, the Active Directory is an LDAP database, and LDAP is a well-defined networking standard. It is probable that future third-party (or Microsoft) Active Directory client add-ons will provide a higher level of integration from heterogeneous clients to the Active Directory.

NOTE: See Chapter 13 for more on integrating Windows 2000 with other operating systems.

Address Book

The Address Book application (included with Windows 95 and 98 as well as with Internet Explorer 4 and later) offers some interesting possibilities for Active Directory integration with other operating systems. According to Microsoft, the Address Book's Find feature (a popular tool for finding people in the local address book or on the Internet) is basically an LDAP search client.

On a computer running Windows 2000 Server or Windows 2000 Professional, you can search directly on the Active Directory using Address Book:

1. Click the Start button and choose Programs | Accessories | Address Book.

2. In the Address Book main window, click the Find People tool button.

3. In the Find People dialog box, click the arrow to the right of the Look In box to reveal search directory choices (see Figure 9-2). Note that Active Directory is one of the search directory choices.

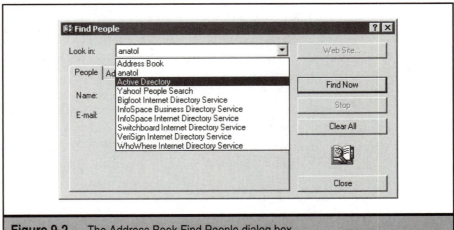

Figure 9-2.   The Address Book Find People dialog box

At the time of this writing, IE 4's Address Book and the Address Book accessory in Windows 95 or Windows 98 do not offer Active Directory as a search directory option in the Look In menu. However, Microsoft may decide to build this functionality into IE and Windows 95/98 versions after the Windows 2000 release.

MANAGING CLIENTS

Windows 2000 provides several convenient tools for managing client computers, and they are worth mentioning here—even though some of them are not, strictly speaking, Active Directory tools.

Microsoft has gathered up many of the client management functions into a pair of useful utilities:

▼ **Computer Management**   This tool manages hardware and software components of the local system. If you wish to configure or monitor some facet of the client configuration that is essentially local and doesn't relate directly to Active Directory or the network structure (such as the client's shared folders, local groups and users, performance logs, event logs, or resource settings), start with this tool.

▲ **Active Directory Users and Computers**   This tool manages the client object and client account as entities within the Active Directory. If you wish to configure or monitor some aspect of the client computer's position within the Active Directory environment, start with this tool.

Of course, many other tools and components that can affect client configuration are available with Active Directory. Windows 2000 clients, for example, are integrated directly into the group policy infrastructure (see Chapter 6 and other chapters that discuss group policy settings). The client computer must also participate in the network, which calls for a range of network configuration tasks.

The next sections discuss the Computer Management tool and Active Directory Users and Computers.

Computer Management Tool

Microsoft gathered up many of the common utilities for administering a computer and placed them with one handy tool called the *Computer Management tool*. The Computer Management tool is one of the purest expressions yet of what Microsoft had in mind for the Microsoft Management Console. You can use Computer Management tools to manage the local computer, a remote computer, a client, or a server.

Microsoft clearly envisions administrators managing their clients by connecting to the client through the Computer Management tool. You can use the Computer Management tool to manage Windows NT 4 clients, Windows 2000 Professional clients, and Windows 2000 Server servers and domain controllers. You can use the Computer Management tool to do the following:

▼   View the event log on the client computer.

■   View system information such as hardware resources.

■   Manage shares, sessions, and open files on the remote computer.

■   View device information through Device Manager.

■   Manage local users and groups.

■   Manage disks and logical drives.

▲   Manage services and applications.

To connect to a client computer from the Computer Management tool, follow these steps:

1.   Click the Start button and choose Programs | Administrative Tools | Computer Management.

2. In the Computer Management main window, right-click the Computer Management icon and select Connect To Another Computer (see Figure 9-3).

3. Select the computer you wish to connect to and click OK.

The computer management tree for the computer you selected appears in the Computer Management main window.

AD Users and Computers

The Active Directory Users and Computers utility provides a topside view of the client's role within the domain. Active Directory Users and Computers is a good place to view the domain structure and see how a Windows 2000 or Windows NT client fits within that structure.

As this chapter has already described, each Windows NT or Windows 2000 client computer is an object within the network

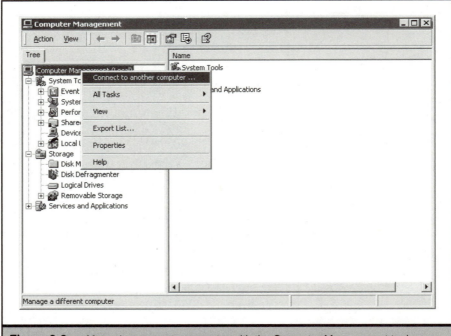

Figure 9-3. Managing a remote computer with the Computer Management tool

with its own attributes and its own computer account. The Active Directory Users and Computers tool primarily reports on the properties of the computer object and computer account within the Active Directory infrastructure.

The following sections describe some important client-management tasks that relate to Active Directory Users and Computers. These tasks include:

▼ Joining a client computer to a domain

■ Managing a computer from AD Users and Computers

■ Specifying a manager for a computer

■ Moving a client computer within a domain

▲ Moving a client computer to a different domain

It is important to note that a computer account as it appears in Active Directory Users and Computers is very similar to a user account: you can disable or reset the account, view the account properties, or perform other account-related tasks. A client computer can become a member of an OU and can be managed through the object security, inherited permissions, and delegation of authority associated with the OU. See Chapter 5, "Users and Groups," for more on managing accounts and delegating authority through Active Directory Users and Computers.

Joining a Client Computer to a Domain

As already described, each client computer must have an account to participate in the domain security system. Windows NT and Windows 2000 computers must have computer accounts. Windows 95/98 computers and other client systems do not fully participate in the domain security system and thus do not require computer accounts.

When a client computer *joins* a domain, a computer account for the client is created in the Active Directory. You can create a computer account for a client directly in Active Directory Users and Computers, or you can create the account by joining the domain from a Windows NT or Windows 2000 client computer.

When you join a domain from the client computer, a computer account in the domain is created automatically. When you create the computer account through Active Directory Users and Computers, the client still must join the domain to participate in the domain's security structure. The advantage of creating a computer account in advance through Active Directory Users and Computers is that, if the computer account is already created, a client-side user does not have to have domain administrative privileges to join the domain. The client user must, however, have administrative privileges on the local client computer to join it to the domain.

To create a computer account in Active Directory Users and Computers, follow these steps:

1. Click the Start button and select Programs | Administrative Tools | Active Directory Users And Computers. Or, access Active Directory Users and Computers from the Microsoft Management Console.

2. Click the plus sign next to the domain to which you would like to add the new computer.

3. Right-click the container or OU that will hold the new computer account. Select New | Computer in the context menu.

4. The New Object–Computer Wizard appears (see Figure 9-4). In the Computer Name box, enter a host name for the computer. This computer name will identify the computer object in the Active Directory environment. The pre–Windows 2000 name (in the next line—refer to Figure 9-4), is a NetBIOS name. The NetBIOS name used to be called a computer name in the Windows NT environment. It identifies the computer to WINS and to all references that require the use of a Windows NT–style Universal Naming Convention (UNC) name. By default, a pre–Windows 2000 computer name will appear automatically, matching the computer name you enter in the first line.

NOTE: Microsoft recommends the practice of matching the NetBIOS name with the host name. Not only does this practice mean you have fewer names to remember, it subtly assists the systems in resolving some of the complex interactions between the Windows NT and Windows 2000 namespaces. If the Windows 2000 name is unreachable or unavailable, Active Directory will often use the NetBIOS name instead.

5. Note that, by default (refer to Figure 9-4), Active Directory requires that whoever is adding this computer account be a member of the Domain Admins group. This setting comes from the default domain policy. Click the Change button to give a different account permission to join this computer to a domain. If the computer is a pre–Windows 2000 computer (a Windows NT computer), check the Allow Pre–Windows 2000 Computers To Use This Account box. Then click Next.

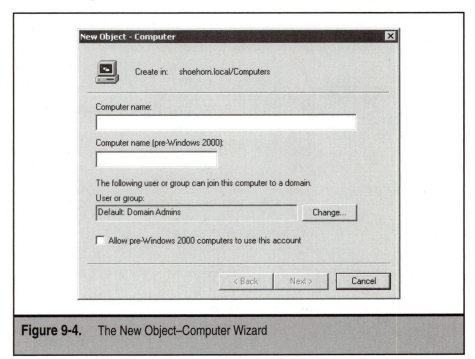

Figure 9-4. The New Object–Computer Wizard

6. The next screen (see Figure 9-5) may ask you whether this computer will be a managed computer. In this case, *managed* means managed by some network management system. Check the system BIOS or consult the vendor documentation to determine the computer's unique GUID/UUID. Then click Next.

7. When the wizard presents a summary of the information you entered, click Finish or Back to go back and change a setting.

NOTE: After you create the computer account, the computer can join the domain using the procedures described later in this section. If the computer account already exists, the client user is not required to supply a domain administrative username and password. However, to change the domain affiliation of the client (as described in the following procedures), the user on the client computer must be an administrator of the client computer.

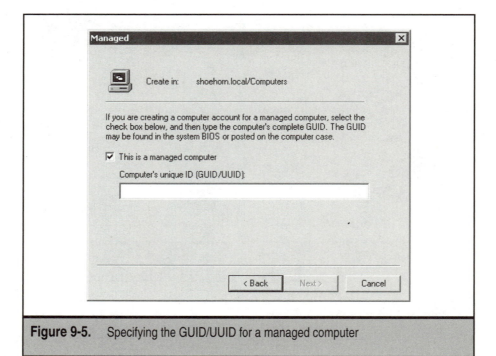

Figure 9-5. Specifying the GUID/UUID for a managed computer

You can also create a domain account by joining the domain from the client. You must have domain administration credentials to join the domain from the client. To join a domain from a Windows 2000 client, follow these steps:

1. Right-click My Computer and select Properties. Or, open the System Control Panel and select the Network Identification tab.

2. In the Network Identification tab (see Figure 9-6), you'll see two options for setting the computer name and joining the domain. (These options will be grayed out if you don't have local administrative privileges for the Windows 2000 computer.)

   ■ Clicking the Network ID button launches a wizard and a brief tutorial that asks a few questions about how the computer will be used. It then provides a summary of the information you'll need to supply. You'll be asked to provide your domain credentials and to enter the computer names.

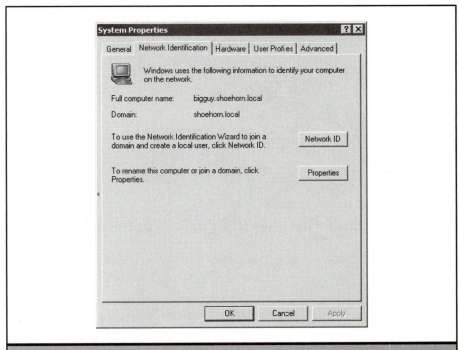

Figure 9-6.   Windows 2000's System Properties Network Identification tab

- Clicking the Properties button dispenses with the niceties and asks you to specify a computer name and a domain name (see Figure 9-7). Clicking the More button lets you set a primary DNS suffix (see Chapter 2, "Active Directory Concepts") and displays the computer's NetBIOS name.

NOTE: The wizard launched by clicking the Network ID button is designed for end users rather than professional administrators. (Remember, you're working from the client end now.) If you've done this kind of task before, just click Properties and make the change. You'll be prompted to supply administrative credentials for the domain.

3. When you are finished, click OK in the System Properties dialog box.

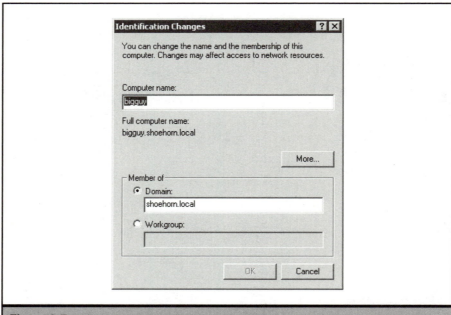

Figure 9-7. The Identification Changes dialog box

To join a domain from a Windows NT 4 computer, follow these steps:

1. Right-click Network Neighborhood and choose Properties. Or, open the Network Control Panel. Choose the Identification tab.

2. The Network Properties Identification tab displays the current NetBIOS computer name and domain or workgroup affiliation. To join a new domain, click the Change button.

3. In the Identification Changes dialog box (see Figure 9-8), enter a new domain name. Check the check box labeled Create A Computer Account In The Domain. Enter the username and password of a domain user with administrative privileges. Note that the Windows NT computer must be able to access the domain to make the change. Click OK in the Identification Changes dialog box.

4. Click OK in the Network dialog box.

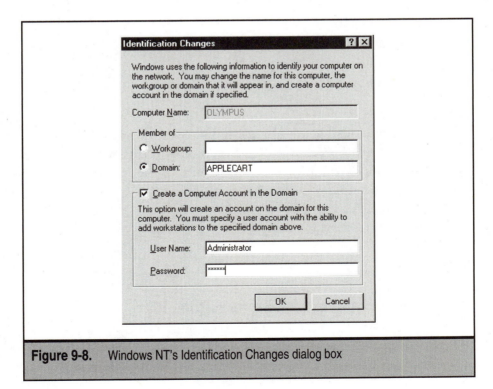

Figure 9-8.   Windows NT's Identification Changes dialog box

It is also possible to add a computer to a domain using the command-line NetDom utility. NetDom is part of the Windows 2000 support tools. See Chapter 7 for a discussion of how to install Windows 2000 support tools.

Use the following command to join a computer to a domain:

```
netdom join computer_name /d:target_domain /ou:targetOU_path
/ud: domain\userID /pd:password /Reboot:time
```

▼ *computer_name* is the name of the computer you wish to add to the domain.

■ *target_domain* is the domain to which you are adding the computer.

■ *targetOU_path* is the path of OUs to the container that will hold the computer account (e.g., OU=philly,OU=BuildingA, OU=Workstations). If an OU path is not specified, the computer account is added to the Computers container.

■ *domain\userID* is the domain name and userID of a user who has sufficient privileges to carry out this operation.

■ *password* is the password of the user specified in the /ud: option.

▲ *time* is the time to reboot, in seconds.

The netdom join command used in the previous code automatically creates a computer account within the new domain. Microsoft points out that this command can produce unpredictable results for a Windows NT computer if the command fails.

The similar netdom add command, used in the following code, creates a computer account, but it does not automatically join the client to the domain:

```
netdom add computer_name /d:target_domain /ou:targetOU_path
/ud: domain\userID /pd:password /Reboot:time
```

Specifying a Manager for a Computer

The Managed By tab (Figure 9-9) in the computer Account Properties dialog box shows you how Active Directory integrates information with OS functionality. The Managed By tab provides contact

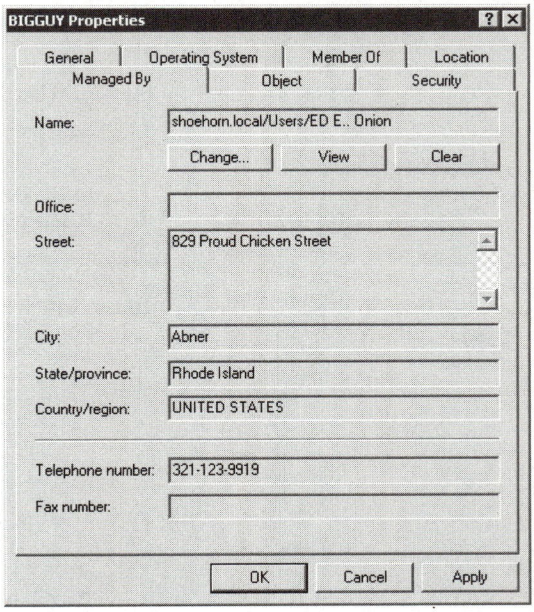

BIGGUY Properties   ? ✕

| General | Operating System | Member Of | Location |
| Managed By | | Object | Security |

Name: shoehorn.local/Users/ED E.. Onion

      Change...   View   Clear

Office:

Street: 829 Proud Chicken Street

City: Abner

State/province: Rhode Island

Country/region: UNITED STATES

Telephone number: 321-123-9919

Fax number:

    OK   Cancel   Apply

Figure 9-9.   The Computer Properties Managed By tab

information for the user who is in charge of managing the object. In the case of a client computer, you can specify the user who has primary responsibility for managing the computer in case the computer requires some attention. An administrative-level user viewing the computer's properties through Active Directory Users and Computers can consult the Managed By tab to determine the name, address, and telephone number of the user who is assigned to manage the computer.

TIP: The Managed By feature is especially useful in large networks when the user viewing the configuration through Active Directory Users and Computers is physically separated from the client computer. The managing user is likely to be someone in the immediate vicinity of the computer who has direct control of the computer's operations.

To specify a manager for a computer:

1. Click the Start button and choose Programs | Administrative Tools | Active Directory Users and Computers. Or, access Active Directory Users and Computers from the Microsoft Management Console.

2. Click the plus sign next to the domain that contains the computer for which you will specify a manager.

3. Click the plus sign next to the container or OU that holds the computer for which you will specify a manager.

4. Right-click the computer name that appears in the right pane and select Properties.

5. In the Properties dialog box, select the Managed By tab (see Figure 9-9), and click the Change button to enter a new managing user.

6. Select a user in the Select User Or Contact dialog box and click OK.

   The manager account name appears at the top of the Managed By tab (as shown in Figure 9-9). Any contact information specified for the manager's account appears automatically in the Managed By tab. See Chapter 5 for more on how to set up a user account and specify user information.

Managing a Computer from AD Users and Computers

The Active Directory Users and Computers Manage option is little more than a shortcut, but it deserves special notice here because it is so nifty. If you right-click a computer icon in Active Directory Users and select the Manage option, the Computer Management tool opens automatically for the computer you selected. You can therefore access all the system management features provided by the Computer Management tools from within Active Directory Users and Computers.

To manage a computer from within Active Directory Users and Computers, follow these steps:

1. Click the Start button and select Programs | Administrative Tools | Active Directory Users And Computers. Or, access Active Directory Users and Computers from the Microsoft Management Console.

2. Click the plus sign next to the domain that contains the computer you would like to manage.

3. Click the plus sign next to the container or OU that holds the computer you would like to manage.

4. Right-click the computer in the right pane and select Manage.

   The Computer Management tool opens for the computer you selected. Note that the name of the computer you selected appears in parentheses beside the Computer Management icon at the top of the tree.

Moving a Client Computer Within a Domain

You can move a computer to a different container or OU within the domain just as you can move a user or group. To move a computer within the domain, follow these steps:

1. Click the Start button and select Programs | Administrative Tools | Active Directory Users And Computers. Or, access Active Directory Users and Computers from the Microsoft Management Console.

2. Click the plus sign next to the domain that contains the computer you would like to move.

3. Click the plus sign next to the container or OU that holds the computer you would like to move.

4. Right-click the computer in the right pane and select Move.

5. When the Move dialog box (Figure 9-10) asks you to select a new container for the object, scroll to the desired container or OU and click OK.

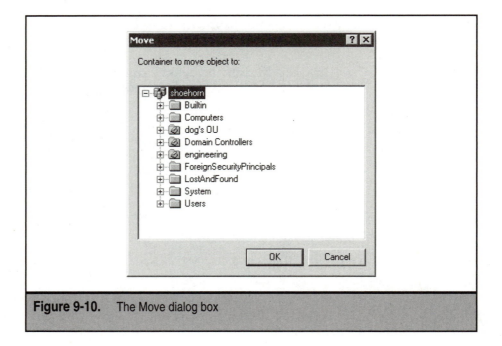

Figure 9-10. The Move dialog box

Moving a Client Computer to a Different Domain

You cannot use Active Directory Users and Computers to move a computer to a new domain. The internal process for moving a computer account to a different domain is vastly more complicated than the process for moving an account to a new container within a domain because the computer must have a new SID and new security arrangements, such as group memberships.

The easiest way to move a computer to a different domain is to join a new domain from the client (as described earlier in this chapter). Joining a new domain, of course, creates a new computer account and does not migrate any existing settings or relationships of the old computer account.

Microsoft also provides a utility called NetDom that is capable of moving a computer account to a new domain. As discussed earlier, NetDom is one of the Windows 2000 support tools. (See Chapter 7 for a discussion of how to install the Windows 2000 support tools.)

NetDom is a command-line utility. To move a computer account to a new domain, use the following command:

```
netdom move computer_name /d:target_domain /ou:targetOU_path
/ud: domain\userID /pd:password /Reboot:time
```

where:

- ▼ *computer_name* is the name of the computer you wish to move.

- ■ *target_domain* is the domain to which you are moving the computer.

- ■ *targetOU_path* is the path of OUs to the container that will hold the computer account (for example, OU=philly,OU=BuildingA, OU=Workstations). If an OU path is not specified, the computer account is added to the Computers container.

- ■ *domain\userID* is the domain name and userID of a user who has sufficient privileges to carry out this operation.

- ■ *password* is the password of the user who is specified in the /ud: option.

- ▲ *time* is the time to reboot in seconds.

The netdom move command retains the existing computer account in the source domain. See Chapter 7 for more on NetDom.

TIP: Microsoft warns that if you are moving a Windows NT computer using NetDom, the operation is not transacted. If the operation fails, the results may therefore leave the computer in the problematic intermediate state of being partly moved.

MANAGING THE NETWORK FROM CLIENTS

Windows 2000 Server and Windows 2000 Advanced Server come with a package of tools that includes many of the Active Directory support tools discussed in this book. The Windows 2000

Administrative Tools can be installed on any Windows 2000 computer, including Windows 2000 Professional clients. You can use the Windows 2000 Administrative Tools to administer the Active Directory network from a Windows 2000 client PC.

The tools included in the Windows 2000 Administrative Tool set are as follows:

▼ Active Directory Domains and Trusts

■ Active Directory Schema

■ Active Directory Sites and Services

■ Active Directory Users and Computers

■ Certification Authority

■ Cluster Administrator

■ Connection Manager Administration Kit

■ DHCP

■ Distributed File System

■ DNS

■ Internet Authentication Service

■ Internet Services Manager

■ QoS Admission Control

■ Remote Boot Disk Generator

■ Remote Storage

■ Routing and Remote Access

■ Telephony

■ Terminal Services Manager, Licensing, and Client Connection Manager

▲ WINS

To install Windows 2000 Administrative Tools on a Windows 2000 computer, follow these steps:

1. Insert the Windows 2000 Server or Windows 2000 Advanced Server CD into the CD-ROM drive.

2. Browse to the \I386 directory.

3. In the \I386 directory, double-click the Adminpak (Adminpak.msi).

4. When the Windows 2000 Administrative Tools Setup Wizard starts, follow the prompts.

To access the Windows 2000 Administrative Tools after they have been installed, click the Start button and choose Programs | Administrative Tools.

SUMMARY

Regardless of how harmoniously your Windows 2000 domain controllers are replicating with each other, you won't get much work done if your network doesn't have any clients. Windows 2000 and Active Directory provide some useful tools for integrating, configuring, and managing client computers. This chapter discussed various client options, such as Windows 95, Windows 98, Windows NT, and Windows 2000 Professional. You learned some of the reasons for upgrading pre–Windows 2000 clients to Windows 2000, and you learned about some of the alternative options for accessing Active Directory features, such as Directory Services Client (for Windows 95/98 systems) and the Address Book utility.

This chapter also examined how to manage client computers using the Computer Management tool and Active Directory Users and Computers. Lastly, you learned about the Windows 2000 Administrative Tools, a set of tools for managing Active Directory that can be downloaded and installed on a client Windows 2000 computer. The next chapter discusses how to use some of those tools (and other tools) to manage the Active Directory schema.

PART III

Mastering Active Directory

CHAPTER 10

Active Directory Schema

The *schema partition* provides the class and attribute definitions used in all parts of the Active Directory. Although the default schema built in to Active Directory does not require modification, you may wish to add classes and attributes to the schema so that you can store your own custom information in the directory database. This chapter takes an inside look at the Active Directory schema and shows how you can add new classes and attributes to the Active Directory.

WHAT IS THE SCHEMA?

The Active Directory schema defines the structure of the directory database. Think of the schema as a key that lets Windows 2000 interpret the contents of the Active Directory. Looking closely at the interplay of classes and objects within any complex data structure can cause an "Escher-esque" dizziness for even the most studious technologist, but it is worth pausing for a moment to consider the difference between the *structure* and the *contents* of a database. As shown in Figure 10-1, the schema is a system of definitions and rules that are referenced by the objects in the directory.

When you add a new user or change a user's name—from Bud to Ralph, for example—you are *not* altering the schema. A directory object such as a user account is an *instance of a schema class* (in this case, the user class). Creating a new instance (by adding a new account) or modifying a value stored with the instance (by changing a username) does not alter the class itself, and therefore does not alter the schema. The type of changes that would require modification of the schema include:

▼ Adding a new attribute to the user class so that Active Directory stores an optional setting for the primary language of the user.

▲ Creating a new class of users that doesn't include some of the default user attributes and contains a collection of special attributes associated with the user's location, primary workstation, and employment history.

As you learned in Chapter 2, "Active Directory Concepts," the schema is an Active Directory partition that is replicated separately from domain data and network configuration data. The schema consists of the following:

▼ **Attributes**   An attribute is a discrete piece of data following a predefined format

■ **Syntaxes**   Datatype and format rules applied to attributes

▲ **Classes**   A collection of attributes. A class serves as a template for an Active Directory object

Attributes and their accompanying syntaxes are gathered into classes. A *class* is a template describing the structure of an *object* (see

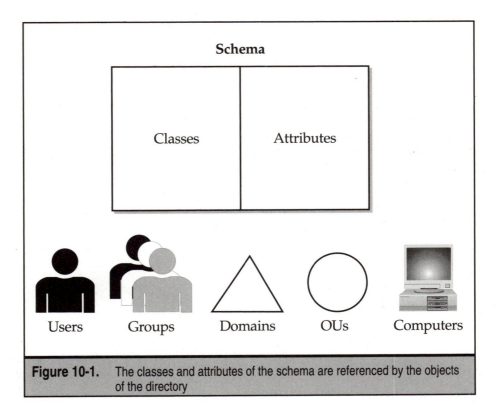

Figure 10-1.   The classes and attributes of the schema are referenced by the objects of the directory

Figure 10-2). Objects are the fundamental storage units of the Active Directory. When you make a change that registers in Active Directory (such as a change in Active Directory Users and Computers), you are creating or altering an object.

NOTE: As mentioned earlier in this section, altering the values stored with an object does not alter the object class stored in the schema.

An entire Active Directory forest shares one schema partition. In other words, all domains and domain controllers throughout the Active Directory network must share a common schema partition, and changes to the schema are replicated throughout the forest. The following sections look closer at attributes, syntax, and classes. Later on in this chapter, you'll learn how to modify the schema for your own network.

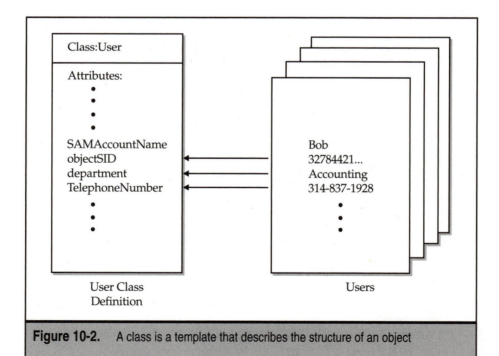

Figure 10-2. A class is a template that describes the structure of an object

Attributes, Syntaxes, and Schema Classes

If you're ready for a few more dizzying facts, you'll notice that schema classes and attributes, like other Active Directory entities, are themselves objects of other schema classes and attributes. This relationship is illustrated in Figure 10-3. In the figure, each attribute in the schema is stored as an object of the class attributeSchema. The attributeSchema class includes attributes such as the following (you can think of these as the properties of an attribute):

▼ The object identifier of the attribute (the attribute's name)

■ The LDAP display name of the attribute

■ The attribute's Global Unique Identifier (GUID)

■ The syntax of the attribute

■ The range of permissible values (the range between the minimum and maximum)

■ Whether the attribute is indexed

▲ Whether the attribute is multivalue (more on that later in the section titled "Attributes")

Each class, on the other hand, is an object belonging to the classSchema class. The classSchema class includes attributes such as the following:

▼ The object identifier for the class (the class's name)

■ The LDAP display name for the class

■ The GUID for the class

■ Attributes that must be present with each instance of the class (mandatory attributes)

■ Attributes that may be present with each instance of the class (optional attributes)

■ The class type (see the later section titled "Classes")

■ The parent classes of this class (see the later section titled "Classes")

▲ The superclass of this class (see the later section titled "Classes")

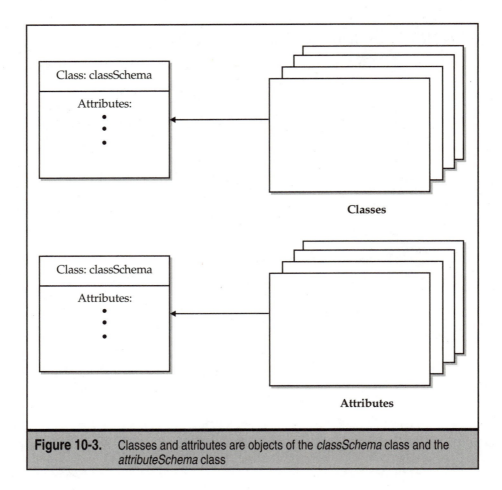

Figure 10-3. Classes and attributes are objects of the *classSchema* class and the *attributeSchema* class

The attributeSchema and classSchema classes can be viewed and managed like other classes in Active Directory.

Attributes

An attribute is a set of specifications defining a chunk of data that will be associated with an object (see "Attributes, Syntaxes, and Schema Classes"). An attribute is not merely a subunit of a class. In fact, an attribute is totally independent of the classes that might reference it (see Figure 10-4). The same attribute may be included in several classes. You must first create an attribute and then associate the attribute with any classes that will reference it.

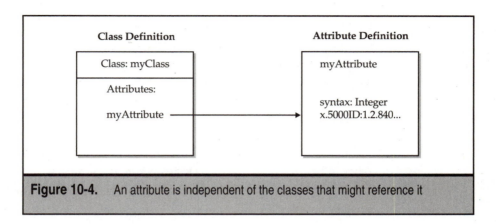

Class Definition	Attribute Definition
Class: myClass	myAttribute
Attributes:	
myAttribute ⟶	syntax: Integer x.5000ID:1.2.840...

Figure 10-4.   An attribute is independent of the classes that might reference it

The default Active Directory schema contains more than 850 attributes. You can add additional attributes to the schema. (See the section "Adding an Attribute" later in this chapter.) However, because an attribute is essentially just a definition, it doesn't really *do* anything until you associate it with a class and then associate Active Directory objects with that class.

The attribute definition includes a setting that specifies whether the attribute should be *indexed*. If the searchFlags attribute of the attribute object is set to 1, the attribute will be indexed. Active Directory automatically generates an index of all indexed attributes. Indexing an attribute helps speed up searches on the attribute. However, generating the index requires processor time, so it isn't a good idea to index an attribute just because you can. The index should contain only attributes that are commonly used in searches. The Active Directory Schema utility lets you mark an attribute as *indexed*. See the later section on "Indexing an Attribute."

TIP: Microsoft notes that it takes longer to modify or create instances of a class if the class has many indexed attributes.

As you'll learn in the next section, the *syntax* of an attribute is the datatype or format of the attribute data. Active Directory attributes are classified as either single-value or multivalue. Each value of a multivalue attribute must follow the rules of the syntax associated with the attribute. The singleValued attribute in the attribute object specifies whether the attribute is a single-valued attribute. (TRUE=single value; FALSE=multivalue). Because of their complexity, multivalue attributes are a little more difficult for the directory to manage. For performance reasons, it is better to avoid indexing multivalue attributes.

TIP: Attribute names that begin with "system" (for example, systemMayContain) are system-only attributes that can't be changed by users.

Syntaxes

A syntax is a datatype or format for an attribute value. Unlike classes and attributes, a syntax is not a directory object. Recognition of syntax options is instead programmed directly into Active Directory.

You specify the syntax for an attribute when the attribute is created. After the attribute is created, you cannot change its syntax. However, for some syntaxes, you can specify a range of permissible values along with the attribute definition. For instance, the Numeric String syntax allows you to specify a minimum and maximum value for the string when you create the attribute. See the later section on "Creating a New Attribute" for more information.

Table 10-1 shows some representative syntax options.

Classes

A *class* is a template that defines the structure for a class of objects. —Hundreds (or thousands) of objects can all belong to the same class. Every object in the Active Directory is associated with a class. The default Active Directory schema contains more than 140 classes.

Much of the class terminology and functionality is inherited from the X.500 directory services specification. In X.500, every class is associated with a class type. The Active Directory class types are as follows:

▼   **Structural classes**   Classes that can actually have instances in Active Directory.

- ■ **Abstract classes**   Classes used to create structural classes.

- ■ **Auxiliary classes**   Classes used to include a predetermined set of additional attributes to a structural or abstract class.

- ▲ **88 classes**   Classes defined prior to the 1993 X.500 standard. (The previous standard was X.500 1988—hence the name.) This category is included for interoperability reasons, though the default directory doesn't include any 88 classes and you can't (and shouldn't) create new 88 classes.

A class inherits properties from a parent class and passes those properties down to child classes. When you create a new class, you specify a parent class for it. The new class will inherit properties from the parent class. By default, every class is a child of a special top-level class called the *top* class. A new class is automatically a child of the top class unless you specify a different parent class. (See the later section "Creating a New Class.")

Syntax	Description
Distinguished Name	Distinguished name of a directory object
Case Sensitive String	Case-sensitive alphanumeric string
Case Insensitive String	Case-insensitive alphanumeric string
Numerical String	A string of digits
Boolean	TRUE or FALSE
Integer	32-bit integer
Large Integer	64-bit integer
Octet String	A string of bytes
SID	A Windows security identifier (SID)

Table 10-1.   Syntax Options

The child class inherits rules and attributes of the parent. You do not have to specify inherited attributes when you create a child class. For instance, if you create a child class of the user class, the child class will automatically be assigned all attributes of the user class. You can then add any additional attributes (that aren't part of the user class) directly to the child.

The attributes associated with a class can be classified as either *mandatory* or *optional* attributes. Mandatory attributes require that a value for the attribute be entered for all instances of the class. When you create a new class, you specify which mandatory attributes and optional attributes you wish to assign to the class. (As the preceding paragraph describes, mandatory and optional attributes can also be inherited from a parent class.) Optional attributes may be added to a class after it has been created; however, mandatory attributes cannot be added to a class once it has been created.

You do not have to create a new class to implement a new attribute, because it's possible to add a new attribute to an existing class. Once an object such as a user account has been created, the class of the object can't be changed. For this reason, Microsoft recommends that if you wish to track some new property of a user account (for instance, the user's height for purposes of assigning office furniture) you add a new attribute to the user class rather than create a whole new child class.

The Schema Cache

When you make a change to Active Directory, you are most likely changing an attribute value for an object. The syntax for that attribute is defined in the schema. Before you can make a change, Active Directory verifies that the change follows the syntax rules defined in the schema (see Figure 10-5). Microsoft did not want every change to every directory setting to require a low-performance, on-disk search of the schema partition, so a copy of the schema is held in memory on Active Directory domain controllers. This RAM-based schema copy is known as the schema cache.

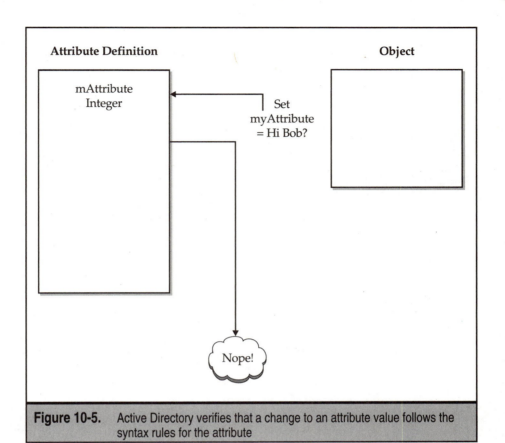

Attribute Definition

Object

mAttribute
Integer

Set
myAttribute
= Hi Bob?

Nope!

Figure 10-5.   Active Directory verifies that a change to an attribute value follows the syntax rules for the attribute

The schema cache, based on the current on-disk version of the schema, is created when the domain controller starts. The schema cache is then used to validate changes to directory objects. If a change is made to the schema itself, that change is first made to the on-disk copy of the schema partition. The schema cache is automatically updated with any changes within five minutes of a change to the on-disk schema copy (see Figure 10-6). It is therefore possible (and, in fact, likely) that if you make a change to the schema and then immediately perform a test to see if the change happened successfully, you will find that the change didn't appear to have happened at all. Active Directory will not fully implement the change until the next schema cache update.

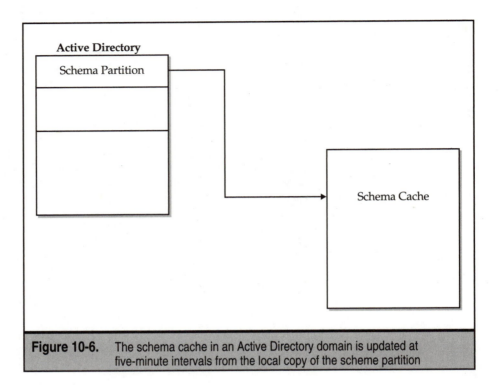

Figure 10-6.   The schema cache in an Active Directory domain is updated at five-minute intervals from the local copy of the scheme partition

NOTE: The five-minute schema cache update interval also assumes that you are testing the change directly at the schema master. If the change has to replicate through the network, delays could be even longer. See Chapter 4, "Understanding Replication," for more on the replication process. A change must first replicate through the network before the on-disk version of each domain controller registers the change. Each domain controller then updates its own schema cache at the five-minute update interval.

You can flush the schema cache and force a reload automatically through the Active Directory Schema application. For a complete discussion of the Active Directory Schema application, see "Working with Active Directory Schema," later in this chapter.

To force a reload of the schema cache:

1. Open Active Directory Schema in Microsoft Management Console (see the section titled "Working with Active Directory Schema").

2. Right-click the Active Directory Schema icon.

3. Choose Reload The Schema in the context menu.

You can also manually update the schema using ADSI Editor (see the later discussion of ADSI Editor in "Working with ADSI Editor"). To force a reload of the schema cache using ADSI Editor:

1. Open ADSI Editor in Microsoft Management Console (see the later section titled "Working with ADSI Editor").

2. Connect to the schema partition (as described in "Working with ADSI Editor"). Right-click the Schema icon. (You may need to click the plus sign next to the ADSI Edit icon.)

3. In the context menu of the Schema icon, choose Update Schema Now.

When the schema cache is updated, the old cache remains in memory temporarily to receive threads that may have started before the time of the update. The new cache and the old cache are thus both in memory at once. Microsoft recommends that you make all schema changes first and then update the schema cache once at the end of the edit session. This prevents the excessive use of memory required to support and manipulate multiple schema caches.

CAUTION: It is important to note that the two preceding procedures update the schema cache from the schema partition that currently resides on the domain controller to which you are connected. These procedures do not replicate a change made on another domain controller. See Chapter 4 for a discussion of how to manually force a replication update.

MODIFYING THE SCHEMA

Since Windows 2000 is still new, the world has not had time to develop a conventional wisdom about when and why it may be useful to edit the schema. It is probable that certain software applications will modify the schema to hold settings necessary for the successful operation of the software. However, the benefits of modifying the schema for everyday operations are a little less certain. Microsoft provides user interface tools for altering the schema, but its a little unclear how and when these tools should be used.

TIP: Microsoft Exchange is an example of a software package that modifies the schema to interoperate with Active Directory. You'll learn more about Exchange with Active Directory in Chapter 13, "Interoperating Active Directory."

The preferred method for modifying the schema, according to Microsoft, is programmatically—through a well-tested script or application. The user interface tools are best suited for occasional troubleshooting, for viewing attribute and object properties, and for interactive schema modification in a testing environment. This part of the chapter discusses the tools Active Directory Schema and ADSI Editor.

As already described, schema attributes and classes are similar to other directory objects, and they can be modified using many of the other tools and procedures used for modifying objects in the Active Directory. See Chapter 8, "Managing Active Directory," for more on modifying directory objects.

TIP: Schema modifications can, of course, facilitate Microsoft's cosmic goal of integrating the network database with the personnel database. You can modify the schema to store all sorts of user information, and that information is then available for directory searches. However, keep in mind that Microsoft advises against using Active Directory as a master copy for personnel data and other information unrelated to the network. There are other ways to track employee medical ID numbers, for example. Don't be in a rush to add new attributes for corporate data unless this use of Active Directory fits with your overall corporate strategy for managing information.

To modify the schema, you must be a member of the Schema Admins group. By default, the built-in Administrator account of the root domain is a member of the Schema Admins group. Other administrative-level users will be able to add the Active Directory

Schema Management Console and view some schema information, but they will not be able to make changes to the schema.

TIP: If you place your current user account in the Schema Admins group, you have to log out and log on again before you can make changes to the schema.

Schema Changes and the Schema Master

As you learned in Chapter 2, "Active Directory Concepts," the master copy of the schema is stored on a single domain controller called the schema master. An Active Directory forest has only one schema master. You can, however, make changes to the schema through a domain controller that is not the schema master. The schema master must be online at the time you make the change. If you modify the schema through a domain controller that is not the schema master, the change is referred back to the schema master and replicated to the network from the schema master.

Microsoft went to great effort to ensure that the schema would not be altered without careful deliberation. One aspect of that schema protection policy is that, by default, you *cannot* change the schema on any domain controller—even the schema master. Before you make a change to the schema through the Active Directory Schema application, you must manually configure the domain controller on which you're working to accept schema changes. As stated in the preceding paragraph, the domain controller that accepts the change does not have to be the schema master. It does, however, have to be configured to accept schema changes.

To configure a domain controller to process schema modifications, follow these steps:

1. Open Active Directory Schema in Microsoft Management Console (see the later section "Working with Active Directory Schema").

2. Right-click the Active Directory Schema icon. Select Operations Master.

3. In the Change Schema Master dialog box (see Figure 10-7), the computer listed in the Current Focus box is the computer to which the Active Directory Schema application is currently connected. To enable this computer to process schema modifications, check the box labeled The Schema May Be Modified On This Domain Controller. Click OK.

4. If you wish to enable schema modification on a different domain controller, right-click the Active Directory Schema icon in Microsoft Management Console and select Change Domain Controller. In the subsequent Change Domain Controller dialog box (see Figure 10-8), click Specify Name and enter the name of the domain controller you wish to make the current focus. Click OK. Go to step 3 to enable schema modifications on this computer.

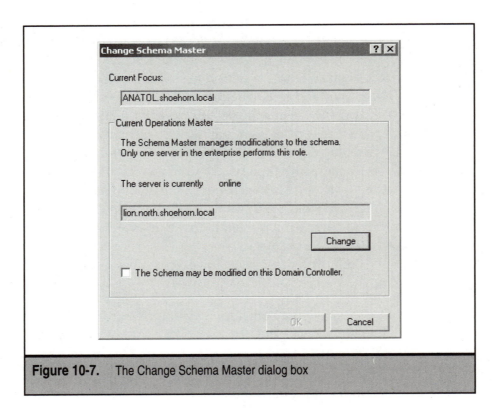

Figure 10-7.   The Change Schema Master dialog box

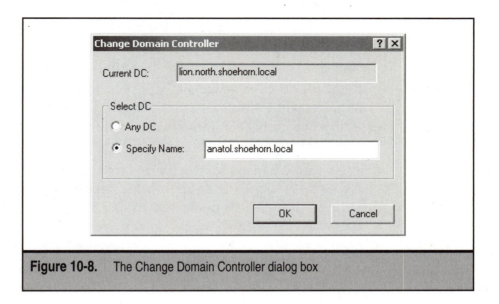

Figure 10-8.   The Change Domain Controller dialog box

NOTE: As stated earlier in this section, it is not necessary to change the schema master role in order to make schema modification. You may, however, choose to change the schema master role someday. It is possible to change the schema master role using the ntdsutil utility (see Chapter 8, "Managing Active Directory"). You can also change the schema master role using the Active Directory Schema application. Caution: Do not change the schema master unless you absolutely have to. Microsoft warns that changing the schema master should be a last resort. If you do reassign the schema master role, do not return the old schema master to the network. You must remove the old schema master from the network if you seize the schema master role.

To change the schema master from Active Directory Schema, follow these steps:

1. Right-click the Active Directory Schema icon in Microsoft Management Console (see the later section "Working with Active Directory Schema").

2. Select Change Domain Controller in the context menu. In the Change Domain Controller dialog box (refer to Figure 10-8), select the Specify Name radio button and enter the name of

the computer that you would like to make into the schema master. (You cannot change the schema master if your current focus is the current schema master.) Click OK.

3. Right-click the Active Directory Schema icon in the Microsoft Management Console (see the later section "Working with Active Directory Schema"). Select Operations Master in the context menu.

4. The Change Schema Master dialog box appears (refer to Figure 10-7). The Change Schema Master dialog box displays the current focus (the domain controller that you're currently connected to) and the current schema master. If these are the same computer, go to step 2 and change the current focus. Click Change.

5. Click OK when you're asked if you want to go through with the change. Active Directory assigns the schema master role to the current focus computer.

Generating an X.500 Object ID

The X.500 specification (upon which the LDAP specification is based) specifies that directory objects should be identified using a globally unique object identifier. Because the point of LDAP is to maximize the interoperability of directory systems, the namespace for these object identifiers (or OIDs) is carefully distributed among issuing authorities, countries, and vendors. Vendors provide their own subdivisions of the namespace and let customers provide additional branches and subdivisions as necessary.

The X.500 is typically a very long number expressed (at least for humans) in dotted decimal format (such as 1.2.840.113556.1). The X.500 object identifier for attributes appears as the attributeID attribute of the attributeSchema object. The X.500 object identifier for classes appears as the governsID attribute of the classSchema object.

Active Directory object identifier IDs begin with the base
1.2.840.113556.1. The reason for this base ID value reveals something
of how the numbering system actually works:

▼ 1 is the number that represents ISO, the root authority.

■ 2 is the number assigned to ANSI.

■ 840 is the number assigned to the USA.

■ 113556 is the number assigned to Microsoft.

▲ 1 is the number Microsoft assigned to Active Directory objects.

Microsoft then provides additional branches for each type of
directory object. Specifically, attributes form a branch with the base
1.2.840.113556.4. Classes form a branch with the base 1.2.840.113556.5.

If you create new classes and attributes, you are supposed to give
them unique identifiers. Your organization can apply for its own
identifier space through the International Standards Organization
(ISO). Or, you can add your own branches to the Microsoft identifier
space. If you want to ensure a unique identifier number within the
Microsoft identifier space, you can use the Object ID Generator
(oidgen.exe) utility in the Windows 2000 Resource Kit to generate
a base identifier for attributes and classes. The Object ID Generator
is a command line utility that requires no parameters.

At the command prompt, type **oidgen**. Your computer will output
two long identifiers in the 1.2.840.112556.1 namespace. One will be
labeled Attribute Base OID and the other will be labeled Class Base OID.
The understanding is that you will start your own numbering scheme
for attributes and classes from these base IDs. These IDs are long to
ensure global uniqueness. In some examples, Microsoft uses a much
shorter ID. You can actually get away with a shorter ID, but, if you
want your system to be fully compliant with X.500, you need to find
a way to ensure uniqueness. Consult ISO (http://www.iso.ch) for
further information.

NOTE: You must install the Windows 2000 Resource Kit before you can use oidgen.exe.

Working with Active Directory Schema

The Active Directory Schema utility is the primary interface provided with Windows 2000 for interactively modifying the schema. Active Directory Schema lets you add, remove, and modify classes and attributes.

Active Directory Schema is located in the system_root\system32 directory of Active Directory domain controllers. You must register the Active Directory Schema DLL before you can use it. To add Active Directory Schema, follow these steps:

1. Log on as an administrator.

2. Click Start and select Run. In the Run dialog box, type **regsvr32 schmmgmt.dll**.

   Alternatively, you can type the preceding command at the command prompt.

3. When a dialog box appears announcing that the operation was successful (that is, if the operation was successful), click OK.

4. Click the Start button and select Run.

5. In the Run dialog box, type **mmc**. Click OK. The Microsoft Management Console appears.

6. In the Microsoft Management Console main window, pull down the Console menu and choose Add/Remove Snap-In.

7. In the Add/Remove Snap-In dialog box, click the Add button.

8. In the Add Standalone Snap-In dialog box, select Active Directory Schema. Click the Add button and then click Close.

9. Active Directory Schema should appear in the Snap-in list in the Add/Remove Snap-In dialog box. Click OK.

10. Active Directory Schema should appear in the Snap-in tree in the Microsoft Management Console main window. To save the console for future use, select the Console menu and choose Save As. Enter a name for the console and choose OK.

Listed beneath the Active Directory Schema icon in the Microsoft Management Console tree are two folders: Classes and Attributes (see Figure 10-9). This is as you would expect, because the schema is essentially a self-referential collection of classes and attributes. If you select the Classes folder, a list of classes appears in the right pane. If you select the Attributes folder, a list of Active Directory attributes appears in the right pane. To view the properties of a class or attribute, right-click the class or attribute in the right pane and select Properties from the drop-down menu.

The following sections describe how to add new classes and attributes and how to view and modify classes and attributes using Active Directory Schema.

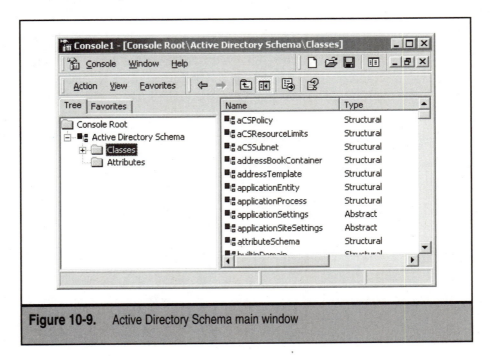

Figure 10-9. Active Directory Schema main window

TIP: A member of the Schema Admins group (such as the Administrator account of the root domain) can assign permissions to other accounts for access to the Active Directory Schema through the Active Directory Schema application. Right-click the Active Directory Schema icon in Microsoft Management Console and select Permissions. See the preceding procedure for a description of how to add Active Directory Schema to Microsoft Management Console.

Viewing and Modifying Attribute Properties

By default, you must be a member of the Schema Admins group to modify attribute properties. Members of the Admins group can open Active Directory Schema and view some schema properties. Members of the Schema Admins group can change the default security to provide greater access to other users and groups.

To view and modify attribute properties, follow these steps:

1. Open Active Directory Schema. (See the previous section titled "Working with Active Directory Schema" for more on adding Active Directory Schema to Microsoft Management Console.)

2. Click the plus sign next to the Active Directory Schema icon to reveal the Classes and Attributes folders. Click Attributes. A list of current Active Directory attributes appears in the right pane.

3. Scroll to the attribute whose properties you wish to view or modify. Notice that the attribute's name, syntax, and description appear in the right pane of the main window.

4. Right-click the attribute whose properties you wish to view or modify and then click Properties.

    The attribute Properties dialog box appears (see Figure 10-10). The settings that can be modified by the user are shown with a white background. Note that many of the settings cannot be modified—especially if you are viewing a built-in attribute from the default Active Directory.

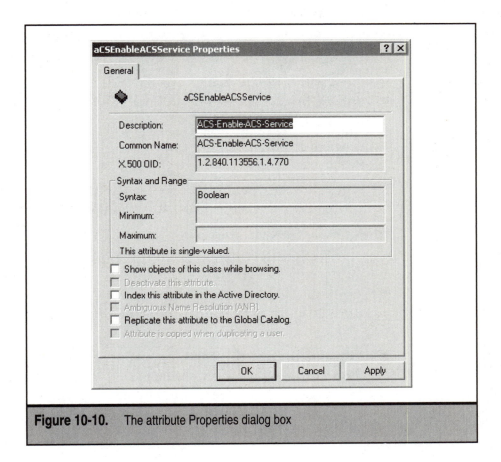

Figure 10-10.   The attribute Properties dialog box

TIP: The settings in the Properties dialog box represent attributes of the attribute object (see the "Attributes, Syntaxes, and Schema Classes" section earlier in the chapter). Recall that the attribute is actually an object that belongs to the attributeSchema class.

The Common Name setting that appears in the attribute Properties dialog box is the LDAP common name that identifies the object in LDAP distinguished name format. (*CN* in the distinguished name stands for *Common Name*.) The earlier section titled "Syntaxes" described the Syntax and Range settings. The check boxes at the bottom of the Properties dialog box offer several important options:

▼ **Show Objects Of This Class While Browsing**

■ **Deactivate This Attribute**   Place the attribute in a deactivated status. See the section titled "Deactivating and Reactivating Classes and Attributes" later in this chapter.

■ **Index This Attribute In The Active Directory**   Index the attribute. See the later section titled "Indexing an Attribute."

■ **Ambiguous Name Resolution (ANR)**   A feature that lets Active Directory resolve differences in naming format (for instance, Tom Jones versus Jones, Tom).

■ **Replicate This Attribute In The Global Catalog**   Place this attribute in the global catalog. See the later section titled "Adding an Attribute to the Global Catalog."

▲ **Attribute Is Copied When Duplicating A User**   For user class attributes only. This setting tells Active Directory to copy the attribute value when a user object is duplicated.

Creating a New Attribute

Active Directory attributes are created independently of class. If you wish to create a new class with new attributes, you must create the attributes first and then add those attributes to the class when you create the class. You can also add new attributes to an existing class.

To create a new attribute, follow these steps:

1. Open Active Directory Schema. (See the previous section titled "Working with Active Directory Schema" for more on adding Active Directory Schema to Microsoft Management Console.)

2. Click the plus sign next to the Active Directory Schema icon to reveal the Classes and Attributes folders. Right-click the Attributes folder and then select Create Attribute.

3. A dialog box warns you that when you create a new attribute, it will become a permanent part of the Active Directory. If you are resolved to press ahead, click Continue.

4. The Create New Attribute dialog box appears (see Figure 10-11). In this dialog box, supply the following information:

- **Common Name**   The LDAP common name for the attribute object. The *common name* identifies the attribute object in the distinguished name (CN = *object_name*—see Chapter 2, "Active Directory Concepts").

- **LDAP Display Name**   The name used for the object in Active Directory searches elsewhere in the user interface.

- **Unique X500 Object ID**   An X500 Object ID for the attribute. See the earlier section titled "Generating an X.500 Object ID."

- **Syntax**   The syntax designation for the attribute. The syntax defines the type and format of the data. See the earlier section titled "Syntaxes."

- **Minimum**   A minimum setting for values associated with the attribute.

- **Maximum**   A maximum setting for values associated with the attribute.

- **Multivalued**   Select this check box if the attribute is a multivalued attribute. Otherwise, the attribute is considered single-valued.

5. When you have finished entering attribute settings, click OK.

As you may have noticed in the preceding section "Viewing and Modifying Attribute Properties," the attribute Properties dialog box contains some additional settings that aren't present in the Create New Attribute dialog box. To configure additional settings for the attribute, such as an attribute description or an index setting, follow the procedure described in the preceding section, "Viewing and Modifying Attribute Properties."

Indexing an Attribute

The Active Directory Schema application lets you optionally index an attribute for faster searches. Indexing an attribute improves

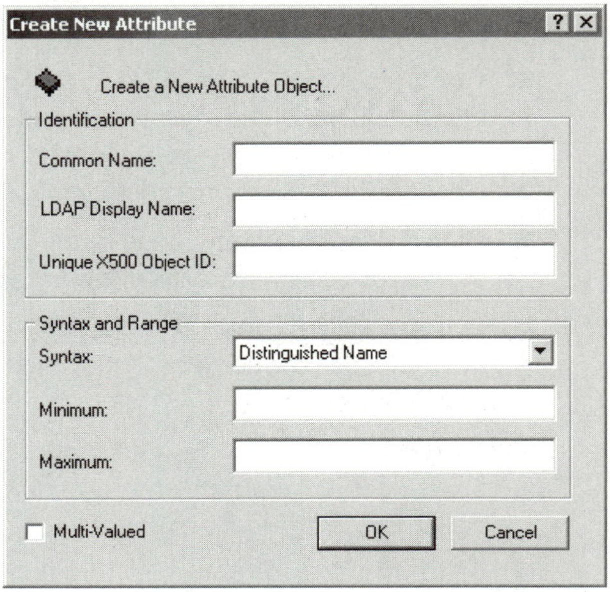

Figure 10-11. The Create New Attribute dialog box

performance for searches that use the attribute, but it takes time to generate the index, so it is best to be selective about what attributes you index. Microsoft recommends the following guidelines:

▼ *Index single-valued attributes.* Multivalued attributes add complexity to the index and require more time and disk space.

■ *Try to index attributes with unique values.* Indexing the countryCode attribute, for instance, does not offer much benefit.

▲ *Limit the number of indexed attributes in a class.* When a new instance of a class is created, indexed attributes within the class require additional processing time.

To index an attribute in the Active Directory, follow these steps:

1. Open Active Directory Schema. (See the previous section titled "Working with Active Directory Schema" for more on adding Active Directory Schema to Microsoft Management Console.)

2. Click the plus sign next to the Active Directory Schema icon to reveal the Classes and Attributes folders. Click Attributes. A list of current Active Directory attributes appears in the right pane.

3. Scroll to the attribute you wish to index. Right-click the attribute and then click Properties.

4. The attribute Properties dialog box appears (refer to Figure 10-10). Click the box labeled Index This Attribute In The Active Directory to select it. Then click OK.

Adding an Attribute to the Global Catalog

As you learned in Chapter 2, "Active Directory Concepts," the global catalog is a subset of Active Directory that is stored on domain controllers, called *global catalog servers,* for fast network searches. Windows 2000 uses the global catalog as part of its normal operations, and users can search for global catalog data directly. The Replicate This Attribute To The Global Catalog setting in the attribute Properties dialog box places the attribute in the global catalog so that it will be available for global catalog searches.

It is important to note that you can search for an attribute even if it isn't in the global catalog. The Windows 2000 search interface applications, such as Windows Explorer, also offer an Active Directory search option, which will turn up attribute settings that aren't in the global catalog. The principal benefit of placing an attribute in the global catalog is that global catalog searches are typically faster.

TIP: The object-oriented terminology is especially confusing around attributes and classes. Note that the Replicate This Attribute To The Global Catalog setting doesn't exactly let you search for the *attribute* as we are using the term in this discussion of schema. It actually lets you search for objects that assign a value for the attribute. For example, the built-in attribute TelephoneNumber is replicated to the global catalog by default. That means you can search for telephone number settings of user objects (such as 316-255-9099), not that you can search for the TelephoneNumber attribute itself, which, in the schema, is actually an object of the attributeSchema class.

To cause an attribute to replicate to the global catalog, follow these steps:

1. In Active Directory Schema, click the plus sign next to the Active Directory Schema icon to reveal the Classes and Attributes folders. Click Attributes. A list of current Active Directory attributes appears in the right pane.

2. Scroll to the attribute you wish to add to the global catalog. Right-click the attribute and then click Properties.

3. The attribute Properties dialog box appears (refer to Figure 10-10). Check the box labeled Replicate This Attribute To The Global Catalog. Click OK.

Viewing and Modifying Class Properties

The Active Directory Schema application provides a view of class properties and lets you change certain settings associated with the class. You'll notice several settings that you can't change, especially for a built-in class that is part of the default Active Directory configuration. You can also add a new class, as described in the next section, "Creating a New Class."

To view and modify attribute properties, follow these steps:

1. In Active Directory Schema, click the plus sign next to the Active Directory Schema icon to reveal the Classes and Attributes folders. Click Classes. A list of current Active Directory classes appears in the right pane.

2. Scroll to the class whose properties you wish to view or modify. Notice that the class's name, type, and description appear in the right pane of the main window.

3. Right-click the class whose properties you wish to view or modify and click Properties.

4. The class Properties dialog box appears (see Figure 10-12). The settings that can be modified by the user are shown with a white background. Note that many of the settings cannot be

modified—especially if you are viewing a built-in attribute from the default Active Directory.

The class Properties dialog box includes the following four tabs:

■ **General**   This tab (see Figure 10-12) displays general information about the class. Many of these settings, such as the common name, class type, and X.500 OID, cannot be changed from this dialog box. However, you can add a description for the class that will appear in Active Directory Schema's main window. You can also check or uncheck

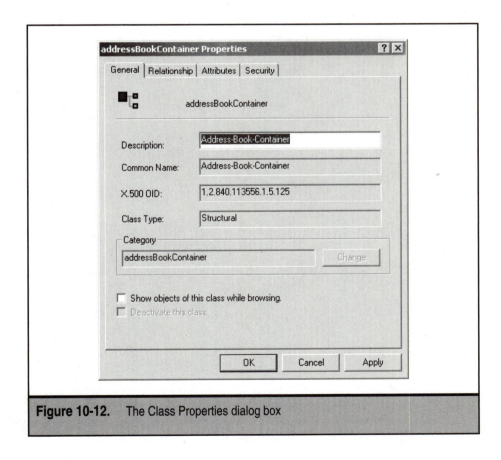

Figure 10-12.   The Class Properties dialog box

Show Objects Of This Class While Browsing. If the class is not part of the original Active Directory configuration, you can check or uncheck Deactivate This Class. See the later section titled "Deactivating and Reactivating Classes and Attributes."

■ **Relationship** This tab (see Figure 10-13) lets you view the parent class and view or edit Auxiliary or Possible Superior class settings. To add an auxiliary or possible superior class, click the corresponding Add button. You can also remove an auxiliary or possible superior class by choosing the class and clicking the corresponding Remove

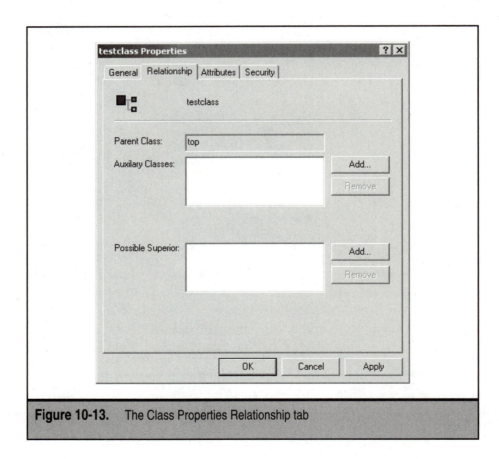

Figure 10-13. The Class Properties Relationship tab

button. See the earlier section titled "Classes" for more on class relationships.

■ **Attributes**   This tab (see Figure 10-14) lets you view mandatory and optional attributes and add or remove optional attributes from the class. To add an optional attribute, click the Add button. Note that if you wish to associate a new attribute with the class, you must create the attribute separately (see the preceding section titled "Creating New Attributes"). See the preceding section on "Classes" for more on mandatory versus optional attributes.

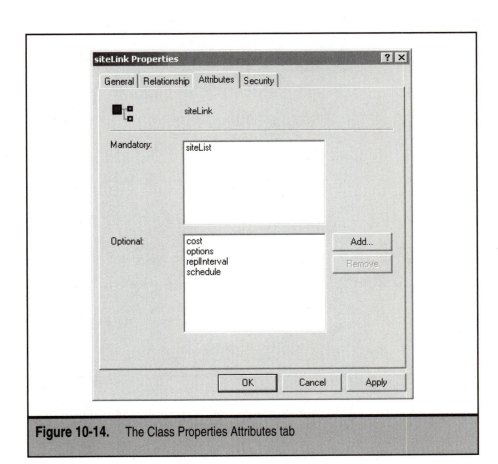

Figure 10-14.   The Class Properties Attributes tab

■ **Security** This tab (see Figure 10-15) lets you assign
permissions to the class object. This tab is similar to security
dialog boxes found elsewhere in the Active Directory
environment. See Chapter 5, "Users and Groups," for
more on setting security for an Active Directory object.

5. When you have finished viewing or modifying the class
Properties dialog box, click OK.

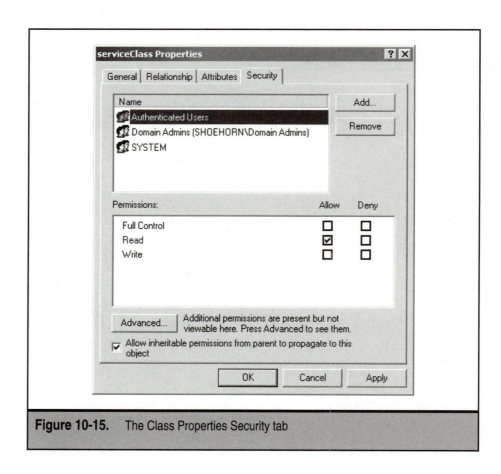

Figure 10-15. The Class Properties Security tab

Creating a New Class

To create a new class from the Active Directory Schema application, follow these steps:

1. In Active Directory Schema, click the plus sign next to the Active Directory Schema icon to reveal the Classes and Attributes folders. Right-click the Classes folder and select Create Class.

2. A dialog box warns you that when you create a new class, it will become a permanent part of the Active Directory. If you are resolved to press ahead, click Continue.

3. The Create New Schema Class dialog box appears (see Figure 10-16). In the Create New Schema Class dialog box, supply the following information:

   - **Common Name**   The LDAP common name for the class object. This name identifies the object in the distinguished name (CN = *object_name*—see Chapter 2, "Active Directory Concepts").

   - **LDAP Display Name**   The name used for the object in Active Directory searches and elsewhere in the user interface.

   - **Unique X500 Object ID**   An X500 Object ID for the class. See the earlier section entitled "Generating an X.500 Object ID."

   - **Parent Class**   A parent class from which the new class will be generated. See the earlier section titled "Classes."

   - **Class Type**   Click the arrow to display a drop-down list of available class types: structural, abstract, auxiliary. See the earlier section titled "Classes."

4. Click Next when you're finished with the preceding settings.

5. The next screen lets you choose mandatory and optional attributes for the class (see Figure 10-17). Click the

corresponding Add button to choose mandatory or optional attributes for the new class. If you want to associate mandatory attributes with the class, do it now. You cannot add these attributes to the class through the Properties dialog box once the class is created. (See the section titled "Viewing and Modifying Class Properties.")

6. Click Finish.

The class Properties dialog box contains additional settings that aren't present in the Create New Class Wizard. To configure additional settings for the class, such as security settings or a description, follow the procedure described in the preceding section, "Viewing and Modifying Attribute Properties."

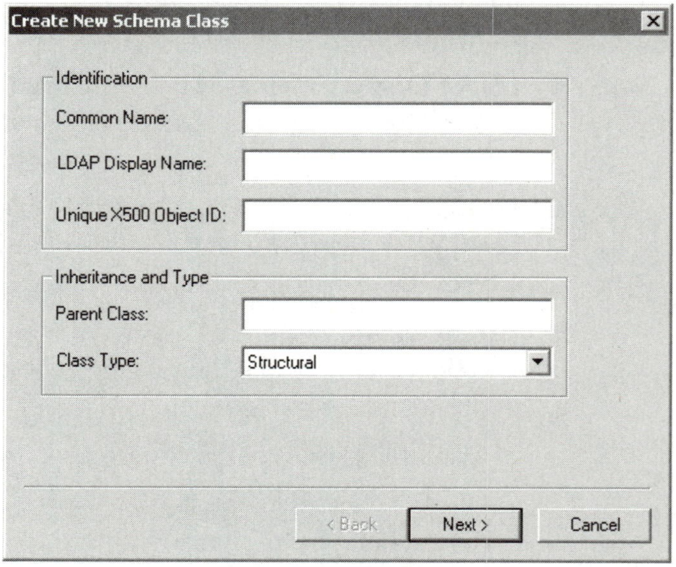

Figure 10-16. The Create New Schema Class dialog box

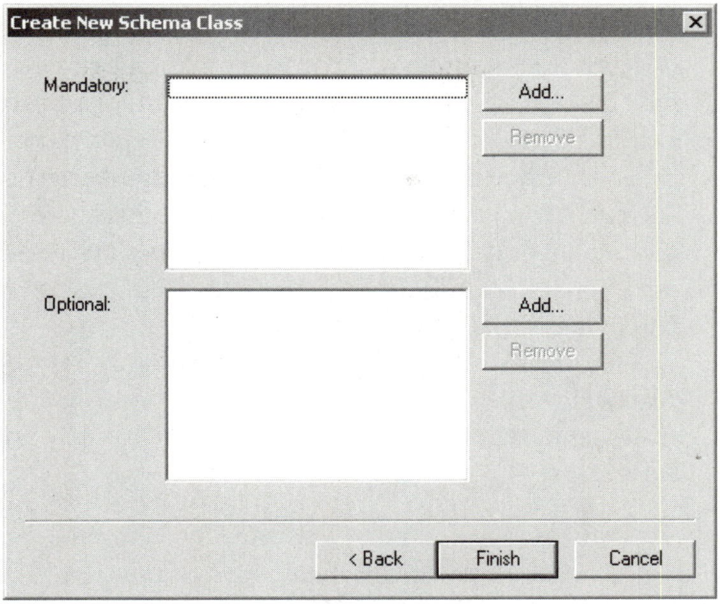

Figure 10-17. Specifying attributes for a new class

Deactivating and Reactivating Classes and Attributes

Because of the complex interdependencies of schema objects, Active Directory does not let you delete attributes and classes in the schema. You can, however, deactivate a class or an attribute. You cannot deactivate built-in attributes and classes that are part of the default Active Directory. In other words, the only attributes and classes you can deactivate are the ones that have been added to your configuration since you installed Active Directory.

For the most part, you cannot deactivate attributes or classes that are referenced in currently active attributes or classes. In other words, you can't deactivate classes that are subclasses, superclasses, or auxiliary classes of active classes, and you can't deactivate attributes that are assigned to currently active classes.

When you deactivate a class, objects created using that class will remain active in Active Directory, but you won't be able to add new objects that use the class. If you don't want the objects of the deactivated class in the Active Directory, you must search for the objects that are instances of the class and delete them as a separate process.

The attributeSchema object and the classSchema object include a Boolean attribute called isDefunct that specifies whether a schema object is activated or deactivated. By default, the value is set to FALSE to signify that the attribute or class is active. Setting this value to TRUE deactivates the attribute or class.

The Active Directory Schema application lets you activate or deactivate a class or attribute from within the user interface. To activate or deactivate a class or attribute in Active Directory Schema, follow these steps:

1. In Active Directory Schema, click the plus sign next to the Active Directory Schema icon to reveal the Classes and Attributes folders. Choose the folder for the schema object you wish to activate or deactivate.

2. Scroll to the schema object you wish to activate or deactivate. Right-click the schema object and then click Properties.

3. In the General tab of the Properties dialog box, check the box labeled Deactivate This Class (or Deactivate This Attribute if you are deactivating an attribute). Note that the box will be grayed out if the schema object is a built-in class or attribute included with the default Active Directory. To reactivate a class or attribute that is currently deactivated, uncheck the check box. Click OK.

Working with ADSI Editor

The ADSI Editor tool (see Chapter 8) lets you view and edit the objects that make up Active Directory. You can use ADSI Editor to view and edit schema objects. The ADSI Editor interface isn't as sophisticated as the interface provided by the Active Directory

Schema tool, but it provides a more uniform view that may be easier to use in some situations.

The purpose of ADSI Editor is to let you view object properties and set values for object attributes. If you're using ADSI Editor to view and modify the schema, the first thing to remember is that the attributes and classes of the schema are themselves objects. When you view classes and attributes in ADSI Editor, you are simply viewing a collection of objects. ADSI makes no effort to portray the classes and attributes of the schema as anything other than a collection of objects belonging to the attributeSchema and classSchema classes.

NOTE: See Chapter 8 for a discussion of ADSI Editor.

To view and edit schema attributes and classes from ADSI Editor:

1. Right-click the ADSI Editor icon in Microsoft Management Console and choose Connect To.

2. In the Connection dialog box (see Figure 10-18) click the down arrow to the right of the Naming Context box and choose Schema. Click OK.

3. Click the plus sign next to the Schema icon that appears below the ADSI Edit icon.

4. Select the folder below the Schema icon with the distinguished name of the schema partition. A list of schema objects appears in the right pane. You'll find the name, class, and distinguished name for each schema object. Note that all the attributes belong to the attributeSchema or classSchema class. The objects belonging to the attributeSchema class are attributes. The objects belonging to the classSchema class are classes. Double-click any schema object to view its Properties.

   The object Properties dialog box (see Figure 10-19) is primarily used to set new values for the attributes associated with the schema object. Note that the attributes you're

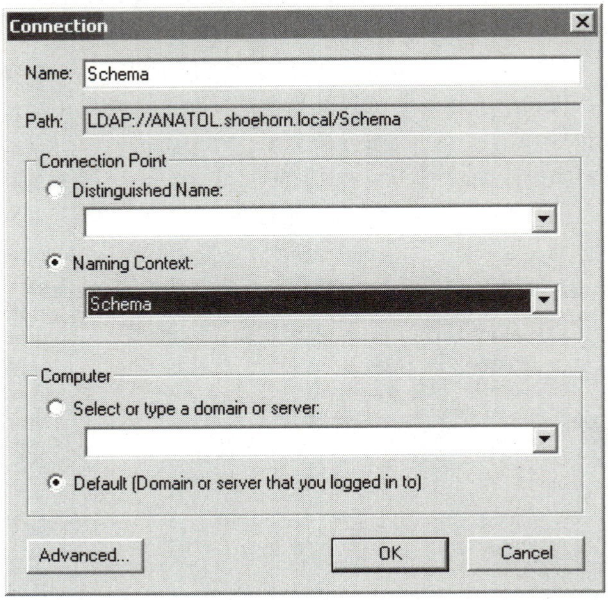

Figure 10-18. Connecting to a domain controller in ADSI Editor

working with in ADSI Editor are not the attributes assigned to the class whose property page you are viewing, but are instead the attributes associated with the schema object itself through its membership in the attributeSchema or classSchema class. Microsoft uses the word "property" in the Attributes tab of the Properties dialog box (refer to Figure 10-14) to avoid confusion. The options are as follows:

- **Select Which Properties To View** The drop-down list lets you choose whether to display mandatory attribute settings, optional attribute settings, or both for the schema object.

- **Select A Property To View** The drop-down list lets you choose an attribute. Note that these are attributes of the classSchema or attributeSchema class (depending on whether the object you're viewing is an attribute or a class).

They are not attributes that belong to the class whose properties you're viewing. They are attributes of the class to which the schema object itself belongs.

■ **Attribute Values**   When you select an attribute, attribute values associated with the object you're viewing appear in the Edit Attribute box. The syntax for the attribute appears in the box marked Syntax. Value(s) assigned to the attribute are shown in the box labeled Values. To change the value associated with the attribute, enter new text in the Edit Attribute box and click Set.

5.   Click OK.

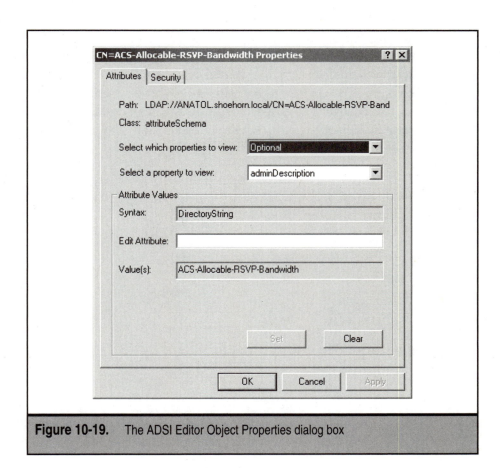

Figure 10-19.   The ADSI Editor Object Properties dialog box

NOTE: Some of the other directory editing tools discussed in Chapter 8 can also be used to edit the schema. These tools include *LDP, CSVDE, and LDIFDE.* See Chapter 8.

SUMMARY

Active Directory is a big, self-replicating database that can disseminate anything you put into it to all parts of the network. By adding new attributes and classes, you can customize Active Directory so that any information you wish to make available to the network is automatically distributed through directory updates. Application vendors will certainly make use of Active Directory as a means of distributing and storing information. This customization will occasionally create conflicts that the network administrator will have to address. The tools and concepts described in this chapter will provide you with some of the background you'll need for addressing those occasional conflicts.

This chapter also described how you can create your own new schema objects, modify schema objects, and view and edit schema object properties.

CHAPTER 11

Active Directory
Security

Network attackers grow more sophisticated every year, and so must network operating systems. The Active Directory environment offers an assortment of powerful new security features. This chapter focuses on Active Directory's support for Kerberos secure authentication. You'll also learn about some interesting network protection measures available through Active Directory's ubiquitous group policy feature, including Windows 2000's TCP/IP security system IPSec.

Kerberos

Support for Kerberos authentication is one of the most important differences between Windows 2000 and Windows NT 4. The Kerberos protocol supports a logon process that is more versatile, more interoperable, and more secure than Windows NT's NTLM authentication. In particular, Kerberos is designed to operate on open, hostile networks (like the Internet) where the user has no control over who may be intercepting messages or attempting to impersonate. Kerberos was developed at MIT as part of the Athena project and has been implemented widely on UNIX-based systems. In addition to providing more secure authentication in unsafe environments, Kerberos also, in part, provides a more network-based security environment for UNIX-like systems. Microsoft already had a network-based security environment in the Windows NT domain, and they should be commended for undertaking the huge task of integrating Kerberos with the Windows security model. (They wouldn't have done it, of course, unless they saw some benefit for the shareholders, but it still seems brave. Many big companies wouldn't have bothered.)

Kerberos authentication provides the following advantages over the NTLM authentication used with Windows NT:

▼ **Tighter security** Traditional authentication methods let the server verify who the client is, but, unlike Kerberos, they didn't let the client verify the server. Kerberos also provides built-in safeguards against the possibility of an unauthorized user impersonating an authorized user.

■ **Efficiency**   Clients are authenticated once for a service and can reuse credentials for the service throughout the logon session without reauthorization from a domain controller. Kerberos also supports a more efficient domain trust system.

▲ **Interoperability**   Windows 2000 Kerberos can interoperate with other Kerberos v5.0 servers and clients. Windows NT had no such mutual logon interoperability.

Windows 2000's Kerberos services work directly with Active Directory. Active Directory domain controllers are automatically configured to provide Kerberos with authentication services, and all Windows 2000 computers are configured to operate as Kerberos clients. The following sections describe how Kerberos works and discuss some of the options for defining and configuring the Kerberos environment.

What Is Kerberos?

Kerberos was developed as an effort to apply the principles of secret key cryptography to real-world network situations. Many discussions of Kerberos either assume the reader already knows what Kerberos is or else launch into an illustrative but oversimplified discussion from the first principle of two computers and a secret. I won't worry about building the whole system logically, but will instead just tell you as simply as I can how the Kerberos system works.

Kerberos is defined in RFC 1510 (by J. Kohl and C. Neuman, September 1993). RFC 1510 describes Kerberos as follows:

Kerberos provides a means of verifying the identities of principals (e.g., a workstation user or network server) on an open (unprotected) network. This is accomplished without relying on authentication by the host operating system, without basing trust on host address, without requiring physical security on all the hosts of the network, and under the assumption that packets traveling along the network can be read, modified, and inserted at will.

Kerberos is based around the principles of cryptography. One important principle of cryptography is the concept of a *key*. A key is a pattern or code that is used to encrypt a message. If you know the key, you can then decrypt the encrypted message so that you can read it. The trick is to ensure that the client and server each receive the key so they can engage in an encrypted session. In Kerberos, a special key server, called a Key Distribution Center (KDC), performs the role of distributing keys. *Kerberos* is the Greek name for the legendary three-headed dog Cerberus who guards the gate to the underworld. The creators of Kerberos named it for that most famous multicranial canine because the protocol, like the dog, has three heads:

▼ **The client**   The computer that is requesting a service.

■ **The server**   The computer that provides the service.

▲ **The KDC**   The computer that issues the session key necessary for the client and server to communicate.

The Kerberos authentication process is the result of an interaction between the client requesting a service, the server providing the service, and the KDC.

Of course, sending the session key around the network in a clear text message serves no purpose, because an intruder could simply intercept the message and extract the session key. It also does not help to encrypt the session key using the session key, because the host would need to have the key already in order to decrypt the message. Therefore, the system actually requires three keys in order to provide secure interaction among client, server, and KDC:

▼ **Session key**   A temporary key used to encrypt messages between a client and a specific service running on a server computer. The session key is generated by the KDC.

■ **Client key**   A key used to distribute a session key to the client. The client key is derived from the user's password and is known only to the client and the KDC. The KDC also uses the client key to encrypt a copy of the session *ticket*, which the client will send to the server to initiate the connection. You'll learn more about the session ticket later in this section.

▲ **Server key**   A key known only by the server and the KDC. The KDC bundles a package of information it wants the server to know (specifically, a copy of the session key and information on the client requesting the connection) and uses the server key to encrypt that package of information into the session ticket. It then encloses the session ticket into a message to the client, encrypted with the client key (see the preceding bullet). The client will be responsible for extracting the session ticket and sending it to the server.

The Kerberos authentication process is shown in Figure 11-1. The need for the session key to pass to the server through the client requires some additional explanation. The easy way for the KDC to perform its role of distributing the session key would have been to

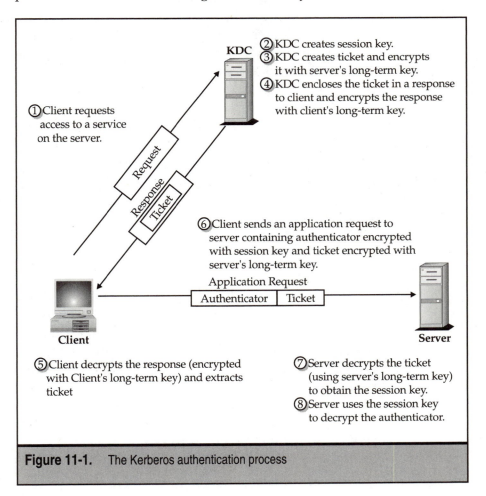

Figure 11-1. The Kerberos authentication process

encrypt the session key in the client key and send it to the client, then encrypt the session key in the server key and send it to the server. The designers of Kerberos, however, realized that on many networks, the server is busy communicating with multiple clients and has neither the RAM nor the time for a separate preliminary exchange with the KDC before each connection. Also, if the client and server each receive the session key separately, it is possible for the client to receive the key and send a request to the server before the key necessary to decrypt the message arrives. For these reasons, Kerberos does not distribute the session key directly to the server.

The KDC uses the server key to encrypt the server's copy of the session key into a structure called a *ticket*. The ticket also contains other information about the client. The contents of the ticket are described in Table 11-1. Note that three of the fields are in unencrypted (plain text) format so the client can store and retrieve the ticket from its ticket cache. The client cannot read the other fields of the ticket because only the KDC and the server have the server key necessary for decrypting the ticket. The client, however, does not have to be able to read the ticket. The client knows only that it must send the ticket to the server (along with *authenticator* information encrypted in the session key) in order to initiate the connection. The server receives the ticket and decrypts it using the server key. The server obtains the session key from the decrypted ticket and uses it to decrypt the client authenticator. The ticket and authenticator provide proof to the server that the client is trusted by the KDC and also supply the server with the session key. All communication between the client and server will be encrypted using the session key. If the client requires authentication of the server, the server then extracts the timestamp enclosed in the ticket, encrypts it using the session key, and returns it to the client. If the client can successfully decrypt this message from the server and determines that the timestamp returned from the server matches the timestamp the client received from the KDC, the client knows

▼ The server has the proper session key (since it was able to encrypt the timestamp message).

▲ The server has the proper server key (since it was able to decrypt the ticket and obtain the timestamp).

Field Type	Field Name	Description
Unencrypted fields	tkt-vno	Kerberos version number (5 for Windows 2000 Kerberos).
	realm	Name of the KDC's realm. (A realm is equivalent to a Windows domain.) KDC can only issue tickets to services in its own realm.
	sname	The server name.
Encrypted fields	flags	The ticket option flags.
	key	The session key.
	crealm	The client's realm (does not have to be the same as the server and KDC's realm).
	cname	Client's host name.
	transited	List of other realms that participated in authenticating the client.
	authtime	The authorization time— timestamp showing the moment when the KDC authenticated the client by issuing a ticket granting ticket (TGT).
	starttime	Time at which ticket becomes usable.
	endtime	Ticket expiration time.
	rnew-till	Maximum limit for Endtime in renewable tickets (optional).
	caddr	Addresses for which the ticket can be used (optional).
	authorization-data	User and group SIDs passed to the service to which the client is connecting (optional).

Table 11-1.   Data Fields of a Kerberos Ticket

This Kerberos authentication process can thwart much of the impersonating and masquerading that occurs on the Internet. It cannot, however, stop all types of attacks. See the section titled "What Kerberos Doesn't Prevent" later in the chapter for more on hacker attacks to which Kerberos is not immune.

In Windows 2000, the client key (known only by the client and KDC) and the server key (known only by the server and KDC) are known as *long-term keys*. The client long-term key is derived from the user's logon password.

NOTE: The analogy of the dog Cerberus is an interesting literary aside that helps to highlight the three parts of the Kerberos authentication process (as opposed to the typical two-part client/server process). However, it should be noted that there is no indication that the three writhing heads of Cerberus ever communicated with each other in any orderly or rational way. Furthermore, a close inspection of the legend raises the question of whether this is indeed the best metaphor for a network security system. Cerberus was not exactly invincible, but was in fact "vinced" on several occasions by heroes who took his fearsome appearance as something of a challenge. Orpheus lulled all three heads to sleep by playing pretty music. Aeneas pacified him with honey cakes. Hercules put a leash on him and walked him around for a while. We'll hope these lapses in the resolve of the hellhound are not an indication of vulnerabilities in its digital namesake.

How Does Kerberos Work in Windows 2000?

In Windows 2000, every Active Directory domain controller is automatically configured to operate as a KDC. You'll find the Kerberos Key Distribution Center Service in Programs | Administrative Tools | Computer Management | Services and Applications | Services. The service starts automatically. Kerberos authentication is integrated seamlessly into the Windows 2000 logon process. Windows 2000 clients will use Kerberos logon if possible. Pre-Windows 2000 clients do not support Kerberos and will instead log on using NTLM authentication.

Authentication requests to the KDC service use the krbtgt account domain account. Before a client can begin requesting tickets from a KDC, it must undergo Kerberos authentication with the KDC itself, as follows:

1. When a user logs on, the user's password is encrypted through a one-way hashing function to derive the client's long-term key. That key is then sent to the domain controller, which, in Windows 2000, also happens to be a KDC.

2. The domain controller/KDC receives the client key from the client and checks it against the copy of the client key stored in the Active Directory. (Active Directory holds the user's password and can thus independently derive the client key using the one-way hashing function. Passwords and client keys are well protected in Active Directory. You cannot display them using directory search tools. Even an administrator cannot obtain a user's password or client key from Active Directory.)

3. The domain controller/KDC issues the client a session key for communication with the KDC and a Kerberos ticket that the client will use for initiating communication with the KDC itself. This ticket is called a ticket granting ticket (TGT), and it is encrypted using the KDC's own long-term key. The client will be able to use the TGT and the KDC session key to communicate with the KDC until the TGT expires or until the user logs off.

The client maintains a cache of tickets it has received from the KDC for access to various network services (see Figure 11-2). The client can continue to use the cached ticket (and its accompanying session key) to communicate with the service until the ticket expires, at which point the client must request a new ticket from the KDC.

In a multidomain environment, the Kerberos authentication procedure is similar but a bit more complicated. When two domains enter into a trust relationship, the Kerberos ticket-granting service of each domain is registered with the KDC of the other's domain. The local domain can then assign a ticket to the KDC in the other domain

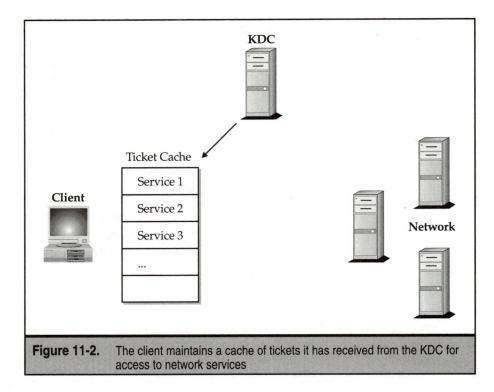

Figure 11-2. The client maintains a cache of tickets it has received from the KDC for access to network services

just as it would assign a ticket to any other service. This ticket is called a *referral ticket,* and the process is as follows:

1. A user in domain A tries to access computer 1 in domain B.

2. The user's workstation asks the KDC in domain A for a session ticket to access a service on computer 1.

3. The KDC in domain A sends the workstation a referral ticket for the KDC in domain B.

4. The workstation asks the KDC in domain B for a request for a session ticket to access a service on computer 1.

5. The KDC in domain B issues a session ticket for the service on computer 1.

If the network includes three or more domains in a tree structure (so that not every domain has a direct trust relationship with every other domain), the workstation may sometimes receive a series of referral tickets from intermediate domains before receiving a session ticket to access the service.

Configuring Kerberos

Kerberos runs automatically on Active Directory domain controllers, so you don't have to configure anything to use it. You can, however, configure a few important options for defining the Kerberos environment. The following sections discuss

▼ Configuring delegation of authentication

■ Turning off Kerberos preauthentication

▲ Setting Kerberos policy

Remember that the Kerberos service can only be used by client computers that support it. Pre–Windows 2000 Microsoft computers (such as Windows NT and Windows 95/98) do not provide built-in support for Kerberos.

Configuring Delegation of Authentication

Often a service must interact with other services on the network in order to perform its role. In Windows NT, a service representing a client could operate under the client's security context when interacting with other services. This concept was known as *impersonation*. The Kerberos *delegation of authentication* feature is similar to impersonation. According to Microsoft, delegation of authentication works under the following three conditions:

▼ The client process, the server process, and the back-end server process (the service accessed by the server process) must be running on Windows 2000 systems in a Windows 2000 domain.

■ The client's account must allow delegation of authentication.

▲ The service's account must allow delegation of authentication.

To configure the client account for delegation of authentication, follow these steps:

1. Select Start | Programs | Administrative Tools | Active Directory Users And Computers.

2. Select the container or OU that holds the user account for which you wish to configure delegation of authentication.

3. Right-click the account name in the right pane and select Properties.

4. In the account's Properties dialog box, select the Accounts tab.

5. In the account's Properties Account tab (see Figure 11-3) scroll through the Account Options list for the entry labeled Account Is Sensitive And Cannot Be Delegated. If this option is checked, remove the check mark. Click OK.

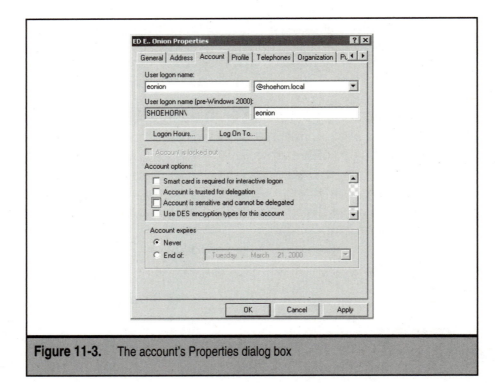

Figure 11-3.   The account's Properties dialog box

By default, many services run under the local system account of the computer on which they're located. In some cases, the service runs under a different account with specific permissions and privileges necessary for operating the service. The steps for configuring a service account for delegation of authentication are different depending on whether the service account is the local system account or a different user account.

If you configure the local system account for delegation of authentication, you allow local system services to request services on other computers. If you don't want to allow delegation of authentication for all local system services, you should configure the service you wish to authorize for delegation of authentication to run under a different service.

To configure the local system account for delegation of authentication, follow these steps:

1. Select Start | Programs | Administrative Tools | Active Directory Users And Computers.

2. Select the container or OU that holds the computer on which the service runs.

3. Right-click the icon for the host computer and choose Properties.

4. In the account's Properties General tab, check the Trust Computer For Delegation box (see Figure 11-4). Click OK.

To configure the service account for delegation of authentication if the service runs on an account that isn't a local system account, follow these steps:

1. Select Start | Programs | Administrative Tools | Active Directory Users And Computers.

2. Select the container or OU that holds the service account of the service for which you're configuring delegation of authentication.

3. Right-click the account name in the right pane and select Properties.

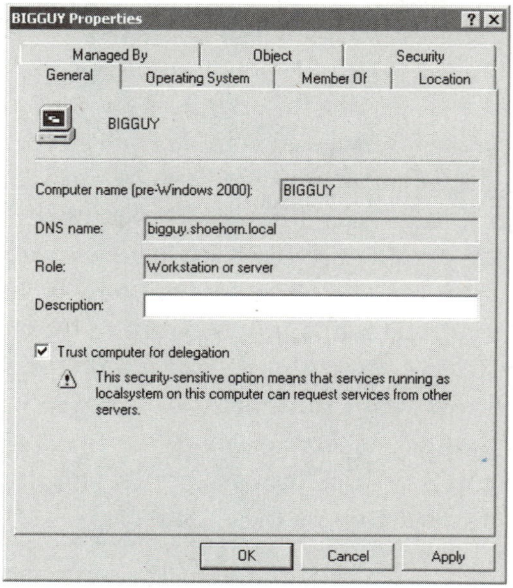

Figure 11-4. The account's Properties General tab

4. In the account's Properties Account tab (refer to Figure 11-3) scroll through the account options list and check the Account Is Trusted For Delegation box. Click OK.

To determine which account the service uses, or to change the account the service uses, check the Services list in the Computer Management utility by following these steps:

1. Select Start | Programs | Administrative Tools | Computer Management.

2. In the Computer Management main window, right-click the Computer Management icon and select Connect To Another Server to select the computer on which the service is running. (Skip this step if the service is running on the system to which you're currently connected.)

3. Click the plus sign next to the Services And Applications icon.

4. Double-click the Services icon.

5. A list of services appears in the right pane. Right-click the service for which you wish to view or configure the account and choose Properties.

6. In the service's Properties dialog box, select the Log On tab (see Figure 11-5). If the Local System Account option is selected, the service logs on to the local system account. Select This Account to configure a different logon account. Click the Browse button to browse for another account. Enter password and confirm the account password. Click OK.

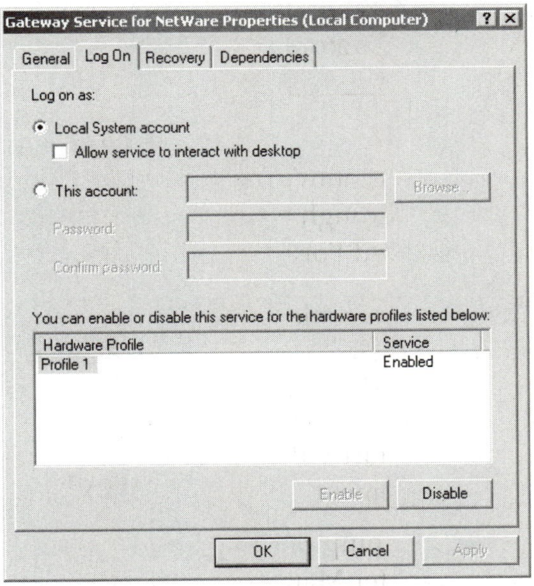

Figure 11-5. The service's Properties Log On tab

Turning Off Kerberos Preauthentication

The earlier section "How does Kerberos Work in Windows 2000?" described the Kerberos authentication process. The client initially sends an authentication request to the KDC and is issued a ticket granting ticket (TGT), which the client will use for authentication with the KDC itself. The Kerberos protocol provides an additional optional layer of security known as *preauthentication*. Preauthentication causes the KDC/domain controller to perform preliminary authentication before issuing a TGT. Preauthentication is considered a defense against password-guessing attacks (see the later section titled "What Kerberos Doesn't Prevent").

By default, Windows 2000 requires all accounts to use preauthentication. However, several Kerberos preauthentication methods are in existence, and not all Kerberos environments support Windows 2000 preauthentication. If all your Kerberos servers and clients are Windows 2000 servers and clients, you do not need to change the default preauthentication setting, but if non-Windows Kerberos clients are not able to successfully interoperate with Windows 2000 Kerberos, you may wish to disable preauthentication for a user account.

To disable preauthentication, follow these steps:

1. Select Start | Programs | Administrative Tools | Active Directory Users And Computers.

2. Select the container or OU that holds the account for which you wish to disable preauthentication.

3. Right-click the Account icon in the right pane and then select Properties.

4. In the account's Properties Account tab (see Figure 11-3), scroll through the Account Options list and select the Do Not Require Kerberos Preauthentication check box. Click OK.

Setting Kerberos Policy

The default security policy (described later in this chapter in the section titled "Understanding Security Policy") includes several Kerberos-related policy settings. You can configure

Kerberos security policy through the Domain Security Policy tool
(Start | Programs | Administrative Tools | Domain Security
Policy) or through the Group Policy Editor snap-in. See Chapter 6
"Group Policy" for more on configuring group policy in Windows
2000. Kerberos policy settings are shown in Table 11-2.

Location	Policy	Description
Computer Configuration\Windows Settings\Security Settings\Account Policies\Kerberos Policy	Enforce User Logon Restrictions	If enabled, client won't receive the session ticket unless the user has Log On Locally or Access This Computer From the Network user rights for the target computer (default: enabled).
	Maximum Lifetime For Service Ticket	Maximum lifetime for session ticket (minutes). Zero setting = never expires (default: 600 minutes).
	Maximum Lifetime For User Ticket	Maximum lifetime for TGT (default: 10 hours).
	Maximum Lifetime For User Ticket Renewal	Maximum total lifetime for a TGT, including renewal (default: 7 days).
	Maximum Tolerance For Computer Clock Synchronization	Maximum allowable difference for which Kerberos will consider the client clock and the server clock synchronized (default: 5 minutes).

Table 11-2. Domain Group Policy Settings

Interoperating Windows 2000 Kerberos

The scions of Kerberos were encouraged but cautious when Microsoft announced that it would incorporate Kerberos into Windows 2000. They remain cautious and some, in fact, are skeptical. Microsoft, however, is upbeat about how Windows 2000 Kerberos interoperates with other Kerberos v5 systems. One principal concern of the critics is the contents of the authorization-data field (refer to Table 11-1), which, in Windows 2000 Kerberos, contains Windows-based security information. The authorization-data field is theoretically optional, but, according to the Kerberos community, Microsoft's use of the field does not strictly comply with the Kerberos standard. The degree of incompatibility is the subject of much discussion. It is important to note, however, that Kerberos is not really designed as a full-blown security architecture. The services to which Kerberos is providing access are operating within the security environment of an operating system, and Kerberos-based ticket delivery services do not guarantee that a client in one environment will have access to a service in another environment.

Microsoft makes the following statements regarding Windows 2000 Kerberos interoperability:

▼ A Windows 2000 client can authenticate to a non-Windows KDC.

■ A non-Windows Kerberos client can authenticate to a Windows KDC.

■ A non-Windows KDC can provide access to resources in a Windows domain if a two-way trust exists between the Windows domain and the KDC's Kerberos realm.

■ A Windows KDC can provide access to resources on a non-Windows Kerberos realm through a service account or through a one-way trust.

▲ See Chapter 7 for information on how to use the NetDom utility to create a non-windows Kerberos ream trusts.

TIP: The Kerberos policy settings (refer to Table 11-2) are configured primarily for Windows 2000 clients. If you experience problems interoperating with other operating systems, try reconfiguring some of these settings or try configuring the account to not require preauthentication.

Windows 2000 Client with a Non-Windows 2000 KDC

A non-Windows 2000 KDC can authenticate a Windows 2000 client. But what then? Microsoft makes a careful distinction between *authentication* and *authorization* when it comes to interoperating Kerberos. The non-Windows KDC can provide access to services running within its own realm; however, if you wish the KDC to provide access to services in the Windows domain, the picture gets a little cloudier.

The non-Windows KDC cannot easily offer a substitute to the Kerberos/Active Directory interoperability supplied by a Windows 2000 domain controller. Windows 2000 uses the authorization-data field of the session ticket (refer to Table 11-1) to provide Windows-based security credentials, such as user and group SIDs. A non-Windows KDC will not supply values for this field, and therefore will be of limited value for providing access to Windows-based services. The Kerberos services do not actually process the authorization-data field. The authorization-data values are instead passed to the application. Most Windows NT/2000-based applications require SID-style authorization, and those applications will not find the authorization information they need in a session ticket offered by a non-Windows KDC.

A solution (sort of) for this problem of supporting a Windows 2000 client and Windows 2000 domain-based services through a non-Windows KDC is to let Active Directory manage the accounts and to use the non-Windows Kerberos realm as something kind of like an account domain (see Figure 11-6). The non-Windows KDC will then use the referral service to pass the ticket request to the Active Directory domain controller. This system requires a trust relationship between the Kerberos realm and the Active Directory domain, and the primary account database must reside in the Windows domain. Also, to provide access to resources in the realm, you must set up some form of account mapping system. The add-on Windows 2000 Services for UNIX package provides username mapping to UNIX security.

Non-Windows Client with a Windows 2000 KDC

According to Microsoft, a Windows 2000 KDC will look like any other KDC to non-Windows clients. You must specify the Kerberos realm (in

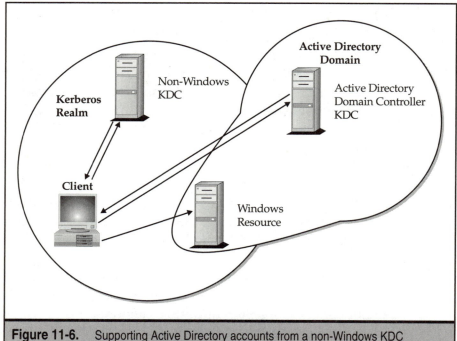

Figure 11-6.   Supporting Active Directory accounts from a non-Windows KDC through referral

this case, use the Windows 2000 domain) and the KDC in the Kerberos client configuration. The default Windows 2000 KDC configuration is designed for supporting Windows 2000 clients. If you need to support non-Windows clients, you may wish to investigate the Kerberos policy settings (see the section titled "Setting Kerberos Policy") and the preauthentication setting (see the section titled "Turning Off Kerberos Preauthentication").

The Windows 2000 KDC will provide access to resources in the Windows 2000 domain and will offer interdomain access to other Windows resources through the cross-domain referral service. You can access resources in the non-Windows realm if a trust relationship exists between the Windows domain and the Kerberos realm. Note that the service you are accessing may perform some form of authorization based on rights assignment. You may need to implement some form of account mapping. The add-on Windows 2000 Services for the UNIX package provides username mapping to UNIX security.

TIP: Note that if you wish to let Windows 2000 domain users access a particular UNIX service, you can create a service account in the Windows 2000 domain that the client-side application will use for contacting the service.

What Kerberos Doesn't Prevent

Kerberos is an ingenious system for tightening security on an open network, but even with Kerberos working one must not become overconfident. RFC 1510 enumerates the following types of attacks from which Kerberos does not provide protection:

▼   **Denial of service**   Some denial-of-service attacks do not require authentication at all, but are in fact designed to *fail* authentication (and to do so many times, thereby tying up the server's attention). Other forms of denial-of-service attacks prevent an authorized authentication from taking place. According to RFC 1510, within the Kerberos protocols there are places "where an intruder can prevent an application from participating in the proper authentication steps."

■   **Password guessing**   Kerberos can't stop an attacker from guessing a bad password. A key is derived from the user's password. An attacker could theoretically intercept a KDE request and process it offline using a dictionary-style attack algorithm to crack the longterm key. If your name is Bob, don't make your password *bob*. Microsoft's best practices for password assignment are given in the note at the end of this section.

▲   **Key discovery**   An attacker who gains access to a key will be able to impersonate the key's owner or impersonate a server that the key's owner is attempting to contact.

RFC 1510 also points out that Kerberos' timestamp features, which are used to prevent replay of intercepted messages, require that the clocks of the KDC, client, and server are at least "loosely synchronized," and that the protocol used to synchronize the clocks should itself be protected from network attack. The RFC does not go into a detailed definition of what the authors mean by "loosely

Maintain Good Password Policies

As corporate computers have become faster and more powerful, the computers and computer programs used to crack passwords have also become faster and more powerful. It is now more important than ever to maintain good password policies. For the record, Microsoft recommends the following rules:

▼ Passwords should be at least seven characters long.

■ Passwords should contain a combination of letters, numerals, and symbols: ! @ # $ % ^ & * ( ) _ - + = { } [ ] : ; " ' < > , . ? / | \. At least one symbol should occupy a position that is not the first or the last character.

■ Passwords should be significantly different from previous passwords.

▲ Passwords should not contain a username or any name, an address, or any common word.

synchronized." This caution is most applicable to heterogeneous Kerberos networks. A native Windows 2000 network maintains sufficient time synchronization to operate Kerberos without additional measures.

UNDERSTANDING SECURITY POLICY

The Active Directory environment relies heavily on group policy to define the security environment. As you learned in Chapter 6, Active Directory lets you apply one or more *group policy objects* to a site, domain, or OU. A group policy object is a bundle of predefined policy attributes. You can mold the Active Directory environment by giving values to these attributes. By strategically applying group policies at each level (site, domain, and OU) you can additionally mold the policy environment and diversify the policy environment, so that each OU has the specific policies it needs and more global policies are set for the domain and site.

Security is one of the central features of group policy. The network administrator can use all the capabilities of group policy (as described in Chapter 6) to define the security infrastructure. Some group policy security settings are reminiscent of Windows NT system policy settings. Others (such as the audit policies and password policies) were collected from other parts of the Windows NT interface. Other security policies, such as Kerberos policies (refer to Table 11-2) and IP security policies, are totally new and have no precedent in earlier versions of Windows.

Although it is possible to set security policy at all policy levels (site, domain, and OU), because the domain is the fundamental security unit of Windows networking, it is probable that organizations will wish to define security policy (perhaps more so than other policies) at the domain level. Active Directory maintains a *domain security policy* that serves as a central location for defining domain security settings. You can access the domain security policy through the Administrative Tools program group (Start | Programs | Administrative Tools | Domain Security Policy). You can also apply security policy settings through group policy objects at each of the policy levels. Some policies (such as password policy) *must* be set at the domain level.

The domain security policy divides security policy attributes into the following groups. This structure is equivalent to Computer Configuration\Windows Settings\Security Settings tree of a group policy object:

▼   Account Policies

■   Local Policies

■   Event Log

■   Restricted Groups

■   System Services

■   Registry

■   File System

■   Public Key Policies

▲   IP security policies on Active Directory

The following sections discuss each of these policy categories. For more on working with group policy in Active Directory environments, see Chapter 6.

Account Policies

The Account Policies section of the group policy Security Settings subtree includes three subsections:

▼   Password Policy

■   Account Lockout Policy

▲   Kerberos Policy

Kerberos policy was discussed earlier in this chapter in the section titled "Setting Kerberos Policy." The password and account lockout policies are similar to the account policy options available through Windows NT Server's User Manager for Domains utility. Account policies can be set *only* at the domain level. Although you may be able to set these options in a group policy object applied to an OU, the OU settings will not take effect. Password and account lockout policies are shown in Table 11-3.

Location	Policy	Description
Computer Configuration\Windows Settings\Security Settings\Account Policies\Password Policy	Enforce Password History	Specifies whether to require that a password be different from previous passwords and the number of previous passwords that will be retained in the password history (default: 1 password remembered).

Table 11-3.   Password and Lockout Policies; *Default* Shows the Default Domain Policy Value

Location	Policy	Description
	Maximum Password Age	Time in days before the user is forced to change the password (default: 42 days).
	Minimum Password Age	Time in days that a user must use the password before changing it (default: 0 days).
	Minimum Password Length	Minimum number of characters in password. Zero value means password not required (default: 0).
	Passwords Must Meet Complexity Requirements	Forces the password to meet a set of complexity requirements supplied by Microsoft. See the discussion later in this section (default: Not Defined).
	Store Passwords Using Reversible Encryption For All Users In The Domain	This setting is to support applications that require access to passwords. Unless such applications exist, do not use this option (default: Not Defined).
Computer Configuration\Windows Settings\Security Settings\Account Policies\Account Lockout Policy	Account Lockout Duration	Number of failed logon attempts before user is locked out (default: Not Defined).

Table 11-3.   Password and Lockout Policies; *Default* Shows the Defult Domain Policy Value *(continued)*

Location	Policy	Description
Computer Configuration\Windows Settings\Security Settings\Account Policies\Account Lockout Policy	Account Lockout Threshold	Duration of lockout (default: Not Defined).
	Reset Account Lockout Counter After	Time in minutes before the logon attempt counter is reset after bad logon attempts (default: Not Defined).

Table 11-3. Password and Lockout Policies; *Default* Shows the Default Domain Policy Value *(continued)*

TIP: The minimum password age is important if you plan to enforce password history. If the minimum age is set to zero days, the user can just change the password many times at once (until the history is exceeded) and then return to an earlier password.

Local Policies

The Local Policies section contains settings that provide or deny access to resources on a local system. These settings do not have to be set through the local computer policy. You can set local policies through a site, domain, or OU group policy object, and the settings will apply to a local computer through the rules of group policy application discussed in Chapter 6.

The Local Policy section includes the following subsections:

▼ Audit Policy

■ User Rights Assignment

▲ Security Options

The default domain policy leaves most of these settings undefined. The attributes for the Audit Policy and User Rights Assignment policies are similar to their Windows NT 4 counterparts. Note that the Audit Policy feature does not configure auditing for specific object but, instead, enables auditing for specific classes of events (object access, policy change, logon, account management, and so forth). As in Windows NT, the User Rights Assignment policies assign a user or group to a particular right (change the system time, logon as a service, back up files and directories, and so forth).

The Security Options section offers a number of miscellaneous security settings. Some of the more interesting Security Options settings are shown in Table 11-4. You may wish to browse through the complete list in Group Policy Editor to see if any of the entries apply to your network.

Location	Policy	Description
Computer Configuration\Windows Settings\Security Settings\Local Policies\Security Options	Allow Server Operators To Schedule Tasks	Specifies whether members of the Server Operators group (in addition to administrators) will be able to schedule tasks using the AT command (does not apply to Task Scheduler).
	Automatically Log Off Users When Logon Time Expires	Specifies whether to log off users automatically when the logon hours for the account are over.

Table 11-4. Security Options Policies

Location	Policy	Description
Computer Configuration\Windows Settings\Security Settings\Local Policies\Security Options	Disable CTRL-ALT-DEL Requirement For Logon	Specifies whether to let the user log on without pressing CTRL-ALT-DEL. CTRL-ALT-DEL suspends background processes and protects against Trojan horse attacks. This setting is not recommended.
	Prevent Users From Installing Printer Drivers	Prevents members of the Users group from installing printer drivers.
	Rename Guest Account	Forces a new name to be associated with the Guest account. (Prevents attackers from logging on as Guest.)
	Rename Administrator Account	Forces a new name to be associated with the Administrator account. (Prevents attackers from guessing the admin username.)
	Shut Down System Immediately If Unable To Log Security Audits	Causes the system to shut down immediately if security auditing fails (prevents attacker from suspending auditing).

Table 11-4. Security Options Policies *(continued)*

Event Log

The Event Log settings configure the Windows 2000 event log. Although the Event Log subtree is part of the domain security settings and is located in the Security Settings group policy object subtree, the event log configuration settings (which include settings for the system log and the application log as well as the security log) are essentially management-related settings. These settings were described in Chapter 8 "Managing Active Directory."

Restricted Groups

The Restricted Groups option lets you specify at the policy level which users must be a member of a specific group. The user(s) is added to the group if he or she is not currently a member. A user who is currently a member of the group but is not specified for the group in the restricted group configuration is automatically removed from the group. The Restricted Group feature also includes a Members Of list that lets you define the groups to which the restricted group should belong. You cannot set restricted group policy for a local computer. The option is only available for sites, domains, and OUs.

To configure a restricted group, follow these steps:

1. Select Start | Programs | Administrative Tools | Domain Security Policy to open the domain security policy. Expand the Security Settings tree. Or, open a group policy object (as described in Chapter 6), expand the Computer Configuration tree, expand the Windows Settings subtree, and then expand the Security Settings subtree.

2. Right-click the folder labeled Restricted Groups and select Add A Group.

3. In the Add A Group dialog box, enter the group name of the group you wish to designate as a restricted group or click the Browse button to browse for the group. If you enter a group in a different domain, don't forget to precede the group name with the domain name domainID\groupID.

4. The group is added to the Restricted Group list in the right pane. Note that, by default, the restricted group has no members and those users who were members of the group previously will be removed from the group unless you intentionally add them in through the Restrict Group configuration. To configure the restricted group, right-click the Group icon in the right pane and select Security.

5. The Configure Membership dialog box appears (see Figure 11-7). To add members, to the group, click the Add button at the dialog box. To remove a member from the Restricted Members list, select the member in the Members Of This Group list and click the Remove button. At the bottom of the dialog box, you'll find a This Group Is A Member Of check

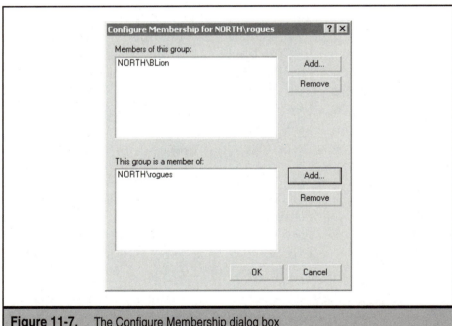

Figure 11-7. The Configure Membership dialog box

box. Click the lower Add button to make the restricted group a member of another group. To remove a group membership, select the group in the list and click Remove.

System Services

The Computer Management utility lets you configure service startup-type settings (automatic, manual, disabled). The System Services group policy option lets you configure service startup type through policy. The policy setting will override any changes imposed directly through the local interface and will restore the policy-based setting. The System Services policy section also lets you define user and group security for the service object. You cannot set system service policy for a local computer. The option is only available for sites, domains, and OUs.

To set system service policy, follow these steps:

1. Select Start | Programs | Administrative Tools | Domain Security Policy to open the domain security policy. Expand the Security Settings tree. Or, open a group policy object (as described in Chapter 6), expand the Computer Configuration tree, expand the Windows Settings subtree, and then expand the Security Settings subtree.

2. Select System Services.

3. A list of services appears in the right pane. To set system service policy, right-click the name of a service and choose Security.

4. In the Security Policy Setting dialog box (see Figure 11-8), check the Define This Policy Setting box. Select a startup type option (Automatic, Manual, or Disabled). Click the Edit Security button to set user and group access security for the service.

5. Click OK.

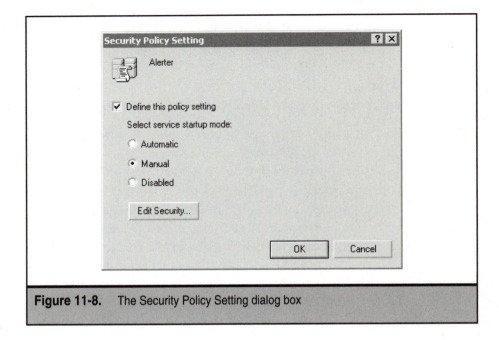

Figure 11-8. The Security Policy Setting dialog box

Registry

The Registry section of the Security Settings policies lets you specify user and group access permissions for Registry keys. You can only set security for keys and subtrees in the HKEY_CLASSES_ROOT, HKEY_LOCAL_MACHINE, and HKEY_USERS trees. You cannot set Registry policy for a local computer. The option is only available for sites, domains, and OUs.

To set Registry policy, follow these steps:

1. Select Start | Programs | Administrative Tools | Domain Security Policy to open the domain security policy. Expand the Security Settings tree. Or, open a group policy object (as described in Chapter 6), expand the Computer Configuration tree, expand the Windows Settings subtree, and then expand the Security Settings subtree.

2. In the Security Settings tree, right-click the Registry folder and choose Add Key.

3. In the Select Registry Key dialog box (see Figure 11-9), select the key for which you wish to set security. Click the plus sign beside the top-level key to browse for a lower-level key. Click OK.

4. In the Database Security dialog box (see Figure 11-10), click the Add button to add a user or group to the access list. Select a user or group in the list at the top of the dialog box and configure security settings for the user in the Permissions list below. Select the Advanced button for additional security configuration options.

5. Click OK.

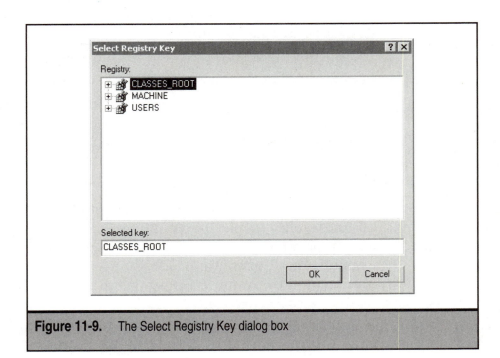

Figure 11-9. The Select Registry Key dialog box

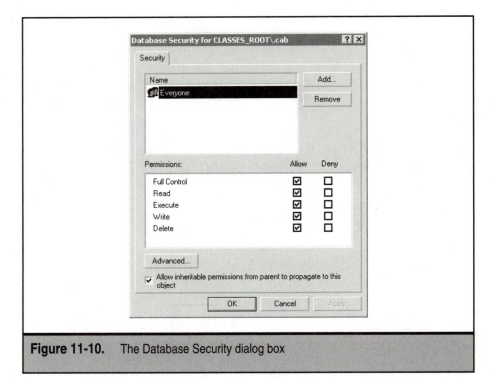

Figure 11-10.   The Database Security dialog box

File System

The File System option lets you set permission for file system objects (NTFS directories and files) at the policy level. To set file and directory policy, follow these steps:

1. Select Start | Programs | Administrative Tools | Domain Security Policy to open the domain security policy. Expand the Security Settings tree. Or, open a group policy object (as described in Chapter 6), expand the Computer Configuration tree, expand the Windows Settings subtree, and then expand the Security Settings subtree.

2. In the Security Settings tree, right-click the File System folder and choose Add File.

3. In the Add A File Or Folder dialog box (see Figure 11-11), browse for the file or folder for which you'd like to configure system policy.

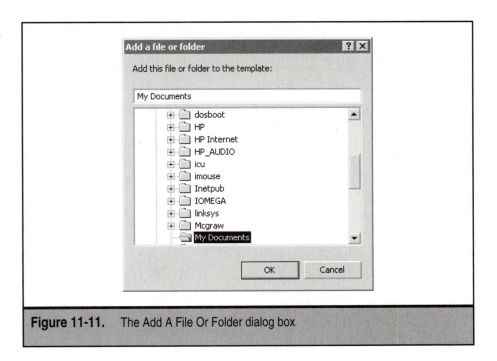

Figure 11-11.   The Add A File Or Folder dialog box

4. In the Database Security dialog box (similar to Figure 11-10), click the Add button to add a user or group to the access list. Configure permissions for a selected user in the Permissions box below. Click Advanced for additional security options.

5. Click OK.

Public Key Policies

The public key policies relate to the Windows 2000 Certificate features. See the Windows 2000 Resource Kit Books Online for more on certificates in Windows 2000.

IP Security Policies

The IP Security feature (IPSec) is one of the more interesting developments in Windows 2000. IPSec is a big topic that requires more discussion than a simple pointer to a policy setting.

IPSec offers secure TCP/IP networking. Unlike Kerberos (which is applied specifically to the authentication process), IPSec secures *all* packets passing among compliant hosts. IPSec communication is similar to the Secure Sockets Layer (SSL) communication that is now common with Internet, except that the applications must have some knowledge of SSL. According to Microsoft, IPSec is implemented entirely below the socket layer and is thus invisible to the application. Windows 2000's IP Security features are integrated into the built-in TCP/IP protocol stack. You can configure this IP security using the IP Security policy settings.

According to Microsoft, IPSec offers the following benefits through a convenient central management scheme:

▼ An open industry TCP/IP security standard

■ Transparency

■ Authentication

■ Confidentiality

■ Data integrity

▲ Dynamic rekeying

As you'll learn in the next section, in order to achieve these benefits, the computer has to *do extra things*. For this reason, there is a performance trade-off for implementing IPSec that may or may not be significant depending on your network conditions. It should be noted, however, that one of the reasons for the development of standards such as IPSec is that large organizations have come to realize that it isn't enough to provide a barrier that keeps outside users from gaining access to the internal network. You also have to contend with threats from the inside. IPSec can protect *any or all* network communications—either internal or external.

How IPSec Works

According to Microsoft, Windows 2000 IP security ensures the following:

▼ **Integrity**   The packet has not been modified in transit.

■ **Authentication**   The packet really came from the computer listed as the source. An attacker can't pretend to be a user or computer trusted by the recipient.

■ **Confidentiality**   Only the intended recipient can read the message. Someone "listening in" by intercepting packets will not be able to read the data.

■ **Nonrepudiation**   The fact that the sender sent the message is documented. The sender can't deny sending the message.

▲ **Anti-replay**   Each packet is unique and can't be reused.

To implement IP security, you define security policies that specify authentication, IP filtering, and other settings. When a Windows 2000 computer sends a packet, the IPSec driver checks to see if any of the IP security policies apply to the packet. If so, the sending and receiving computer engage in a security negotiation through the Internet Key Exchange (IKE) protocol. This negotiation results in the establishment of a security agreement (SA) between the two hosts. The security agreement defines the parameters necessary for supporting secure communication between the hosts.

By default, the hosts participating in an IP security negotiation use the Diffie-Hellman computation to decide on a key to use for encrypted communication between the hosts. The key is never sent across the network directly.

IP security policies can be added to the default domain policy, to local computer policies, or to other group policy objects. The following sections assume you are creating and editing domain IP security policies. Steps for creating and editing local computer policies are similar. Windows 2000 includes an IP Security Policy Management MMC snap-in. The Setup Wizard for the snap-in asks if you wish to edit IP security for the local computer, for the current domain, or for another domain and creates a snap-in for the appropriate default object. You don't have to use the snap-in to edit IP security policy. You can edit IP policy directly from the Domain Security Policy utility or from Group Policy Editor. See Chapter 6 for more on implementing group policy in Active Directory domains.

TIP: To install the IP Security Policy Management snap-in, select Start | Run and enter **mmc** in the Run dialog box. In Microsoft Management Console's Console menu, select Add/Remove Snap-In. Then, click the Add button and browse for IP Security Policy Management.

Configuring IP Security Policy

By defining IP security policies, you can configure when and how the computers on your network will implement security policy through IP security.

An IP security policy is a collection of one or more *IP security rules* (see Figure 11-12). An IP security rule consists of the following elements:

▼ **IP filter lists**   A collection of IP filters. (Actually, the policy specifies a list of IP filter lists and each list is a collection of IP filters.)

■ **Filter action**   The action that should take place for a packet that satisfies the filter list.

■ **Authentication method**   Authentication method that will be used to establish a trusted connection between the computers. The default is Kerberos. You can also specify a certificate authority or enter a preshared key.

■ **Tunnel setting**   IPSec tunnel endpoint.

▲ **Connection type**   A setting that specifies whether the rule applies to all connections, LAN connections, or remote access connections.

The basic idea behind IP security is to identify a group of IP addresses and then define the actions that will take place when one of these addresses appears. A group of IP addresses is specified through an IP filter. The filter can identify a packet by protocol and

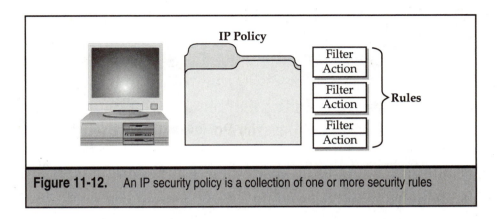

Figure 11-12. An IP security policy is a collection of one or more security rules

by source address or destination address using any of the following identification criteria:

▼ My IP address

■ Any IP address

■ Specific DNS name

■ Specific IP address

▲ Specific subnet

One or more filters can be combined into a filter list, and one or more filter lists can be associated with an IP security policy. In keeping with the Active Directory philosophy, elements such as filter lists and filter actions can be applied to a policy but are otherwise independent of any particular policy. Once you create one of these elements, you can use it in more than one policy. It is possible to create filters, filter lists, and filter actions from within the IP security Policy Setup Wizard, but to do so you'll need to pass through a disorienting tangle of embedded wizards or optional Properties dialog boxes. You may opt to create policy elements from within the Policy Setup Wizard once you're familiar with the procedure, but for purposes of this discussion, I will show how to create filter lists and filter actions separately and then discuss how to combine these elements into IP policies.

Creating and Editing IP Filter Lists

An IP security policy must include one or more filter lists. A filter is a collection of source or destination DNS names, IP addresses, or IP subnets with optional information on the protocols to which the filter applies. The following filter lists are installed by default:

▼ **All ICMP Traffic**   Identifies all Internet Control Message Protocol (ICMP) traffic regardless of source or destination address.

▲ **ALL IP Traffic**   Identifies all IP traffic regardless of source or destination address.

The ALL IP Traffic option lets you create rules that will always apply regardless of the address or IP protocol. The ICMP Traffic option lets you create rules that will apply to ICMP packets. (ICMP is used for reporting delivery problems and other network errors.)

CREATING A FILTER LIST   If you wish to apply a different filter list to an IP security policy, you must create the filter list. To create an IP filter list for an Active Directory domain, follow these steps:

1. Select Start | Programs | Administrative Tools | Domain Security Policy to open the domain security policy. Expand the Security Settings tree. Or, open a group policy object (as described in Chapter 6), expand the Computer Configuration tree, expand the Windows Settings subtree, and then expand the Security Settings subtree.

2. Right-click the IP Security On Active Directory icon and select Manage IP Filter Lists and Filter Actions.

3. The Manage IP Filter Lists And Filter Actions dialog box appears. To add a new filter, click the Add button.

4. In the IP Filter List dialog box (see Figure 11-13), enter a name and description for the new filter. Administrators often ignore

description fields. In this case, it is worth your while to enter a description of the Filter list. If the list contains an assortment of IP address entries, it may not be easy to recall why you created it. The filters included in the Filter list are shown at the bottom of the IP Filter List dialog box. To add a new filter, click the Add button. If you uncheck the Use Add Wizard checkbox, the options will be similar to the options in steps 5–10, but you'll perform the configuration through a Properties dialog box. (See the next procedure on editing Filter list properties.)

5. The IP Filter Wizard starts. Read the first frame and click Next.

6. The next frame asks you to identify source address(es) to which the filter applies. You can specify the computer's own address, any IP address, a specific DNS name, a specific IP address, or a specific IP subnet. Choose an address type. If you choose a specific IP address, IP subnet, or DNS name, the wizard will ask for the necessary addressing information. Click Next.

7. The next frame asks you to identify destination address(es) to which the filter applies. You can specify the computer's own

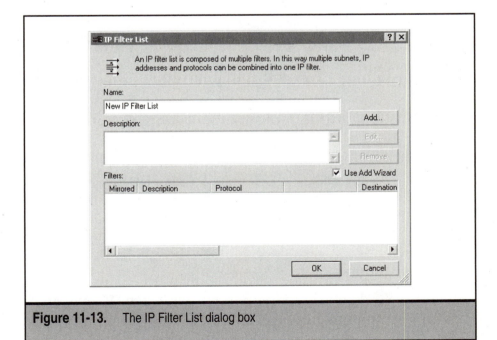

Figure 11-13.   The IP Filter List dialog box

address, any IP address, a specific DNS name, a specific IP address, or a specific IP subnet. Choose an address type. If you choose a specific IP address, IP subnet, or DNS name, the wizard will ask for the necessary addressing information. Click Next.

8. The next frame asks you to choose the TCP/IP protocol to which the filter applies. Options include TCP, UDP, ICMP, etc. Note that you can also choose Any (which applies the filter to all TCP/IP protocols) or Other (which lets you specify a port address to which the rule applies). Enter the necessary information and click Next.

9. The next frame announces that you have finished creating the filter. Check the Edit Properties box if you wish to edit the filter properties on completion of the wizard. Click Next.

10. When you complete the Add Filter Wizard, you return to the IP Filter List dialog box (see step 4). The filter you just created should appear in the Filters list. To add another filter, click the Add button and repeat steps 5–9. To edit the properties of a filter, select the filter and click the Edit button. To finish creating the Filter list, click Close.

11. The Edit button in the IP Filter List dialog box (refer to Figure 11-13) summons the Filter Properties dialog box (see Figure 11-14). The Filter Properties dialog box offers choices similar to choices you'll face when creating a filter (see steps 5–9).

EDITING A FILTER LIST To Edit a filter list, follow these steps:

1. Select Start | Programs | Administrative Tools | Domain Security Policy to open the domain security policy. Expand the Security Settings tree. Or, open a group policy object (as described in Chapter 6), expand the Computer Configuration tree, expand the Windows Settings subtree, and then expand the Security Settings subtree.

2. Right-click the IP Security On Active Directory icon and select Manage IP Filter Lists And Filter Actions.

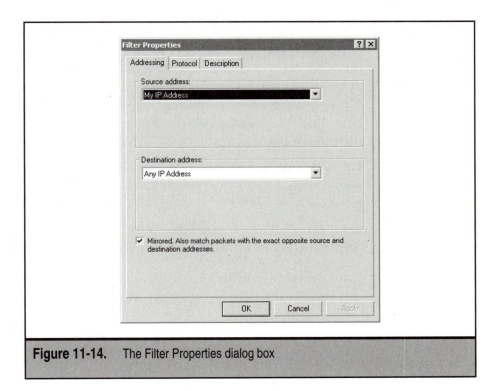

Figure 11-14.   The Filter Properties dialog box

3. The Manage IP Filter Lists And Filter Actions dialog box appears. Select a filter list and choose Edit.

4. In the IP Filter List dialog box (refer to Figure 11-13), edit the Filter list name or description. To edit one of the filters associated with the Filter list, select the filter and choose Edit. The Filter Properties dialog box appears (refer to Figure 11-14). The options are similar to the options for creating a new filter (see steps 5–9 of the preceding procedure). The tabs of the Filter Properties dialog box are as follows:

   ■ **Addressing**   Lets you specify source and destination address information.

   ■ **Protocol**   Lets you specify the protocols that will be filtered.

   ■ **Description**   Lets you specify a description for the filter.

A pair of filter configuration properties deserve special notice. First, in the Addressing tab (refer to Figure 11-14), you can specify whether or not the filter will be *mirrored*. Mirroring means that the filter will also apply to packets with opposite source and destination addresses from the entries you specify. Filters are mirrored by default. You can disable the Mirrored attribute in the Addressing tab.

The Filter Properties dialog box's Protocol tab (see Figure 11-15), lets you specify a specific port address for the TCP and UDP protocols.

5. In the IP Filter List dialog box, choose a new filter to edit and click the Edit button. Or, select OK to close the IP Filter List dialog box.

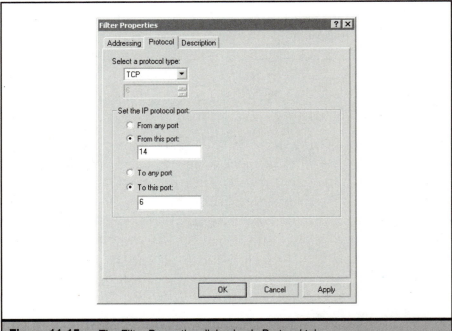

Figure 11-15.   The Filter Properties dialog box's Protocol tab

Creating and Editing Filter Actions

A filter action is a description of the actions that will take place when a packet is discovered that matches the filter criteria. The following filter actions are installed by default:

▼ **Permit**   Permit packet to pass even if it isn't secured.

■ **Request Security (Optional)**   Attempt to establish a secure session but allow unsecure traffic to pass if a secure session can't be established.

▲ **Require Security**   Accepts unsecured requests initially, but then requires the client to negotiate a secure session. Does communicate with unsecure clients.

You can create a rule that applies any of these filter actions to a default Filter list or to a Filter list that you create. You can also create your own filter actions.

CREATING A FILTER ACTION   To create a filter action, follow these steps:

1. Select Start | Programs | Administrative Tools | Domain Security Policy to open the domain security policy. Expand the Security Settings tree. Or, open a group policy object (as described in Chapter 6), expand the Computer Configuration tree, expand the Windows Settings subtree, and then expand the Security Settings subtree.

2. Right-click the IP Security On Active Directory icon and select Manage IP Filter Lists And Filter Actions.

3. The Manage IP Filter Lists And Filter Actions dialog box appears. Select the Manage Filter Actions tab.

4. In the Manage Filter Actions tab (see Figure 11-16), click the Add button to add a new filter action. Note that you can uncheck the Use Add Wizard checkbox to add a filter action without the Filter Action Wizard. If you elect not to use the

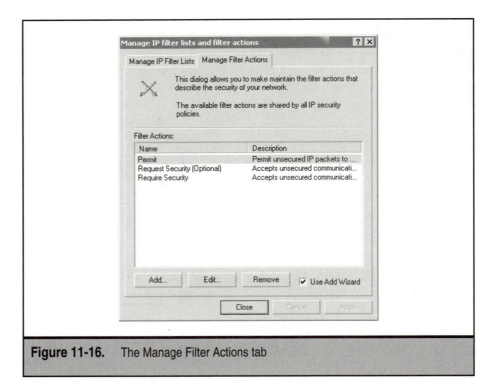

Figure 11-16. The Manage Filter Actions tab

wizard, you'll configure the new filter action through a Properties dialog box. The options are similar to the options in the following steps:

5. The Filter Action Wizard starts. Read the first frame and click Next.

6. In the next frame, enter a name and description for the filter action.

7. In the next frame (see Figure 11-17), select whether this filter action will permit all traffic that meets the filter criteria, block all traffic that meets the filter criteria, or negotiate security for a request that meets the filter criteria. If you select Permit or Block, you have already specified an action and there isn't much more to decide. Click Next and go to step 10. If you elected to negotiate security, you'll need to configure the parameters necessary for the security negotiation. Click Next and go to step 8.

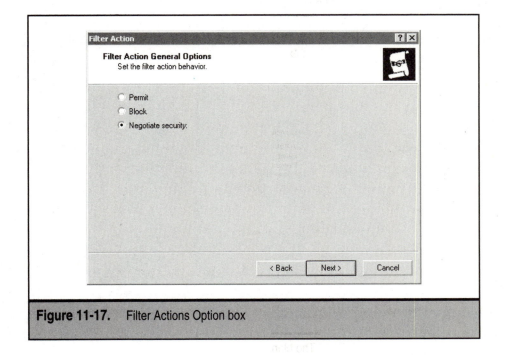

Figure 11-17.   Filter Actions Option box

8. If you chose to negotiate security in step 7, the next frame asks you whether or not this filter action will include communication with computers that do not support IPSec. If you select Fall Back To Unsecured Communication, the computer will accept a lesser level of IP security (or no IP security) if the other host does not support IPSec. Click Next.

9. The next frame (see Figure 11-18) asks you to choose one of the following security method options:

   ■ **High (Encapsulated Secure Payload)**   Provides encryption, authentication, and protection from modification. Because this option provides encryption of message data, it is considered the highest security level. It also requires the highest processing overhead. If you are configuring a server that experiences high demand, consider whether this level of security is necessary. Microsoft recommends testing production conditions before deployment.

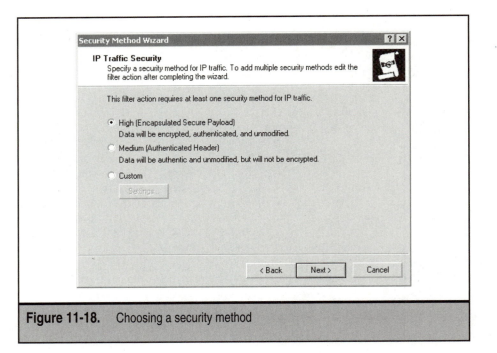

Figure 11-18. Choosing a security method

- **Medium (Authenticated Header)** Provides authentication and protection from modification.

- **Custom** Lets you set a custom integrity algorithm, encryption algorithm, and session key renewal settings.

If you choose Custom and click the Settings button, the Custom Security Method Settings dialog box appears (see Figure 11-19). Enter the desired values for integrity and encryption algorithms and session key renewal. Note that you can check either the Authentication Header protocol (AH), which doesn't provide encryption, or the Encapsulated Secure Payload protocol (ESP), which does provide encryption. Click OK. Click Next in the IP Traffic Security screen (refer to Figure 11-18).

10. The next screen announces that you have finished creating a filter action. Check the Edit Properties box if you wish to go immediately to the filter action's Properties dialog box. Click Finish.

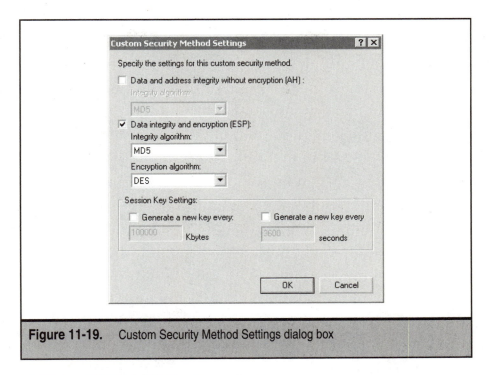

Figure 11-19.   Custom Security Method Settings dialog box

EDITING A FILTER ACTION   To edit a filter action for a domain security policy, follow these steps:

1. Select Start | Programs | Administrative Tools | Domain Security Policy to open the domain security policy. Expand the Security Settings tree. Or, open a group policy object (as described in Chapter 6), expand the Computer Configuration tree, expand the Windows Settings subtree, and then expand the Security Settings subtree.

2. Right-click the IP Security On Active Directory icon and select Manage IP Filter Lists And Filter Actions.

3. The Manage IP Filter Lists And Filter Actions dialog box appears. Select the Manage Filter Actions tab.

4. In the Manage Filter Actions tab (refer Figure 11-16), select a filter action and click the Edit button.

5. The filter action's Properties dialog box appears (see Figure 11-20). In the Properties dialog box, select whether

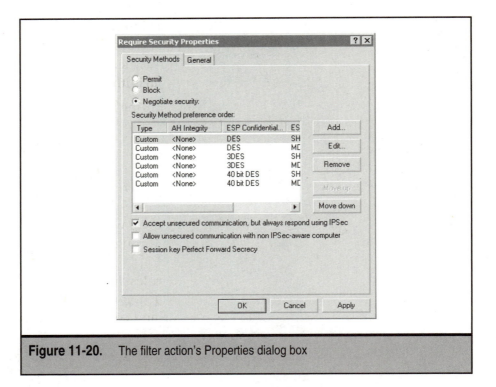

Figure 11-20.   The filter action's Properties dialog box

to permit or block the packet or whether to negotiate security. If you elect to negotiate security, you can specify a preference order for security methods. To add a new security method, click the Add button. (If you elect to add a custom security method, you'll use the Custom Security Method settings dialog box (refer to Figure 11-19) to configure the settings for the security method. See step 9 of the preceding procedure.

6. The filter action's Properties dialog box (refer to Figure 11-20) also offers the following options:

■ **Accept Unsecured Communication But Always Respond Using IPSec**   This option is analogous to the Require Security built-in filter action described earlier in this section.

■ **Allow Unsecured Communication With NonIPSec-aware Computer**   This option is analogous to the Request Security (Optional) built-in filter action described earlier in this section.

- **Session Key Perfect Forward Secrecy** This option specifies that a key will not be used to generate additional keys. It improves security but increases overhead in some cases by requiring additional authentication.

7. When you have finished configuring the filter action properties, click OK.

Creating an IP Security Policy

Creating a security policy is easy if you have already defined the necessary Filter lists and filter actions. If you haven't defined Filter lists and filter actions, you can create them while you create the security policy, but you'll have to flip through several embedded wizards to do so.

A security policy is a collection of rules. Each rule is a specific association of a Filter list with a filter action with accompanying settings for authentication, tunneling, and connection type.

CREATING AN IP SECURITY POLICY To create an IP security policy for a domain, follow these steps:

1. Select Start | Programs | Administrative Tools | Domain Security Policy to open the domain security policy. Expand the Security Settings tree. Or, open a group policy object (as described in Chapter 6), expand the Computer Configuration tree, expand the Windows Settings subtree, and then expand the Security Settings subtree.

2. Right-click the IP Security On Active Directory icon and select Create IP Security Policy.

3. The IP Security Policy Wizard starts. Read the first screen and click Next.

4. In the next screen, enter a name and description for the IP security policy. Click Next.

5. The next screen asks if you would like to include the default response rule in the security policy. Leave the box checked to include the default response rule. Uncheck the box to leave the default response rule out of the policy. Click Next.

6. If you elected to include the default response rule in step 5, the next screen asks you to choose an authentication method to use with the default response rule. The default is Kerberos. You can alternatively specify a certificate authority or enter a preshared key. Click Next.

7. The next screen says you have completed the IP Security Wizard. Note that, so far, all you've done is created a policy and (optionally) placed the default response rule in that policy. To add other rules to the policy and configure the policy setting, you'll need to edit the policy. The last screen asks if you'd like to edit the policy immediately after completing the wizard. The default is Yes. If you leave this box checked, proceed to step 3 of the next procedure after this step. Click Finish.

ADDING A RULE TO AN IP SECURITY POLICY To add a rule to an IP security policy, follow these steps:

1. Select Start | Programs | Administrative Tools | Domain Security Policy to open the domain security policy. Expand the Security Settings tree. Or, open a group policy object (as described in Chapter 6), expand the Computer Configuration tree, expand the Windows Settings subtree, and then expand the Security Settings subtree.

2. Select IP Security On Active Directory. The list of existing policies appears in the right pane. Right-click an IP security policy and choose Properties.

3. The policy's Properties dialog box appears (see Figure 11-21). In the Rules tab, you'll see a list of the IP Security rules that are currently installed with the policy. A rule is an association of a Filter list with a filter action along with other settings for authentication, tunneling, and connection type. If you just created the policy, the Rule list could be empty or it could contain the default response rule. To add additional rules, click the Add button. Note that the Policy Properties dialog box (refer to Figure 11-21) includes a Use Add Wizard checkbox. You can add a new rule either through a wizard or

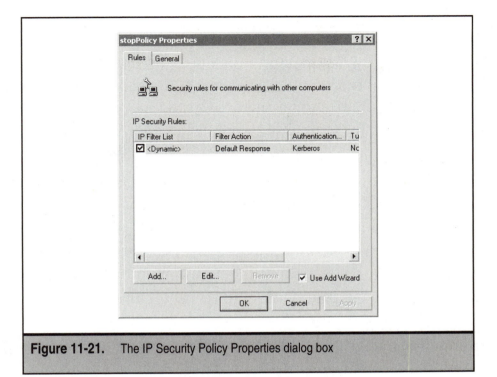

Figure 11-21.   The IP Security Policy Properties dialog box

by directly configuring the new rule's Properties dialog box. The following steps assume you're using the Security Rule Wizard (the default). If you elect to add a rule without using the Add Rule Wizard, you'll configure similar settings through the dialog box described in step 11.

4. The Security Rule Wizard starts. Read the first screen and click Next.

5. In the next screen, choose whether this rule will be used in IP tunneling and, if so, select a tunnel endpoint IP address. Click Next.

6. In the next screen, select whether this rule will apply to all network connections, local area network connections, or remote access connections. Click Next.

7. In the next screen, choose an authentication method that will apply to the rule. Kerberos is the default. Alternatively, you

can specify a certificate authority or enter a preshared key. Click Next.

8. The next screen (see Figure 11-22) asks you to choose an IP Filter list for the rule. Select one of the current Filter lists or click Add to install a new Filter list. See the previous section entitled "Creating and Editing Filter Lists." Click Next.

9. The next screen asks you to select a filter action for the rule. Select one of the current filter actions or click Add to install a new filter action. See the previous section titled "Creating Filter Actions" and "Editing Filter Actions." Click Next.

10. The next screen tells you that you have completed the Rule Wizard. A check box asks if you wish to edit the rule properties. To edit rule properties before returning to the policy's Properties dialog box, leave the check box checked. Click Finish.

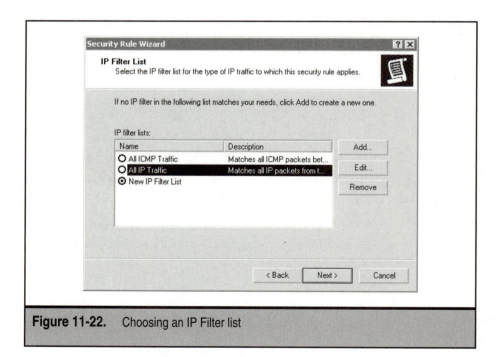

Figure 11-22.   Choosing an IP Filter list

11. If you elected to edit the rule properties in step 10, the new Rule Properties dialog box appears (see Figure 11-23). The tabs of the Rule Properties dialog box offer options similar to the Security Rule Wizard options described in steps 4–10.

12. When you have finished adding the new rule, you are returned to the policy's Properties dialog box (see to Figure 11-21). To add another rule, click the Add button and repeat steps 4–11. To edit the properties of a rule, select the rule and click the Edit button.

13. Select the General tab in the Policy Properties dialog box to edit the name and description of the policy. The General tab also lets you configure policy update settings and key exchange settings.

14. Click Close to close the policy's Properties dialog box.

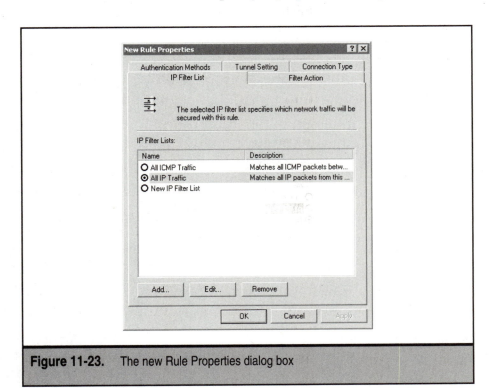

Figure 11-23.   The new Rule Properties dialog box

SUMMARY

This chapter took a close look at some important security features of the Active Directory environment. You learned about Windows 2000's support for Kerberos authentication, including some background on Kerberos and a discussion of what you can and can't do with Windows 2000's Kerberos. You learned how to configure Kerberos policy and other settings. This chapter also discussed some group policy settings that will help you tighten security on your network. One of the most important security features of Windows 2000 is IP Security, which lets you protect TCP/IP communications for the whole network. This chapter described how to create IP Security policies.

CHAPTER 12

Scripting Active Directory

If Active Directory is Microsoft's answer to NetWare, then Windows Scripting Host is its answer to UNIX. Windows 2000 still can't match the rich and versatile UNIX scripting environment, but 2000 is a giant step closer to a scriptable operating system than its NT predecessors. This chapter is not a tutorial on Java or VBScript, but it will help you get started scripting in the Active Directory environment.

SCRIPTING IN THE ACTIVE DIRECTORY ENVIRONMENT

Since the days of the very nonscriptable Windows 3.1, Microsoft has been working to make it easier to automate and customize Windows. In the old days, the customizing consisted of what you could achieve through the limited MS-DOS command language. The DOS-style command language is still around in Windows 2000, but you now have other more powerful and versatile alternatives.

Many of the advances have come through the integration of Windows Scripting Host. Windows Scripting Host, as you will learn later in this chapter, is not a scripting language itself but is rather a scripting environment—a hosting application that matches up a script with a scripting engine. Windows Scripting Host provides built-in support for VBScript (a script-based descendent of Microsoft's Visual Basic) and JScript (Microsoft's ActiveX-enabled Java derivative). Windows Scripting Host is also capable of supporting other third-party scripting engines.

Through the built-in support for VBScript and JScript, you can write flexible and compact text-based utilities for any number of routine administration tasks. In fact, many of the utilities included with Windows 2000 were written in VBScript. (See the section titled "Built-in Scripts" later in this chapter.)

NOTE: This chapter doesn't attempt to provide a tutorial on how to program with VBScript or any other scripting language. Microsoft provides some big, comprehensive help files on VBScript and JScript at the Windows scripting home page: http://msdn.microsoft.com/scripting. Writing in VBScript is faster and easier than writing in a full programming language such as Visual Basic or C++. You do have to know a little about programming, though. This ain't MS-DOS!

You can also use VBScript and JScript (as well as the MS-DOS command language) for writing startup, logon, logoff, and shutdown scripts. Active Directory greatly enhances (and therefore complicates) the Windows logon/logoff scripting capability through the group policy feature, which lets you attach startup, logon, logoff, and shutdown scripts to group policies applied to a site, domain, OU, or computer.

TIP: If your organization is planning a large-scale migration to the Active Directory environment (from Windows NT or from some other networking system), you may be especially interested in scripting as a means of batch-processing users and other objects into the directory.

Interfaces

The scripting languages used with Windows 2000 are typically lean and light—designed to provide the maximum functionality for a minimum amount of code and minimal use of system resources. Many of the control structures, file input/output, and type checking of a full programming language are left out of a scripting language. The Windows scripting languages are, instead, designed to interact directly with COM-based Windows applications and derive much of their power from the ability to open Windows-based applications such as Excel and Word and actually *do* things. In the Active Directory environment, the script communicates through the COM interface to interact with application-based COM objects and through the Active Directory Services Interface (ADSI) to interact with the Active Directory (see Figure 12-1).

Programming books on COM and OLE—which some authors say is the same thing as COM and others say is closely related— are available at most technical bookstores. Microsoft also provides references and white papers on creating COM objects. See http://www.microsoft.com/com/.

An interesting recent development is Microsoft's Windows Script Component Wizard, which lets you create custom, reusable COM components in VBScript, JScript, or any other ActiveX-enabled scripting language. You can download the Script Component Wizard from http://msdn.microsoft.com/scripting. The Script Component Wizard (see Figure 12-2) provides the part-time scripter a taste of the automated programming environment common now within the world of software development. You can specify a scripting language, enable error checking or debugging, and add properties, methods, and events to the component.

Microsoft provides interfaces to the Active Directory through the Active Directory Services Interface (ASDI). ASDI is one aspect of Windows scripting that you haven't encountered prior to

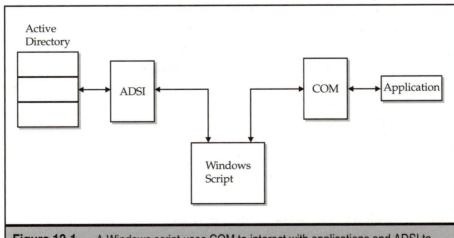

Figure 12-1.   A Windows script uses COM to interact with applications and ADSI to interact with the Active Directory

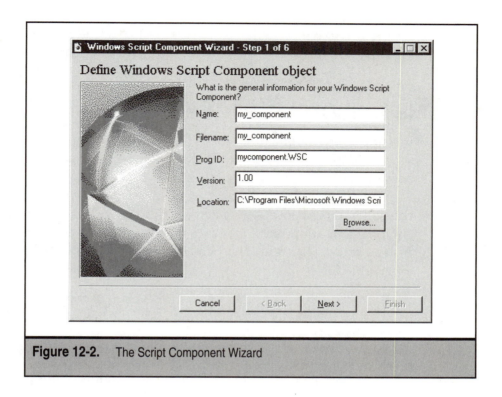

Figure 12-2.   The Script Component Wizard

Windows 2000—and a part of the picture you may not find in
VBScript references until the dust settles from the Windows 2000
release. The best source on ADSI at this time is the downloadable
Active Directory Software Developer's Kit available at the Windows
scripting home page: http://msdn.microsoft.com/scripting.

ADSI addresses not only scripting but all forms of programming,
providing structures, functions, and interfaces for accessing the
Active Directory from within an application or script.

TIP: Microsoft actually recommends that you use well-tested programs and
scripts for critical directory changes (such as changes to the schema) rather
than relying on ADSI Editor and the other directory-editing tools.

Microsoft provides several sample scripts that show how to
write scripts that will interact with the COM interface and the
ADSI interface. The Windows sample scripts are available at
http://msdn.microsoft.com/scripting. You can also learn a great

deal about Windows scripting by analyzing some of the scripts that are supplied with Windows 2000 and the Windows 2000 Resource Kit. See "Built-in Scripts," later in this chapter.

WHAT IS WINDOWS SCRIPTING HOST?

It is important to remember that Windows Scripting Host is not a scripting language. It is not even a scripting engine, although the scripting engines VBScript and JScript are included with Windows Scripting Host. Windows Scripting Host is more like a script controller. Its purpose is to match a script file with the scripting engine that is supposed to execute that script file (see Figure 12-3).

You can invoke Windows Scripting Host from either of two executable files:

▼ **cscript.exe**   The command-line version of the scripting host that accepts DOS-based command switches and is invoked from the command prompt.

▲ **wscript.exe**   The Windows-based version of the scripting host configured and invoked through the Windows Run command or through file associations in the Windows environment.

You'll learn more about these two scripting-host options later in this chapter.

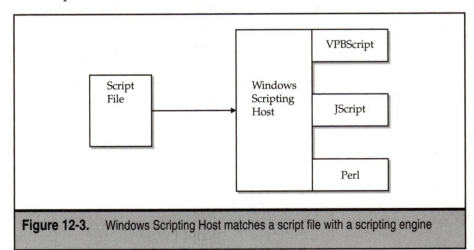

Figure 12-3.   Windows Scripting Host matches a script file with a scripting engine

You invoke Windows Scripting Host by executing either cscript.exe or wscript.exe and specifying the name of the script file:

```
wscript my_script.vbs
```

The advantage of this architecture is that it spares the user from having to learn the details of every possible scripting format. The user does not have to know where the scripting engine is located and what options or arguments are required for invoking the engine directly. *All* scripts are invoked and configured through cscript or wscript.

Behind the scenes, each scripting engine is registered with Windows Scripting Host. The Windows 2000 Registry contains the data necessary for Windows Scripting Host to associate the script file with the appropriate script engine.

NOTE: ·Ready-to-use scripting engines for the Visual Basic scripting language VBScript and for Microsoft's Java scripting language (JScript) are included with Windows Scripting Host. You can also register other ActiveX scripting engines. The Windows 2000 Resource Kit, for instance, includes an ActiveX-based Perl version called ActivePerl. To register a third-party scripting engine, consult the vendor documentation.

You can also execute a VBScript or JScript by double-clicking the Script File icon in a Windows user interface utility such as Windows Explorer, Network Neighborhood, or My Computer. As you might expect, this browse-and-click capability is a consequence of the Windows file association feature. The .vbs and .js file extensions are each associated with the Windows-based scripting host wscript.exe, so, by default, double-clicking the icon for a .vbs or .js file launches the scripting host.

Configuring Script Files

To view the properties for a VBScript or JScript file, right-click the file and choose Properties. The Script Properties dialog box appears, as shown in Figure 12-4. The Script Properties dialog box contains the following tabs:

▼ **General**   The General tab includes a summary of file-related information, such as the file size and path. You can specify whether to make the file read-only or hidden. Of particular interest is the Opens With setting (next to the Change button in Figure 12-4). Note that the file is configured to open with the Microsoft Windows-Based Script Host. (You can't read all the text in the figure.) This is another way of saying the script file is configured to open with wscript.exe by default. Notice that this Opens With setting is in the same region of the property page with the Type Of File setting. If you click the Change button, you will change the file association for the file type (other files with the same extension will also change).

■ **Security**   The Security tab specifies permissions for the script file. It is similar to other security sheets in the Active Directory

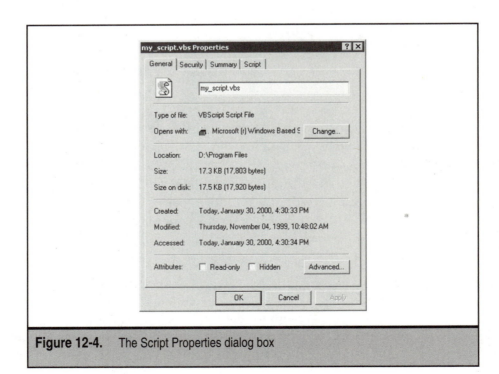

Figure 12-4.   The Script Properties dialog box

environment. It is sometimes useful to set access permissions for a script to prevent unauthorized users from executing or modifying the script. See Chapter 5, "Users and Groups," for more about Active Directory permissions.

▲ **Script**   The Script tab (see Figure 12-5) provides additional configuration settings. The most noteworthy of these settings is the checkbox labeled Stop Script After Specified Number Of Seconds. Beneath this check box is a field where you can specify the number of seconds. The purpose of this is for cases in which the script may hang or become embroiled in an infinite loop. Some scripts may also include a BatchMode setting that lets you configure the script to execute in batch mode.

When you change one of the settings in the Script tab and click Apply or OK, Windows 2000 creates a .WSH file with script file

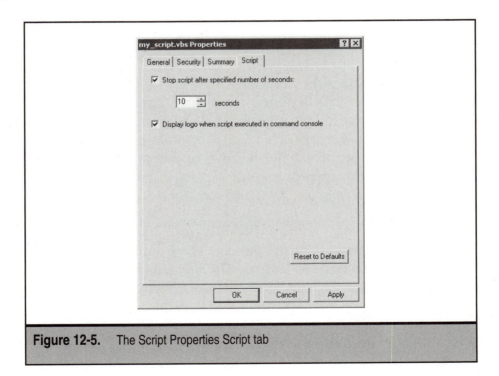

Figure 12-5.   The Script Properties Script tab

configuration settings. The .WSH file is similar in format to an INI or a PIF file. A sample .WSH file is as follows:

```
[ScriptFile]
Path=\\olympus\McGraw\ActiveDir\Docs\Chap12\scripts\CHART.VBS
[Options]
Timeout=10
DisplayLogo=1
```

You can specify a .WSH file directly as a script file argument for wscript.exe or crscript.exe, or you can double-click the .WSH file to execute it. When you execute a .WSH file, Windows Scripting Host reads the configuration options and then executes the script specified in the path.

NOTE: The BatchMode setting in the .WSH file specifies whether the file should be run in batch mode. When no BatchMode setting is present, the default is to run in interactive mode (equivalent to BatchMode=0). The setting BatchMode=1 calls for the file to run in batch mode.

cscript.exe

Cscript.exe is the command-line version of the Windows scripting host. Cscript is designed to run in the Windows 2000 command window or in DOS-style .bat files. Some built-in scripts are written specifically to run in the cscript environment. When you run a script under wscript, a dialog box may appear and tell you to run the script under cscript instead.

The format for the cscript command is as follows:

```
cscript script_name [options..] [script parameters...]
```

The options are cscript options. These optional settings (sometimes called host parameters) specify additional information for the scripting host. Options are preceded with a double slash (//).

Script parameters are parameters that are passed to the script. These parameters relate to specific details of each individual script and therefore vary from script to script.

Cscript command options include the following options. You'll notice that some of these options are reminiscent of the .WSH file options described in the preceding section:

▼ **//B** Specifies that the command should run in batch mode. Batch mode suppresses error messages and user prompts.

■ **//I** Specifies that the command should run in interactive mode (this is the default setting).

■ **//T:time_in_sec** Time-out period in seconds. The script will execute for the specified time and then terminate. (The default is no predefined time-out period—the script will run as long as it wants to.)

■ **//logo** Displays a logo when the script executes.

■ **//nologo** Prevents the logo from appearing when the script executes.

■ **//H:default_script_host** Defines the default scripting host executable (cscript.exe or wscript.exe). By default, Windows 2000 executes scripts using wscript.exe. This option lets you change the default. Note that this option *does not* specify which executable to use to run a specific script. This option is not specified along with a script file. It just sends an instruction to Windows 2000 to change the default.

■ **//S** Saves the command-line options specified in this command.

▲ **//?** Displays command options and other usage information.

wscript.exe

The Windows-based scripting host executable wscript.exe does not have a list of command-line options like the options described in the previous section for cscript.exe. You configure wscript options through the Script File Properties dialog box (as described in the previous section titled "Configuring Script Files"). By default, VBScript and JScript files are configured to open with wscript.exe. You can run wscript.exe by double-clicking a VBScript or JScript file (or any other script file with a file association mapped to wscript.exe). You can also run wscript from the Run command (Start | Run). Or, you can enter the name of a script file with an extension mapped to wscript.exe at the Run command.

If you start wscript from the Run command, the format is simply as follows:

```
wscript script_file
```

where *script_file* is the path and name of the script file you wish to execute.

Setting the Default Scripting Host

By default, VBScript and JScript scripts run with the Windows-based scripting host wscript.exe. You can, however, change the default setting so that these script files run under cscript by default.

To change the default scripting host executable, enter the following command at the command prompt:

```
cscript //H:host_name
```

where host_name is the name of the new default host (cscript or wscript). For example, to change the default host to cscript, use the following command:

```
cscript: //H:cscript
```

Debugging Scripts

Microsoft makes a script debugger that you can use to troubleshoot problems with VBScript and JScript files. The Microsoft script debugger is available at the Windows scripting Web site: http://msdn.microsoft.com/scripting.

It is worth noting that a version of the script debugger is also built into Internet Services Manager, the management utility for Windows 2000's Internet Information Server (IIS). The Internet Services Manager version is designed primarily for debugging

Web-related client-side and server-side scripts. To access the IIS script debugger, follow these steps:

1. Select Start | Programs | Administrative Tools | Internet Services Manager.

2. In the Internet Services Manager tree, right-click an application virtual directory. Select Properties.

3. In the Properties dialog box, select the Virtual Directory tab and click the Configuration button.

4. In the Application Configuration dialog box, select the App Debugging tab.

5. In the App Debugging tab (see Figure 12-6), enable server-side and/or client-side debugging. You can also configure script error message options.

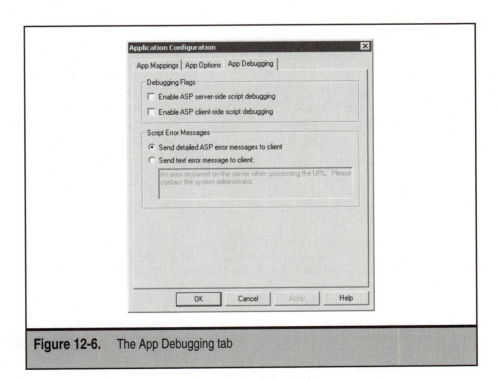

Figure 12-6.   The App Debugging tab

LOGON SCRIPTS

The traditional logon script was a script that ran when a user sat down at a computer and automatically configured any customizable aspects of the user environment. This definition is still appropriate in Windows 2000, but Active Directory adds considerable complexity to the task of customizing the user environment. You could argue, that some of the innovations in the NT/2000 user environment, such as user profiles, system policies, and group policies, have reduced the need for logon scripts. However, logon scripts have not gone away. In addition to a logon script applied specifically to a user, the Active Directory environment also supports startup, logon, logoff, and shutdown scripts applied through any of the group policy levels. It is therefore possible to apply a number of automated scripts to the user environment from a number of different sources.

You can use logon scripts and other environment scripts to create network connections, set environment variables, display messages, execute programs, and log information. Some administrators use logon or logoff scripts to perform an automatic backup of user data. With Windows 2000's support for VBScript and JScript, your possibilities of what you can do in a script have increased greatly: you can reach into the Active Directory itself, open Microsoft Word and write a log entry, or even send an email message.

Policy scripts are part of a group policy object and are applied in the order of group policy application:

1. Local computer policy

2. Site policy

3. Domain policy

4. OU policies

Although it is possible to add startup, logon, logoff, and shutdown scripts at each of these policy levels, script proliferation can lead to some confusion. It is best to strive for a uniform strategy for how to apply policy scripts. The best practices for scripts are similar to those for other group policy objects. Apply the script to the widest possible base and (if possible) try to avoid the situation where later scripts are undoing or contradicting settings from earlier scripts. Networks that use OUs as a kind of de facto resource domain—with most of the management occurring at the OU level—may wish to use OU policy as the sole vehicle for applying policy scripts.

After all policy scripts have executed, the logon script applied specifically to the user account runs. Because this script is the last to execute, it has the power to change or override settings from other scripts. The user logon script in Windows 2000 has a role similar to the role it had in Windows NT 4, and it is similarly configured through the User Properties dialog box. On many networks, it will undoubtedly remain the primary means of assigning a logon script due to the general inscrutability of the group policy feature. However, if you plan on applying the same script to an entire class of users, group policy is far simpler in the long run. Note, for instance, that when a user moves to a different location (and therefore moves to a new OU that requires a new logon script), the user logon script must be changed manually but the applicable OU-level policy script will adjust automatically to the appropriate script for the new environment.

The following sections describe how to configure user logon scripts and policy scripts.

NOTE: See Chapter 5, "Users and Groups," for more on setting properties for user accounts. See Chapter 6, "Group Policy" for more on the group policy feature.

User Logon Scripts

You can designate a user logon script through the User Account Properties dialog box. The Add New User Wizard does not offer a choice of specifying a logon script when the account is created.

To specify a user logon script, follow these steps:

1. Select Start | Programs | Administrative Tools | Active Directory Users And Computers.

2. In the Active Directory Users And Computers main window, browse to the OU or container that holds the user account to which you'd like to add a logon script.

3. Right-click the user account and choose Properties.

4. In the User Properties dialog box, select the Profile tab.

5. In the Profile tab (see Figure 12-7), enter the path to the user logon script.

Policy Scripts

As you learned in Chapter 6, you can configure startup, logon, logoff, and shutdown scripts to execute through the Active Directory group policy features. These policy scripts allow you to define the user environment through a script without ever tying the script directly to a user's account.

To add a script to a group policy object, follow these steps:

1. Right-click a site, domain, or OU in Active Directory Sites And Services or Active Directory Users And Computers and choose Properties.

2. In the Properties dialog box, select the Group Policy tab.

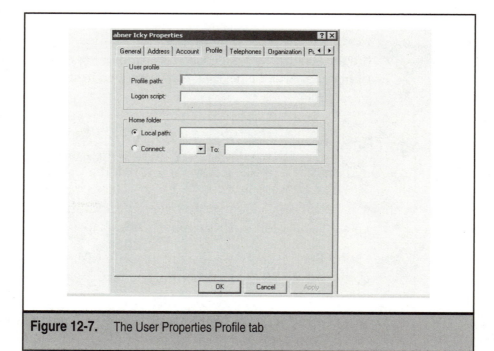

Figure 12-7. The User Properties Profile tab

3. To create a new group policy object, click New. To add a script to an existing group policy object, select the object in the Group Policy tab and choose Edit. For more on creating and modifying group policy objects, see Chapter 6.

4. To add a startup or shutdown script for the computer, expand the Computer Configuration tree and then expand the Windows Settings subtree. Select Scripts (Startup/Shutdown). Icons for a startup script and a shutdown script appear in the right pane.

5. Double-click one of the icons in the right pane (Startup or Shutdown). For instance, double-click Startup. A dialog box appears with a list of all Startup scripts configured for the policy object. To add a startup script, click the Add button. The Add A Script dialog box appears (see Figure 12-8). Enter a script name or click the Browse button to browse for a script. Enter any parameters in the box labeled Script Parameters. When you are finished, click OK.

6. The script you entered should appear in the Properties dialog box. Click Apply or OK.

7. To add a logon or logoff script, expand the User Configuration tree and expand the Windows Settings subtree. Select Scripts (Logon/Logoff). Double-click the Logon or Logoff icon in the right pane. Add the new script as described in steps 3 and 4.

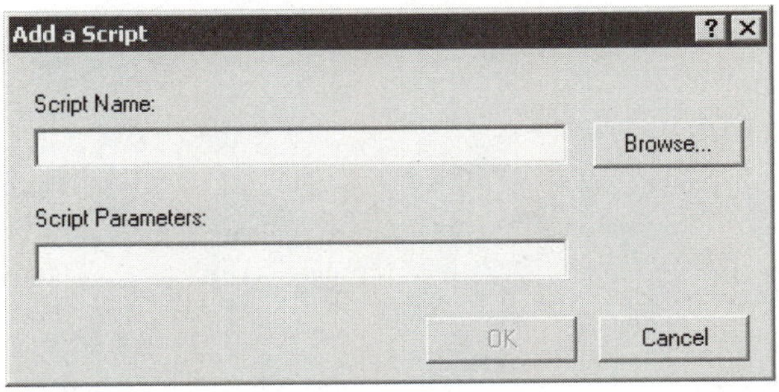

Figure 12-8.   The Add A Script dialog box

In addition to letting you configure policy scripts, Group Policy Editor also lets you configure settings that describe how policy scripts will be processed. The policies shown in Table 12-1 are included with the default administrative templates.

Location	Policy	Description
Computer Configuration \Administrative Templates\ System\Logon	Run logon scripts synchronously	Tells Windows to run all logon scripts before enabling the desktop environment. In other words, Windows Explorer doesn't open until the last script has run. This setting takes precedence over the similar user configuration setting (shown later in this table).
	Run startup scripts asynchronously	Tells Windows to run startup scripts simultaneously. By default, one startup script does not start until the previous startup script is finished.
	Run startup scripts visible	Displays startup scripts as they execute. By default, Windows 2000 computers do not display executing startup scripts.
	Run shutdown scripts visible	Displays shutdown scripts as they execute. By default, Windows 2000 computers do not display executing shutdown scripts.
	Maximum wait time for group policy scripts	Tells Windows the maximum time to wait for group policy scripts to run on this computer.

Table 12-1. Group Policy Settings Relating to Policy Scripts

Location	Policy	Description
User Configuration \Administrative Templates\ System\Logon/ Logon/Logoff	Run logon scripts synchronously	Tells Windows to run all logon scripts before enabling the desktop environment. In other words, Windows Explorer doesn't open until the last script has run.
	Run legacy logon scripts hidden	Tells Windows not to display logon scripts written for Windows NT. By default, Windows NT batch files execute in a command window. This policy makes NT-based logon scripts run hidden.
	Run logon scripts visible	Displays logon scripts as they execute. By default, Windows 2000 computers do not display executing logon scripts.
	Run logoff scripts visible	Displays logon scripts as they execute. By default, Windows 2000 computers do not display executing logon scripts.
	Run these programs at user logon	Not truly a script-related setting, but included here for perspective. Use this setting to cause a program to run at user logon with or without a logon script.

Table 12-1.   Group Policy Settings Relating to Policy Scripts *(continued)*

BUILT-IN SCRIPTS

Microsoft wrote many VBScripts for Windows 2000 Server. Some of these programs are included with the Windows 2000 Server implementation or with the Windows 2000 Resource Kit. These scripts are useful not only for the ready-made functionality they provide, but also as examples of how to program in VBScript. You can open any of these scripts in Notepad to see the source code.

The scripts in the Inetpub\AdminScripts directory are designed to operate with Internet Information Server (the Windows 2000 Web server) in a Web-based scripting environment. Some sample Web-related scripts are located in the Inetpub\ iissamples directory.

The Windows 2000 Resource Kit includes several useful scripts—most of them for management and migration. Table 12-2 shows some of the Resource Kit scripts. By default, these scripts will be installed to the Program Files\Resource Kit directory. To reach these scripts through the Start menu, make sure the Resource Kit is installed and then select Start | Programs | Windows 2000 Resource Kit | Tools | Remote Administration Scripts. The extensive use of VBScript for the tools of the Windows 2000 Resource Kit is testament to the importance of VBScript and to its versatility.

EXECUTING SCRIPTS AUTOMATICALLY

A script file written for a registered scripting engine executes when you double-click the File icon in a Windows interface application such as Windows Explorer. If even that is too much trouble, you can also use any of the following methods to make a script run automatically:

▼ Make the script a logon script for the user account or execute the script from a logon script for the user's account. See Chapter 5, "Users and Groups."

■ Reference the script as a startup/logon/logoff/shutdown script in a group policy object or execute the script from another script that is configured as a startup/logon/logoff/shutdown script.

■ Add a script (or any program for that matter) to the policy setting.

■ Enable the group policies Computer Configuration\Administrative Templates\System\Run These Programs At

Script	Description
CheckBios.vbs	Displays system BIOS information
Chkusers.vbs	Checks for users that satisfy criteria you specify
CreateUsers.vbs	Creates user accounts
Desktop.vbs	Displays desktop properties of a computer you specify
Drives.vbs	Displays information on physical disks
Fileman.vbs	Performs operations on a file, such as renaming, copying, or taking ownership
Group.vbs	Displays the list of groups in a domain
Listdomains.vbs	Displays a list of all domains in the namespace
ListPrinters.vbs	Displays properties of printers installed on a computer
ListSpace.vbs	Displays disk space information
Modifyldap.vbs	Modifies LDAP policies
Modifyusers.vbs	Modifies user accounts
NetConnections.vbs	Displays information on network connections
Schemadiff.vbs	Compares two different schema and lists differences
Service.vbs	Manages services on a computer (starts, stops, removes, lists dependencies)
Share.vbs	Creates and deletes shares and displays share information

Table 12-2.   Some Scripts Included with the Windows 2000 Resource Kit

User Logon, or User Configuration\ Administrative Templates\ System\Run These Programs At User Logon.

■ Place the script in the Start Menu\Programs\Startup folder of a user profile.

▲ Configure the Windows 2000 Task Scheduler to run the script.

Of course, most of the preceding methods just run the script when the user logs on or logs off. The Task Scheduler is the best way to run scripts at a specific time or time interval.

Task Scheduler is an application that lets you run programs and scripts to run at a certain time or on a certain regular schedule. You can use Task Scheduler to execute a script (or any application for that matter) automatically.

To schedule a script or program in Task Scheduler, follow these steps:

1. Select Start | Programs | Accessories | System Tools | Scheduled Tasks.

2. Click the Add Scheduled Task icon in the Scheduled Tasks main window (see Figure 12-9).

3. The Scheduled Task Wizard starts and announces that you are about to schedule a task. Click Next.

4. The next screen asks you to choose the program you wish to schedule. Select a program from the available list, or click the Browse button and browse to the program or script you would like to schedule. Select the program or script and choose Open.

5. In the next screen (see Figure 12-10), choose a scheduling option for the task (Daily, Weekly, Monthly, One Time Only, When My Computer Starts, or When I Log On.) Click Next.

6. The next screen asks for additional scheduling information, depending on the scheduling option you chose in step 4. Choose the time you'd like the program to execute, the start

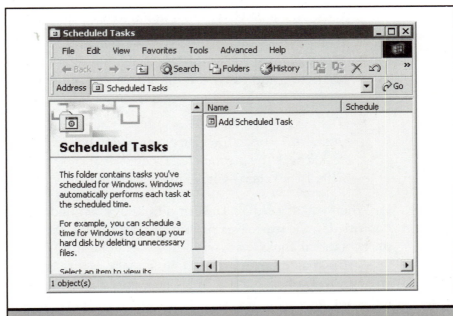

Figure 12-9.   The Scheduled Tasks main window

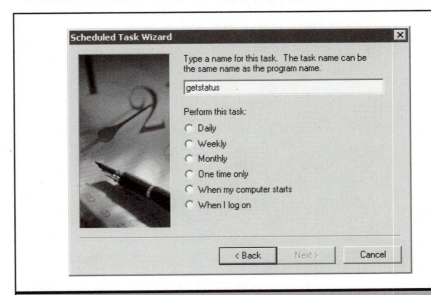

Figure 12-10.   Choosing a scheduling option

data, and so forth. When you have configured the necessary information, click Next.

7. The task must run under the credentials of a user. Enter the username and password for the user account you'd like to use to run the task. Confirm the password. Click Next.

8. The next screen displays a summary of information you entered. To open the Properties dialog box for the scheduled task, check the box labeled Open Advanced Properties For This Task When I Click Finish. Click Finish.

When you schedule a task through the Scheduled Task Wizard (as described in the preceding procedure), an icon for the task appears in the Scheduled Tasks main window (refer to Figure 12-9). To view the Properties dialog box for the scheduled task, right-click the Task icon and choose Properties. The Task Properties dialog box has the following tabs:

▼ **Task** Displays general information about the task, such as the program that will run and the account it will run under.

■ **Schedule** Lets you view and modify the schedule for the task.

■ **Settings** Additional configuration settings related to the task (see Figure 12-11).

▲ **Security** Security settings for the task object.

If you schedule a script to run through the Task Scheduler, the script will run with the default scripting host (wscript or cscript). If you are scheduling a script that must run under cscript, make sure you make cscript the default. See the section titled "Setting the Default Scripting Host," earlier in this chapter.

NOTE: See Task Scheduler Help for more information on scheduling tasks.

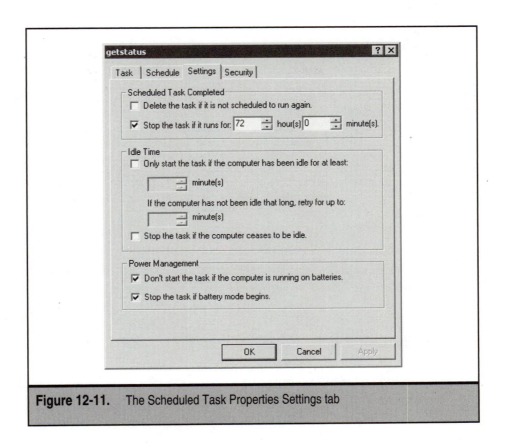

Figure 12-11.   The Scheduled Task Properties Settings tab

RUNNING UNIX SCRIPTS IN WINDOWS 2000

ActivePerl, the Perl interpreter found in the Windows 2000 Server
Resource Kit, runs Perl scripts in Windows 2000. If you are porting
existing Perl scripts to the Windows 2000 environment, modifications
may be necessary.

For greater and more seamless portability of UNIX-based
applications and scripts into Windows 2000, try the add-on Microsoft
Interix package. Microsoft claims that Interix lets you run UNIX
applications and scripts in Windows 2000 without changing any
code. Contact Microsoft for details on how to obtain Interix.

SUMMARY

This chapter introduced the Windows 2000 scripting environment. Windows 2000 offers a rich environment for custom scripting. Scripts can access:

▼ The COM interface for interacting with COM-based Windows applications.

▲ The Active Directory Services Interface (ADSI) for interacting with Active Directory.

Windows 2000 not only supports the .bat files and user logon scripts found in Windows NT, but also adds built-in VBScript and JScript capability through the Windows Scripting Host. Windows Scripting Host also supports other ActiveX-enabled scripting engines. You learned about the two incarnations of Windows Scripting Host: wscript (for Windows-based scripts) and cscript (for command-line scripts).

Another important aspect of the Windows 2000 scripting environment is Active Directory's support for multiple levels of startup, logon, logoff, and shutdown scripts through the group policy feature.

Lastly, this chapter described some of the built-in scripts included with Windows 2000 Server and showed how you can configure scripts (and other programs) to run automatically through the Task Scheduler.

CHAPTER 13

Interoperating Windows 2000

As networks become more integrated, the need for interoperable systems becomes more pronounced. Although some might think that Microsoft has no competitors in the world of operating systems, Microsoft does not share that opinion. Like any contemporary and successful operating system, Windows 2000 must be capable of interoperating with other systems. This chapter discusses NetWare, Macintosh, and UNIX in the world of Windows 2000. You'll also learn how to integrate Active Directory with Microsoft's own Exchange directory system.

Most of Windows 2000's interoperability components do not relate directly to Active Directory (although this chapter mentions some add-on components that interface the Active Directory with NetWare and UNIX). You will, however, need to contend with these interoperability issues if you're configuring an Active Directory network. This chapter will help you find your way through Windows 2000's interoperability features.

WINDOWS 2000 AND NETWARE

Windows 2000, like its predecessor Windows NT, is designed to interoperate with Novell NetWare. You can share files and directories with NetWare clients and access NetWare resources from Windows 2000 clients. Like NT Server, Windows 2000 Server can act as a gateway to provide Microsoft clients access to NetWare resources. The following sections describe how to interoperate NetWare with a Windows 2000 network.

Configuring Windows 2000 for NetWare

Microsoft made NetWare connectivity a high priority for Windows NT 4. Windows 2000 inherits all that NetWare functionality. Configuring Windows 2000 for NetWare is similar to configuring Windows NT for NetWare—once you find your way through changes in the user interface. The following sections discuss these topics:

▼ Installing NWLink

■ Creating a gateway to NetWare resources

■ Connecting to a NetWare volume

■ Adding a NetWare printer

▲ Sharing files with NetWare clients

Later sections introduce some of the advanced NetWare functions you have to pay extra for, such as the add-on Microsoft Directory Synchronization Service.

Installing NWLink

Microsoft's NWLink protocol (actually it is called NWLink IPX/SPX/NetBIOS Compatible Transport Protocol) is the protocol that Windows systems use to operate on NetWare networks. Because IPX/SPX is a proprietary protocol, Microsoft had to give its version a different name, but for all practical purposes you can think of NWLink as a version of IPX/SPX.

NOTE: If you're wondering whether NWLink is perfectly compatible with IPX/SPX, the answer depends upon whom you ask. Microsoft seems to believe that it is. If Novell agrees, it certainly isn't admitting it. The effectiveness of NWLink is nonetheless remarkable, and one would have to guess that part of the reason for the enormous success of Windows NT 4 was its ability to interoperate simply and reliably with NetWare systems.

If you are setting up your Windows 2000 system to participate in a NetWare network, you probably already know more than you need to know about protocol configuration on IPX/SPX networks. Each local subnet must have a network number and frame type. By default, NWLink can autodetect the network number and frame type and configure the network adapter accordingly. Microsoft recommends you allow the NWLink protocol to autodetect the frame type and network number if possible. Occasionally, however, autodetection doesn't work. A misconfigured computer, for example, can cause neighboring computers to guess the wrong frame type and number for the local network. If necessary, you can manually configure a frame type and network number for the network through the NWLink configuration.

TIP: Some network applications have been known to misbehave if you don't assign a number and frame type. A manually configured frame type can improve performance because the receiving computer knows the frame type of an incoming packet automatically.

The best way to determine the network number and frame type assigned to the network adapter is to type **ipxroute config** at the command prompt. If the adapter displays a frame type and network number you aren't expecting, try the manual configuration option.

The network number associated with the network adapter is sometimes referred to as the *external* network adapter. The IPX/SPX world also uses the concept of an *internal* network number. The internal network number is a logical designation used on routed networks to identify computers that provide network services. By default, the internal network number is 00000000. You do not have to set an internal network number unless your computer offers services to a NetWare network through the NetWare-based Service Advertising Protocol (SAP). Some SAP-enabled applications set the internal network number automatically.

You must be a member of the Administrators group to install NWLink:

1. Choose Start | Settings | Network And Dial-up Connections.

2. Right-click the Local Area Connection icon and choose Properties.

3. In the Local Area Connection Properties dialog box, click the Install button.

4. In the Select Network Component Type dialog box, select Protocol, and then click Add.

5. In the Select Network Protocol dialog box, select NWLink IPX/SPX/NetBIOS Compatible Transport Protocol and click OK.

Once you have installed NWLink, you may wish to configure NWLink properties. The NWLink IPX/SPX/NetBIOS Compatible Protocol Properties dialog box lets you configure the following:

▼ *An internal network number for the network interface.*   Network services that use the SAP agent to advertise on the NetWare network require an internal network number. Consult your NetWare documentation for more on assigning internal network numbers.

■ *Auto or manual frame type detection.*

▲ *Frame type options for manual detection.*

Again, you must be a member of the Administrators group to configure NWLink properties:

1. Choose Start | Settings | Network And Dial-up Connections.

2. Right-click the Local Area Connection icon and choose Properties.

3. In the Local Area Connection Properties dialog box, select NWLink IPX/SPX/NetBIOS Compatible Transport Protocol and click the Properties button.

4. In the NWLink IPX/SPX/NetBIOS Compatible Transport Protocol Properties dialog box (see Figure 13-1), enter an internal network number. Select Auto Frame Type Detection or Manual Frame Type Detection. If you select Manual Frame Type Detection, click the Add button and add the frame types you'd like to detect. Options include Ethernet 802.2, Ethernet 802.3, Ethernet II, and Ethernet SNAP.

5. Enter a network number for the frame type. Click the Add button again to add frame types.

6. Click OK.

If the Routing and Remote Access utility is installed on the Windows 2000 Server on which you configure NWLink, the server can act as an IPX router. Use the Routing and Remote

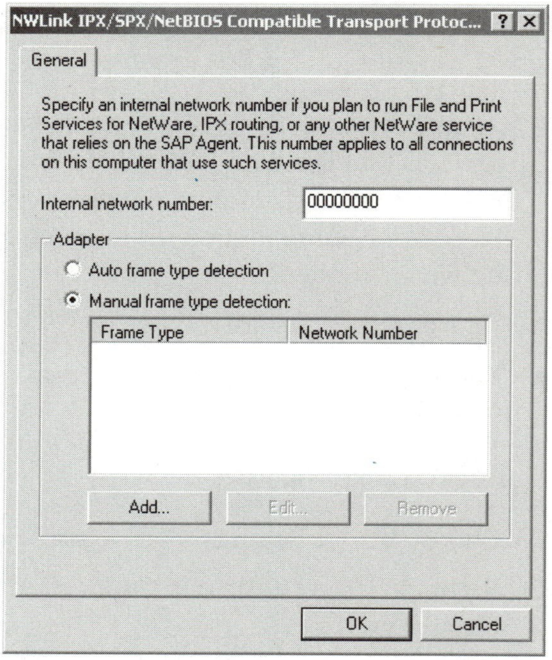

Figure 13-1.   Enter an internal network number in this dialog box

access utility in the Administrative Tools group (see Figure 13-2) to configure IPX routing. Routing and Remote Access will also take care of advertising services hosted on the Windows 2000 server to the IPX/SPX network through SAP. If you wish to advertise services through SAP, but you don't have Routing and Remote Access running on the Windows 2000 server, install the SAP agent service.

You must be a member of the Administrators group to install SAP agent:

1. Choose Start | Settings | Network And Dial-up Connections.

2. Right-click the Local Area Connection icon and choose Properties.

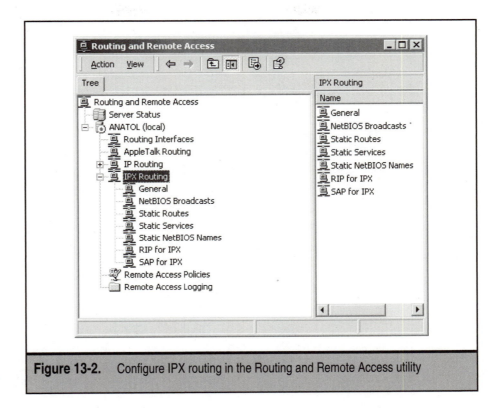

Figure 13-2.   Configure IPX routing in the Routing and Remote Access utility

3. In the Local Area Connection Properties dialog box, click the Install button.

4. In the Select Network Component Type dialog box, choose Service and click the Add button.

5. In the Select Network Service dialog box, choose SAP Agent and click OK.

6. Click Close in the Local Area Connection Properties dialog box.

Creating a Gateway to NetWare Resources

Gateway Service for NetWare (GSNW) enables a Windows 2000 server to act as a gateway to NetWare resources (see Figure 13-3). Through Gateway Service for NetWare, you can configure your network so that NetWare volumes appear as Windows directory shares on the

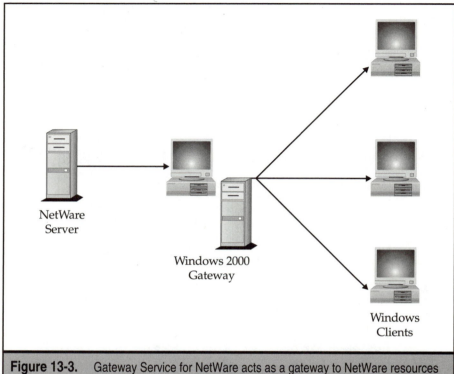

NetWare
Server

Windows 2000
Gateway

Windows
Clients

Figure 13-3.   Gateway Service for NetWare acts as a gateway to NetWare resources

GSNW server computer. Windows clients (Windows 95, Windows 98, Windows NT, Windows 2000) can access NetWare files, print, and direct services through the gateway without the need for NetWare client software.

To install Gateway Service for NetWare, follow these steps:

1. On the NetWare network, create a user account that the Windows 2000 server will use to gain access to NetWare resources.

2. On the NetWare network, create a NetWare group called **NTGATEWAY**. Give the group the necessary rights so that group members will have access to resources shared with the Windows 2000 gateway. Add the user account you created in step 1 to the NTGATEWAY group.

3. On the Windows 2000 server, remove any NetWare redirectors installed on the system, such as Novell client software.

4. On the Windows 2000 server, choose Start | Settings | Network And Dial-up Connections. (You must be a member of the Administrators group to do this.)

5. Right-click the Local Area Connection icon and choose Properties.

6. In the Local Area Connection Properties dialog box, click the Install button.

7. In the Select Network Component Type dialog box, select Client and click the Add button.

NOTE: Gateway Services for NetWare is both a client and a server. Note that, for installation purposes, it is listed as a client in the Select Network Component Type dialog box.

8. In the Select Network Client dialog box, choose Gateway (And Client) Service For NetWare and click OK.

9. The Select NetWare Logon dialog box (see Figure 13-4) asks you to select a preferred server or a default tree and context. The options in this dialog box allow the client portion of the Gateway (and Client) Service for NetWare to attach to a NetWare network. Enter a preferred server if you want the Windows 2000 server to attach to a bindery-based NetWare server. Enter a default tree and context if you want to access NDS-based NetWare resources. Note that you don't have to choose a preferred server or a default tree and context.

10. When Windows 2000 informs you that you have to reboot for the changes to take effect, click OK.

When you reboot your Windows 2000 computer, the GSNW appears with the Control Panel applications. You can use the GSNW Control Panel to create gateways or to configure Gateway Service for NetWare settings.

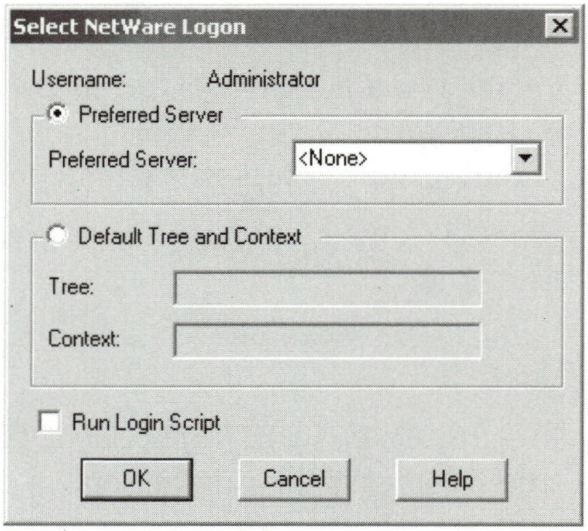

Select NetWare Logon [X]

Username: Administrator

◉ Preferred Server

Preferred Server: <None>   ▼

○ Default Tree and Context

Tree: [   ]

Context: [   ]

☐ Run Login Script

[OK   ]   [Cancel]   [Help]

Figure 13-4.   The Select NetWare Logon dialog box

To configure Gateway Service for NetWare (after you have installed it and restarted the system), follow these steps:

1. Select Start | Settings | Control Panel.

2. Double-click the GSNW icon.

3. The Gateway Service for NetWare dialog box appears (see Figure 13-5). You can enter a preferred server or default tree and context. Also, you can set print options or elect to run a user login script.

TIP: Microsoft warns that, if you are using Gateway (and Client) Services for NetWare to log into a NetWare network and you plan to run a login script, you need to enter the 32-bit Windows command prompt *cmd.exe*. Don't use the 16-bit *command.com*. The file should begin with *#cmd*.

After you have installed and configured Gateway (and Client) Services for NetWare, you still haven't yet shared anything. You must specifically configure a gateway to make NetWare resources accessible to Microsoft clients. If you are connecting to an NDS network, the NetWare resource must be in the same container with

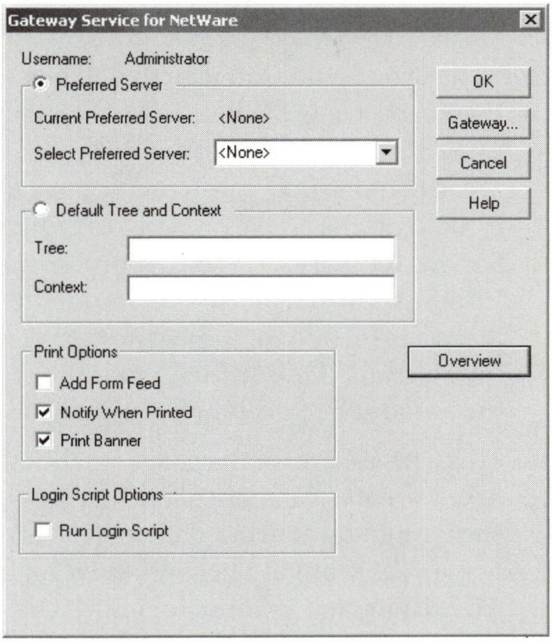

Figure 13-5.   The Gateway Service for NetWare dialog box

the NTGATEWAY group you created when you installed Gateway Service for NetWare (see the procedure earlier in this section).

You must configure the gateway before you can share resources through it. To configure the gateway, you must associate the gateway with the gateway account you created on the NetWare network when you installed Gateway Service for NetWare (see the procedure earlier in this section). You must configure the gateway only once for the server. After that, you can simply add shares to the gateway.

To configure the gateway and share a NetWare volume, follow these steps:

1. Make sure Gateway Service for NetWare and NWLink are installed and configured on your system.

2. Select Start | Settings | Control Panel.

3. Double-click the GSNW icon.

4. The Gateway Service for NetWare dialog box appears (refer to Figure 13-5). In the dialog box, click the Gateway button.

5. In the Configure Gateway dialog box (see Figure 13-6), check the Enable Gateway box. Enter a name for the gateway account. The gateway account name and password should match the account name and password you used for the account you created on the NetWare network when you installed Gateway Service for NetWare (see the procedure earlier in this section). Windows 2000 will use this account to gain access to the NetWare resources. If the gateway account will authenticate through an NDS network, enter the distinguished name of the account in NetWare's distinguished name format.

6. To create a share for the gateway, click the Add button. You'll be asked to enter the share name that will appear to Microsoft clients and the network path to the NetWare volume. If you wish to map the share to a network drive, enter the default drive letter. Click Unlimited to admit unlimited concurrent users or click Allow to set a maximum number of concurrent users. Click OK.

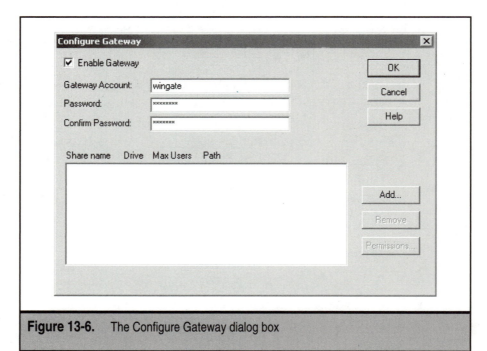

Figure 13-6. The Configure Gateway dialog box

After you have configured the gateway, the next time you wish to add a share, you can just open the Configure Gateway dialog box (shown in Figure 13-6) and click the Add button. You don't have to create a new gateway or reconfigure the gateway account.

To configure permissions for a Gateway Services for NetWare share, follow these steps:

1. Select Start | Settings | Control Panel.

2. Double-click the GSNW icon.

3. The Gateway Service for NetWare dialog box appears (refer to Figure 13-5). In the dialog box, click the Gateway button.

4. In the Share list, select the share for which you would like to configure permissions. Click the Permissions button.

5. In the Permissions dialog box, select a user or group and configure the appropriate permissions. To add a new user or group to the permissions list, click Add.

Connecting to a NetWare Volume

GSNW includes a client module that lets the Windows 2000 Server computer act as a client on a NetWare network. This module is (basically) the Client Service for NetWare client included with Windows 2000 Professional. With Gateway (and Client) Services for NetWare installed, you can access NetWare resources directly. You don't need to use a gateway to access NetWare resources if your computer includes NetWare client software such as Gateway (and Client) Services for NetWare. Novell also provides client software for Microsoft clients.

To access a NetWare shared volume directly, follow these steps:

1. Make sure NWLink and a suitable NetWare client (such as Gateway [and Client] Services for NetWare) are installed on your system.

2. Double-click My Network Places on the desktop. (You can also access My Network Places through Windows Explorer.)

3. Double-click the Entire Network icon. In the right pane, select Entire Contents.

4. Double-click the NetWare Or Compatible Network icon.

5. The NetWare network appears. Double-click an NDS tree or a NetWare computer to view the available resources.

6. Browse to the resource you'd like to access. To map a network drive to the resource, select the resource and choose Map Network Drive from the Tools menu.

Adding a NetWare Printer

If Gateway Services for NetWare is installed on a Windows 2000 Server computer (or if Client Services for NetWare is installed on a Windows 2000 Professional computer), you can add a NetWare printer directly through the Add Printer Wizard.

To share a NetWare printer with Microsoft clients, follow these steps:

1. Make sure Gateway Service for NetWare is installed and configured on your Windows 2000 Server system.

2. Select Start | Settings | Printers.

3. In the Printers window, double-click the Add Printer icon.

4. The Add Printer Wizard starts. Click Next.

5. In the next screen, select the option for Network Printer. Click Next.

6. In the next screen, select the option labeled Type The Printer Name. Enter the name of the printer in NetBIOS name format: *printserver**sharename*. Or leave the Name field blank and browse for the NetWare printer in Shared Printers.

7. Follow the remaining instructions in the Add Printer Wizard. Click Finish.

The printer you create will be added to the Printers folder. You can configure properties for the printer as you would for other network printers in the Printers folder. Right-click the Printer icon and select Properties to configure printer properties. Go to the Security tab to configure permissions for the printer.

You can also connect to a NetWare printer through the command prompt. Use the net use command to map a local lpt port to the NetWare print queue:

net use lpt2 *server**print_queue*

where *server* is the name of the NetWare server and *print_queue* is the name of the print queue.

Then create a printer that prints to the port you mapped to the NetWare print queue. If the printer is on an NDS network, enter the tree and path to the shared printer with the net use command. Consult your NetWare documentation for more information.

Sharing Files and Printers with NetWare Clients

Microsoft provides an add-on product called File and Print Services for NetWare that enables a Windows 2000 computer to emulate a NetWare server. You can use File and Print Services for NetWare to make Windows 2000 directories, files, and printers available to NetWare clients. To obtain File and Print Sharing for NetWare, contact Microsoft.

TIP: You can also make Windows directories available to non-Microsoft clients through Windows 2000 Server's Web Sharing feature. Web Sharing uses Internet Information Server (IIS) to provide Internet-style access to directory contents.

Services for NetWare

Microsoft plans to provide an add-on package for NetWare-related services and utilities. The Services for NetWare package provides enhanced interoperability between Windows 2000 and NetWare systems. The package contains the following:

▼   **Microsoft Directory Synchronization Services (MSDSS)**   A package that synchronizes the NDS directory with the Active Directory.

- ■ **File Migration utility**   A utility that migrates NetWare files and directories—along with their accompanying permissions—to Active Directory.

- ■ **File and Print Services for NetWare v5.0**   Described earlier in the section "Sharing Files and Printers with NetWare Clients." File and Print Services for NetWare v5.0 is for Windows 2000 systems.

- ■ **File and Print Services for NetWare v4.0**   Described earlier in the section "Sharing Files and Printers with NetWare Clients." File and Print Services for NetWare v4.0 is for Windows NT 4 systems.

- ▲ **Directory Service Manager for NetWare**   A service that lets you manage bindery-based NetWare servers through Windows. Account information is copied to Windows and changes are propagated back to the NetWare servers.

The most interesting of these features (especially for a book on Active Directory) is Microsoft Directory Synchronization Services (MSDSS). MSDSS actually lets Active Directory and the NDS directory coexist and share information. You can manage directory objects from either or both directories and the changes will be synchronized. Microsoft reportedly decided to include MSDSS because beta testers complained that the Directory Service Manager for the NetWare product did not do enough to allow management of NetWare resources from within the NetWare environment. MSDSS allows the NDS network to be managed as before and invisibly synchronizes the NDS directory with Active Directory.

Contact Microsoft for more on obtaining Services for NetWare.

WINDOWS 2000 AND UNIX-BASED SYSTEMS

Windows 2000 comes with lots of built-in support for UNIX-based systems. Part of that support comes through the greater TCP/IP environment that is the bloodstream for Active Directory. Windows 2000's DNS and DHCP services support UNIX clients as well as

Microsoft clients, and the Internet technologies built into Windows 2000 through Internet Information Server (such http and ftp services) are as accessible from a UNIX client as they are from any other client. Windows 2000 also includes some TCP/IP diagnostic utilities that support interoperations with UNIX-based systems, including ping, lpq, arp, and tracert (which is basically the UNIX utility traceroute). Chapter 11, "Active Directory and Windows 2000 Security" also describes Kerberos authentication, which you can use to implement unified network authentication for Windows and UNIX systems. These services and utilities are only part of Microsoft's support for UNIX interoperability. Some additional features, which you'll learn more about in the following sections, include these:

▼ **Connectivity utilities**   Client utilities that let you copy files and execute commands on UNIX systems.

■ **Printer services**   You can access Windows printers from UNIX clients, or you can access a UNIX-based network printer or print server through a Windows printer.

■ **Telnet server**   Windows 2000's Telnet server offers remote access to UNIX-based (as well as Windows-based) Telnet client computers.

■ **Simple TCP/IP services**   A group of small UNIX services that support UNIX clients who are looking for these services.

▲ **Services for UNIX**   An add-on package not included with Windows 2000 that supports NFS, password synchronization with UNIX systems, username mapping, NIS to Active Directory migration, UNIX utilities such as grep and vi, and the Korn shell.

This chapter discusses these Windows features for promoting interoperability with UNIX-based systems. Of course, the UNIX world is also hard at work promoting its own brand of connectivity with the Windows environment. And more third-party products appear every day as the industry prepares for the next great battle in the war of the worlds.

Connectivity Utilities

Windows 2000 comes with a number of built-in TCP/IP utilities. Basic TCP/IP diagnostic utilities, such as ping and tracert (trace route) are included with Windows 2000. It also includes some client connectivity utilities that are designed to provide connectivity to a server that is running the corresponding server utility. These are standard UNIX-based utilities that have been around the UNIX world for years. Most UNIX-based systems have the capacity to receive connections through these utilities if configured to do so. Windows 2000's TCP/IP connectivity utilities include the following:

▼ **File Transfer Protocol (FTP) client** Lets the computer connect to an FTP server to transfer files.

■ **Lpr—Line Printer Daemon client** Sends print jobs to UNIX-based Line Printer Daemon (LPD) print servers.

■ **Remote Copy Protocol (RCP) client** Copies files to and from a server running the remote shell daemon.

■ **Rexec** Executes processes on a UNIX-based server running the Rexec daemon.

■ **Rsh** Executes commands on a UNIX-based server running the Remote Shell daemon.

■ **Telnet—Telnet Client** Lets the user open a terminal session on a Telnet server.

▲ **TFTP—Trivial File Transfer Protocol client** Lets the computer connect to a TFTP server to transfer files.

FTP is used often on the Internet. Telnet is common for in-house connections or dial-up access. RCP, Rexec, and Rsh are three of the Berkeley remote access utilities that developed from Berkeley Systems Design (BSD) UNIX. It is important to remember that these utilities have been around for some time, and they were developed before a billion people hooked up to the Internet. Most of them don't have the kind of security one typically requires today in open environments. If you have concerns about security, use these utilities in a protected setting or through a virtual private network (VPN).

TIP: The add-on Services for UNIX package (discussed later in this chapter in the section titled "Services for UNIX") includes the server software for some of these utilities. A Telnet server is included with Windows 2000 Server. Internet Information Server (or IIS—the Internet server included with Windows 2000) provides an FTP server service.

File Transfer Protocol

The File Transfer Protocol (FTP) provides file transfer services over a TCP/IP network. FTP is popular throughout the world, and many graphics-based FTP client packages bear little resemblance to the original UNIX command utility. The FTP client included with Windows 2000, however, is a command-based utility that seems very much oriented toward its precursors in the UNIX world.

To use the Windows 2000 FTP client, go to the command prompt and type the FTP command to start the FTP command shell. You can optionally specify the FTP server to which you'd like to connect in the FTP command:

ftp *[-v] [-n] [-i] [-d] [-g] [-s:filename] [-a] [-w:windowsize] [host_name]*

- ▼ *-v* suppresses responses from remote computer.

- ■ *-n* disables autologin.

- ■ *-i* suppresses intermediate prompts during transfer of multiple files.

- ■ *-d* turns on debugging.

- ■ *-g* enables FTP to use wildcards.

- ■ *filename* is a text file containing the FTP commands you'd like to execute (see Table 13-1).

- ■ *-a* tells FTP to use any local interface.

- ■ *windowsize* is the buffer size (overrides the default size of 4096).

- ▲ *host_name* is the name or IP address of the FTP server to which you are connecting.

NOTE: Optional parameters are shown in brackets: [ ]. Don't type the brackets!

After you start FTP, the FTP> prompt appears at the command line. From the FTP command prompt, enter any of the commands listed in Table 13-1. All FTP servers may not accept all of these commands, but you can usually find a way to move between directories and transfer files. If you are looking for more information on a given command, use the ? command for help:

```
FTP> ? append
```

Command	Description	Parameters
!	Escapes FTP.	None.
?	Displays Help.	Command you want help with (optional).
append	Appends local file to remote file.	Filename of local file; filename of remote file. If remote filename isn't given, use same name as local file.
ascii	Sets transfer type to ASCII (default setting).	None.
bell	You can configure a bell to ring after a successful file transfer. Command toggles the current bell setting.	None.
binary	Sets transfer type to binary.	None.

Table 13-1.   FTP Commands

Command	Description	Parameters
bye	Exits FTP.	None.
cd	Changes directory.	Remote directory name.
close	Ends the current FTP session.	None.
debug	Toggles debugging feature.	None.
delete	Deletes file on remote computer.	Filename on remote computer.
dir	Displays contents of directory on remote computer.	Directory name (optional). If no directory name is given, current directory is assumed.
disconnect	Disconnects from the remote computer but stays in FTP.	
get	Copies file from remote computer to local computer.	Remote filename. Local filename (optional—otherwise same name is assumed).
glob	Specifies whether wildcards can be used in path. Command toggles setting.	None.
hash	Toggles hashmark printing.	None.

Table 13-1.   FTP Commands *(continued)*

Command	Description	Parameters
help	Displays command description.	Command name (optional). Otherwise, you get help for all commands.
lcd	Changes current directory on local computer.	Directory name.
literal	Sends arguments to a remote FTP server.	Argument(s).
ls	Lists files and subdirectories on remote computer.	Directory name (if no directory is given, defaults to current directory).
mdelete	Deletes file(s) on remote computer.	Filename(s).
mdir	Writes lists files and subdirectories on remote computer to local file.	Directory on remote computer. Filename of output file on local computer. Use – to write output to screen.
mget	Copies file from remote computer to local computer.	Filename(s) of files to copy
mkdir	Creates a directory on the remote computer.	Directory name.

Table 13-1. FTP Commands *(continued)*

Command	Description	Parameters
mls	Writes list of files and subdirectories on remote computer to local file.	Directory on remote computer. Filename of output file on local computer Use – to write output to screen
mput	Copies files from local computer to remote computer.	File name(s).
open	Connects to a specified FTP server.	DNS name or IP address or remote server. (Optional) port number for contacting remote FTP service.
prompt	Toggles (on/off) prompt for each file in a multiple file transfer.	None.
put	Copies one local file from local computer to remote computer.	Filename.
pwd	Outputs name of current directory on remote computer.	None.
quit	Ends FTP session and exits FTP.	None.

Table 13-1.   FTP Commands *(continued)*

Command	Description	Parameters
quote	Sends argument to remote FTP server (same as literal).	Argument.
recv	Copies file from remote computer to local computer (same as get).	Filename.
remotehelp	Displays help from remote source.	FTP command you need help with.
rename	Changes the name of remote file.	Current filename. New filename.
rmdir	Deletes a directory on remote computer.	Directory name.
send	Copies file from local computer to remote computer (same as put).	Local filename. (Optional) remote filename—defaults to same name.
status	Displays status of FTP connections.	None.
trace	Enables display of route for each FTP packet (toggles on/off).	None.
type	Displays or changes current file type.	Desired file type (binary or ASCII). If no type given, command outputs the current file type.

Table 13-1. FTP Commands *(continued)*

Command	Description	Parameters
user	Sends logon information to remote computer.	Username. Password and account can be specified after username if required. Otherwise, remote FTP may prompt for additional logon information.
verbose	Toggles (on/off) verbose mode for FTP prompts and responses.	None.

Table 13-1.   FTP Commands *(continued)*

LPR

This command sends a print job to an LPD (Line Printer Daemon) server. See the section "Interoperating Printers with UNIX," later in this chapter, for more on Windows 2000's UNIX printing service.

lpr -S *server_name* -P *printer_name* [-C *class*] [-J *print_job*]
[-o *file_type*] *filename*

▼ *server_name* is the name of the print server.

■ *printer_name* is the name of the printer.

■ *class* is the job classification comment that will appear on the burst page.

■ *print_job* is the name of the print job.

■ *file_type* is an optional file type specification. The default is text. For binary files, use –O l (capital O, lowercase L).

▲ *filename* is the name of the file you wish to print.

Rcp

Rcp copies files from the client to and from a server running the remote shell daemon rshd or copies files between two other computers running rshd.

rcp *[-a] [-b] [-r] [-h] file1 file2... destination*

▼ *-a* specifies ASCII mode (optional).

■ *-b* specifies binary mode (optional).

■ *-r* copies the contents of subdirectories within the specified directory.

■ *-h* is a parameter that must be included if the file you're transferring is a hidden file.

■ *file1 file2* are the files you wish to copy. These parameters can take several forms:

■ *filename* If you just specify a filename, the current directory is assumed.

■ *path/filename* To copy a file in a different directory, include the path.

■ *host_name:path/filename* Copies a file from the specified host.

■ *host_name.username:path/filename* Copies a file from the specified host using the specified user account.

▲ *destination* is the destination for the files. The destination can either be a filename (with or without path) or a directory path. Note that, if you are copying more than one file, the destination must be a directory.

Rexec

Rexec runs a command on a server that is running the rexec daemon.

rexec *host_name [-l username] [-n] command*

▼ *host_name* is the name of the rexec server on which you'd like to run the command.

■ *username* is a username to use to run the command on the remote computer.

■ *-n* redirects input to NULL.

▲ *command* is the command you wish to execute.

Rsh

Rsh executes commands on a remote server that is running the rsh daemon rshd.

rsh *host_name [-l username] [-n] command*

▼ *host_name* is the name of the rsh server on which you'd like to run the command.

■ *username* is a username to use to run the command on the remote computer.

■ *-n* redirects input to NULL.

▲ *command* is the command you wish to execute.

Telnet

The Telnet client application establishes text-based terminal sessions with a Telnet server. It can communicate with the Telnet server included with Windows 2000, but it is also designed to interoperate with other third-party and UNIX-based Telnet server applications. Telnet applications come in many sizes and intensities. The version included with Windows 2000, like the FTP client, seems more like a UNIX application than like something in Windows.

To start Telnet, go to the command prompt and type **telnet**. You can optionally include a computer and port number to initiate a Telnet connection at the same time you start the command shell:

telnet *[hostname or IP address] [port_number]*

Once you have started the telnet command shell, you can type any of the commands shown in Table 13-2. Once you establish a connection with another computer, the commands you type at the Telnet prompt will be sent to the remote Telnet server. To escape to the local command shell, press CTRL-].

The set command lets you set certain configuration options. Set command options are shown in Table 13-3. The option follows the set command on the same command line, like so:

```
set ntlm
```

The NTLM option offers you the interesting possibility of logging in without supplying a username and password. NTLM is a Microsoft authentication protocol that can obtain login information directly from the security database. In other words, if the remote user currently has the necessary domain security credentials for accessing

Command	Description
close	Closes the current Telnet connection
display	Displays current configuration settings
help	Displays a description of commands
open	Opens a Telnet connection; requires DNS name or IP address of Telnet server
quit	Quits Telnet
set	Configures settings (see Table-13.3)
status	Displays current connection status
unset	Turns off NTLM, LOCAL_ECHO, and CRLF settings: unset ntlm
?	Displays a description of commands

Table 13-2.   Telnet Client Command Options

Option	Description
NTLM	Turns on NTLM authentication
LOCAL_ECHO	Turns on local echo of remote commands
TERM [type]	Terminal type (type options include ANSI, VT100,VT52, and VTNT)
CRLF	Send both CR and LF

Table 13-3. Set Options for Telnet Client

the Telnet server, the NTLM authentication occurs invisibly. Of course, the NTLM option requires that both client and server support NTLM. This option works well for Windows 2000 clients accessing Windows 2000 Server servers, but if you're attempting to access a UNIX-based Telnet server, you won't be able to use NTLM authentication.

TFTP

TFTP transfers files between a TFTP client and a remote TFTP server. TFTP is faster and simpler, but less versatile and less reliable, than FTP. Whereas FTP is widely popular, TFTP doesn't get much attention outside of the UNIX world.

tftp *[-i] host_name [get] [put] file [destination]*

▼ *-i* specifies binary transfer mode (otherwise, ASCII is assumed).

■ *host_name* is the remote computer (if you're using put) or the local computer (if you're using get).

■ *get* copies a file from the remote computer to the local computer.

■ *put* copies a file from the local computer to the remote computer

- *file* is the path and filename of the file you wish to copy.

▲ *destination* is the destination path and filename (if omitted, the filename is the same as the source name and the file is copied to the current directory).

Interoperating Printers with UNIX

Print Services for UNIX (also called Lpdsvc) is the Windows 2000 equivalent to the UNIX Line Printer Daemon (LPD) service. TCP/IP Print Server Service makes Windows 2000-based printers appear to UNIX clients as UNIX LPD printers.

Print Services for UNIX supports clients that use the LPR network printing utility. The LPR utility is found on most UNIX-based systems, and it is included with the Windows NT and Windows 2000 TCP/IP utilities. Microsoft states that Print Services for UNIX supports all LPR clients that are compatible with RFC 1179.

Once Print Services for UNIX is installed, it automatically makes all shared printers available to LPR clients. See the previous section entitled "LPR" for more on how to print to an LPD server such as Print Services for UNIX from Windows 2000's built-in LPR utility. Syntax varies among LPR clients. The printer name or print queue name referenced in the lpr command is the share name of the Windows 2000 printer (which may be, but is not always, the name of the printer). The Windows 2000 *must* be shared on the network if you wish to print to it using lpr.

To use Windows 2000 as an LPD print server, you must install Print Services for UNIX:

1. Select Start | Settings | Network and Dial-up Connections.

2. In the Network and Dial-up Connections main window, select the Advanced menu and select Optional Networking Components.

3. In the Windows Optional Networking Components dialog box, select Other Network File and Print Services and click the Details button.

4. In the Other Network File and Print Services dialog box, check Print Services for UNIX. Click OK.

5. In the Windows Optional Networking Components Wizard, click Next.

6. Windows 2000 prompts for a CD or for the location of the Windows 2000 Server installation files. Insert the CD or click OK to browse for the installation files. If you are locating the files on the network, it may not be enough to just point to the share. You may need to specify the I386 folder of the installation files.

Windows 2000 also lets you add a TCP/IP printer port (for printing to TCP/IP network printers) or an LPR port (for printing to printers attached to UNIX-based printer servers). You can use a TCP/IP or LPR port to create a Windows logical printer that prints to a TCP/IP printer or a UNIX-based LPD printer on the network.

To add a network printer through a TCP/IP port, follow these steps:

1. Click Start | Settings | Printers.

2. In the Printers window, double-click Add Printer.

3. The Add Printer Wizard starts. Click Next.

4. The next screen asks if you want to create a local or network printer. Select Local Printer, Make sure the box labeled Automatically Detect And Install My Plug And Play Printer is not checked. Click Next.

5. The next screen asks you to select a printer port. Select Create A New Port. Click the disclosure triangle on the right side of the text box to reveal port options. Select Standard TCP/IP port. Click Next.

6. The Add Standard TCP/IP Printer Port Wizard starts. Click Next and follow the instructions. The TCP/IP network printer must be online and properly configured in order to complete the wizard.

To add a printer on a UNIX-based print server, follow these steps:

1. Make sure Print Services for UNIX is installed (see the procedure earlier in this section).

2. Choose Start | Settings | Printers.

3. In the Printers window, double-click Add Printer.

4. The Add Printer Wizard starts. Click Next.

5. The next screen asks if you want to create a local or network printer. Select Local Printer, Make sure the box labeled Automatically Detect And Install My Plug And Play Printer is not checked. Click Next.

6. The next screen asks you to select a printer port. Select Create A New Port. Click the disclosure triangle on the right side of the text box to reveal port options. Select LPR Port. Click Next.

7. In the Add LPR Compatible Printer dialog box, enter the IP address or DNS name of the print server computer in the box labeled Name Or Address Of Server Providing Lpd. Enter the printer or print queue on the print server computer in the box labeled Name Of Printer Or Print Queue On That Server. Click OK.

8. Follow the remaining instructions to complete the installation.

Telnet Server

Windows 2000 comes with a built-in Telnet server to support remote clients for text-based Telnet login sessions. Of course, you are telnetting to a Windows 2000 system, not a UNIX system, and the commands you use in the Telnet session will be Windows 2000 commands.

NOTE: Windows 2000's Telnet server with the add-on Services for UNIX Korn shell offers some intriguing possibilities for a UNIX-like look and feel.

Windows 2000's built-in Telnet server supports two simultaneous Telnet sessions—enough for occasional remote administration, but not enough for large-scale Telnet deployment. If you need additional client access, install the Telnet server included with the add-on Services for UNIX package (described later in this chapter in the section titled "Services for UNIX"), or purchase a third-party Telnet server application.

The built-in Telnet service is installed automatically with Windows 2000 Server, but it is configured to start manually. You must start the Telnet Service in order to use it. Windows 2000 offers three ways to start the Telnet service:

▼ Using the Net Start command from the command line

■ Through the Services tree of the Computer Management utility

▲ Using the Telnet Server Admin utility

The first two of these methods are the same techniques you'll use to start any service in Windows 2000. From the command prompt, type **net start tlntsvr** to start the Telnet server service (tlntsvr). You can then stop the service by typing the net stop command: **net stop tlntsvr**

You can also start Telnet through the Computer Management utility. The services tree of the Computer Management utility is reminiscent of the Services Control Panel of NT days. Computer Management not only lets you start and stop the service, but it also provides a convenient interface for configuring startup options. You can configure Telnet to start automatically when the system starts, and you can configure other service-related settings, such as what to do in the event of a service failure.

To start or stop Telnet or configure Telnet startup options:

1. Select Start | Programs | Administrative Tools | Computer Management.

2. In the Computer Management main window, click the plus sign beside Services and Applications.

3. From the Services and Applications subtree, select Services.

4. A list of services appears in the right pane. Scroll to Telnet. Right-click Telnet and choose Properties.

5. In Telnet Properties dialog box (see Figure 13-7), click the Start button in the General tab to start Telnet. You can also pause or stop Telnet if it is already started.

6. If you wish to set up Telnet to start automatically when the system starts, click the triangle to the right of the Startup Type box and select Automatic.

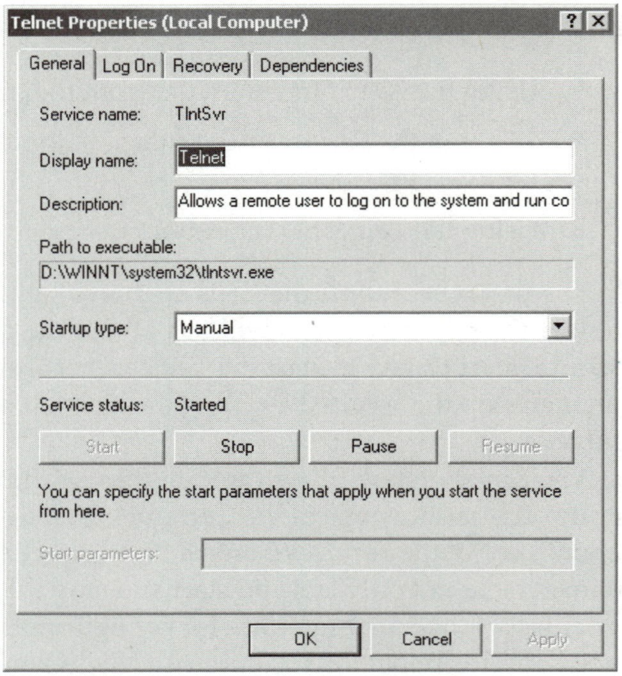

Figure 13-7. The Telnet Properties dialog box

7. Click the Log On tab to configure the login account for the Telnet service (the default is the System account).

8. Click the Recovery tab to choose a course of action in the event of a service failure.

9. Click OK.

The third way to start the Telnet service is also the preferred method for administering Telnet once it is running: through the Telnet Server Administration utility. The Telnet Server Administration utility is a text-based and menu-driven utility that isn't much like the other administrative tools in the Windows 2000 Administrative Tools folder. The text-based format of the Telnet Server Administration utility, however, makes it usable from within Telnet itself, and this was probably why Microsoft designed this utility to operate from within a command window (although Microsoft is not very good about documenting *how to get to* this utility from the command window).

To start the Telnet Server Administration utility from within Windows, follow these steps:

1. Choose Start | Programs | Administrative Tools | Telnet Server Administration

2. A command window opens with the Telnet Administration utility started (see Figure 13-8).

Telnet Administration utility's top-level menu includes six options, "UNIX-ly" numbered 0–5:

▼ **0)**   Quit this application.

■ **1)**   List the current users.

■ **2)**   Terminate a user session.

■ **3)**   Display / change registry settings.

■ **4)**   Start the services.

▲ **5)**   Stop the service.

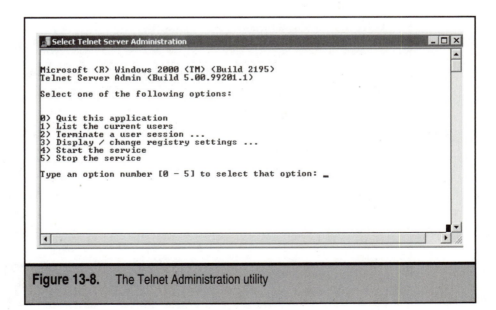

Figure 13-8.   The Telnet Administration utility

To select an option, type the appropriate number and press ENTER. Most of the options are self-explanatory, except for the Display/Change Registry Settings option, which requires some commentary. This option leads to a series of additional options. The reference to "Registry settings" is a little misleading, or, at least, is no truer here than it is for any other utility. You are not left to roam the Registry. You can, however, configure a few specific settings that are associated with Registry keys. Selecting this option leads to a secondary menu with the choices shown in Table 13-4.

Number	Name	Description
0	Exit this menu	Returns to the top-level menu.
1	AllowTrustedDomain	A 0 value excludes domain users (allows only users in local database). A 1 value (default) allows access from domain users and users from trusted domains.
2	AltKeyMapping	A 0 value maps VT100 CTRL-A to CTRL-A. A 1 value (default) maps VT100 CTRL-A to ALT.
3	DefaultDomain	Default domain. Use period (.) to set the default domain to the local domain.
4	DefaultShell	Path and filename for default shell. The default setting is the Windows 2000 command shell.

Table 13-4. Telnet Server Admin Display/Change Registry Settings Options

Number	Name	Description
5	LoginScript	Path and filename for the Telnet session login script. A default script is located in system_root\System32\login.cmd.
6	MaxFailedLogins	Maximum number of failed login attempts before a connection is terminated (default is 3).
7	NTLM	Authentication options. NTLM is a Microsoft authentication protocol that uses the local security environment for authentication and doesn't require a login username and password:
		0 means NTLM isn't required. The user is prompted for username and password, which are returned as plain text.
		1 means try NTLM first, and if that doesn't work, prompt for username and password.
		2 (default) means only use NTLM authentication.
8	TelnetPort	Specifies the port for incoming Telnet requests (default is port 23).

Table 13-4.   Telnet Server Admin Display/Change Registry Settings Options *(continued)*

The Telnet Server Administration utility is actually the executable file tlntadmn.exe. You can alternatively start the Telnet Server Administration utility by typing **tlnetadmn** from the command prompt or from within a Telnet session.

TIP: If you have problems establishing a Telnet session from the network, the problems may be related to Telnet's authentication options. Your Telnet client may not support NTLM communication. Try changing the NTLM setting (see Table 13-4) to 0 and see if you can log in. If that doesn't work, try using 1. If you type in a username and password from the Telnet prompt, watch your case. Also, the Telnet protocol doesn't deal well with a backspace for corrections. If you make a mistake in your username or password and then backspace to correct it, the login might fail even if you got it right the second time.

Simple TCP/IP Services

Windows 2000 includes a group of TCP/IP services—dubbed the Simple TCP/IP Services—for supporting UNIX-based clients that expect these services.

▼ **Character Generator**   Sends printable ASCII characters to line printers.

■ **Daytime**   Sends current time information.

■ **Discard**   Discards all messages received on a given port.

■ **Echo**   Echoes messages received on a given port.

▲ **Quote for the Day**   Returns quotes from a quote file (system_root\System32\Drivers\Etc\Quotes). Note that *quote* is not used in quotes. These are real quotes—like "To be or not to be." The purpose is to provide for a cheery login.

These services are included with Windows 2000 Server to provide support for UNIX-based clients that use them. Microsoft states specifically that you should not install the Simple TCP/IP services ". . . unless you specifically need this computer to support communication with other systems that use these protocol services."

To install Simple TCP/IP Services, follow these steps:

1. Select Start | Settings | Network and Dial-up Connections.

2. In the Network and Dial-up Connections main window, select the Advanced menu and choose Optional Networking Components.

3. In the Windows Optional Networking Components Wizard, select Networking Services and click the Details button.

4. In the Networking Services dialog box, select the Simple TCP/IP Services check box. Click OK.

5. In the Windows Optional Networking Components Wizard, click Next.

6. Windows 2000 prompts for a CD or for the location of the Windows 2000 Server installation files. Insert the CD or click OK to browse for the installation files. If you are locating the files on the network, it may not be enough to just point to the share. You may need to specify the I386 folder of the installation files.

TIP: The Windows NT implementation of the character generator (chargen) was notoriously susceptible to denial-of-service attacks. A hacker could use this service to flood a network segment with charged broadcasts and bring traffic to a standstill. Microsoft provided a hot fix in NT days that presumably has been included in the Windows 2000 version, but watch out for this one.

Services for UNIX

Services for UNIX is Microsoft's boldest attempt yet to integrate Windows with UNIX. Services for UNIX offers an amazing array of UNIX connectivity tools and services. Although Services for UNIX isn't included with Windows 2000 Server, it is such an important tool for UNIX interoperability that it deserves some mention here.

Services for UNIX is an add-on package available separately through Microsoft. Microsoft states that Services for UNIX supports Digital UNIX, Hewlett-Packard HP-UX 10.1+, and Sun Solaris SPARC 2.5.1+. They don't mention the L word, and they don't mention other open system UNIX-based systems such as BSD. However, most of the utilities and services of Services for UNIX are fairly standard UNIX features, and it isn't hard to imagine that you'll find considerable support for them in Linux and among other UNIX variants.

Some highlights of the Services for UNIX package include the following:

▼ **NFS**   Services for UNIX includes both client and server support for the UNIX-based Network File System (NFS).

■ **Telnet server**   The Telnet server included with the Windows 2000 distribution supports only two simultaneous connections. The Telnet service included with Services for UNIX supports larger-scale Telnet deployments.

■ **UNIX utilities**   Services for UNIX includes over 60 classic UNIX utilities, such as grep, sed, vi, and find, as well as file and directory commands like mkdir, rm, and ls.

■ **Password synchronization**   Lets you synchronize UNIX and Windows passwords

■ **Username mapping**   Lets you map UNIX usernames with Windows usernames.

■ **NIS to Active Directory Migration Wizard**   Migrates Network Information Service (NIS) files to Active Directory, providing a convenient migration path for UNIX users and groups to become assimilated into the Active Directory environment.

▲ **Korn shell**   Yes, you read it correctly. Services for UNIX actually lets you use the UNIX-based Korn shell to operate a Windows 2000 system.

For more on obtaining the add-on Services for UNIX package, consult the Microsoft Web site.

WINDOWS 2000 AND MACINTOSH

Windows 2000 Server includes a number of features designed to provide for the efficient integration of Macintosh clients and networks. Perhaps the most significant advance in Microsoft/Macintosh interoperability has nothing to do with Windows 2000 and happened, instead, on the Macintosh end. That extremely significant advance is the transition of the Mac OS (along with almost every other operating system) to the TCP/IP networking protocol. In Windows NT days, Macintosh integration centered primarily around the AppleTalk protocol. In today's world, however, most Macintosh clients speak TCP/IP. Windows 2000's File Service for Macintosh and Print Service for Macintosh can operate through TCP/IP as well as AppleTalk.

The following sections describe how to set up Windows 2000 File Service for Macintosh and Print Service for Macintosh. Of course, some integrated networks have AppleTalk subnets that are operating fine as they are, and some organizations will still wish to configure Windows 2000 Servers to communicate with AppleTalk clients. Windows 2000 Server participates in an AppleTalk network and acts as an AppleTalk router. Windows 2000 Server can also act as an AppleTalk gateway, simultaneously routing and converting AppleTalk frames to and from TCP/IP.

Windows 2000 Server's Macintosh support features include the following:

▼ AppleTalk routing

■ File services

■ Print services

■ ATCP remote access protocol

■ Apple standard authentication

■ Secure Logon for Macintosh clients

▲ Administrative tools

The following sections provide some details on Windows 2000's Macintosh support. If you're looking for additional information, Microsoft provides extensive commentary on Mac support services in the Windows 2000 online documentation. See "AppleTalk Network Integration" in the Network Interoperability section of online Help. Or, see the Interoperability section of the "Internetworking Guide" in the Windows 2000 Resource Kit Books Online.

File Services for Macintosh

As the preceding section mentioned, Windows 2000 can provide file sharing for Macintosh clients over either TCP/IP or AppleTalk. If both TCP/IP and AppleTalk are installed, the connection will first be attempted using TCP/IP. AppleTalk must be installed if you want the Windows 2000 server to appear in Macintosh browse lists. AppleTalk will be installed automatically when you set up File Services for Macintosh.

To use File Server for Macintosh, you must have an available NTFS partition. File Server for Macintosh can share files only on NTFS partitions. You'll also need to install File Server for Macintosh client software on the Macintosh client.

The steps for configuring Windows 2000 Server as a Macintosh file server are as follows:

1. Install File Services for Macintosh.

2. Set File Services for Macintosh configuration options. For instance, configure login security for Macintosh clients or create Mac-related file associations.

3. Set up Microsoft-accessible folders on the Windows 2000 computer.

4. Install Microsoft authentication software on the Macintosh client.

The following sections discuss the tasks associated with sharing files for a Macintosh client.

TIP: You can manage File Services for Macintosh from the command prompt using the Macfile command. The Macfile command has four primary options and many parameters: *macfile server* manages the File Services for Macintosh server; *macfile volume* manages Macintosh-accessible volumes; *macfile directory* manages directories on Macintosh-accessible volumes; and *macfile forkize* manages Macintosh file and data resource forks. See Windows 2000 Help for more on the *macfile* command.

Installing File Services for Macintosh

To install file services for Macintosh, follow these steps:

1. Choose Start | Settings | Control Panel. Open the Add/Remove Programs Control Panel.

2. In the Add/Remove Programs Control Panel, select Add/Remove Windows Components. Wait for the Windows Components Wizard to appear. (In some early versions of Windows 2000, the Windows Components Wizard had the habit of sometimes opening in the background. If you don't see it, check the task bar.)

3. In the Windows Components Wizard, select Other Network File And Print Services and click the Details button.

4. In the Other Network File And Print Service dialog box (see Figure 13-9), select the Files Services For Macintosh check box. Click OK.

5. Click Next in the Windows Components Wizard. Windows 2000 will install File Services for Macintosh. You may be prompted for the Windows 2000 CD or a Windows 2000 installation share.

If TCP/IP is installed on the Windows 2000 Server machine, the Windows Component Wizard automatically configures Apple Filing Protocol (AFP) over TCP/IP. The AppleTalk protocol is also installed automatically when you install File Services for Macintosh.

Configuring File Services for Macintosh

After you install File Services for Macintosh, you can configure File Server for Macintosh through the Computer Management tool.

To configure File Server for Macintosh, follow these steps:

1. Install File Server for Macintosh (as described in the preceding procedure).

2. Choose Start | Programs | Administrative Tools | Computer Management.

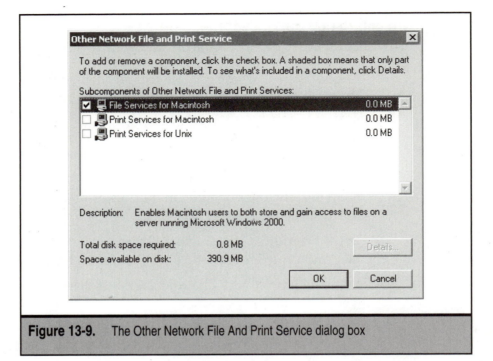

Figure 13-9. The Other Network File And Print Service dialog box

3. In the Computer Management main window, expand the System Tools subtree.

4. Right-click Shared Folders and choose Configure File Server For Macintosh.

5. The File Server for Macintosh Properties dialog box appears. In the Configuration tab (see Figure 13-10), you can enter a server name for the computer that will be used by AppleTalk clients. You can also enter a login message that will appear when a Mac user logs in. You can also set a limit for the number of simultaneous Mac sessions. The Security section offers a check box that lets you choose whether or not Mac clients will be able to save the password for the Windows 2000 Server. The Enable Authentication drop-down box offers the following options:

- Microsoft Only

- Apple Clear Text

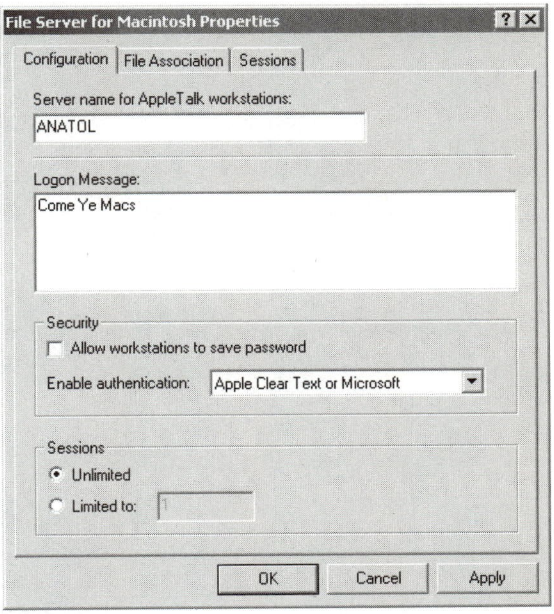

File Server for Macintosh Properties   ? X

Configuration | File Association | Sessions

Server name for AppleTalk workstations:

ANATOL

Logon Message:

Come Ye Macs

Security
☐ Allow workstations to save password

Enable authentication: Apple Clear Text or Microsoft ▼

Sessions
● Unlimited
○ Limited to: 1

OK   Cancel   Apply

Figure 13-10.   The File Server For Macintosh Properties Configuration tab

- Apple Encrypted
- Apple Clear Text Or Microsoft
- Apple Encrypted Or Microsoft

NOTE: The preceding authentication choices are the choices that will be available on the server end. The client software may restrict the authentication options. Also, as you will learn later in this section, you can set an authentication option for the each Microsoft-accessible volume.

The File Association tab (see Figure 13-11) maps Windows file extensions to Macintosh file extensions. The point of associating file extensions is so the correct icon will appear on the Mac for a file shared from the Windows 2000 computer. Specify Mac file creator and type settings in the With Macintosh Document Creator And

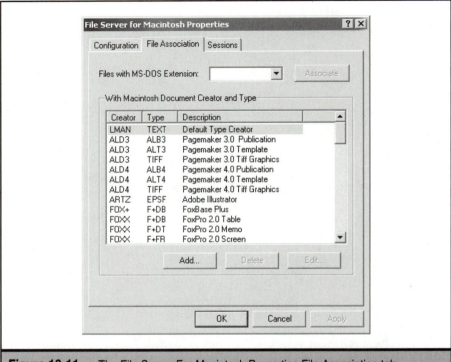

Figure 13-11. The File Server For Macintosh Properties File Association tab

Type box. Select or enter a DOS file type in the Files With MS-DOS Extension box, and then choose a Mac file type and click the Associate button. You can associate multiple DOS extensions with a single Mac file type. To add a new Mac file type, click the Add button.

NOTE: File extension associations do not affect files that have already been created. The association will apply to new files only.

The Sessions tab gives a summary of usage information and lets you send a message to Mac users.

Sharing Folders for Macintosh Clients

After you have completed the task of installing and configuring File Services for Macintosh, you can share folders with Macintosh clients. To create a Macintosh-accessible volume, follow these steps:

1. Select Start | Programs | Administrative Tools | Computer Management.

2. In the Computer Management window, expand the System Tools subtree.

3. Double-click the Shared Folders icon.

4. Right-click Shares and choose New File Share.

5. The Create Shared Folder Wizard appears (see Figure 13-12). Enter a share name, a description, and a Macintosh share name. Click the Browse button to browse for the folder you wish to share. The folder must be on an NTFS partition or a CDFS (CD drive) volume. In the Accessible From The Following Clients section, select the Apple Macintosh check box. Note that, by default, Microsoft Windows is also selected. Click Next.

6. In the next screen (see Figure 13-13) choose the share permissions you'd like to apply to the share. To set custom permissions, select Customize Share And Folder Permissions and click the Customize button. Click Finish.

NOTE: The permissions you assign in the Create Shared Folder Wizard are share permissions. They restrict access to folders and files through the share. These permissions do not affect local access to the folder or access through a different share.

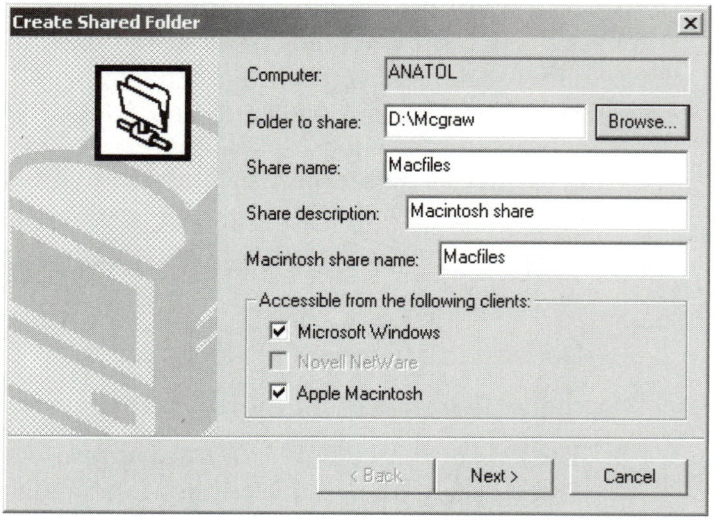

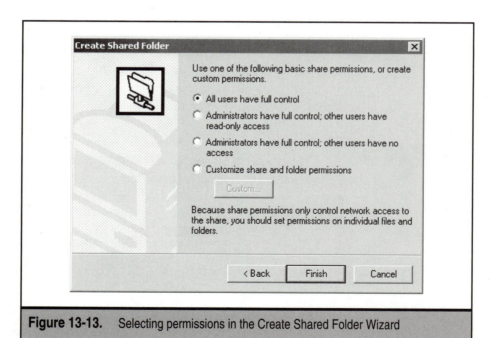

Figure 13-12. The Create Shared Folder Wizard

Figure 13-13. Selecting permissions in the Create Shared Folder Wizard

The share you create will be listed as a shared folder in the Computer Management main window (see Figure 13-14). To view share information, double-click the Shares folder in the Computer Management subtree System Tools | Shared Folders. If you elected to make the share accessible from Windows and Macintosh (see step 5 of the preceding procedure), separate shares will be created for Windows and Macintosh clients. In Figure 13-14, note that the Macintosh Share icon is different from the normal Share icon. The little sharing hand seems to be holding an old Macintosh computer (circa 1986) with a tiny and unappealing gray-scale screen.

Right-click the Share icon to manage or modify the current settings. To stop sharing the Macintosh-accessible volume, select Stop Sharing. To view or modify share properties, click Properties.

The Share Properties dialog box for a Microsoft-accessible share is shown in Figure 13-15. The General tab displays the share name and path and lets you configure a user limit and security settings. The security settings include the following:

▼ **Password**   A password for the Microsoft-accessible volume.

■ **This Volume Is Read-Only**   Specifies that users will not be able to modify files or directories through the share.

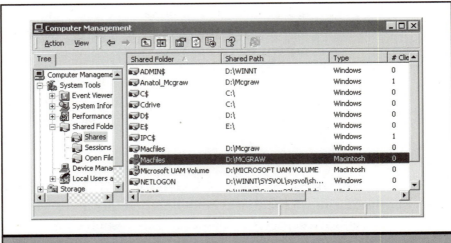

Figure 13-14.   Viewing shares in the Computer Management utility

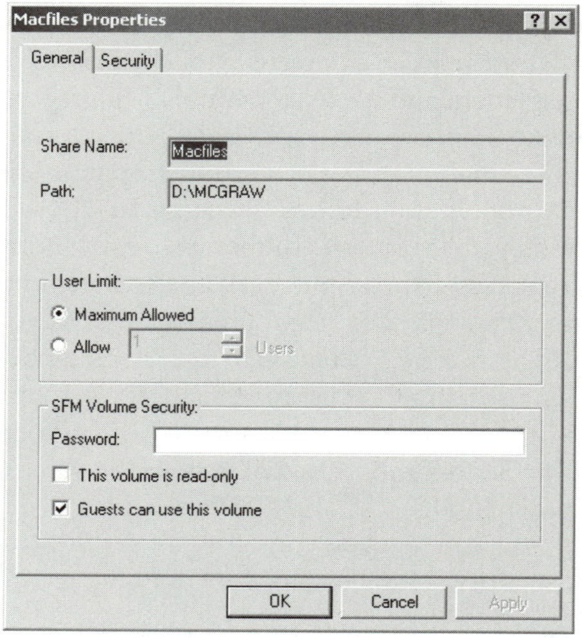

Figure 13-15. The share Properties dialog box for a Mac-accessible volume

▲ **Guests Can Use This Volume** Specifies that the volume
Mac users who do not have credentials on the Windows 2000
network will be able to access the volume through the
Windows 2000 Guest account.

The Security tab provides security settings for the file share object.
These settings are similar to security settings elsewhere in the Active
Directory interface.

Setting Up the Macintosh Client for Microsoft Authentication

The Macintosh client uses authentication files and a Mac-based
authentication process to gain access to resources. A software module
on the Macintosh computer called the User Authentication Module
(UAM) accepts login information from the user and forwards that

information to the server to which the user is trying to connect. The Macintosh Chooser typically uses a built-in UAM. Microsoft, however, has its own UAM software, which, according to Microsoft, provides more secure authentication. When Files Services for Macintosh is installed, a special folder called the Microsoft UAM volume is created. The Microsoft UAM volume, which is automatically shared to Mac clients, includes an installer application that will download the necessary UAM software to the Macintosh client.

To configure the Macintosh client for Microsoft authentication, follow these steps:

1. From the Macintosh computer, open the Apple menu and double-click Chooser.

2. In the Chooser, select AppleShare.

3. Select the AppleTalk zone where the Windows 2000 Server resides. Select the Windows 2000 Server and click OK.

4. Click Registered User or Guest.

5. Click the Microsoft UAM Volume.

6. Close the Chooser.

7. The Microsoft UAM volume should appear on your desktop. Double-click Microsoft UAM volume.

8. Double-click the file labeled MS UAM Installer.

9. If a Welcome screen appears, click Continue.

Once you have installed the Microsoft UAM, users connecting to Windows 2000–based volumes will have the option of using Microsoft Authentication.

If the Macintosh has an earlier version of Microsoft UAM, it is a good idea to upgrade. If you plan to use Windows 2000's AFP over TCP/IP feature for file sharing over TCP/IP networks, you must use the latest version of Microsoft UAM (v5.0). According to Microsoft, Microsoft UAM 5.0 requires AppleShare Client 3.8 or newer, or Mac OS 8.5 or newer. The Microsoft UAM volume also contains an older version of Microsoft UAM for older clients. If the Mac client doesn't meet the requirements for MS UAM v5.0, Windows 2000 will install an older version of the Microsoft UAM. However, if the older version is installed, you won't be able to use File Services for Macintosh with TCP/IP.

> **TIP:** If you plan to use Microsoft authentication, you must also enable it on the server side. See the previous section title "Installing File Services for Macintosh."

Print Services for Macintosh

Windows 2000's Print Services for Macintosh is designed to provide the following functions:

▼ Macintosh clients can print to Windows-based local or network printers installed on the Windows 2000 computer.

▲ Windows clients can use the Windows 2000 Server to print to AppleTalk-based PostScript LaserWriter printers.

Print Services for Macintosh requires the AppleTalk protocol. AppleTalk is installed automatically when you install Print Services for Macintosh or File Services for Macintosh.

Installing Print Services for Macintosh

To install Print Services for Macintosh, follow these steps:

1. Choose Start | Settings | Control Panel. Open the Add/Remove Programs Control Panel.

2. In the Add/Remove Programs Control Panel, select Add/Remove Windows Components. Wait for the Windows Components Wizard to appear. (In some early versions of Windows 2000, the Windows Components Wizard had the habit of sometimes opening in the background. If you don't see it, check the task bar.)

3. In the Windows Components Wizard, select Other Network File And Print Services. (Don't check or uncheck the box—just select the line.) Click the Details button.

4. In the Other Network File And Print Service dialog box (refer to Figure 13-9), select the Print Services for Macintosh check box. Click OK.

5. Click Next in the Windows Components Wizard. Windows 2000 will install Print Services for Macintosh. You may be prompted for the Windows 2000 CD or a Windows 2000 installation share.

Windows 2000 installs AppleTalk on your system automatically if it isn't already present.

Setting Up a Macintosh-Accessible Printer

If Print Services for Macintosh is running, printers installed on the Windows 2000 are automatically available to Macintosh clients. (If the printer on the Windows 2000 computer is a network printer, you may need to change the login account for the Print Services for Macintosh service. See the following section.)

It is also possible to configure the Windows 2000 Server computer so that Mac-world printers located on the AppleTalk network are available to Windows and Macintosh clients. The strategy for accomplishing this is a little like the old concept of mapping a printer port to a network printer to support DOS applications. Essentially, you set the AppleTalk network printer up as a local printer on the Windows 2000 computer and define a special port (called an AppleTalk printing devices port) to connect the logical printer on the Windows 2000 computer with the AppleTalk printing device on the AppleTalk network.

To install an AppleTalk printer, follow these steps:

1. Install Print Services for Macintosh (see preceding section).

2. Choose Start | Settings | Printers.

3. In the Printers window, double-click Add Printer.

4. The Add Printer Wizard thanks you for calling it to life. Click Next.

5. In the next screen, the Add Printer Wizard asks you to choose a local or network printer. Select Local Printer. If the printer is

a plug-and-play printer attached to the Windows 2000 computer, select Automatically Detect And Install My Plug And Play Printer. Click Next.

6. The next screen asks you to choose a printer port (see Figure 13-16). Choose Create A New Port and select AppleTalk Printing Devices.

7. The next screen asks you to select the AppleTalk printing device you wish to install as a printer. Click the AppleTalk zone that contains the printing device and select the printing device. Click OK.

8. Answer the remaining questions from the Add Printer Wizard and click Finish.

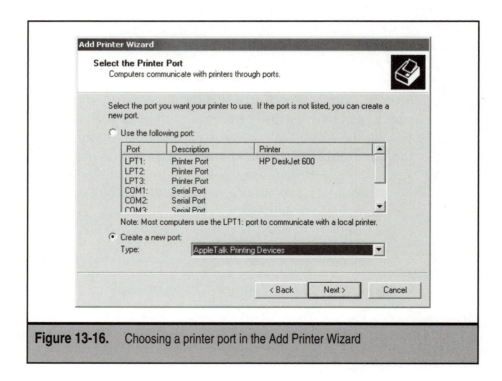

Figure 13-16. Choosing a printer port in the Add Printer Wizard

Setting Up a User Account for Macintosh Print Jobs

The Macintosh environment typically does not provide a built-in means of authentication for users accessing printers. Windows 2000, on the other hand, considers a printer to be a resource and provides similar security for printers as it provides for other resources.

The Print Services for Macintosh service (which Mac clients use to access printers on the Windows 2000 computer) is assigned to the System account by default. The System account has unlimited access to the local system but does not have access to other computers. Microsoft recommends that, if you want to restrict a Macintosh user's access to printers, you configure the Print Services for Macintosh service to use a different account. You can then configure the security settings for this account to grant or deny access to specific printing resources.

TIP: Because the System account does not provide network access, it may not let Mac users print to a network printer installed on the Windows 2000 computer. If you can't print to a printer on the Windows 2000 computer that is actually a network printer (pointing to another Windows computer on the network), use the following procedure to assign Print Services for Macintosh to a different account.

To change the account for the Print Services for Macintosh service, follow these steps:

1. Select Start | Programs | Administrative Tools | Computer Management.

2. In the Computer Management main window, expand the Services and Applications subtree and select Services.

3. In the Services list, find the Print Server for Macintosh service.

4. Double-click Print Server for Macintosh.

5. In the Print Server for Macintosh Properties dialog box, select the Log On tab.

6. In the Log On tab (see Figure 13-17), select This Account and enter the name of an account you wish to use for accessing Print Server for Macintosh. Enter a password and then confirm it. This password will be used by Macintosh users to access the service.

7. Click OK in the Printer Server for Macintosh Properties dialog box.

Capturing a Macintosh Printer

Windows administrators are accustomed to a very controlled arrangement in which the print service on a printer server machine controls access to the printing device and the administrator retains control of the print device by controlling the logical printer object on the print server computer. In the Mac world, things typically aren't quite as formal. You can install an AppleTalk printer on the

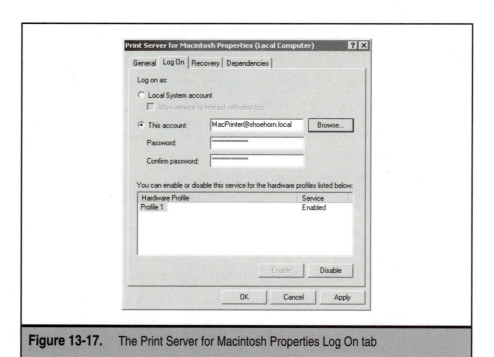

Figure 13-17. The Print Server for Macintosh Properties Log On tab

Windows 2000 computer and the Windows 2000 computer will serve as a print server for that AppleTalk printer, but that doesn't mean that Macintosh users can't still print to the printing device directly. If you want the Windows 2000 computer to have sole control over the printing device (as it would with a Windows-based printing device), you can *capture* the printing device.

To capture or release an AppleTalk printing device, follow these steps:

1. Make sure the AppleTalk printing device is installed as a Windows 2000 printer. See the earlier section titled "Setting Up a Macintosh-Accessible Printer."

2. Select Start | Settings | Printers.

3. In the Printers window, right-click the Printer icon for the printer you wish to capture and select Properties.

4. In the Printer Properties dialog box, select the Ports tab.

5. Select the port for the AppleTalk printing device and choose Configure Port.

6. To capture the port, select Capture This AppleTalk Printing Device check box. To release a port that has already been captured, deselect the Capture This AppleTalk Printing Device check box.

Supporting AppleTalk

A Windows 2000 computer can participate in an AppleTalk network and even act as an AppleTalk router. The following sections discuss

▼ Installing the AppleTalk Protocol

■ Configuring AppleTalk

▲ Setting up AppleTalk routing

Consult your Macintosh documentation for additional information on configuring Macintosh networks.

Installing the AppleTalk Protocol

If you install File Services for Macintosh or Print Services for Macintosh, the AppleTalk protocol is installed automatically. You can, however, install AppleTalk without installing File Services for Macintosh or Print Services for Macintosh. You may, for instance, wish to use your Windows 2000 computer as an AppleTalk router without setting up file and print services.

To install the AppleTalk protocol, follow these steps:

1. Select Start | Settings | Network and Dial-Up Connections.

2. In the Network and Dial-Up Connections window, right-click a Network Connection icon and select Properties. The Network Connection icon represents a network interface such as an Ethernet adapter. Choose the interface for which you would like to configure the AppleTalk protocol. The default name for a network interface is Local Area Connection. Note that if you are installing AppleTalk so that you can use your Windows 2000 computer as a router, you will most likely have an additional network adapter, such as a LocalTalk, EtherTalk, or a second Ethernet adapter.

3. In the Connection Properties dialog box, click the Install button.

4. In the Select Network Component Type dialog box, click Protocol and then click Add.

5. In the Select Network Protocol dialog box, select the AppleTalk protocol and click OK.

6. Click Close in the Local Area Connection dialog box.

When the AppleTalk protocol is installed, it is automatically configured for all LAN connections. To disable AppleTalk for a LAN connection, right-click the Connection icon and deselect the AppleTalk Protocol check box in the Connection Properties dialog box.

Configuring AppleTalk

To set AppleTalk configuration settings, follow these steps:

1. Make sure AppleTalk is installed, either by installing File Services for Macintosh or Print Services for Macintosh, or by

installing AppleTalk directly (as described in the preceding section, "Installing the AppleTalk Protocol").

2. Right-click the connection for which you wish to configure the AppleTalk protocol. For instance, right-click Local Area Connection and choose Properties.

3. In the Connection Properties dialog box, select AppleTalk Protocol and click the Properties button.

4. The AppleTalk Protocol Properties dialog box appears (see Figure 13-18). The AppleTalk Protocol Properties dialog box offers the following choices:

    ■ **Accept Inbound Connections On This Adapter**   Select the check box to accept inbound connections.

    ■ **This System Will Appear In Zone**   Select a default zone.

5. Click OK.

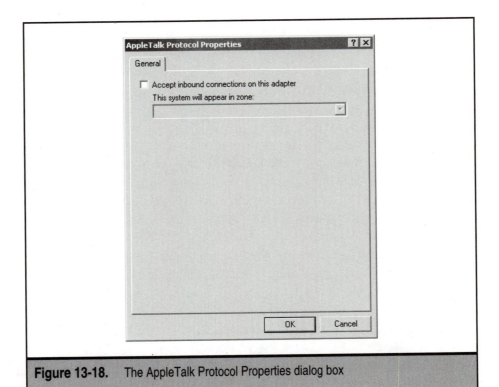

Figure 13-18.   The AppleTalk Protocol Properties dialog box

Setting Up AppleTalk Routing

If you wish to use the Windows 2000 as a router on an AppleTalk network, you must configure AppleTalk routing.

To configure AppleTalk routing, follow these steps:

1. Select Start | Programs | Administrative Tools | Routing and Remote Access.

2. In the Routing and Remote Access window, right-click the name of the server and choose Configure And Enable Routing and Remote Access.

3. In the Routing and Remote Access window (see Figure 13-19), double-click the server you wish to configure as an AppleTalk router. Right-click AppleTalk Routing.

4. Select Enable AppleTalk Routing in the context menu.

5. In the Adapters list, select an adapter. Click the Properties button.

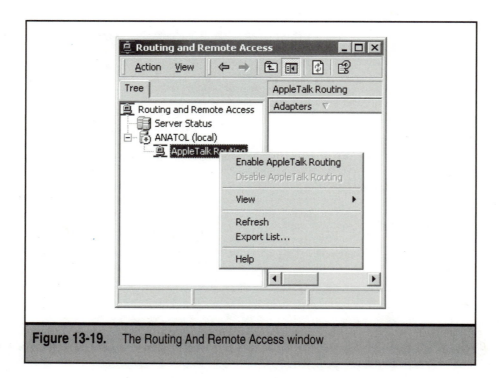

Figure 13-19.　The Routing And Remote Access window

6. In the Adapter Properties dialog box, configure routing properties such as seed routing and network number allocation. Consult your Macintosh documentation for more on configuring Macintosh networks.

ACTIVE DIRECTORY IN THE MICROSOFT EXCHANGE ENVIRONMENT

Many networks already have an operational directory system that maintains and distributes user and contact attributes for the Microsoft Exchange Server mail service. Microsoft provides a feature that lets you synchronize Exchange Server and Active Directory attribute information. This service has the obvious benefit of letting you enter a user attribute (such as a user's e-mail address) only once. Synchronizing with Exchange also offers the following benefits:

▼ **Unified administration**   You can manage contact and delivery information for both environments from a single location.

■ **Extending Active Directory features to Exchange**   By managing Exchange Server from Active Directory, you can manage Exchange data by the attribute. For instance, you can give a group permission to change a user phone number without giving the group permission to change the username.

■ **Simplified migration**   You can copy user attributes directly from the Exchange environment rather than having to enter them into the Active Directory.

▲ **Third-party migration**   You can migrate third-party directory information into Exchange, and then replicate the information from Exchange into Active Directory.

A diagram of the Exchange synchronization process is shown in Figure 13-20. You create a connection agreement that defines how the Exchange and Active Directory environments are connected and how data is exchanged. You must designate a *bridgehead* server for each end of the connection agreement. The Exchange-connector bridgehead

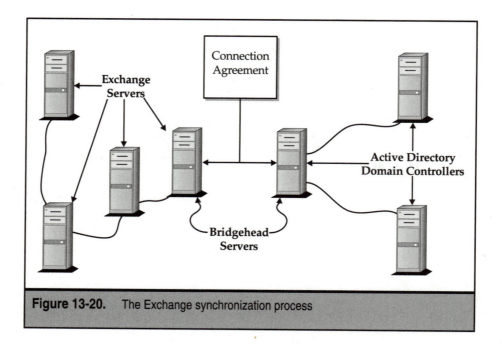

Figure 13-20. The Exchange synchronization process

server is unrelated to the replication bridgehead servers discussed in Chapter 4, "Understanding Replication," but it is the same idea. The bridgehead server receives the updates from the connection and distributes those updates throughout the environment. The connection agreement is managed through a computer that is running the Active Directory Connector service (which is sometimes called MSADC for Microsoft Active Directory Connector). The Active Directory Connector service typically runs on a domain controller, but it is possible to run the Active Directory Connector service on a member server. Note that if you run the Active Directory Connector service on a member server, you must still use an Active Directory domain controller as the Windows bridgehead server for the connection.

You can create multiple connection agreements for managing Exchange/Active Directory synchronization on a large or complex network. For purposes of bandwidth optimization, you can even create different connection agreements to synchronize different Active Directory objects or attributes.

The Connector service distinguishes among three different types of connections:

▼ **Two-Way**   Changes in either directory are written to the other directory.

■ **Windows to Exchange**   Changes in Active Directory are written to Exchange.

▲ **Exchange to Windows**   Changes in Exchange are written to Active Directory.

The connection type you choose depends on your design of the connector architecture and on how you intend to manage the systems. If you are more comfortable making mail and contact changes through the Exchange interface, choose the Exchange to Windows option to update the Active Directory with changes made in Exchange. If you are more comfortable making mail and contact changes through the Active Directory interface, choose the Windows to Exchange option to update Exchange with changes you make through Active Directory. If you'd like to be able to make a change in either environment, choose Two-Way.

The basic idea behind this synchronization is as follows:

▼ Exchange mailboxes map to Active Directory users.

■ Exchange custom recipients map to Active Directory contacts.

▲ Exchange distribution lists map to Active Directory groups.

When you set up a connection agreement, you specify which containers will be synchronized. A connection agreement maps an Exchange container to an Active Directory OU (see Figure 13-21). If you map a parent container to an Active Directory OU, child containers will be synchronized, and the necessary child containers will be created within the OU to receive the synchronization updates (see Figure 13-22).

Objects within a container that is specified in a connection agreement are mapped to corresponding objects in the corresponding container. Actually, attributes attached to the corresponding objects are mapped. This may seem like an amazing feat, but it is actually simpler than it sounds. Since the same company created both Active Directory and Exchange (Microsoft), they were able to ensure that the mail-related objects mapped fairly efficiently. Table 13-5 shows

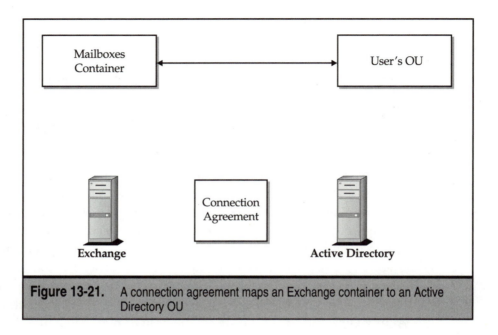

Figure 13-21. A connection agreement maps an Exchange container to an Active Directory OU

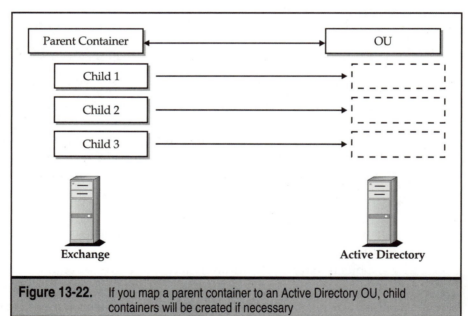

Figure 13-22. If you map a parent container to an Active Directory OU, child containers will be created if necessary

Object Class	Exchange Attribute	Windows 2000 (Active Directory) Attribute
User object in AD (Mailbox object in Exchange)	givenName Folder-Pathname DXA-task home-MDB Assoc-NT-Account	givenName folderPathname mDBOverHardQuotaLimit msExchHomeServerName objectSID
Contact object in AD (Custom object in Exchange)	Manager target-address protocol-Settings	Manager targetAddress protocolSettings
Group object in AD (Distribution List object in Exchange)	home-MTA owner oOF-Reply-To-Originator Report-To-Owner	msExchExpansionServerName managedby oOFReplyToOriginator reportToOwner
All Object Classes	company employeeNumber telephoneNumber postalAddress uid cn Admin-description Extension-Attribute-1	company employeeID telephoneNumber streetAddress mailnickname displayName description extensionAttribute1

Table 13-5.   Exchange to Active Directory Attribute Mappings

examples of some of the Exchange attribute to Windows attribute mappings. Many additional mapped attributes have exactly the same (or a very similar) name in both environments. For instance, the Exchange security-Protocol attribute maps to the Windows 2000 securityProtocol attribute. For more on attribute mappings, see "Synchronizing Active Directory with Exchange Server Directory Service" in the Windows 2000 Resource Kit Books Online Deployment Planning Guide.

Organizing and Optimizing Connection Agreements

You have a wide range of options for connecting Windows 2000 networks to Exchange sites through connection agreements. You can connect multiple Exchange sites to a single Active Directory domain. You can connect multiple Active Directory domains to a single (or multiple) exchange sites.

NOTE: You cannot connect more than one Exchange organization to a single Active Directory forest.

If your directory generates a large amount of synchronization traffic, you can spread the load by synchronizing one container through one connection agreement and another container through a different connection agreement. The connector service can be running on a domain controller or on a member server. If your directory is large, Microsoft recommends running the connector service from a member server to minimize the effect of domain controller resources.

NOTE: If local performance is not a problem, however, and if you are more concerned about network traffic, placing the connector service on a domain controller can reduce the total amount of network traffic necessary to support the system.

If you have a multisite or multidomain network, the location of connector service servers and bridgehead servers deserves some additional attention. As you might guess, since the connector draws information that resides on the domain partition, you must have a separate connection agreement for each domain. Also, on multidomain networks, the connector runs global catalog searches to ensure that it is not duplicating information found in a different domain. For this reason, it is a good idea to place the connector service server on the same LAN segment with a global catalog server, as well as on the same segment with the domain controller that is acting as a bridgehead server. It is equally important that the Exchange bridgehead be well connected to the connector service server and the Windows bridgehead.

TIP: Microsoft offers a formula for calculating the size a connector service synchronization event:
Active Directory to Exchange: 51KB + 14KB per changed object
Exchange to Active Directory: 61KB + 26KB per changed object

When you begin Exchange directory synchronization on a large network, a giant tsunami of synchronization can occur at the outset because so many objects and attributes need to be synchronized in order to bring the two directories to accord. If you are attempting to synchronize a large directory, Microsoft recommends that you devise a plan to stagger the deployment of connection agreements across sites and domains so as to minimize the effects of traffic caused by the initial synchronization.

Implementing an Exchange Server Connection

The following sections discuss some of the procedures you'll need for integrating your Exchange environment with Active Directory. Consult the Windows 2000 Resource Kit Books Online and your Microsoft Exchange documentation for more information.

Installing the Connector Service

The Active Directory Connector service requires Microsoft Exchange Server v5.5. If you plan to deploy Exchange Server v5.5 on a Windows 2000 system, you need Exchange Service Pack 2.

To install the Active Directory Connector service, follow these steps:

1. On the Windows 2000 Server CD or a Windows 2000 installation share, browse to the directory Valueadd\MSFT\MGMT\ADC.

2. In the Valueadd\MSFT\MGMT\ADC directory, double-click Setup.exe.

3. The Active Directory Connector Installation Wizard starts. Click Next.

4. In the next screen, select whether you wish to install the Active Directory Connector service and/or the Active

Directory Connector Management components. Select Active Directory Connector service.

5. The next screen asks for a destination folder. Accept the default or enter a folder name. Click Next.

6. Specify an account and password for the account the Active Directory Connector service will run under. Click Next.

7. The connector service installs.

NOTE: Microsoft states that, to avoid conflicts with Active Directory, you should reassign the LDAP port address on the Exchange server.

Configuring Connection Agreements

You create and configure connection agreements through the Active Directory Connector Management tool, which you install when you set up the Active Directory Connector service (see the preceding section "Installing the Connector Service"). Active Directory Connector Management is a Microsoft Management Console utility.

To set up a connection agreement, follow these steps:

1. Install the Active Directory Connector service and the Connector Service Management components (see the preceding section "Installing the Connector Service").

2. Select Start | Programs | Administrative Tools | Active Directory Connector Management.

3. In the Active Directory Connector Management main window, right-click the icon for a computer with the connector service and choose New | Connection Agreement.

4. The connection agreement's Properties dialog box opens (see Figure 13-23). Configure the properties for the new connection as desired.

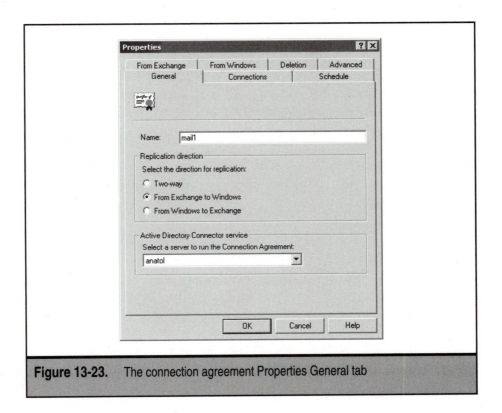

Figure 13-23. The connection agreement Properties General tab

The seven tabs of the connection agreement Properties dialog box are described in the following list.

GENERAL   Enter a name for the connection agreement (required). Choose a direction for the replication (Exchange to Windows, Windows to Exchange, or two-way). Choose a connector service server that will enter into the connection agreement.

CONNECTIONS   The Connections tab (see Figure 13-24) provides information on the servers (the Windows server and the Exchange server) at either end of the connection agreement. The Windows server is the server running the connector service. Both the Windows

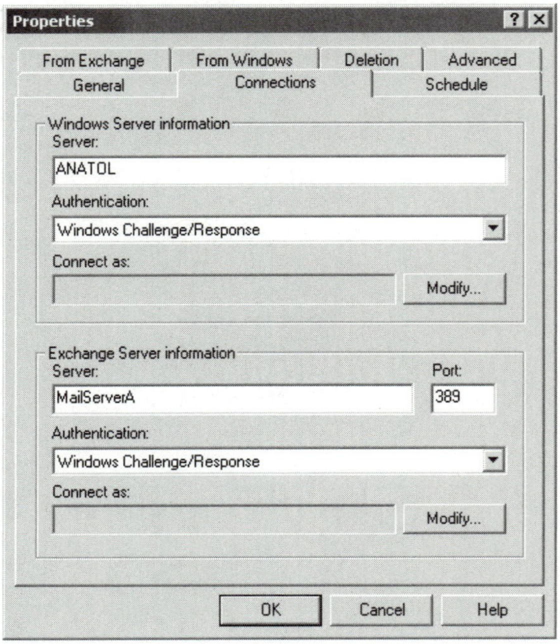

Figure 13-24. The connection agreement Properties Connections tab

server and the Exchange server run NT/2000-based operating systems, and both require login credentials in order to access the system. The Connect As box displays the name of the account that the service will use to access information on each machine. Click the Modify button to specify an account name. The account you specify must have the necessary permissions for carrying out the assignment. Those permissions will depend on the direction of the connection you are establishing. The connector service must have write access to a directory into which it will be writing changes. For instance, if you choose to replicate changes from Exchange to Windows, the connector service permissions for the Windows side must allow write access to the Active Directory.

SCHEDULE The Schedule tab (see Figure 13-25) lets you establish a schedule for the synchronization. By default, the connector service

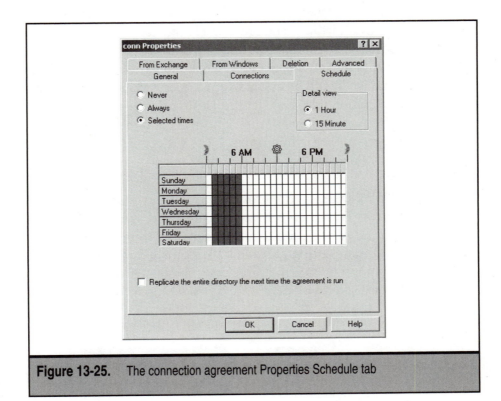

Figure 13-25.   The connection agreement Properties Schedule tab

polls for directory changes every five seconds during the time specified in the Schedule tab. The Detail View options (1 hour and 15 minutes) don't have anything to do with the schedule, but just control the gradations of the schedule graphic. You can choose to perform replication never, always, or at the times shown in the schedule. Click a block of time in the schedule to select it. Note the check box at the bottom labeled Replicate The Entire Directory The Next Time This Agreement Is Run. You can use this option to force a replication of all mail-related items in the directory rather than just the objects that have changed.

TIP: You can change the default five-second delay between synchronization cycles through the Registry setting HKEY_LOCAL_MACHINE\System\ CurrentControlSet\Services\MSADC\Parameters. The setting Sync Sleep Delay (secs) accepts a DWORD value for the number of seconds between cycles.

FROM EXCHANGE   The From Exchange tab (see Figure 13-26) lets you choose the Exchange containers whose contents you'd like to replicate to Active Directory. Click the Add button to add a container to the list. You'll be asked to specify an Exchange server and provide login credentials. The Default Destination setting gives the distinguished name of the Windows container to which the directory changes will be synchronized. The Objects list lets you define the types of objects that will be synchronized.

FROM WINDOWS   The From Windows tab lets you choose the Active Directory containers whose contents you'd like to replicate to Exchange. Click the Add button to add a container to the list. The Default Destination setting gives the distinguished name of the Exchange container to which the directory changes will be synchronized. The Objects list lets you define the types of objects that will be synchronized.

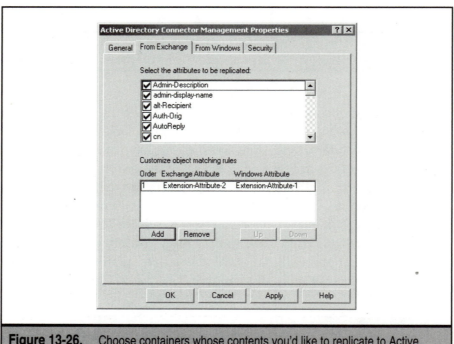

Figure 13-26.   Choose containers whose contents you'd like to replicate to Active Directory in this tab

DELETION   In the default configuration, deletions are not replicated between the directories. In other words, if you delete an object in Active Directory, the corresponding Exchange object is not deleted. Instead, the deletions are recorded in files on the connector service server computer. (Deleted Active Directory objects are listed in the file NT5.ldf. Deleted Exchange objects are listed in the file Ex55.csv. The files are located in the directory *system_root*\System32\MSDAC\ *connection_agreement_name*.) The Deletion tab lets you change this default behavior and configure the connector service to delete objects. Be sure you know what you're doing if you elect to delete objects with the connector service. Even though you no longer need an object in Exchange, you may still find reasons for keeping the object in the Active Directory.

ADVANCED   The Advanced tab lets you set the page size for connector service replication. The Advanced tab also lets you declare whether a connection agreement will be the *primary* connection agreement for the exchange organization or Windows domain. The primary connection agreement is the connection agreement that is designated to replicate new objects that are created in the source directory to the destination directory. (Note that it would be kind of pointless and confusing for all connection agreements to attempt to replicate the same newly created object.) This setting designates one connection agreement to replicate newly created objects. If no primary connection agreement is defined, new objects won't be replicated, but replication will still occur for updates of existing objects. The Advanced tab also offers a setting that lets you decide what to do if a mailbox is created in Exchange for which there is no corresponding Windows account. You can create a Windows contact (the default), create a new user account, or create a disabled user account.

Customizing Object and Attribute Replication

You can choose which attributes will replicate between the directories and create custom matching rules that tell which Exchange object to map to which Windows attribute based on a common attribute value.

To customize attribute synchronization, follow these steps:

1. With Active Directory Connector service and the Connector Service Management utility installed on your computer, choose Start | Programs | Administrative Tools | Active Directory Connector Management.

2. In the Active Directory Connector Management utility, right-click the Active Directory Connector Management icon and select Properties.

3. In the Active Directory Connector Management Properties dialog box, click the From Exchange tab (see Figure 13-26), and select the Exchange attributes you'd like to replicate to corresponding attributes in Active Directory. Note that all the attributes in the list are selected by default. To remove an item from the list, deselect it. The Matching Rules list (at the bottom of the dialog box) lets you specify a custom association between an Exchange attribute and a Windows attribute. An object will be replicated if the settings for the attributes specified in the Matching Rules list match. Click the From Windows tab to configure similar settings for Windows to Exchange replication.

4. Click OK.

Managing the Active Directory Connector

The way that you manage your mail-related directory objects will depend on how you define your connection agreements. If you're planning on one-way connections from Exchange to Windows, you'll need to add and modify mail-related objects through Exchange. If, on the other hand, you plan on one-way connections from Active Directory to Exchange, you'll need to manage mail-related objects through Active Directory. If you plan to use two-way synchronization, you can work from either side.

The earlier section titled "Configuring Connection Agreements" described the Active Directory Connection Management utility, which you can use to configure and manage connection agreements.

You can configure mailbox-related user properties through Active Directory Users and Computers. When Active Directory Connector management tools are installed, Exchange extensions are copied to the Active Directory schema so that Exchange-related settings can be managed through Active Directory Users and Computers. Microsoft Exchange Server must be running on your network in order for Exchange extensions to take effect. Also, you must make sure Advanced Features is selected in Active Directory Users And Computers to view Exchange-related settings. If the connection agreement is configured properly, you should see E-mail Addresses, Exchange, and Exchange Advanced tabs in Active Directory Users and Computers.

Managing from the Client

The Connector Service Management utility, described in the earlier section titled "Configuring Connection Agreements," can be installed on a Windows 2000 Professional computer. If you run the Setup Wizard from a Windows 2000 Professional workstation, you can elect to add the Active Directory Connector Management utility to the workstation.

Logging Connector Service Events

You can configure the Active Directory Connector service to log information to the event log.

To configure connector service logging, follow these steps:

1. With Active Directory Connector service and the Connector Service Management utility installed on your computer, choose Start | Programs | Administrative Tools | Active Directory Connector Management.

2. In the Active Directory Connector Management utility, right-click a connector service server computer and click Properties.

3. In the Connector Properties dialog box, select the Diagnostic Logging tab (see Figure 13-27) and choose one or more event

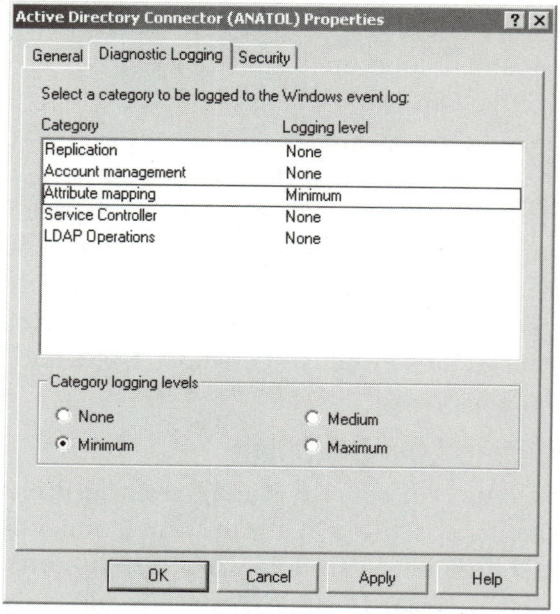

Figure 13-27. The Active Directory Connector Properties Diagnostic Logging tab

logging categories. For each category, choose a logging level: None, Minimum, Medium, or Maximum. The categories are

- **Replication**   Logs replication events.

- **Account Management**   Logs attempts to write or delete an object during synchronization.

- **Attribute Mapping**   Logs attempts to map attributes from one directory to corresponding attributes in the other directory.

- **Service Controller**   Logs attempts to start or stop the connector service.

- **LDAP Operations**   Logs connector-related LDAP operations.

4. Click OK or Apply.

SUMMARY

Windows 2000 is designed for heterogeneous networks, and it includes built-in features that allow it to interoperate with NetWare, Macintosh, and UNIX-based systems. This chapter discussed interoperability and Windows 2000. You learned about NWLink and Gateway Services for NetWare. You learn about Services for Macintosh, Services for UNIX, and a collection of useful TCP/IP connectivity utilities. You learned how to install printers and share files with non-Microsoft clients, and, last of all, you learned how to synchronize Active Directory with the Microsoft Exchange Directory service.

Index

▼ A

A G DL P strategy, 138, 139, 141
A records, 48–50
access control lists (ACLs), 134, 137
access token, 134
Account Policies section, 400–402
ACLs (access control lists), 134, 137
ACPI (Advanced Configuration and Power Management Interface), 309
Active Directory
    backing up, 258–261
    concepts, 17–36

considerations for, 208–209
database considerations, 208–209
deployment process, 206–250
described, 4
DNS and, 40–68, 208
environment, 3–16
important setup procedures, 250–255
introduction to, 1–36
managing, 257–304
modifying, 265–280
need for, 207–209
operating modes, 19–21
replication and, 82–93

Active Directory, *continued*
rollout for, 230
scripting, 433–458
setting up, 205–255
system requirements, 231–232
TCP/IP and, 39–79
test site for, 209–211
upgrade considerations, 210
upgrade paths, 231–232
Windows 2000 and, 12
Windows NT and, 4–16, 208, 209
Active Directory Connector, 520, 525–526, 532–534
Active Directory Connector Management utility, 526–531
Active Directory Domains and Trusts tool, 248–249
Active Directory Installation Wizard, 237–239, 254
Active Directory Migration Tool (ADMT), 227, 245
Active Directory network, 21–31. *See also* networks
considerations for, 215–222
installing, 224–225
migrating NetWare network to, 229
migrating Windows NT network to, 225–229
planning for, 212–214
requirements, 213–214
Active Directory Schema. *See* schema
Active Directory Schema utility, 343

Active Directory Services Interface (ASDI), 436–437
Active Directory Sites And Services utility, 70, 184
Active Directory Software Developer's Kit, 437
Active Directory Users and Computers utility, 316, 318–330
ActivePerl, 439, 457
ActiveX, 439
Add A File Or Folder dialog box, 410, 411
Add A Group Property Link dialog box, 194–195
Add A Script dialog box, 449
Add Monitored Server Wizard, 118, 119
Add Printer Wizard, 288, 472, 490, 511
Add/Remove Snap-in dialog box, 189, 191
Address Book application, 315
Adm subdirectory, 186
.adm template files, 186
administrative templates, 192–193
Administrative Tools group, 15
ADMT (Active Directory Migration Tool), 227, 245
ADSI Editor, 266–272
adding objects, 271–272
adding to Microsoft Management console, 267
deleting objects, 272
editing attributes, 268–271, 371–373
editing classes, 373–375

reloading schema cache, 349
working with, 372–376

Advanced button, 268

Advanced Configuration and Power Management Interface (ACPI), 309

Advanced dialog box, 268, 269

AFP over TCP/IP, 501, 509

AH (Authentication Header) protocol, 424

Alpha processor, 231

Apple Filing Protocol (AFP) over TCP/IP, 501, 509

AppleTalk printer, 511–512, 514–515

AppleTalk protocol, 499, 500, 515–519

applications. *See* software

Apply Group Policy permission, 195–197

appmgr.dll file, 188

ASDI (Active Directory Services Interface), 436–437

attributes, 342–344
    Active Directory and, 32–33
    adding, 338
    adding to global catalog, 363–364
    associated with classes, 346
    attributeSchema class, 341, 342
    creating, 360–361
    customizing replication, 531–532
    deactivating, 371–372

described, 12–13, 339
    editing, 373–375
    indexing, 361–363
    mapping, 521–523
    properties for, 358–360
    reactivating, 371–372

Attributes folder, 357

attributeSchema class, 341

Authentication Header (AH) protocol, 424

authenticator, 382

authoritative restore, 259, 264–265

 B

backing up Active Directory, 258–261

BackOffice applications, 213

backup domain controllers (BDCs), 5, 19–20, 225–226

Backup utility, 258–259

bandwidth, 10–11

BatchMode setting, 442

BDCs (backup domain controllers), 5, 19–20, 225–226

bind operation, 274

BIND versions, 68

BIOS, 309

Block Policy Inheritance setting, 187–188

Bridge All Site Links option, 109–111

bridgehead servers
  configuring, 113–115
  connection agreements and, 519–520
  described, 11, 22
  intersite replication and, 103, 104
  vs. Intersite Topology Generator, 113
Browse For A Group Policy Object dialog box, 189, 190
built-in scripts, 451–452

▼ C

canonical name format, 35, 36
CD drive (CDFS) volume, 505
CDFS (CD drive) volume, 505
CDO (Collaborative Data Objects) interface, 103
Cerberus, 380, 384
Change Domain Controller dialog box, 352, 353
Change Operations Master dialog box, 302
Change Schema Master dialog box, 301, 352
character generator (chargen), 497
child classes, 345–346
chkupgrd.exe utility, 309
class attributes, 32–33
class types, 344–345
classes, 344–346

attributes associated with, 346
classSchema class, 341–342
creating, 338, 369–371
deactivating, 371–372
described, 12–13, 339, 340
editing, 373–375
properties for, 364–368
reactivating, 371–372
Classes folder, 357
classSchema class, 341
client key, 380–382, 384
clients, 305–333. *See also* computers
  connecting to, 317–318
  joining to domains, 319–326
  Macintosh clients, 314
  managing, 316–331
  managing network from, 331–333
  moving to different domain, 330–331
  moving within domains, 329–330
  Netware clients, 314
  options for, 306–316
  other networking systems, 314
  Telnet clients, 314, 485–487
  UNIX-based clients, 314
  Windows 95/98 clients, 306–308, 312–314
  Windows 2000 clients, 306–308, 311–312
  Windows NT clients, 306–308, 312

clonepr.dll, 226, 228, 244

ClonePrincipal tool, 226, 228, 244

cn attribute, 32

CN (Common Name) setting, 359–360

Collaborative Data Objects (CDO) interface, 103

COM interface, 436

commands. *See also specific command names*
FTP commands, 478–483
NetDom commands, 326
repadmin commands, 116–117

comma-separated value (CSV) format, 280

Common Name (CN) setting, 359–360

common.adm template, 193

Computer Management utility
account operations, 390–391
connecting to client computer, 317–318
described, 316
Macintosh operations, 501–505
system management, 328–329
Telnet operations, 491–492
troubleshooting with, 240, 241

computer policies, 185

computers. *See also* clients
associating server objects with, 77–78

connecting to client computer, 317–318
joining client computer to domain, 319–326
managing, 328–329
moving to different domain, 330–331
moving within domain, 329–330
specifying manager for, 326–328

conf.adm template, 192, 193

config.pol file, 180

configuration partition, 23

Configure DNS Server Wizard, 52

Configure Membership dialog box, 406

Configure Your Server Wizard, 52–53

configuring
desktops, 297, 298
DHCP service, 49–50
DNS service, 52–53
DNS zones, 53–65
File Services for Macintosh, 501–504
global catalog servers, 252
GPO policies, 182–184
IP Security policy, 414–416
Kerberos, 387–393
preferred bridgehead server, 113–115
primary zone, 58
script files, 439–442

configuring, *continued*
    site link bridges, 109–112
    site links, 104–114
    sites, 70–71, 73–74
    software installation
        properties, 295–296
    trusts, 246–250
    Windows 2000 for NetWare,
        460–473
    zone properties, 61–63
connection agreements,
    93, 519–531
Connection dialog box, 268, 269
connection objects, 93,
    96–100, 104
containers, 6, 254. *See also* objects
Create New Attribute dialog
    box, 362, 363
Create New Class Wizard, 372
Create Shared Folder
    Wizard, 505
cross-link trusts, 247
cscript.exe, 438, 439, 442–443
CSV (comma-separated value)
    format, 280
CSVDE tool, 279–280
Custom Security Method Settings
    dialog box, 425

D

Database Security dialog
    box, 409, 410

dc attribute, 32
dcpromo.exe utility
    creating domain controllers,
        224, 236–238
    demoting domain
        controllers, 254–255
    described, 223
    promoting servers, 228
debugging scripts, 444–445
default policy, 176, 178–179
Delegation of Control feature,
    170–172
Delegation of Control Wizard,
    171–172, 253
deleting
    groups, 163–164
    objects, 272
    user accounts, 156–157
    zones, 64
Deployment Planning
    Guide, 206, 250
deployment process, 206–250
deployment utilities, 244–245
desktop, managing, 297–300
Device Manager, 240
DFS (Distributed File Service),
    222, 307
DHCP servers, 243–244
DHCP service, 49–50, 211
Diffie-Hellman computation, 413
Direct Replication Partner
    icon, 119–120
directory replication.
    See replication

Directory Service Migration Tool, 229

Directory Services Client, 307, 313–314

Directory Services restore mode, 239

Disk Quotas feature, 284–285

distinguished names, 32, 33–36, 272, 278

Distributed File Service (DFS), 222, 307

distribution groups, 135, 136

DNS console, 53, 65–67

DNS (Domain Name System)
    Active Directory and, 40–68
    configuring DNS service, 52–53
    configuring DNS zones, 53–65
    described, 40–44
    dynamic updates, 48–50
    integration of, 8–10
    migrating data to Windows 2000, 67–68
    name resolution, 41–44
    naming conventions, 46
    naming objects, 31–32
    NETBIOS and, 208
    problems with, 203, 242–244
    testing DNS functions, 211
    zones, 46–48

.dns extension, 47

DNS namespace, 45–46

DNS records, 41, 42

DNS servers
    Active Directory and, 9, 40
    adding to management console, 66
    configuring, 53–67
    DNS name resolution and, 41–44
    installing, 52–53
    interoperating with, 68
    Microsoft DNS Server, 40
    problems with, 203
    removing from management console, 66
    requirements, 214
    test system and, 211
    zones and, 46–47

DNS/WINS integration, 9

Domain Controller Security Policy tool, 179

domain controllers
    creating, 236–239
    demoting, 254–255
    policy settings for, 178, 179
    problems with, 243
    processing schema modifications, 351–353
    replication and, 11, 120
    requirements, 213
    specifying for GPO changes, 197–201
    SRV records and, 50
    system clock, 232

domain local groups, 8

domain master, 26

Domain Name System. *See* DNS
domain naming master,
    214, 301–302
domain partition, 23
Domain Security Policy tool, 179
domain tree, 7
domains
    adding to zones, 63
    described, 46
    joining client computers
        to, 319–326
    master account domains, 227
    moving clients to different
        domains, 330–331
    moving clients within,
        329–330
    multidomain networks,
        27–31
    network considerations,
        215–216
    policy settings for, 178
    resource domains, 227–228
    switching to native
        mode, 251–252
    types of, 45
DOS, 434, 438
drivers, 240, 309, 310
dynamic DNS server, 9
dynamic updates, 48–50

▼ E

edb.chk file, 258
edb*.log file, 258

Encapsulated Secure Payload
    (ESP) protocol, 424
error messages
    error log, 240
    "Failed to Open Group
        Policy Object," 203
ESP (Encapsulated Secure
    Payload) protocol, 424
Event Log settings, 405
event logs, 240, 405, 533–534
Event Viewer, 240, 242
Excel spreadsheets, 280
expanded ring topology, 95
explicit trusts, 247, 248–249
exporting objects, 275–279
external trusts, 247, 248

▼ F

"Failed to Open Group Policy
    Object" error, 203
fault tolerance, 10–11
fde.dll file, 188
File and Print Services for
    NetWare, 473
File Replication Service
    (FRS), 222
File Server for Macintosh, 500
File Services for Macintosh,
    500–510
File System option, 410–411
File Transfer Protocol. *See* FTP
files. *See also specific file names*
    .adm template files, 186

file policy, 410–411
managing, 280, 283–285
protecting, 284–285
replication log files, 121–125
.zap files, 294–295
zone files, 55, 56, 60
Filter Action Wizard, 421–422
filter actions, 421–427
Find Domain Controllers
window, 99
Find feature, 315
Find People dialog box, 315
Find Shared Folders dialog
box, 283
folders. *See also specific folder*
names
folder policy, 410–411
folder redirection policy,
297, 298–300
for group policies, 197,
198–200
managing, 280–285
publishing, 280–283
sharing for Macintosh
clients, 505–508
forest, 7, 26, 338, 351, 524
forestwide replication
topology, 91–92
FQDN (fully qualified domain
name), 45
FRS (File Replication
Service), 222
FTP commands, 478–483

FTP (File Transfer Protocol),
314, 477–483
fully qualified domain name
(FQDN), 45

 G

Gateway Service for NetWare
(GSNW), 465–471
global catalog, 14–15, 363–364
global catalog servers
configuring, 252
domain partitions
and, 23, 25
infrastructure masters
and, 27, 213
intrasite replication and, 94
multidomain networks
and, 214
replication topology and, 92
requirements, 214
universal groups and, 139
globally unique identifiers
(GUIDs), 26, 34–35
GPCs (group policy
containers), 186
GPOs (group policy objects)
adding scripts to, 448–449
associating with
containers, 181
configuring policies for,
182–183
creating, 181–182, 449

GPOs, *continued*

described, 175, 176, 179

disabling subtrees for, 202

linking, 194–195

specifying domain controller for, 197–201

GPT (Group Policy Template) folder, 186

gptext.dll file, 188

gpt.ini file, 186

group policies, 173–204. *See also* policies

in Active Directory, 176–180

compatibility issues, 307–308

controlling, 197

creating snap-in, 188–191

described, 174–175

extensions, 188

filtering, 195–197

folder redirection policy, 297, 298–300

implementing, 175

interaction between, 187–188

Kerberos policy, 392–393, 400

links and, 187, 194–195

listed, 198–200

location of, 186, 197, 198–200

managing files and folders, 283–285

managing software, 289–296

managing user desktop, 297–300

multidomain environments and, 30–31

network considerations, 221

options for, 191–201

printer-related settings, 286–288

processing order of, 184–186

purpose of, 175

security policy, 398–431

setting up, 180–188

settings for policy scripts, 450–451

strategies, 201–203

tips for, 221

.zap files and, 294–295

group policy containers (GPCs), 186

Group Policy Domain Controller setting, 201

Group Policy Editor, 449–451

group policy feature, 6–7, 8, 30–31

group policy objects. *see* GPOs

Group Policy Template (GPT) folder, 186

group policy templates, 192

Group Policy window, 182, 191–192

groups, 135–141

Active Directory groups, 138–140

adding to other groups, 161–162

adding users to, 146–149

administrators group, 141

backup operators group, 141

built-in groups, 138, 140–141

changing group type, 136
computer local groups, 137
creating, 159–161
deleting, 163–164
distribution groups, 135, 136
domain local groups,
    137, 140
global groups, 8, 137,
    139, 140
granting permissions
    through, 136–137
guests group, 141
managing, 142–164
moving, 163
network considerations,
    220–221
overview, 134–135
permissions and, 134–141
predefined groups, 140–141
properties, 162–163
removing from other
    groups, 161–162
removing users from,
    146–149
restricted groups, 405–407
scope of, 137–138
security groups, 134, 135,
    136–140
types of, 8
universal groups, 20,
    137, 138–140
users group, 141
GSNW (Gateway Service
    for NetWare), 465–471
GUIDs (globally unique
    identifiers), 26, 34–35

H

Hardware Compatibility List
    (HCL), 240
Help topics, 240–241
high watermark settings, 87, 88
host records, 48–50

I

Identification Changes dialog
    box, 324, 325
IIS (Internet Information Server),
    103, 444–445, 473
IKE (Internet Key Exchange)
    protocol, 413
impersonation, 387
importing
    objects, 275–279
    security templates, 194
incremental zone transfer, 46–47
inetcorp.adm template, 193
inetres.adm template, 192
inetset.adm template, 193
infrastructure masters, 27, 28,
    213, 302–303
installing
    Active Directory network,
        224–225
    Directory Services
        Client, 313–314
    DNS server, 52–53
    File Services for Macintosh,
        501
    NWLink, 461–465

installing, *continued*
Windows 2000, 232–250
Windows 2000
Administrative Tools,
331–333
Windows 2000 Support
Tools, 115, 250–251
Interix package, 457
Internet Explorer, 312, 315, 316
Internet Explorer policies, 193
Internet Information Server (IIS),
103, 444–445, 473
Internet Key Exchange (IKE)
protocol, 413
Internet RFCs, 34
intersite replication, 102–104
Intersite Topology Generator,
103, 113
intransitive trusts, 7
intrasite replication, 94–102
IP addresses, 40–42, 57
IP filter lists, 416–420
IP Filter Wizard, 417
IP Security feature (IPSec),
411–431
IP Security Policy Management
MMC snap-in, 413, 414
IP Security Policy Wizard,
427–428
IP security rules, 414
IPSec (IP Security feature),
411–431
IPX routing, 463–464
IPX/SPX. *See* NWLink
iteration, 44

▼ J

Java scripting language.
See JScript
.js extension, 439
JScript
debugging scripts, 444–445
described, 434, 435
executing, 439
properties for, 439–442

▼ K

KCC. *See* Knowledge
Consistency Checker
KDC (Key Distribution Center),
380–386, 395–396
Kerberos protocol, 378–398
configuring, 387–393
described, 379–384
explicit trusts, 250
external trusts, 248
limitations, 397–398
policy settings, 392–393, 400
vs. NTLM authentication,
378–379
Windows 2000 and, 384–387,
394–397
Key Distribution Center (KDC),
380–386, 395–396
keys, 379–384, 397
Keywords button, 282

Knowledge Consistency
Checker (KCC)
checking replication
topology, 100
intrasite replication
and, 94–98
replication and, 92–93
replication topology
and, 82, 91
Korn shell, 498

 L

LANs, 218–219
LDAP Data Interchange
Format Data Exchange.
See LDIFDE tool
LDAP (Lightweight Directory
Access Protocol) service, 9, 32,
272–275, 314
LDAP queries, 51
LDAP records, 272–275
LDAP server, 9, 10
LDAP service, 354
LDAP/X.500 format, 32
LDAP/X.500 naming
conventions, 34
LDIF files, 279
LDIF format, 279–280
LDIFDE tool, 275–279
ldp.exe utility, 272–275, 307
Lightweight Directory Access
Protocol. *See* LDAP
Line Printer Daemon (LPD)
client, 483

links
GPO links, 194–195
site links, 104–114
WAN links, 29, 71, 218, 219
Local Policies section, 402–404
local policy, 176–178
Local Security Policy tool, 178
Log On To button, 153
logoff scripts, 446, 449
Logon Denied button, 153
Logon Hours dialog box, 154
logon scripts, 446–451
logs
event logs, 240, 405, 533–534
replication logs, 121–125
transaction logs, 258
long-term keys, 384
LPD (Line Printer Daemon)
client, 483
Lpdsvc, 488–490
lpr command, 483

 M

Macfile command, 500
Machine subdirectory, 186
Macintosh clients, 498–519
AppleTalk support, 515–519
File Server for Macintosh,
500
File Services for Macintosh,
500–510
Microsoft Authentication
for, 508–510

Macintosh clients, *continued*
Print Services for Macintosh, 510–515
sharing folders, 505–508
support for, 314
TCP/IP and, 499, 500, 501, 509
Managed By feature, 326–328
management console
adding ASDI Editor to, 267
adding DNS servers to, 66
removing DNS servers from, 66
Managers GPO, 197
master account domains, 227
messages. *See* error messages
meta-data, 127–129
Microsoft Active Directory Connector (MSADC), 520, 525–526
Microsoft BackOffice suite, 213
Microsoft Directory Synchronization Services (MSDSS), 473, 474
Microsoft DNS Server, 40
Microsoft Exchange, 519–534
connection agreements, 524–525
managing Active Directory connector, 532–534
schema and, 350
server connection, 525–532
Microsoft Management Console (MMC) meta-tool, 15
Microsoft Office applications, 309

migration, 29, 225–229
mirroring, 420
mixed mode, 19–21, 219, 251–252
MMC (Microsoft Management Console), 15
Move dialog box, 155, 329–330
Move Tree utility, 254
movetree.exe, 244
MSADC (Microsoft Active Directory Connector), 520, 525–526
MS-DOS, 434, 435
msicuu.exe, 244
multidomain networks, 27–31, 215–216, 227

N

native mode, 19–21, 219, 251–252
NDS directory, 474
NDS networks, 468–470, 473, 474
nested groups, 20, 161
nested OUs, 217–218
NetBIOS, 5, 8–9, 208
NetBIOS name, 320, 321
NetBIOS name resolution, 208, 214
netdom add command, 326
netdom join command, 326
netdom move command, 331
netdom trust command, 250
NetDom utility
adding computers to domains, 326

creating trust relationships, 226, 229, 249–250

moving clients, 330–331

netdom.exe, 244

Netlogon share, 180

NetMeeting policies, 193

NetWare clients, 460–474

configuring Windows 2000 for, 460–473

connecting to shared volumes, 471–472

File and Print Services for NetWare, 473

services for, 473–474

sharing files, 473

sharing printers, 472–473

sharing volumes, 469–471

NetWare networks, 208, 229

Network and Dial-Up Connections control panel, 242

Network control panel, 242

Network File System (NFS), 498

Network ID button, 323, 324

network IDs, 60

Network Information Service (NIS), 498

Network Monitor utility, 115, 131–132

networks

Active Directory network details, 21–31

considerations for, 215–222

designing, 212–213

domains and, 215–216

group policy and, 221

groups and, 220–221

installing Active Directory network, 224–225

LANs, 218–219

managing from clients, 331–333

mixed mode vs. native mode, 219

multidomain networks, 27–31, 215–216, 227

NDS networks, 468–470, 473, 474

NetWare networks, 208, 229

OUs and, 216–218

planning for, 212–214

reasons for dividing into sites, 69

replication and, 69, 222

requirements for, 213–214

sites and, 218–219

users and, 220–221

Windows NT networks, 225–229

New Object dialog box, 106, 281

New Object–Computer Wizard, 320–322

New Zone Wizard, 54–60

NFS (Network File System), 498

NIS (Network Information Service), 498

nonauthoritative restore, 259, 262–263

nonsecurity group, 8

nontransitive trusts, 7

nslookup utility, 242

NT system policy, 176, 179–180
NTConfig.pol file, 180
ntds.dit file, 258
Ntdsutil utility, 263, 264, 265
NTFS partitions, 234–235, 500, 505
NTLM authentication, 378–379, 384, 486–487
NWLink, 461–465

▼ O

Object ID Generator utility, 355, 356
object identifiers (OIDs), 354
objectGUID, 34–35
objects
    adding, 271–272
    ADSI Editor for, 266–272
    connection objects, 93, 96–100
    customizing replication, 531–532
    delegation of control and, 170–172
    deleting, 272
    described, 340
    editing attribute settings, 268–271
    exporting, 275–279
    importing, 275–279
    inheritance and, 168–170
    moving, 254
    naming in Active Directory, 31–36
    ownership of, 167–168
    permissions for, 166–167
    viewing attribute settings, 268–271
    X.500 objects, 354–356
Offline Files feature, 284
oidgen.exe utility, 355, 356
OIDs (object identifiers), 354
operations masters, 23–27, 300–303
optimizing connections, 95
Options dialog box, 124–125
organizational units. *See* OUs
originating updates, 85, 86
ou attribute, 32
OU policy, 447
OUs (organizational units)
    connection agreements and, 521–522
    creating, 252–253
    delegating control of, 253
    described, 6–7
    multiple domains and, 28, 29
    nesting, 217–218
    network considerations, 216–218
    organization of, 217
    security and, 217

▼ P

packet sniffer. *See* Network Monitor utility
parent classes, 345–346

parent-child trusts, 247
partitions
     described, 23
     directory partitions, 125–127
     FAT partitions, 168, 169,
          234–235
     forestwide directory
          partitions, 91
     NTFS partitions, 234–235,
          500, 505
     schema partitions, 23, 336
passwords. *See also* security
     authoritative restore
          and, 265
     Directory Services restore
          mode, 239
     minimum password age, 402
     password filtering, 21
     password guessing, 397
     PDC emulator and, 24–25
     policies for, 398, 400–402
PDC emulators
     described, 24–25
     reassigning, 302–303
     requirements, 213
PDCs (primary domain
     controllers), 5, 19, 225, 227
performance
     connector service and, 524
     database and, 238
     domain controllers and, 10
     monitoring, 129–131
     replication, 124, 125
Performance Monitor utility, 115,
     129–131

Performance Statistics
     option, 124
Perl, 439, 457
Permission Entry dialog box, 170
permissions, 164–172
     common permissions,
          164–166
     Delegation of Control
          feature and, 170–172
     Gateway Services for
          NetWare share, 471
     groups, 134–141
     inheritance of, 168–170
     objects, 166–167
     ownership and, 167–168
     propagating, 169–170
     scripts, 440–441
     users, 134–135
pilot site, 211–212
ping utility, 242
pointer (PTR) records, 48–50
Poledit.exe, 180
policies. *See also* group policies
     in Active Directory, 176–180
     defined, 176
     file policy, 410–411
     folder policy, 410–411
     Group Policy Editor,
          449–451
     IP Security policies, 411–431
     Kerberos policy, 392–393,
          400
     password policies, 398,
          400–402
     public key policies, 411

policies, *continued*
　registry policy, 408–410
　system service policy,
　　407–408
　types of, 176–180
policy environment, 177
policy scripts, 446–447, 448–451
Policy Setup Wizard, 415
preferential replication, 25
primary domain controllers. *See*
　PDCs
Print Services for Macintosh,
　510–515
Print Services for UNIX, 488–490
printers
　AppleTalk printers, 511–512,
　　514–515
　group policy settings,
　　286–288
　managing, 286–289
　printer location tracking,
　　288–289
　publishing, 286
　sharing Macintosh printers,
　　510–515
　sharing NetWare printers,
　　472–473
　sharing UNIX printers,
　　488–490
pruning, 286
PTR (pointer) records, 48–50
public key policies, 411
publishing
　folders, 280–283
　printers, 286
　software, 291, 293–294

 R

RCP (Remote Copy Protocol)
　client, 484
RDN (relative distinguished
　name), 33–34, 35
records, 64–65, 272–275
recursion, 42–45
referral ticket, 386
Registry Editor, 267
Registry section, 408–410
Registry.pol file, 186
relative distinguished name
　(RDN), 33–34, 35
relative ID (RID), 25–26
relative identification (RID)
　master, 25–28, 213, 302–303
remote access, 20
Remote Copy Protocol (RCP)
　client, 483
remote procedure call (RPC),
　103, 104
remote shell daemon (rshd), 484
repadmin utility, 115–117
replicated updates, 85
replication, 81–132
　Active Directory and, 82–93
　Active Directory partitions,
　　24
　bridgehead servers
　　and, 11, 22
　connection objects, 93,
　　96–100
　customizing, 531–532
　described, 82–85

forcing manual replication, 101–102

intersite replication, 92, 102–104

intrasite replication, 94–102, 103

KCC and, 92–93

managing, 115–117

Microsoft goals for, 84

monitoring, 115, 117–132

multiple domains and, 29

network considerations, 222

Network Monitor utility, 131–132

network performance and, 69

Performance Monitor utility, 129–131

performance of, 124, 125

preferential replication, 25

repadmin utility, 115–117

Replication Monitor utility, 117–129

RPC vs. SMTP, 104

between sites, 92, 102–104

tools for, 115–132

replication log files, 121–125

Replication Monitor log, 131

Replication Monitor main window, 120–121

Replication Monitor Options dialog box, 123–124

Replication Monitor utility, 115, 117–129

replication restore, 259, 261–262

replication topology, 91–92

checking, 100

described, 21, 82–84

forestwide replication topology, 91–92

global catalog servers, 92

illustrated, 82

KCC and, 82, 91

res1.log file, 258

res2.log file, 258

resource domains, 5, 227–228

resource records, 41

Restore Wizard, 262

restoring Active Directory, 259–260, 261–265

Restricted Groups option, 405–407

Rexec utility, 484–485

RFC 1123, 46

RFC 1510, 379, 397–398

RFC 1995, 46–47

RFC 2253, 33

RFCs, 34

RID (relative ID), 25–26

RID (relative identification) master, 25–28, 213, 302–303

root, 45

Routing and Remote Access utility, 463

RPC (remote procedure call), 103, 104

rsh daemon (rshd), 485

rsh utility, 485

rshd (remote shell daemon), 484

rshd (rsh daemon), 485

▼ S

SA (security agreement), 413
SAP agent, 463, 464–465
SAP (Service Advertising
    Protocol), 462
Schedule dialog box, 108–109
Scheduled Task Wizard, 454–456
schema, 335–376
    described, 13–14, 338–349
    making changes to, 351–354
    manually updating, 349
    modifying, 349–376
    reassigning schema master,
        300–301
Schema Admins group,
    350, 351, 358
schema cache, 346–349
schema classes, 341–342
schema master, 13, 14, 26, 214,
    351–354
schema partition, 23, 336
scope, 137–138
Script Component Wizard,
    436, 437
scripting, 433–458. *See also*
JScript; VBScript
    in Active Directory
        environment, 434–438
    ActivePerl, 439, 457
    ASDI, 436–437
    COM interface, 436–437
    interfaces for, 435–438
    Interix package, 457

Script Component Wizard,
    436, 437
script.exe, 442–443
setting default scripting
    host, 444
Windows scripting home
    page, 435, 437, 444
Windows Scripting Host,
    434, 435, 438–445
wscript.exe, 443–444
scripts
    built-in scripts, 451–452
    configuring, 439–442
    debugging, 444–445
    executing automatically,
        452–457
    logoff scripts, 446, 449
    logon scripts, 446–451
    Perl scripts, 457
    policy scripts, 446–447,
        448–451
    sample scripts, 437, 452, 453
    shutdown scripts, 446, 449
    startup scripts, 446, 449
    subdirectory for, 186
    UNIX scripts, 457
    user logon scripts, 447–448
    Web-related scripts, 452
Scripts subdirectory, 186
search function, 275–276, 315
Secure Sockets Layer (SSL), 412
security, 377–432. *See also*
passwords
    Active Directory and, 6–8

group policy settings, 398–431

integrated zones and, 48

IP Security feature, 411–431

Kerberos protocol, 378–398

NTLM authentication, 378–379, 384

OUs and, 29, 217

script files and, 440–441

software and, 296

Windows 2000, 134–135

Windows NT, 134–135

security agreement (SA), 413

security descriptor, 134

security groups, 134, 135, 136–140

Security Options section, 403–404

security policies, 192

Security Policy Setting dialog box, 407, 408

Security Rule Wizard, 429–431

security rules, 415

Security Settings tree, 178

security templates, 192, 194

Select Group Policy Object Wizard, 189

Select Registry Key dialog box, 409

server key, 380–382, 384

server objects, 77–78

servers. *See also* DNS servers
bridgehead servers, 11, 22, 113–115
DHCP servers, 243–244

managing in DNS console, 65–67

placing in sites, 76–78

promoting, 228

synchronizing directory partitions with, 125–127

Telnet servers, 485–487, 490–498

Windows 3.5 server, 232

Windows 3.51 server, 232

Windows 4.0 server, 232

WINS servers, 214

Service Advertising Protocol (SAP), 462

Services for UNIX, 477, 490, 497–498

Services for UNIX Korn Shell, 490

session key, 380–382

shortcut trusts, 247–248

Show Attribute Meta-Data option, 127–129

/showmeta command, 117

/showreps command, 117

/showvector command, 116

shutdown scripts, 446, 449

Simple Mail Transfer Protocol. *See* SMTP

Simple TCP/IP Services, 496–497

simplified ring topology, 83, 94

site link bridges, 109–112, 110

site links
configuring, 104–114
creating, 105–106

site links, *continued*
    defined, 104
    properties for, 107
    vs. connection objects, 104
sites, 69–78
    adding server objects to, 77
    associating subnets with,
        72–73
    changing name of, 70
    configuring, 70–71, 73–74
    creating, 71–72
    default site, 70
    delegating control of, 74
    described, 11, 22, 69
    dividing networks and, 69
    network considerations,
        218–219
    placing servers in, 76–78
    replication between, 92,
        102–104
    replication within, 94–102
SMTP (Simple Mail Transfer
    Protocol), 103–104, 132
SOA (Start of Authority)
    records, 62
software
    assigning, 290–293
    managing, 289–296
    publishing, 291, 293–294
    security and, 296
    upgrades, 296
spreadsheets, 280
SRV records, 9, 10, 40, 50

SSL (Secure Sockets Layer), 412
stamps, 89–90
Start menu, 297
Start of Authority (SOA)
    records, 62
startup scripts, 446, 449
subnets, 69–78
subtrees, 202
/sync command, 116
Synchronization command, 127
synchronous processing, 185
syntaxes, 339, 344
system clock, 232
System Information utility, 240
System Policy Editor, 180
system policy feature, 176,
    179–180
system requirements
    Active Directory, 231–232
    Microsoft Office
        applications, 309
    Windows 2000 Professional,
        308–311
System Services option, 407–408
system state backup, 258,
    259, 260–261
system state restore
    operation, 260
/system32 subdirectory, 188
System.adm template, 193
system.adm template, 192
SysVol folder, 180, 222,
    238–239, 265

T

Task Scheduler, 454–457
taskbar, 297
TCP/IP
    Active Directory and, 39–79
    AFP over TCP/IP, 501, 509
    checking configuration, 242
    DNS servers and, 41
    IP Security feature for, 411
    Macintosh clients and, 499, 500, 501
    Simple TCP/IP Services, 496–497
    site definition features and, 71
    for UNIX-based clients, 496–497
    utilities for, 476–488
Technicians GPO, 197
Telnet clients, 314, 485–487
Telnet Server Administration utility, 492–496
Telnet servers, 485–487, 490–498
templates, 192–194
test site, 209–211
TFTP (Trivial File Transfer Protocol) client, 487–488
ticket granting ticket (TGT), 385, 392
tickets, 380, 382–383, 385–387
Transitive Replication Partner icon, 119
transitive trusts, 7

tree-root trusts, 246–247
Trivial File Transfer Protocol (TFTP) client, 487–488
troubleshooters, 240–243
troubleshooting. *See also* error messages
    debugging scripts, 444–445
    DHCP, 243–244
    DNS, 203, 242–244
    domain controllers, 243
    drivers, 240
    Kerberos protocol, 394
    Telnet sessions, 496
    tools for, 240–241
    Windows 2000 installation, 239–244
trust path, 247
trusts, 7, 246–250

U

UAM (User Authentication Module), 508–510
universal groups, 8, 20, 137, 138–140
Universal Naming Convention (UNC), 8
UNIX scripts, 457
UNIX-based clients, 314, 474–498
    Print Services for UNIX, 488–490
    Services for UNIX, 477, 490, 497–498

UNIX-based clients, *continued*
TCP/IP services, 496–497
Telnet server, 490–496
utilities for, 476–488, 498
update collisions, 84, 85
update sequence numbers
(USNs), 85–90, 128
updates
computer group policies, 185
conflict resolution for, 89–90
dynamic updates, 48–50
originating updates, 85, 86
replicated updates, 85
user policies, 185
upgrade.txt file, 310
UPN suffix, 144
UPNs (user principal names),
35–36, 157–159
URL-based name format, 35
URLs. *See* Web sites
Use Any Available Domain
Controller option, 201
User Authentication Module
(UAM), 508–510
user logon scripts, 447–448
user policies, 185
user principal names (UPNs),
35–36, 157–159
User subdirectory, 186
userPrincipleName attribute, 35
users
adding to groups, 146–149
copying user accounts,
145–146

creating, 143–146
deleting accounts for,
156–157
disabling accounts for,
156–157
managing, 142–164
managing desktop for,
297–300
moving, 154–155
network considerations,
220–221
overview, 134–135
permissions and, 134–135
properties, 149–154
removing from groups,
146–149
renaming accounts for,
156–157
USNs (update sequence
numbers), 85–90, 128

 V

.vbs extension, 439
VBScript
built-in scripts, 451–452
debugging scripts, 444–445
described, 434, 435
executing, 439
properties for, 439–442
virtual private network
(VPN), 476

Visual Basic scripting language.
See VBScript
VPN (virtual private
network), 476

▼ W

WAN links, 29, 71, 218, 219
watermark settings, 87, 88
Web Sharing feature, 473
Web sites
COM objects, 436
Hardware Compatibility
List, 240
Windows 2000 hardware
updates, 309
Windows 2000
installation, 236
Windows 2000 Readiness
Analyzer tool,
309–310, 311
Windows scripting, 435,
437, 444
WfW systems, 214
win32log file, 310
Windows 3.5 server, 232
Windows 3.51 domain
controller, 231
Windows 3.51 member
server, 232
Windows 3.51 server, 232
Windows 4.0 domain
controller, 231

Windows 4.0 member server, 232
Windows 4.0 server, 232
Windows 95/98
creating policy file, 180
group policy and, 307–308
installing Directory Services
Client, 313–314
NetBIOS name
resolution, 214
Windows 95/98 clients, 306–308,
312–314
Windows 2000, 459–535
Active Directory and, 12
client options for, 306–308
compatibility information,
240
configuring for NetWare,
460–473
group policy, 173–204
installing, 232–250
interoperating, 459–535
Kerberos protocol and,
384–386, 394–397
Macintosh clients, 498–519
migrating DNS data to,
67–68
NetWare clients, 460–474
running UNIX scripts in, 457
security overview, 134–135
troubleshooting, 239–244
UNIX-based clients, 474–498
Web sites for, 236
Windows 2000 Active Directory
domain, 22

Windows 2000 Administrative
Tools, 311–312, 331–333
Windows 2000 clients, 306–312,
323–324
Windows 2000 domain
controllers, 19–21
Windows 2000 Domain
Manager, 244
Windows 2000 Professional, 288,
308–311, 533
Windows 2000 Readiness
Analyzer tool, 309
Windows 2000 Registry, 439
Windows 2000 Resource Kit, 451,
452, 453
Windows 2000 Server
adding secondary zone
to, 56–58
adding standard primary
zone to, 54–56
configuring as Macintosh
file server, 500
configuring DNS service
on, 52–53
migrating DNS data
to, 67–68
Windows 2000 Setup
Wizard, 233
Windows 2000 Support Tools,
115, 117, 244, 250–251
Windows 2000 Support Tools
Setup Wizard, 251
Windows Components
Wizard, 501, 510–511
Windows File Protection
feature, 284–285

Windows Installer Cleanup
utility, 244
Windows Internet Naming
Service. *See* WINS
Windows Media Player
settings, 193
Windows NT
Active Directory and, 4–16,
208, 209
character generator
(chargen), 497
client options for, 306–308
creating policy file, 180
group policy and, 307–308
limitations of, 5–6
Microsoft support for, 209
multiple domains and, 227
NetBIOS name
resolution, 214
NTLM authentication,
378–379, 384
security overview, 134–135
Windows NT 4 domain
controllers, 19–21
Windows NT clients, 306–308,
312, 325–326, 331
Windows NT DNS Server, 68
Windows NT network, 225–229
Windows NT Server 4, 4–5
Windows Scripting Host,
434, 435, 438–445. *See also*
scripting; scripts
Windows.adm template, 193
winnt32.exe program, 236, 310
winnt.adm template, 193
winnt.exe file, 236

WINS name resolution, 62
WINS servers, 214
WINS (Windows Internet
  Naming Service), 9
wizards
  Active Directory Installation
    Wizard, 237–239, 254
  Add Monitored Server
    Wizard, 118, 119
  Add Printer Wizard, 288,
    472, 490, 511
  Configure DNS Server
    Wizard, 52
  Configure Your Server
    Wizard, 52–53
  Create New Class
    Wizard, 372
  Create Shared Folder
    Wizard, 505
  Delegation of Control
    Wizard, 171–172, 253
  Directory Services Client
    Wizard, 313
  Filter Action Wizard,
    421–422
  IP Filter Wizard, 417
  IP Security Policy Wizard,
    427–428
  New Object–Computer
    Wizard, 320–322
  New Zone Wizard, 54–60
  Policy Setup Wizard, 415
  provided by ADMT, 245–246

  Restore Wizard, 262
  Scheduled Task Wizard,
    454–456
  Script Component Wizard,
    436, 437
  Security Rule Wizard,
    429–431
  Select Group Policy Object
    Wizard, 189
  Windows 2000 Setup
    Wizard, 233
  Windows 2000 Support
    Tools Setup Wizard, 251
  Windows Components
    Wizard, 501, 510–511
wmp.adm template, 193
wscript.exe, 438, 439, 443–444
wsecedit.dll file, 188
.WSH file, 441–442

 X

X.500 object ID, 354–356
X.500 specification, 354
X.500 standard, 32

 Z

.zap files, 294–295
zone files, 55, 56, 60
zone transfers, 47, 58, 62

zones, 46–48
  Active Directory–integrated
    zones, 58–59
  adding domains to, 63
  choosing zone type, 55
  configuring DNS
    zones, 53–65
  configuring properties
    for, 61–63
  delegating, 64
  deleting, 64
  described, 46–47

DNS servers and, 46–47
forward lookup zones,
  54, 56, 59
incremental zone
  transfer, 46–47
integrated zones, 48
New Zone Wizard, 54–60
primary zones, 53, 58
reverse lookup zones, 59–61
secondary zones, 56–58
standard primary zones,
  53–56, 59–61